A Diction
TROUT

A Dictionary of
TROUT FLIES

AND OF FLIES FOR SEA-TROUT AND GRAYLING

A. Courtney Williams

SIXTH EDITION
WITH AN ADDITIONAL SECTION
ON MODERN FLIES BY
T. DONALD OVERFIELD

A & C Black . London

A & C BLACK (PUBLISHERS) LIMITED
35 BEDFORD ROW, LONDON WC1R 4JH

SIXTH EDITION (PAPERBACK) 1986
FIRST EDITION 1949
SECOND EDITION 1950
THIRD EDITION 1961
FOURTH EDITION 1965
FIFTH EDITION 1973

Williams, A. Courtney
A dictionary of trout flies and of flies
for sea-trout and grayling.—6th ed.
1. Flies, Artificial
I. Title   II. Overfield, T. Donald
799.1'2   SH451

ISBN 0-7136-5603-4

ISBN 0 7136 5603 4

Printed in Great Britain
by Butler & Tanner Ltd, Frome, Somerset

CONTENTS

ILLUSTRATIONS

between pages 416 and 417

INTRODUCTION

It is now some years since *Trout Flies: A Discussion and a Dictionary* was published and although it was well received and the demands of some anglers have been sufficiently insistent to make another edition possible, that book never satisfied me enough to make me feel that a revised edition would merit the approval that I would wish for it.

It is, therefore, with the publishers' approval and co-operation, that *A Dictionary of Trout Flies, and of Flies for Sea-Trout and Grayling* now appears in place of an amended version of the original book, of which little but the plates now remains, and the value of that feature has been enhanced by the addition of others. The new book has been planned around the "List of Natural and Artificial Flies" which figured prominently in the other volume, although the new list, except in its general form, is very different from the original one. Except in one or two instances, the whole of the matter has been entirely re-written and greatly extended, a few unimportant patterns being deleted and a large number added. In addition over 400 carefully selected dressings have been included with a commentary on many of them.

That the original fly "dictionary" was appreciated was made very evident from the number of letters which reached me following the publication of *Trout Flies*, letters which in some cases began a correspondence which has continued ever since and from which I have derived a great amount of pleasure and not a little knowledge of artificial and natural flies, much of which has now been incorporated in this book.

The more or less universal desire to know more about artificials, what they represent, and how and when they should be used, was easily understandable, but it was a surprise to me to find that so many readers were interested in the natural insect and that so many were anxious to have the dressings of the artificial patterns. It had been my opinion that the dressings could be of interest and value only to the relatively few fishermen who tie their own flies.

That this view was incorrect has been made very clear to me, for requests for another book to include the dressings have come from anglers at home and overseas, especially from the U.S.A. I am hopeful that those now provided will satisfy these many correspondents since the dressings given have been selected with a good deal of care from the thousands available. And I am sufficiently optimistic to believe that the details furnished about some of the lesser known patterns such as the Grey Duster, Dogsbody, Welsh Partridge, and Paragon, will enable anglers in this country at any rate, to tie flies which will account for many a good fish. That they should be afforded a reasonable test and be used intelligently goes without saying, but if these provisos are adhered to, I feel confident that the patterns mentioned above (and many others) will not be found wanting. It is as well to bear in mind, however, that the artificial fly which will kill on all rivers and at all times has yet to be invented.

At this juncture it will be wise for me to offer my credentials to the reader since the Introduction seems to be the most suitable place to do so. There are folk, amongst whom I number myself, who are voracious readers, by which I mean that we read everything; the advertisements on hoardings, the labels on sauce bottles, and even those affecting announcements in magazines which kindly inquire about our health and whether we feel sluggish and out of sorts. It is only natural, therefore, that when we settle down to a book that we should read every word of it, from the publisher's blurb on the front to the advertisements on the back of the jacket. On the other hand, there are people who read a book in such a perfunctory manner that invariably they ignore the Introduction, dismissing it as being of no consequence.

To my mind this is a mistaken view, for it is in this preliminary canter that the author is most likely to reveal something of himself. In the case of a technical book that is surely most desirable because every reader must wish to know the writer's qualifications for undertaking the task he has set himself. How else (except in the case of an established author) is it possible for the reader to assess his views and theories at their true value?

In the last few years we have been favoured with a spate of books on fly-fishing, some of which have been excellent, but others of which have been little more than reiterations of what has been said (and generally said better) many times before, plus a few instructional notes of doubtful value. In view of all that has been written about angling in the last half-century, this is possibly inevitable, although at the same time I cannot help but feel that some of those who have written about fly-fishing in recent years seem to know too little about their subject, whilst others would appear to have learnt too much in too short a period.

Time was, I suppose, when most of us who have fished for longer than we care to remember, knew far more about some aspects of our sport than we do now, for as one grows older in experience, one realizes that where angling is concerned, the certainties of yesterday may be the doubts of to-day. To be dogmatic about fishing is to court disaster for no sport is subject to so many contradictions. No sooner do we convince ourselves that such-and-such a theory is absolutely unassailable than some circumstance arises which completely disproves it. And therein, perhaps, lies much of the fascination of angling.

Dangerous as it may be for those who live in glass houses to throw stones at their neighbours or, indeed, for those who live in stone houses to throw glass (lest they cut themselves in the process), I have taken the risk because I feel tolerably certain that most fly-fishers share my opinion.

Personally I can make no claim to be a very expert fisherman, nor yet an entomologist except in an amateurish sort of way. But of experience, I have had plenty, for thanks to a very early initiation into the art, it is now some forty years since I took my first fish on a fly. My age was certainly under ten at the time and the fish was only a minute salmon parr which took a fly almost as large as itself. The circumstances are engraven on my memory because, in spite of my vociferous protests, my father made me return this monster to the river! But small as was that fish, it was large enough to inoculate me with the fishing virus which passing years have failed to eradicate and for which, thank goodness, there is said to be no cure. Probably it was already in my blood before the incident referred to above, since my forebears were anglers, due in part to the fact that about 150 years ago my great-grandfather, Polycarp Allcock, set up his sign as a hook-maker and thus laid the foundations of the tackle firm which was later to become the largest concern of its kind in the world. The business has remained in the family ever since and through my connection with it and also, of course, through my previous books, I have been brought into contact with an unusually large number of fishermen. And as a direct consequence, I have enjoyed unique opportunities of casting my flies over many of the best trout and salmon waters in this country, as well as on the Continent, and during one brief but memorable visit to the U.S.A. and Canada.

Among those rivers which it has been my good fortune to fish are many with names which are familiar to all fishermen for they include the Exe and Otter, Test, Anton, Itchen, and Kennet; Colne, Windrush, and Evenlode; Dove, Derwent, Wye, and Manifold, Teify, Towy, and

Usk; Teme, Corve, Lugg; Onny, Clun, Tanat; Mawddach, Dovey,
Dysynni and Dee; Swale, Eden, Eamont; Teviot, Tummel, and Tweed.

Some of the best sport of all has been provided, however, by little
and lesser-known rivers like Leicester's Sence and Yorkshire's Skeeby
Beck, whilst many of the most enjoyable days have been spent on
minor Welsh waters—on streams such as the Alwyn, Ceirog, Lledr,
Conway, Llugwy, Ogwen, Monnow, and Irfon, to name but some
of them.

My object in referring to these waters is not to boast of the number
I have fished (which could be of no interest to readers), but solely to
emphasize that my experience has not been confined mainly to one
particular river, or indeed, to any one part of the country, for I deem
that to be of some importance when one is writing about artificial flies
and the methods of using them. Like all other trout anglers, I have, or
course, my own favourite streams (not always those which hold the
most or the largest fish) to which I return again and again. Nevertheless, circumstances and choice have ever tended to turn me into a
peripatetic fisherman and consequently my experience has been more
varied than specialized. It should be noted, in explanation of some
anomalies, that this book was written over a period of three fishing
seasons.

In these wanderings with rod and line in various parts of the country
I have naturally made many good friends, and my sincere thanks are
due to several of them who have gone to considerable trouble to assist
me in compiling this book: to H. D. Turing and C. V. Hancock, to
whom I have often turned for advice, and to many others; more
especially to one who is usually regarded as being the greatest living
authority and writer upon the artificial trout fly, for the time and
patience he has expended in helping and advising me with certain portions of this work. Whilst respecting his desire that he should remain
anonymous, it would be ungenerous of me did I not express to him
my gratitude for all the information and encouragement he has so
freely given. The debt I owe to several friends who helped me with the
List of Flies is mentioned elsewhere, whilst for information about
natural insects, my thanks are extended to Major John Evans and Mr.
D. E. Kimmins who never grumble about the many queries with which
I ply them. My grateful thanks are due to the editors and pro-
prietors of the following for allowing me to use information which
has appeared in their columns: *The Country Sportsman, The Field,
The Fishing Gazette, The Journal of the Flyfishers' Club,* and *The*

Salmon and Trout Magazine. The frontispiece is reproduced, by kind permission of the author and his publishers from the lithograph by Daumain reproduced in Lt.-Col. Antoine Vavon's *La Truite* (Maurice Dormann et Cerf, Etampes).

If the reader finds a little original information in this book, as I trust he will, the credit must be given to one or other of the experts referred to above; if there are errors and omissions, as well there may be, the blame must be laid on myself.

A. COURTNEY WILLIAMS

Stratford-on-Avon, 1948

To

THE MEMORY OF MY FATHER
ALFRED WILLIAMS
1848–1925
who taught me how to cast a fly

and to all
Fathers and Mothers, Uncles and Aunts
who instil in the Younger Generation
a Love of Sport

PART I

PART I

I. On Catching More Fish

The standard of fly fishing is almost certainly higher to-day than at any period in the past, although I feel sure that with but little trouble to himself, the average fly-fisher could greatly improve his technique and could catch many more fish than he does. And one of my objects in this book is to suggest how this can be done.

By "average" fisherman is meant one who is neither a novice nor an expert and who generally kills about as many fish as do the majority of others who fish the same water. The expert, however, will consistently take more fish than other rods, season after season, and is seldom defeated by water and weather conditions. In fact, his great skill becomes most apparent when conditions are such as to make most others give up fishing because they feel that it is hopeless.

To improve one's fishing so as to be able to kill more trout or more grayling is one thing; to become an expert is another. It demands not only deep knowledge gained by study and experience, but also certain natural gifts (including keen eyesight) which are not vouchsafed to everybody. Great technical skill obviously plays some part, but contrary to generally accepted ideas, I do not think that the chief difference between the expert and the ordinary sort of fly-fisher lies mainly in the more skilful manner in which the former handles his gear.

He is able, of course, to place his fly just where and how he wants it, and in a manner calculated to command the admiration and respect of the less gifted. But to what extent does it give him an advantage over them?

Admittedly authorities have long stressed the necessity of presenting a fly to a fish correctly, but it seems to me that the importance of this matter has been a little exaggerated. There was a time when reasonably correct presentation was not as easily attained as it is now, for the limitations of old-fashioned rods and lines made it difficult to cast a fly in anything like a satisfactory manner, and the writers of those days could not possibly have visualized the high level of casting which is general to-day.

If it is conceded, as I think it will be, that the average fly-fisherman can cast pretty well; is reasonably careful about taking cover in order to avoid scaring fish, and has a fair theoretical and practical knowledge of fly-fishing, it becomes necessary to seek other reasons to account for the super-efficiency of the expert.

I would suggest that there are at least three—tactics, concentration, and the selection of the right fly.

Tactics can only be determined by a study of water, weather, and the ways of trout, and obviously success or failure must largely depend upon the soundness of the tactics and methods employed. In this respect knowledge and experience must count for much, although most experts also possess a natural "flair" for fishing, which plays some part. To be able to get inside the mind of a trout is a gift denied to most anglers but is a quality which seems to be highly developed in a few.

Concentration is in quite a different class because it is something which every angler can cultivate if he so wishes. That it is of importance is generally appreciated, although the average angler does not practise it to the same degree as does the expert. The latter, when fishing, always concentrates completely. Rarely does he miss a fish through an ill-timed strike; rarely is there a hatch of any insect which he does not note immediately it occurs: rarely a movement on the water which escapes him. He is fully absorbed in his task, always on the alert, and ever ready for any eventuality which may arise.

Compared with this impressive demonstration of concentration, the methods of most of us are definitely casual. I wonder how many fishermen can truthfully say that they have never missed a fish through turning to speak to someone at the critical moment? And how often, following a period of quiescence, when a trout unexpectedly attacks the fly, do many of us strike seconds too late through being caught totally unprepared?

It is not, of course, every fisherman who aspires to become an expert, or who is willing to make of fishing the rather strenuous affair that the expert must of necessity make of it. At the same time, without following his methods too slavishly, it should be possible for most average anglers greatly to improve their fishing solely by concentrating more than they normally do. It is a habit which can be cultivated with advantage.

Important as I judge concentration to be, the choice of the right fly is of no less consequence. And in this matter, the expert scores heavily because his knowledge and experience permit him to select the best pattern without hesitation, whilst other anglers may be obliged to rely upon some general or fancy pattern, or else find the best fly by a process of trial and error, losing valuable time in so doing.

The correct choice and size of artificial fly must so often be the deciding factor in the size of a catch that the subject must be dealt with at some length. Before doing so, mention must be made of one other trait which all experts possess—enthusiasm. It is of real importance as without it, no fly-fisher can ever hope to rise above the mediocre.

Having thus briefly touched upon the several qualities which seem to me to be necessary in the make-up of a fly-fisher who is wishful of rising above the average, I must, in all fairness, confess that personally I have never had any ambition to become one of those superlative anglers of whom other fishermen speak with the deference and respect due to their great skill. Probably this is because of my natural laziness which has deterred me from making the effort required. There are men who have found it easy to reach the top class but for the most the road is a long one. Sometimes one meets an exceptionally gifted fly-fisher who gets a great many fish in what would seem to be a carefree haphazard manner and who is quite unlike the popular conception of an ultra proficient angler.

One such comes to my mind. He fishes the Welsh border streams and can always be relied upon to take more trout and grayling than any of the local or visiting anglers who fish the same waters. His rod is old and mis-shapen, his reel clatters and shudders, and his line, from which most of the dressing has long since departed, remains on the reel from one year to another. Stowed away in his pockets are a couple of spare casts and a match box holding his flies. These are confined to two patterns, a Herefordshire Alder, and of late, a Grey Duster, and he uses them (and no others) from the first week of the season until the last. He never carries a net and it is to be doubted whether he knows the name of any of the natural flies he sees on the water, as he will not be bothered with details of that sort. One can only attribute his success to the fact that he has a natural gift for catching fish. That indefinable quality is found but rarely and the great majority of us have to gain what proficiency we may by the hard way.

To some extent this may be said of all field sports, although I feel that it is truer of fishing than of other sports since they are concerned with animals of which there is no special difficulty in making a close study, because, unlike fish, they inhabit the same element as ourselves. It is this circumstance which makes it so much easier to predict the behaviour and reactions of animals and birds than those of fish.

There is, of course, something to be said for not taking our fishing too seriously for when it ceases to be an amusement and a relaxation, it loses much of its charm. There are many anglers who will agree with Robert Hartman when he says that "although fishing gives rise to a variety of emotions and a wide range of absorbing interests, it is not a profession, but an entertainment which should be approached with a light heart, a light step, and a light rod". That, however, in no way conflicts with the fact that the more we learn about the science and the greater our knowledge of everything connected with it, the easier and more enjoyable it becomes. In fact, one of the most satisfying and enchanting things about angling is that one's knowledge of it can never reach finality. However much we may study the art, there will always be more problems ahead, new fields to conquer, fresh roads to explore.

II. On the Importance of the Fly

To the fly-fisher, the artificial fly must ever be a vital link in his outfit. The most expensive rod, reel and line, will avail him but little if the fly he chooses fails to attract fish. One of the greatest anglers I ever knew, the late Canon C. F. Eagles of Coughton (Warwickshire) was wont to use an old dilapidated greenheart rod, a child's brass reel, which had cost only eighteen pence when he had bought it twenty or more years before; and a heavy gut (or more often gut-substitute) cast which looked more suitable for grilse than trout. Yet on this crude gear he killed an incredible number of fish each year. His great gifts included skill, patience, and wonderful eyesight, but perhaps more than anything else, it was his ability to select the right fly which gave him so much success.

Yet anglers there are, and numbers of them, who will go to a great amount of trouble to secure an outfit to suit them and who select each individual item of it with great care, but who, when at the waterside, are quite content to leave the choice of the fly to some friend or ghillie who may, or may not be, competent to advise them. Or if no one is at hand to offer assistance, they will pick out a fly for no reason at all beyond that they know it to be a celebrated pattern, although it should be obvious that no fly, however great its reputation, can be expected to take fish under all conditions or on every river. Were that the case we should all catch many more fish than we do!

The ability to select the right fly—that is the pattern and size which is most likely to take fish in the conditions which prevail—can be attained only by study and experience. Sound systematical knowledge in the choice of his fly cannot fail to increase the fisherman's chance of catching trout. It often marks the difference between the average sort of angler and the expert. To my mind, it is of far greater importance than the actual presentation of the fly which according to most authorities is the main factor which separates the expert from the ordinary fisherman. Although the performance of the average angler may not be near that of the adept, he can usually cast his fly sufficiently well to avoid too many mistakes. Mistakes will, of course, happen at times but it is really surprising how often one can make quite serious errors of judgment without putting down a feeding fish. The average man, too, will get his fly tangled up in bushes, trees and other snags, and he may do it a little more frequently than the more experienced fisherman, but these trials are common to all anglers, including the most expert. If a man can cast moderately well and fails to take as many trout as others who fish the same water, the answer nearly always lies in the fly.

It may be argued that on some particular water well known to him, any fly-fisherman worthy of the name will have a pretty clear idea of the patterns which are most likely to be successful. This is true enough, but few of us fish the same water all our lives; and what happens when we find ourselves on a strange river? Then the guess which is easy enough to make on the water we know, is likely to be hopelessly wrong. In fact, I should say that the test of a really good fisherman is that on a strange water he should be able to take as many fish as the local anglers.

It does not appear to me to be possible to escape the conclusion that methodical knowledge alone can save us from wasting time and effort and from the ignominy of coming back "clean" when others' creels are comfortably full.

How then can the beginner set about obtaining the necessary knowledge? As a start, it seems to me that some study of trout-fly entomology is essential if one is to be able to recognize the flies and insects on the water. And when there are no flies on the surface or near the river, one ought to know enough about the habits and diet of trout to be in a position to determine the sub-surface food they are likely to be taking.

Reading books on the subject, and the regular examination of the stomach contents of fish we catch, will teach us a lot. But even when natural insects can be recognized with some degree of certainty, the selection of the artificial pattern may still depend upon a number of factors such as the season of the year, light, wind, temperature, barometric pressure and the height, colour and temperature of the water. The fisherman who can weigh up these accurately and can appreciate what they mean to fish, will be filling his basket while a better performer with the rod will be engaged in that fruitless and annoying occupation of constantly changing flies. Although the task may sound a formidable one, a little intelligence should enable one to grasp the significance of these several factors, so that by a mental process of elimination, the choice of a likely killing fly can be undertaken with some degree of confidence.

Far be it from me to suggest that my modest contribution in this book will solve the problem for every reader, although I am not unhopeful that it may provide him with food for thought and serve as a basis for further study of an interesting subject.

In a brief summary of the many things a fly-fisher should know if he is to be able to make a swift diagnosis of what fly is most likely to tempt fish at any specific time, it is not possible to consider in detail such factors as "rise-forms" for example, however useful they may be to the angler who can understand and profit by them. I only refer to them at all in order to emphasize the desirability of studying everything which may be of assistance in determining the best pattern to employ. And it must be obvious that the ability to discover the natural fly on which a fish is feeding merely by the form of its rise, cannot help but be useful; and it can often be done, even if the science is not an absolutely accurate one.

It must be said, however, that it is perhaps only of interest to the advanced fly angler and then only if he regularly fishes the chalk streams, or other placid waters, for on the majority of our rivers with their rough, fast flow, the form of a rise is not always easy to establish.

The theory is that trout rise in different ways to different species of insects and that the form of the rise can conveniently be divided into three main sections, as follows: (*a*) Supersurface rises made to insects standing on the water or just above it. (*b*) Flush rises made to insects held in the surface film. (*c*) Subsurface rises made to insects under water such as nymphs, shrimps, and the larvae and pupae of many flies. The latter type of rise is again sub-divided into one which breaks the surface film and into another in which it only makes a bulge in it.

Space will not permit me to pursue the subject further, but enough has been said, I hope, to indicate that the manner in which a trout rises is worth noting, for it may provide a valuable clue to the species of insect the fish is taking.

There have been many attempts made to formulate rules as to the type and colour of artificial fly to employ according to the conditions of the day and the river, but almost all these "short cuts" designed to make the lot of the fly-fisherman easier, must be rejected because of their lack of reliability. No dictum is more often quoted, for instance, than that of Stoddart—that a bright fly should be used on a bright sunny day and a dark fly on a dull one. Apart from the fact, generally overlooked, that Stoddart was referring only to salmon flies, not many anglers will agree with this theory. Where trout are concerned, some fishermen believe that the exact opposite is the case and personally I think that it is impossible to lay down any hard and fast rule of this nature. The only exception I would allow is that in thick, muddy, or peat-stained water, a really dark-coloured fly appears to be easier seen by fish than a light one. Whenever the river is so thick as to make it difficult for trout to see a fly, it is my habit to put on a Williams Favourite, fished wet, although any other black fly would probably do just as well; as long as the fish can see a fly at all, it brings good results.

The ability to recognize and correctly name the standard artificial patterns at least, is practically essential for any fly fisherman and, in that matter, this book should be of some little assistance to those who are unable to differentiate between the flies in their possession. A survey of the dressings, together with the comments which accompany them, should also help the tyro to understand something of the structure of an artificial fly, from which he should have no great difficulty in eventually deducing the function which any specific pattern is intended to fulfil.

When he can do this, he will have made sufficient progress to avoid serious errors and will find himself invested with some degree of confidence; and confidence is a necessary and powerful weapon in the hands of any angler.

Without this confidence (which is the result of knowledge), the fly-fisher has to rely on general patterns, variants, and fancies. All these are good in their proper place but even should they bring success, it is surely as well in fishing as in everything else, to have a clear understanding of what one is doing and much more important, of the reason for doing it. And the reason for putting on a fancy or general pattern is, all too often, because the angler is at a complete loss to know what to use. In these circumstances, whether his choice of fly proves to be a good one or otherwise, becomes purely a matter of chance.

There are occasions without number, of course, when these nondescript patterns are extremely useful and when their employment is fully justified but I do not believe that they should be used solely because the angler is devoid of all other ideas and turns to them as a pleasant help in time of trouble! On most rivers (chalk streams excepted) general and fancy flies may possibly account for more trout than those of the exact imitation order but the danger lies in the temptation to use them *as a matter of course*, when on certain occasions, a closer copy of the fly on the water would bring many more fish to the net.

Although it is not possible for anyone to say *with certainty* that under certain conditions such-and-such a fly is bound to take fish, knowledge, plus experience, should enable any fly-fisherman to choose a pattern which, to put the matter at its lowest level, should reduce his chances of failure and provide some definite prospect of success.

Clearly no angler, whether he fishes the wet or the dry fly, can hope to imitate the insect on the water if he is unable to identify it. Catching the natural fly and matching it up with a pattern in one's box cannot be recommended, since many artificials which well represent some natural insect as seen by the fish, may, in our eyes, bear very little resemblance to it.

If one is to take a reasonably intelligent interest in one's fishing in order to extract from it the fullest possible amount of satisfaction and the maximum degree of profit, some study of the natural fly is essential. The entomology of the trout fly is not the difficult subject it is often thought to be and without making any pretensions to be an expert entomologist myself, I am sure that mastering its rudiments is worth all the time and trouble it entails, for apart from any benefit it confers upon the fisherman, it is in itself a science of absorbing interest.

To deal with it in a brief manner can be a little dangerous but for the purposes of this book, I have felt bound to attempt it and can only hope that the real entomologist will not be too critical of any shortcomings which may result. My aim has been to provide sufficient information to enable the reader to identify the commoner insects he is likely to find on or near the water; to be able to select the appropriate imitations, and to catch fish on them.

To be able to do this appears to me to be a much more satisfactory procedure than to choose a pattern at random, hoping that it may appeal to the fish. More satisfactory, because the trout is defeated by a predetermined plan instead of by a lucky chance. On this subject, T. J. Hanna once made some pertinent observations which I cannot do better than repeat. "It should always be remembered", he wrote, "that the man who puts up, say, a Butcher, when the blue-winged olive is on in force, has missed the whole point of fly-fishing. He, poor fellow, is more to be pitied than scorned, for he has deliberately acknowledged his defeat. Fly-fishing is a riddle and he has confessed his inability to read that riddle. Thereafter, fishing must be to that man a mere recreation and the only satisfaction he is likely to get is the killing of a few fish; but the pleasures of angling cannot be weighed in pounds and ounces on a spring balance."

Necessary as I hold some knowledge of the natural insect to be, it does not follow that to take fish, a close imitation of it is required. On the contrary, as I have already pointed out, on most rivers and brooks, except the chalk streams, an impressionistic suggestion of the natural fly is sufficient. Yet although the fish in most waters are not as fastidious as those of the Test, undue liberties may not be taken with them. When the same conditions obtain, one pattern will take fish when another fails, not once or twice, but constantly every season, and consequently the artificial should always be selected with care and in accordance with the conditions of the moment.

The problems which face the wet fly-fisherman are more difficult of solution and I am inclined to think experience is his best guide although some knowledge of entomology is perhaps of even greater importance to him than it is to the dry fly man.

Lake flies are in a category to themselves. The diet of lake trout is rather different from that of river fish, although quite as varied. Sometimes they will take flies off the surface freely and a dry fly will then account for many fish, since on the whole trout which inhabit lakes are less shy than their brethren of the rivers; but much of their food is of the underwater variety and consists of snails, shrimps, water-lice and the larvae of gnats and when they are devoting their attention to these, only a sunken fly is likely to tempt them. I think that it is true to say that almost any artificial fly which kills well on rivers will also take trout in lakes although some of the best lake patterns are useless on rivers.

To sum up, my own opinion is that one can rub along with little or no knowledge of entomology; and with experience, it is often possible to make a fairly accurate guess as to the patterns which will attract fish. But if the choice and size of fly is dictated by a full understanding and appreciation of the conditions of the moment (and for this the ability to recognize the natural insect on the water is, to say the least, a tremendous help) then one will consistently catch more fish.

It must surely be agreed by every school of thought that fish are able to distinguish one fly from another. Were this not so, the whole art of the fly-dresser would be so much wasted effort. For that reason alone, if for no other, the artificial should never be selected in a haphazard manner.

As some consolation to any reader who may feel a little awed at the thought of all he must learn in order to become a first-class fly-fisherman, I will quote the last verse of some amusing

lines, entitled "Heresy" which appeared some years ago in, I
think, the *Journal of the Fly-Fishers' Club:*

> But I am afraid
> That I do not care a rap or even a hoot
> For I am a heretical brute
> Who does not believe
> That in order to achieve
> A dish
> Of fish
> (Provided one can detect
> The approximate colour of the insect)
> It is necessary to be an entomologist
> An icthyolo- or any other variety of a gist.

My only comment is that any angler who feels the same as the
author of the above, may certainly achieve a dish of fish, but
were he also an icthyologist and an entomologist, the chances are
that he would acquire a very much larger dish! To adapt oneself to conditions should not be beyond the power of any
angler of ordinary intelligence and to gain a working knowledge
of entomology is not, in reality, the formidable task it may at
first appear. The importance of these things cannot be over-
estimated and it would be easy enough to give dozens of
examples to prove this.

We all know that there are occasions when trout are very un-
accommodating and will not rise, but even then a good fisherman should generally be able to find a way of tempting some of
them. I am very certain that were I a better entomologist,
icthyologist, and fly-dresser, my visits to the water would be far
more consistently productive than they are.

III. ON THE TROUT'S MENU

So far the relation of the artificial fly to the natural insect has
been considered but little reference has been made to the latter.
At this point, therefore, it becomes necessary to emphasize the

fact that the natural winged fly forms but a small part of the trout's diet. He lives on many other things: on plankton, microscopic algae, vegetable matter, the nymphae and larvae of a great variety of insects, on molluscs and crustaceans of many sorts, on beetles, grubs, spiders and caterpillars, and on other small fish such as minnows, sticklebacks, and the fry of many species, not excluding those of his own, for every trout is a cannibal by nature.

The fly-fisher obviously cannot hope to imitate successfully a tenth part of this varied menu, although it is feasible that a wet fly may often be taken for one or other of the many forms of sub-surface life on which fish habitually feed. Nevertheless imitations need not be confined to those of the up-winged duns. They may be usefully extended to cover insects like moths, caterpillars, beetles, bugs, and scores of flies of the great diptera order. Possibly some readers will feel that I am inclined to pay too much attention to flies and insects of this sort and that it is only the ephemeridae which are of any real account. In that case, it is to be feared that they will view with horror my recommendations to imitate many creatures which are far from being *persona grata* amongst chalk stream anglers, such horrors for instance as caterpillars, the larvae of gnats, and copies of corixae and water-lice.

But I remain unrepentant, because it is my conviction that from Halford's time onwards so much of our best fishing literature has emanated from those who fish the chalk streams, that the ephemeridae have assumed an exaggerated and unwarranted importance in the minds of the numerous fishermen whose sport is generally confined to other waters than those of the south. When one reads so much, and so frequently, of the b.-w.o., iron blue dun, olives, and pale wateries, it becomes easy to fall into the error of thinking that they are the only flies worth serious consideration.

It simply is not true! Outside the few chalk streams, on almost every river, brook, beck, and lake throughout the British Isles, these upright-winged duns are of less importance to the fly-fisherman than are insects like the black gnat, march brown, alder, sedges, perlidae, crane-flies and such oddments as moths, shrimps, and many sorts of beetles, all of which are welcomed by fish in waters where food is generally scarce.

If I have stressed this point, it is because it is not always fully appreciated; neither is it one which is of interest only to the wet fly man as is so often suggested. A copy of almost any insect can be fished dry in most instances just as well as wet. An artificial daddy-long-legs, for example, when fished on the surface can provide just as much interest as the most delicate little Red Quill, and strange as it may seem to some, under certain conditions, it will account for more fish.

Not for one minute would I recommend that an artificial daddy-long-legs should be used when duns are on the water in force or during a fall of spinners. That would be sheer stupidity, but the "daddy" and many similar flies used at the right time, are of great value to the majority of fly-fishermen. They should not, and indeed, cannot be ignored.

Perhaps a better example of my meaning is provided by a fall of caterpillars which is an annual event on some streams, when myriads of these creatures come floating down on invisible threads from trees overhanging the river. When they reach the water, they create a great furore amongst trout which line up to take advantage of these juicy morsels. Perhaps the real purist would close his eyes in order to avoid seeing such an unfortunate phenomenon and would immediately move away to find other fish to fry. But on the majority of our rivers every rising fish is worthy of the fly-fisherman's attention and if the trout insist on taking small caterpillars, the logical course would seem to be to use an imitation of them.

After all the first axiom of every fly-fisher is to use a copy of the natural fly fish are taking, and there does not appear to me to be any valid reason why that old-established principle should be ignored just because that "fly" happens to be, say, a nymph —or a caterpillar!

Admittedly, if at the same time, there is a hatch of up-winged duns which are attracting fish, most anglers would prefer to use a floating pattern of a dun. But on most rivers, this rarely happens and finding trout taking the falling caterpillars must be accounted a welcome discovery; and one, in my opinion, of which it is right and proper for the fly-fisherman to take full advantage.

IV. ON THE TYPES OF RIVERS

One of the first things which a beginner has to realize is that there are several types of rivers each demanding different treatment from the fly-fisher. Mr. G. H. Rountree has summed up the matter admirably in *The Field* in these words: "It seems to me that speaking generally, there are three types of rivers in the British Isles. First, those that have large and regular hatches of fly (and corresponding falls of spinners), the flies hatching at one time being mainly of one species. On such streams the fish wait for the hatch and fishing between hatches is virtually useless. When the hatch is on the fish have a definite taste for the fly of the moment. On such streams fairly exact imitation pays handsome dividends.

"Secondly come the rivers on which there are comparatively large hatches at irregular intervals with other flies of varied kinds hatching out almost individually all the time. During one of the big hatches the fish become very nearly as particular as those of the first type of river, but as they cannot rely on the date of the next big meal, they do not take fly between hatches. At such times they take whatever passes the door and a good 'general' pattern of artificial is probably better than too specific a pattern, and even a 'fancy' is good. The third type of river seldom gets a real hatch at all, but is equally seldom devoid of flies. Here the fisherman's choice of fly becomes secondary to his ability to find and stalk his fish. Any feather confection which looks as though it might exist in nature will account for a fish or two."

The first type of river is, of course, the chalk stream and as that term is used so frequently in this book, it may be as well to define it. Broadly speaking, a chalk stream is so named because it rises in and/or flows through chalk deposits, quite irrespective as to whether it provides good or bad fishing. To which rivers the appellation can be correctly applied is not so easily determined, since so many of them must be classed as "doubtful", by which is meant that they may have their source in a chalk formation and then run through limestone, peat, etc., or vice versa.

When speaking of chalk streams in England, most fly-fishers mean those south-country rivers which rise in the Downs and flow into the Channel, although exceptions must be made to this rule. Of the latter, the Kennet is perhaps the most notable example, and to take another, I believe that the Driffield Beck in Yorkshire is a "purest of the pure" chalk stream.

All these true chalk rivers have the same general characteristics; few tributaries, much silt, much weed, and a prolific food supply. All this, however, is only partly due to their origin. Some of it is also due to their steady unbroken flow through rich pasture land. A chalk stream with a different fall might be altogether different in character to the south-country rivers, although it would still be a chalk stream. Although I am sure that fishermen generally accept without quibble the rather restricted definition of a chalk stream as meaning a river like the Test or Itchen, it seems wise to confirm that it is in this sense that the term is employed in this book, in order to avoid any confusion in the minds of readers.

Broadly speaking all other rivers and brooks fall into one of the two other classes already mentioned and there is little need to say much about them at this point beyond that they call for different methods of fly-fishing which are discussed in detail later on. Every angler should be able to decide without much difficulty to which type any river or stream conforms and accordingly determine the sort of artificial fly which is most likely to prove successful. For this reason I have purposely omitted those lists of "Flies for Rivers" and "Flies for Months" which are to be found in many books and catalogues because it seems to me that they often confine the fly-fisher's choice to unnecessarily narrow limits and deter the beginner (for whom they are intended) from using a perfectly suitable pattern merely because it does not happen to be amongst those recommended.

V. On Fly-fishing Methods

The two principal methods of fishing the artificial fly are, of course, wet and dry; or, in other words, the choice lies between the use of a fly fished below the surface of the water and one which floats upon it.

It is not my intention to sing the praises of dry fly-fishing as compared with wet, or vice versa, because each has a place and every angler must decide for himself, according to the conditions of the moment, which method is more likely to produce satisfactory results. The weather, the season, the state and character of the water have all to be taken into consideration, and the wise fisherman will make use of one or other method accordingly.

And here it becomes necessary for me to confess that in this respect I do not follow my own advice, because except for sea-trout (and salmon), my use of the wet fly is confined to an occasional day in the early spring when the cold keeps trout near the bottom. For the rest of the season, I prefer the floating fly, not necessarily because it takes more fish, but because to my mind, it is by far the most entertaining form of fly-fishing and the one which provides the greatest amount of interest and pleasure. That this view is widely held is clear, because the popularity of the dry fly increases every year. It has invaded some of the oldest strongholds of the wet fly-fisherman and is fast becoming the accepted manner of fishing on many rivers where not so many years ago, any man using a floater would have been put down as a crank.

Having thus defended my allegiance to the dry fly method, my qualifications to write about the wet fly may well be suspect, so let me hasten to add in extenuation, that for the first ten or twelve years of my angling life, I used nothing but the sunken fly. My tutor was my father, than whom no man was a better exponent of that style of fishing; and his teaching stood me in good stead when later I was so fortunate as to be stationed for a year in the north and was able to spend part of every day during the whole of the season, fishing one or other of the Yorkshire rivers. My companion for much of that time had fished the Yorkshire rivers all his life and was one of the greatest wet fly experts it has been my privilege to meet. Nearly his equal, was an Irish-born brother officer who frequently fished with us. Ironically enough, it was this experience more than anything else which caused me to adopt the dry fly, because it brought home to me my incompetence with the sunken fly when fishing in the company of expert exponents of that art. It seemed to me then, that to fish the wet fly as it should be fished, was a most difficult accomplishment and nothing which has happened since has caused me to revise that opinion. I still believe that fishing the wet fly properly calls for more skill than fishing a floater, although possibly fishing the up-stream worm in low clear water is more difficult than either! To catch fish on the sunken fly presents no great difficulty, but to get the best out of it, as do the real wet fly experts, is a very different matter. I well remember fishing a long glide on the Swale and feeling well pleased with my efforts which produced a brace of trout. My pride was soon humbled when the friend referred to above, *following behind me* down the same piece of water, accounted for another five fish.

To-day there are numbers of anglers who learned to fish dry and have had no experience of any other method. That they are thereby sometimes placed at a disadvantage, they are the first to admit, but they plead that to "fish the water" with a fly one cannot see, must be dull and uninteresting. Each man is entitled to make his own choice so that I will only point out that there are times when the wet fly is likely to pay higher dividends. And that is never more true than in the first few weeks of the season, before the water has warmed up, and when natural insects are often conspicuous only by their absence. Even then, to be quite fair, it must be said that occasions arise when the floating lure may produce better results. April of last year provided me with a striking example of this.

Following a particularly severe winter, my first visit to a Shropshire river was made towards the middle of the month in cold dull weather, with a nip of east in the wind and with the water temperature not many degrees above freezing. In three days' fishing, not one trout was seen rising and there were no insects of any sort either on or near the water.

In these adverse conditions, trout were where one would expect them to be—or the bottom—and obviously a well-sunken fly was indicated. But although different wet patterns were tried in turn, not one of them succeeded in attracting a fish and consequently, late on the first afternoon a change was made to dry fly. This was a policy born of desperation and was quite unjustified by the conditions which would scarcely have been less propitious for the use of a floater. Yet within half an hour, a brace and a half of sizeable trout were in the creel and on the following days fair catches were recorded, all the fish being taken on either the Grey Duster or a Dogsbody.

An examination of the stomach contents of some of the trout taken, showed that they had been feeding exclusively on caddis larvae. Why then they should have risen to a fly on the surface and totally ignored a sunken one, appears to me to defy any logical explanation; but fishing is prone to such anomalies.

It is usual to believe, as already mentioned, that there are only two methods of fly-fishing, but this belief is not strictly correct and needs some qualification. The Rev. Edward Powell, almost alone amongst angling writers, has pointed out that, in reality, there are two forms of dry fly-fishing, the first as it is (or should be) practised on most rivers, and the second as it is practised on the chalk streams; and the two styles are poles apart.

This fact is still not generally appreciated but it is of considerable importance and some little space must therefore be devoted to it. To commence with, it is necessary to compare the characteristics of the chalk streams with those of most other waters, as then it will be evident why widely divergent methods of fishing them are required.

The great majority of our chalk streams are situated in the south, and are moderately big spring-fed rivers, too deep for wading except in the upper reaches, and running quietly through flat and rich water-meadows, with clear banks almost flush with the water. Normally these rivers are gin clear and support great beds of weeds which are carefully cut each year and which harbour tremendous numbers of nymphs and other larvae. Perhaps, more than anything else, it is this wealth of insect life which makes the chalk streams so dissimilar to other rivers. The regular and enormous hatches of ephemerids which these waters enjoy, is directly due, of course, to the presence of such quantities of beneficial weeds.

As these hatches (and the subsequent fall of spinners) occur pretty consistently throughout the season, the patient angler can almost always rely on finding fish rising at some period of the day. He is thus able to cast over selected feeding fish, confident in the knowledge that if his fly is a reasonably close imitation of the fly on the water, he should creel a brace or more of heavy specimens. On the chalk streams, anglers refer to "*the* rise": on other rivers, fishermen speak of "*a* rise".

These big trout of the Test, Itchen, and Kennet, are shapely, well-educated fish, which although mostly stew-fed, fight well enough, although possibly in a less intelligent manner than their smaller brethren of the rough fast streams. On account of the great amount of food available to them, they tend to become fastidious feeders, and because of the relatively slow flow of the river and its extreme clarity, they have ample opportunity of examining everything which is offered them. Unless it is a passably good imitation of the particular insect which is interesting them at the time, they will certainly perceive the deception and reject it.

In these circumstances, the use of the right pattern becomes a *sine qua non*, and it follows that unless the fisherman is able to identify the fly on which the fish are feeding, he is definitely handicapped. Most of those who fish the chalk streams are capable of recognizing the more usual insects, and if they are unable to do so, the river keeper will generally be able to help them, for some of these keepers are sound entomologists.

To mount the right pattern is essential, but that is only half of the story. In addition it must be faultlessly presented. Finding just the pattern which the trout will take is not always easy, although this difficulty is offset by the fact that comparatively few patterns are required on the chalk streams, for they are almost entirely confined to imitations of duns, spinners, and sedges. The great majority of the numerous general and fancy flies, as well as the many copies and suggestions of the Coleoptera, Diptera, and Lepidoptera, all effective on other rivers, are virtually useless.

As I have already indicated it was for the special conditions found on the chalk streams that Halford evolved his system of dry fly-fishing and for which he designed so many artificial patterns. Clearly his methods and flies were never intended for general use on other waters where conditions might be altogether different, and on which, therefore, they might prove unsuitable. In saying that, no criticism of Halford is intended or implied, for the debt fly-fishers (whether they be of the wet or dry school) owe to him is well-nigh incalculable.

I remember reading a description of the chalk streams some years ago, in which they were contemptuously described as providing "drawing-room fishing for city millionaires". There may be a few anglers who feel that way about them, and there may be a grain of truth in it, although they are none the worse for that. On what other rivers in the British Isles, or for that matter in any part of the world, is it possible to see a line of dimples on the surface of the water, stretching as far as the eye can see, and each denoting a feeding trout of an average weight of nearly a couple of pounds?

In some other countries like New Zealand, Canada, and South Africa, fish of several times that weight are taken with some frequency; but they are not free risers as are the trout of the chalk streams; and if they are taken on fly at all, more often than not, it is from a river estuary or a lake, and on a well-sunken lure.

It would be idle to deny that some of the southern chalk streams are not as good as they used to be. Water-extraction by municipal undertakings, extensive drainage schemes, the activities of catchment boards and agricultural committees, shortage of labour, heavy taxation and greatly increased maintenance costs have all had their effect on the fishing. On some stretches little or no re-stocking is being undertaken and stews once full of young fish now lie derelict. In some cases "keepering" has been curtailed or has ceased to exist and consequently weeds have not received the attention they require. In these circumstances the fishing has naturally deteriorated, but it would be quite wrong to accept this as a general picture for it is only true of some fisheries. Many riparian owners and lessees by exercising foresight and good management (and often that trait so beloved by Englishmen—compromise) have successfully overcome most of the difficulties which have beset them with the result that most of the erstwhile famous stretches have suffered but little and the fishing they offer to-day is at least comparable with that enjoyed in the hey-day of the Halfordian era. These south-country streams still hold a big head of fish and whilst it is true that the average weight of the fish has declined in the last thirty years, it remains considerably higher than that of most British rivers. There must be very few waters in this country where it is the usual practice to return to the water all trout of under one and a half pounds (or even two pounds); that on the chalk streams it is possible to do this and still retain a reasonable number of fish, disproves the suggestion that these waters are "finished". Nothing could be further from the truth especially when it is remembered that to the majority of anglers the glory of the chalk streams lies not only in the number and size of the fish they hold, but also in the beauty of the rivers themselves and the quiet rich water-meadows through which they flow.

Chalk-stream fishing and dry fly-fishing are so inexorably bound together in the minds of all fishermen that it is not easy to separate them, necessary as it is to do so. Let me quote what my friend, Cyril Hancock, has written of these waters: "Without them the history of fly-fishing would have been different the world over; for the art of the dry fly in all its fullness could hardly have been developed on lesser streams."

That is very true and in it will be found the reason why for over half a century, whenever anglers fall to discussing the floating fly, they instinctively think of the chalk streams. And that is why most of us are inclined to forget that nowadays the dry fly is fished on almost every river in the country and that its use is not confined to the chalk streams which are few in number and are fished by a relatively small number of fishermen.

The rivers, brooks, and becks of the rest of England, Scotland, Wales, and Ireland are of much more importance to the average dry fly angler, although in character they are different to the chalk streams in almost every respect.

They are of many types, these rivers of mountain, moorland, woodland, and valley, for some come rushing down from the high hills, forcing their way past rocks and boulders, whilst others pursue a more gentle course over stones and gravel, their little white-capped waves constantly dissolving into long shallow glides and deep pools.

All of them possess certain common characteristics. For the most part, these trout streams of the north, the west and the Midlands, flow rapidly between high banks, which force the angler who would not be seen by the fish, to get down to the level of the water or right into it; in fact, the profusion of trees and bushes growing along the banks, often makes wading a necessity.

Another characteristic of most of them is the manner in which the height and colour of the water will vary with every change of weather, so that conditions seldom remain exactly the same for many days at a time. Many are subject to sudden spates. Heavy rain will cause them to rise several feet in the course of an hour, only to fall again just as rapidly when the weather has cleared. Some of the smaller waters, quite considerable streams, holding good trout in the spring and autumn, will become little more than a trickle during a prolonged drought.

But it is in the habits and food of the fish that we find the greatest divergencies between them and the chalk streams. Even the behaviour of the trout is apt to be very different.

On most rivers, if an angler is lucky enough to come across a fish rising with some regularity, he should find little difficulty in creeling it. That is, of course, if it is not one of those irritating fish which will rise at your fly with a rush, and having missed it, refuse to come again a second time, however hard you try to tempt him. Apparently his suspicions have been aroused, although for no reason which is obvious, and there is nothing to be done but to try him again an hour or so later, when as likely as not, the same annoying experience will be repeated!

A very different state of affairs is found on the chalk streams, for here we encounter the steady riser, and to the fly-fisher who has had no experience of these southern waters, there would seem to be no difficulty about tempting him. It is, therefore, a shock to find that he ignores every pattern you show him and an even greater surprise to discover that as long as you continue to present the fly properly, he will continue to pick off the natural insects which float alongside your counterfeit. Unlike his relatives in other rivers, this trout is highly educated and unless the fisherman can discover the one particular fly on which the fish is feeding and can put up a good imitation, he will do better to look for a more accommodating and less experienced specimen. On the chalk streams, this should not be difficult, but elsewhere, on waters where the diet is necessarily of a more varied nature and is mostly found below the surface, one may go a long way before finding another rising fish.

Few rivers, of course, are entirely devoid of ephemeroptera, but since suitable weeds do not thrive in them, they do not enjoy the regular and substantial hatches of up-winged duns which are a feature of the Test and similar streams.

That on most rivers the ephemerids are of no great account (and consequently the fish have to subsist on a wide variety of other insects), constitutes one of the more important differences between them and the chalk streams, on which the exact opposite is the case.

As under normal conditions on most of our rivers and brooks, the small and spasmodic hatches in evidence will be those of many sorts of insects, without any one species noticeably predominating, the fisherman can scarcely put up an imitation of the "fly on the water", because that term pre-supposes a reasonably large hatch of some definite fly. Should he decide to try a copy of one of the many kinds of insects on the river, he will probably find that it fails to attract fish since, when they are taking flies at all, they are devoting their attentions to one particular species and ignoring the rest. And with so many different types of flies on the water (many of them land-bred insects which have got there by accident), and with only scattered and irregular rises being made to them, it is by no means easy to discover what the trout are taking. Except on rare occasions, such as when the mayfly is on, the fish which sucks in one fly after another, is uncommon outside the chalk stream.

In the circumstances outlined above, which seem to me to be the usual ones, the dry fly man's best hope would appear to·lie in some general or fancy pattern, designed to suggest a number of insects; and this is the plan which most fly-fishers are forced to adopt. That represents one great departure from chalk-stream practice, whilst a second is that, since rises are infrequent and dispersed over a wide area, it becomes necessary to "fish the water" far more often than to "fish the rise". These then are what I conceive to be the usual tactics which have to be followed on most waters, but they must be modified according to circumstances. There can be no greater mistake than to follow them blindly as do some anglers, amongst whom there are no greater offenders than those who boast that they use the same pattern throughout the whole season. Is not that the acme of foolishness? That it saves thought, time, and trouble, I do not doubt, but nothing will convince me that it is the best, or even a sound way to catch fish.

The same observation may be made of the man who never uses anything but a general or fancy pattern and who seeks to justify this lazy habit by saying: "After all, when fish are in a taking mood, does it really matter what fly one uses? And when they are not, it matters still less!" That argument must have been propounded time after time; in fact, the thesis is hoary with old age, but to the beginner it spells danger because of its obvious plausibility. On the face of it, it would seem to bear a grain of truth, but when examined closely, a flaw becomes apparent. How often are trout and grayling in a "taking mood"? I venture to say that for by far the greater part of any season, the fly-fisher has to work hard to tempt fish and that "any old pattern" will not solve the problem.

The keen angler who wishes to make the most of his opportunities, is always being forced by circumstances to change his fly, sometimes frequently, according to the conditions of the moment. He may find that it will pay to change from a floater to a wet pattern, or vice versa, and that sometimes a nondescript pattern, which bears no resemblance to anything at all, may prove profitable. On a beck, the use of two (or even three) floaters, instead of the normal single fly, will occasionally alter his luck, but all the time the fly-fisher must be planning and trying a different method of attack if he wants to induce fish to rise to his fly when they are disinclined to do so.

Nevertheless, on every river, brook, and lake, there are periods when, for a time, fish will show a marked preference for some particular insect. A hatch of march browns, of sedges, or of olives, to take a few common examples, may induce trout to feed on them exclusively for such time as it lasts in any strength, and there are occasions when for periods they will take nothing but black gnats. These are the times to dispense with the maid-of-all-work and to substitute a more definite imitation of whatever fly is interesting the fish.

During every season, there are odd occasions when some species of fly or beetle may cause fish to rise in an irresponsible manner. When the grannom is hatching, trout will look at nothing else, and the same applies to the gravel-bed and to a fall of ants. In Wales, there are weeks when the natural coch-y-bondhu beetle is a factor to be reckoned with, especially on lakes, whilst in the north, when the stone-fly and creepers are abroad, fish feed on them to the exclusion of all other insects. The same is true, of course, of the mayfly on those rivers and lakes where it occurs, for it causes trout to become absolute gluttons and for a fortnight or so, as far as fish are concerned, no other fly exists.

One is tempted to wonder what sort of sport is enjoyed by the man who steadily perseveres with some fancy pattern during periods of this sort and I imagine that there can be only one answer.

The crystal-clear streams of the south with their wealth of surface food make the employment of a really small artificial fly imperative, for it must approximate to the size of the natural insect it is designed to imitate. Chalk-stream fish often find that the simplest way to secure the maximum amount of food with the minimum of effort, is to take up some strategic position which enables them to pick every fly off the surface of the river as it floats down to them. The presence of large numbers of duns and spinners, plus many sedges in the evenings, ensures an ample food supply right through the spring and summer without the necessity of going in search for it. In fact, there is so much food either on or just under the surface, that bottom feeding is of no greater interest to the fish.

Contrast this with the situation on other rivers on which owing to the irregularity and general scarcity of surface food, trout have no option but to rely mainly on a sub-surface diet and consequently pay little heed to what is happening above them. In these circumstances, a large artificial fly is more likely to attract their attention than a small one which would probably pass over them unnoticed. This contingency is more likely to happen than might at first be apparent, because swift, broken, and often coloured, water, makes it difficult for any fish to see a small object moving very rapidly on the surface. A fly, whether fished wet or dry, can therefore be tied on a hook at least two sizes larger than would be suitable for the clear southern rivers, and many of the most successful anglers known to me use flies tied on size 10 hooks during May, although a smaller size proves more effective in the early spring and in low summer water.

 This, being a generalization, is a dangerous theory, for I am well aware that on larger slow-flowing rivers, better results may accrue from the employment of smaller flies. That, however, does not conflict with my view that on fast rough waters, rather larger patterns than those generally recommended, may be used with advantage.

It should be clear, therefore, that in view of the conditions the dry-fly angler is likely to encounter on the majority of waters, he will have a disappointing time if he follows Halford's dicta too rigidly. Quite 95 per cent of our rivers and streams demand a rather different technique to that which is eminently suited to the chalk streams.

Although it will not be of general interest, it may be mentioned that conversely, and to an even greater degree, the patterns of floating flies which are suitable for the greater part of the country are unlikely to take many fish on the Hampshire and Wiltshire rivers. For many years now, through the kindness of friends, I have fished a few of the chalk streams with some regularity and, as an inveterate experimenter, I have tried most of the patterns which have proved consistently good killers on other rivers. On occasions some success has been achieved with a variant, but, on the whole, the record is one of failure.

I speak, of course, of general and fancy patterns, and not of flies which are specific imitations of natural insects, although for reasons which will be obvious, not all of the latter are effective on chalk streams. My own conviction, founded on experience, is that fishing on the chalk streams is as different from dry fly-fishing on other rivers, as is, dare I say, chalk to cheese?

VI. On Dry-Fly Waters and Dry-Fly Methods

The strength of Halford's influence, even to-day, can best be appreciated by the admission (although it may be only a mental one) which many fly-fishers make, that there are no real dry-fly waters outside the chalk streams. We know that it is not true, but so great was the spell woven by Halford that our conviction is generally half-hearted. Halford was responsible for the cult of the dry fly and he wrote solely of its employment on the chalk streams; ergo, the chalk streams are the only ones suitable for dry fly-fishing!

Halford, of course, did not suggest anything of the sort, so that any argument on the above lines is fallacious. What he did was to write of a style of fishing well suited to those rivers which he regularly fished himself, but nowhere did he insinuate that the floating fly could be exploited with success on those rivers alone.

Nevertheless an idea was born that only on the Test, Itchen, Anton, and suchlike waters, could the dry fly be used profitably, and to-day, some fifty years later, this myth dies hard.

That this should be the case is curious, for dry fly-fishing is now regularly practised in every part of the United Kingdom, yet there is still a feeling that it is only an apology for the real thing. It is almost impossible to escape this conclusion and only this year one of our leading weekly journals devoted to sport replied to a correspondent, with all the weight of editorial authority behind it, that there was no real dry fly-fishing to be had anywhere in Wales! That is pure bunkum and I can only suppose that we have become so accustomed to reading and hearing of "typical dry-fly water" when a chalk stream is meant, that we half-believe that nothing but a limpid spring-fed chalk river like the Test is suitable for dry fly-fishing.

Reason should tell us that this must be nonsense and that the floating fly can be used to advantage on stretches of the majority of rivers and brooks throughout the whole of the British Isles, just as long as the water is not so cloudy as to prevent the fish from seeing a fly on the surface. As I interpret the phrase "dry-fly water", it can only mean water on which the floating fly can be used with good results; to pretend that Hampshire and Wiltshire have an absolute monopoly of rivers of that nature is surely absurd.

Some readers may look upon that statement as rank heresy and will quote the Test and the Itchen, etc., as being classical examples of dry-fly streams. Because of the nature of those rivers, I would fully agree that they provide the best dry fly-fishing in Britain and probably the most pleasant trout fishing to be found in the world. But I am equally convinced that the floating fly will not kill fish on them one whit better than it will on many a little mountain stream, which pounding its way 'twixt rock and boulder, is the direct antithesis of a chalk stream. On this type of swiftly flowing river, the dry fly will give immeasurably better sport than any sunken one and although it may be next to impossible to "fish the rise" in approved chalk-stream style, this is more than counterbalanced by

the fascination of watching a small floating fly riding the wave-
lets and sailing jauntily along on the top of the little rapids. It is
a type of dry fly-fishing far removed from that practised in the
south and it could not be otherwise, for conditions are so different as to demand an entirely separate technique, although one
still fully capable of providing a great deal of pleasure and sport.

The same is true of dry fly-fishing on the little brooks which
run through the fertile valleys of the lowlands, although since
so many of them are heavily bushed and overgrown, the method
of fishing them is quite different to that suitable for a mountain
stream. In a large proportion of them, fishing is almost out of
the question during the summer months, owing to the stream
degenerating into little more than a trickle with, here and there,
a deep hole, but up to the end of May and again towards the
end of the season, good trout may often be taken from them.
The occasional two-pounder is not unknown and all the fish
take the fly readily.

It is an established fact that on these heavily bushed little
brooks (and the majority seem to be of that ilk in varying
degrees), the floating fly will always account for more trout than
a wet one; and although it is not necessary to go into details
here, there are good reasons why this should be so.

All fly-fishing on these small brooks is difficult and calls for
a deal of bending and crawling and a high degree of accuracy in
casting, but if the angler has the requisite amount of patience
and can retain his sense of humour in adversity, he will enjoy
some good sport and a lot of fun.

When a fish is seen to rise, or heard to do so, as is more often
the case, a careful survey must be made of the terrain, and time
devoted to evolving a plan as to how best a fly can be put over
him. Even a slight miscalculation may result in disaster, for
extracting fly and cast from a branch or bush which overhangs
the water, or from some obstruction in it, may be quite enough
to scare the trout which will also disturb others in his frightened
progress upstream. And such mishaps may easily occur for there
will inevitably be plenty of casting over and under branches and
between or round intervening bushes, so that in the course of a

day many a cast and fly will be lost, albeit in exchange for some increase in skill, since there can be nothing more calculated to improve a man's casting or to teach him control of rod and line, than dry fly-fishing on a small and much-overgrown brook. In fishing "little waters" of this nature, the angler can seldom be more than a few yards away from his quarry, so that short casts are essential and the necessity for keeping out of sight becomes absolutely vital.

It is sometimes said that on this type of brook, fish will take any fly offered them because they are used to such a great variety of flies, insects, and beetles which fall into the water from the trees and bushes which everywhere overhang it. There is some truth in this, although as in the case of all waters, there is generally some pattern which the trout will take more freely than others and consequently any time spent in studying the general conditions and noting what flies are on the water, will always be amply repaid.

A good many anglers find greater pleasure in fishing a brook of the nature described above, to any "super-flumina", and in some ways it may provide dry fly-fishing at its very best—a very different type of fishing to that practised on the Test, although even that wonderful river can provide no more exciting sport and none more full of interest. Fishing the floating fly on a heavily bushed brook is an exacting sort of pastime but one that is never without interest and the reward of the angler who can master it, is frequently a nice bag of surprisingly good trout.

Up to the time of Halford's death, dry fly-fishing was little practised outside the chalk streams. Here and there, some stalwart adventurer would be found demonstrating its possibilities in the most unlikely places, but on the whole it made but slow headway amongst the many anglers who had been brought up on the wet fly.

Its introduction was necessarily gradual, but it gathered momentum rapidly and since the early nineteen-twenties, the cult of the floating fly has made remarkable progress. To-day, there must be few rivers in the British Isles where a man fishing dry would be regarded as somewhat eccentric, as he would have been not so many years ago; and, indeed, amongst the younger generation of fly-fishers of to-day, there will be found a considerable proportion who have never used a wet fly and have no desire to do so. I record that fact although I do not commend it.

In my own lifetime, the dry fly has invaded such strongholds of the sunken lure as parts of Scotland, Wales, Ireland, and Yorkshire. In Ireland especially, one might expect the wet fly to hold its own, yet even in the western parts of that country, the dry fly has made in-roads. In his *Irish Reminiscences*, Mr. Maurice Headlam refers to a friend who, fishing in the south-west, caught within a fortnight, no less than a hundred trout, averaging two pounds each, all of which were taken on a floating fly; and Viscount Grey once expressed the opinion that in May, the River Suir provided the finest dry fly-fishing in the whole of the United Kingdom.

On lakes, the supremacy of the wet fly is seldom seriously challenged, although on all still waters there are days and times when the dry fly will prove the more successful, and this is especially true of hot summer days and evenings, when there is no breeze and the water is like a sheet of glass. In such conditions, it will be pretty obvious that dry fly-fishing will offer the better chance of success, but it must not be thought that these are the only sort of conditions which justify the employment of a floater. The fact is that on most small lakes, reservoirs and pools, there are not many occasions when it cannot be profitably used, especially when there is a little ripple on the water.

In a much-fished lake, the dry fly will often account for the best fish. Possibly from long experience, they become suspicious of wet patterns, for many a time I have taken good trout on a floater after offering them a number of sunken flies without eliciting any response. One angler known to me has never fished a wet fly on a lake in his life and he kills as many fish as those who use nothing else. It is true that at times he finds it pays better to fish more in the surface film than on it, but his fly is never wholly out of sight, and incidentally he seldom uses anything but a hackled pattern.

As is the case on rough streams, the lake fisherman does not, as a rule, get many chances to cast over rising fish, although there will be rather more opportunities of doing so than on a river. If he spots a fish rising and can very quickly cast his fly near the centre of the ring it sets up, there is indeed an excellent chance that the trout will take it. If he is unable to put a fly across it promptly, he will be well advised to cast where he saw the rise for some reasonable period, because the likelihood is that the trout will return to the same place within the space of five minutes or so. And I know of no fish so likely to take a floating fly as a lake trout feeding on the surface when there is sufficient breeze to cause a ripple.

When lake fish are not rising at all, one can only keep on casting until a trout is moved. It is possible that one may fail to connect on the first occasion but if the angler continues to cast over him, the chances are that the fish will come again before long. If the day proves a blank, there is always reason to be optimistic about the evening, for on most still waters in summer, a dry Sedge pattern is wonderfully reliable and towards night-fall, it will invariably offer more chance of success than any wet fly.

On the whole, and in spite of the general opinion that wet patterns are far more killing on lakes, it will be appreciated that good sport may be had with the dry fly, although this is more true of small lakes and pools than of very large sheets of water. I must confess that my efforts at fishing the floating fly on the bigger Scottish lochs have not met with much success.

Having said so much in favour of the dry fly, I would not suggest that either on river or lake, it is ever likely to supplant the wet fly entirely. The latter has its own place in the established order of fly-fishing, and since on most rivers and lakes, it regularly accounts for the greater number of fish, it is never likely to lack adherents.

On the great majority of our rivers, it must be admitted that wet fly-fishing is the more logical procedure. Trout find the bulk of their food on or near the bottom and pay little attention to insects on the surface. A hatch of fly in any strength on rough rivers is a comparatively rare occurrence and one to which fish are so little accustomed, that often it fails to arouse their enthusiasm. The long unbroken procession of duns floating along the surface, so commonly seen on the chalk streams, is so unusual on other rivers that there is nothing to induce trout to take up a favourable position from which they can wait for the insects to be carried to them. The probability is that when a hatch occurs, it will be all over before the trout have realized its possibilities. There must always be exceptions such as those provided by a hatch of, say, march browns or mayflies, and in these cases, it will most probably be a more prolonged affair and the fish will react accordingly. Nevertheless, as a general rule, fish which develop a taste for winged flies on the surface (as a change from their usual diet of nymphs and other larvae) must needs search for them and not many trout will trouble to do this as a regular habit, chiefly because they can obtain sufficient nourishment on or near the bottom with far less expenditure of energy. And no trout will ever use a fraction more energy than is absolutely essential.

Because trout and grayling are, for the most part, sub-surface feeders, it does not mean that they are above picking odd flies off the surface of the water when any happen to come within their line of vision. There can be no doubt that when fish are not inclined to rise, they will still take surface food if it is so placed that they can see and secure it without undue effort.

This fact is often ignored by anglers who favour the wet fly, but were it not true, the multitudes of fishermen who use nothing but a floater would find it so unremunerative on most waters, that they would have to abandon it in favour of the sunken fly. That they do not, is sufficient proof that fish which are not rising may be induced to do so.

To fish the dry fly successfully on rivers other than the chalk streams, demands rather different methods to the four cardinal principles laid down by Halford. To cast over a rising fish is naturally desirable when the opportunity to do so presents itself, but such chances are infrequent and when they do occur, casting may be anything but an easy straightforward affair. More often

than not, the trout which rise with some degree of regularity do
so underneath the branches of trees overhanging the water, and
to cover the fish properly a difficult tricky cast is required.

In just the same way as trout of the chalk streams select a
favourable station from which they can wait for insects to be
carried to them, trout in rough rivers take up a pitch under
overhanging trees and bushes.

Not only do these provide some shade and protection, but
their foliage serves to attract insects and there is always a chance
that caterpillars and suchlike oddments will fall from them into
the water.

When no fish are to be seen rising, it is a sheer waste of time
for the dry-fly angler to wait for them to do so. If anything
approaching a general rise occurs at some period of the day, so
much the better, but the chances of this happening are not likely
to be great. One must fish the water, searching out all the likely
places where trout may lie, very much after the style of the wet-
fly man, although, of course, fishing upstream and keeping the
fly on the surface. As we have already seen, results will depend
largely upon the correct choice of fly. And it will not always, or
even generally, be an imitation of an ephemerid.

When fishing the floating fly in this manner, it is of vital
importance to concentrate on every cast for one never knows
just when or where a fish will take the fly. A very quick strike
may be necessary, for on the whole, the active little trout of the
fast rivers are amazingly quick. Unlike the fat and lazy fish
which, inhabiting the gently flowing streams, generally rise to
the fly in a deliberate manner, they are inclined to dash at the
lure and will often seize and eject it again before the fisherman
has even thought of striking. This is not always the case, for fish
seem to rise in a different way at different times; and the species
of insect will also determine their behaviour, but as a general
rule on most rivers with a rapid flow, it is almost impossible to
strike too quickly.

I am a little afraid of this word "strike" because it is apt to
give a beginner a wrong impression and he will strike a heavy
fish with such force as to break his cast. Personally I doubt

whether I ever strike in the sense of lifting the rod-top to any appreciable degree. A sharp turn of the wrist sufficient to tighten the line is all that is necessary. My own experience suggests that quite a large proportion of fish which take a sunken fly, hook themselves, and the big trout of the quietly flowing waters take a floater as if they meant to have it at any cost. But on any swift river, trout are generally prone to pluck at a dry fly in a most disconcerting manner and unless the angler's brain and wrist work in unison, more trout will be missed than hooked.

If the sole aim is to kill the maximum number of fish, then the judicious employment of a wet or dry fly according to the conditions has everything to recommend it, but in actual practice, the wet-fly fisherman generally remains faithful to his own style. The dry-fly angler, too, is of much the same persuasion, although possibly he is rather more inclined to vary his methods and to try a sunken pattern occasionally. This may result in the capture of a fish or two, but it is unlikely to alter his opinion that as a method of taking fish the wet fly lacks interest.

I do not imagine that there can be any general dissent about the floating lure providing the most fascinating way of fishing for trout and grayling, if for no other reason—and there are several more—than the fisherman is able to see the fish actually taking the fly, a performance which can never fail to raise a thrill, even in the most unemotional angler, however often he may see it enacted. And it is beyond dispute that dry fly-fishing becomes more popular every year, due largely to the increasing recognition of the fact that there are few rivers, brooks, and lakes, in the whole of Great Britain on which it cannot be undertaken with a reasonable amount of profit and a great deal of pleasure.

VII. ON FLIES AND FLY-DRESSERS

There is no lack of literature on the history of fly tying throughout the ages and it is not my intention to do more here than briefly to touch upon it. As long as artificial flies have existed, fly-dressers have attempted to copy the living insect, although ideas on how this should be accomplished have naturally differed, and, from time to time, have undergone many changes.

In the course of years, the type of artificial fly and the materials used for its construction have been subject to alterations but the best of the older dressings have survived to keep company with those of later days. The result has been that copies of any one particular insect have tended to multiply in each generation and in the natural course of events, they must continue to do so.

The standard wet patterns which originated for the most part in the North and Midlands, whilst composed of colours which resemble those of the flies they were designed to represent, were evolved for use on the rough tumbling streams of Yorkshire and Derbyshire and were intended to suggest flies being carried along turbulent waters in a submerged or semi-submerged condition. They suited perfectly, and still do, the style of angling employed and the nature of the rivers on which they were used. The old-time fly-dressers were ever mindful of the fact that the style of any artificial fly must be governed by local conditions and that colour and size must be modified according to the state of the sky and water.

Towards the end of the nineteenth century, the cult of the dry fly made its appearance and Halford produced his long series of flies suitable for this style of fishing on the chalk streams. Up till that time the dry fly had been used in a desultory manner only, and by few fishermen. The popularity it was later to enjoy was due largely to Halford. Faced with the difficulty of attracting trout in the clear limpid waters of the chalk streams, he worked out precise imitations of certain natural flies as we see them, and the models he evolved were beautiful examples of meticulous accuracy. For the conditions and method of fishing for which he designed his floating flies, many have never been bettered. That others have lost the reputation they once enjoyed is probably because Halford was too narrow in his outlook and lacked that quality so necessary to every artist—imagination. His "exact imitation" created great interest because it was an advance on anything which had been done before in that direction, but it did not prove to be the final answer to the problem as was thought at the time. Before Halford, the type of water and the method of fishing had decided the general appearance of the artificial fly almost as much as did the shape and colour of the natural insect, but whilst he did not ignore the first, I feel that he laid far too much emphasis on the second.

To-day the fly-tier uses more imagination in order to produce a pattern which *will appear to the fish* as a copy of a live insect. To obtain this result, he does not look upon the natural fly as a laboratory specimen, each part of which must be examined under a microscope and carefully copied to the smallest detail. He secures it by more impressionistic methods in which the blending of the materials to suggest the tints of the living insect forms an important part. His hackled patterns in particular must appear to the uninitiated to bear but little resemblance to the flies they are intended to imitate but the modern fly-tier ("designer" would be a better and a more accurate word) has a freer conception of how best to suggest the diaphanous translucency of many water-bred insects.

If there is a tendency to produce more hackled patterns than in the past as I opine there is, it is because the present-day fly-dresser is satisfied that they permit him to reproduce in a more natural manner the transparent delicacy of the living insect. He believes that the required degree of translucency and iridescency can be better suggested by bright steely hackles than by the lightest of feathered wings. These observations refer in the main to floating flies more than to wet patterns; the latter are pretty well standardized, the dry fly is still in a state of evolution.

That all artificials must be tied in relation to local conditions is still generally agreed. Every fly-fisher knows the pattern which proves deadly on some streams and far less effective, or even useless, on others. The reason may not be evident to the ordinary angler and it is the solving of this, amongst other problems, which helps the fly-dresser to design successful patterns.

The average amateur fly-dresser who builds up a fly, as fancy dictates, from any materials which may be at hand, can hardly expect the result to be particularly effective. All of us do it, I suppose, but although this procedure provides us with some pleasant amusement and has a certain interest attached to it, it is scarcely the best way of evolving a killing pattern; and I feel quite sure that few of the flies with names known to every angler, were created in this haphazard manner.

To produce a beautiful building one has to know something of architecture as well as how to lay bricks. In exactly the same way, the "how" of fly-dressing is comparatively simple, but the "why and wherefore" demands a good deal of study.

In selecting dressings for the flies mentioned in this book, it has been my endeavour to choose those which seem most likely to prove reliable for general use, whether they were designed or recommended by the older school of fly-tiers like Ronalds, Pritt, or Halford, or by the "moderns" such as G. E. M. Skues, Lunn, T. J. Hanna, Lock, Woolley, Eric Taverner, or Edward Powell.

Of the great fly-fishermen and fly-dressers to which reference is frequently made in this volume, F. M. Halford, the originator of the exact imitation theory and the father of English dry fly-fishing, is too well known to call for more than a passing reference. Suffice it to say that his books created the same tremendous interest in natural and artificial trout flies as did those of Alfred Ronalds in a previous generation. The reputation of many of his patterns has suffered in the course of years but his influence on dry fly-fishing was incalculable and even to-day it is almost as great as it was during his lifetime.

Of the others, Roger Woolley is a professional fly-dresser and a particular competent one, who has made a life study of the natural insect. Also a professional, Thomas J. Hanna is an Ulsterman who obviously has little use for dogma and tradition and whose work is full of originality. A naturalist and an angler, he has shown that he is never afraid of breaking new ground and it is that trait, allied to his highly developed sense of the effects which can be obtained by fur, feather, and wool, which has enabled him to produce a number of valuable patterns.

Edward Powell, the rector of a small Shropshire parish, is

another enthusiast who has designed several general and fancy patterns of exceptional merit. A very expert fly-fisher himself, he knows a lot about the likes and dislikes of trout and grayling and a lot more about the best means of securing the colouring and effects he requires in his patterns. Although most of his flies are of the impressionistic variety, the results he secures are sometimes devastating in their efficiency.

William Lunn, a river keeper on the Test, did not originate any flies until he took up fly-tying late in life, but in a short time he accomplished a great deal. He had, I feel, a quite extraordinary flair for creating killing patterns and his Houghton Ruby and his Lunn's Particular will long remain as monuments to his intuition and skill. Not the least merit of his patterns is that none call for rare or unusual feathers, for Lunn relied almost entirely on material which was readily available.

Skues, in my opinion, is in a class by himself. His reputation is unassailable and his books on fly-fishing are models of clearness and lucidity which will be read long after the present generation of anglers has passed away. Possibly as a fly-designer he may lack something of the fire and imagination of Powell or Hanna, but he is the thoroughly efficient artist with a great understanding of the material in which he works; a supreme master of his craft whose every move is founded upon sound reasoning. Perhaps his long life in the legal profession has contributed to this, but whether this be so or not, the fact remains that of all the many good patterns he has given us, none were the result of chance or guesswork. Each and all were developed on rational lines as a result of knowledge, observation, experience, experiment, and a little inspiration. John Lock and his son, Ernest, were both highly skilled fly-tiers. The latter, who died in 1947, was also an exceptionally good angler, well known on the Itchen and the Dove. The flies tied by the Locks were of a characteristic order, having short cut hackles and being rather heavily hackled according to modern standards. But they all floated well and were good killing, hard-wearing patterns which cocked beautifully, due to the superb winging. Just how this was accomplished was Lock's secret, which was not revealed even by careful examina-

tion. Unwaxed silk was used and the wings were very firmly tied
and well spaced out, with the white silk in between them. The
most celebrated fly associated with these two dressers is, of course,
Lock's Fancy, which I believe was invented by the elder Lock.

Rather surprisingly several famous flies were originated by
anglers who were not fly-tiers themselves. Examples which
occur to me are the Peter Ross, that great lake pattern, which
was invented by an angler of that name, and Greenwell's Glory,
the dressing of which was suggested to Jimmie Wright (himself
responsible for creating several well-known salmon flies) by
Canon Greenwell.

Although only a few of the originators of celebrated flies have
been mentioned above, there are, of course, a number of others
who have invented highly successful patterns. The names of
many of them will be found in the "List of Flies" in connection
with those patterns for which they were responsible.

To make any attempt to mention the origin of every fly must
be out of the question, because as most fly-fishers well know,
a great number of our standard patterns were evolved in the
dim and distant past. Some date back to the fifteenth century or
even earlier, and many to the days of Walton and Cotton, and
the names of those who invented them have long been lost. In
many cases too, it is probable that no one person invented them
but that, like Topsy, they "just growed".

If no mention is made of that great anonymous army of professional fly-tiers, it is because that, with a few outstanding exceptions, their lot is not to create new patterns but to tie established
ones to the great and lasting benefit of all fly-fishermen.

Most of these craftsmen, and craftswomen, carry out their
duties in our tackle factories, unheralded and unsung, but with
an efficiency, deftness, and speed which no amateur could hope
to rival. A smaller number are in business on their own, or are
to be found plying their art in the back room of tackle shops
in many a town and hamlet throughout the British Isles. The
work of most of them is of a high order and the products they
make are exported to almost every country in the world. All
and each of them deserve the thanks of every man who ever uses

an artificial fly, for without them, fly-fishing would be brought almost to a standstill.

Only occasionally does one hear of a new and highly successful fly being invented by any of the hundreds, perhaps thousands, of amateurs who tie their own flies, with the exception of some half-dozen (or fewer) whose genius has received recognition.

Why this is so, I do not know, for of the beautiful work of some amateurs there can be no question. Some of the most perfectly tied flies I have ever seen were the work of amateurs like Sir Gerald Burrard, Mr. R. G. B. Gardiner, Dr. T. E. Pryce-Tannatt, and General Sir John Taylor, to mention but a few known to me who, without doubt, are supreme masters of this craft.

They each have their own individual style and to compare these is a matter of considerable interest, for to me (and I imagine to most fly-fishers) an artificial fly is something rather more than a mere article of commerce or just a type of bait for fish; it is (or should be) a work of art. Like a picture, one can examine its proportions, perspective, structure, and colouring. Yet it must be agreed that it is not always the most perfectly tied or best groomed pattern which will necessarily kill the greatest number of fish. Sometimes a roughly tied specimen will do quite as well, although perhaps the roughness is generally of the deliberate and studied variety, for the fly which is merely carelessly dressed is seldom much of a success.

What must always be of importance is the quality, selection, and mixing of the materials. Substitutes for the correct feathers and dubbings are apt to be like most makeshifts, only rather more so!

First-class hackles, in particular, are not easy to come by, but the difference between a good hackle and a poor one often represents the difference between a full creel and an empty one.

Fly-dressing is a fascinating hobby and one of those crafts in which the amateur can vie with the professional. The latter, of course, works immeasurably quicker; he (or more often, she) will tie three or four patterns whilst even a skilled amateur will be producing one. But however beautifully a fly is tied it can never be a perfect specimen if it is not made of the best materials, and that is a matter in which all the advantage lies with the amateur.

VIII. ON FLY-TYING

The Author's Recommended Books
  Fly-Tying: Principles and Practice, Sir Gerald Burrard.
  How to Tie Flies for Trout and Grayling, McCleland.
  Fly-Tying for Trout, Eric Taverner.
  Modern Trout Fly Dressing, Roger Woolley.
  Dry-Fly Entomology, Halford.
  Dry-Fly Fisherman's Entomology, Mosely.
  Troutfisher's Entomology, Wauton.
  What Fly Is That?, by "PPP".

Recommended Contemporary Books
  The Flytiers Manual, Mike Dawes. A step-by-step guide to nearly 400 fly patterns.
  Flytying Techniques, Jacqueline Wakeford. 350 colour photographs show all stages in flytying, from basic techniques to advanced ones.
  Robson's Guide, Kenneth Robson. A stillwater trout fly pattern book, with the dressings, history, and colour photos of the finished fly.
  200 Popular Flies, Tom Stewart. A very useful patterns book for trout, sea-trout and salmon.
  Fly Dressers' Guide, John Veniard. A basic textbook on techniques and standard patterns, with over 600 dressings.
  The Super Flies of Still Water, John Goddard. 60 selected "most productive" patterns, illustrated, with background information.
  Trout Flies of Stillwater, and *Trout Fly Recognition,* John Goddard. Authoritative guides to the natural fly life for stillwaters and rivers respectively, with lists of dressings.
  Sea-trout Fishing, Hugh Falkus. An expert guide to all aspects of sea-trout fishing; includes effective sea-trout patterns.

IX. On Maintaining the Purity of the Breed

Certain patterns of flies have become standardized because there is universal agreement about the dressing and it follows that in these cases the correct tie should always be followed. Yet one often sees examples of flies which have little likeness to the patterns whose name they bear. That this should happen is regrettable and there is little excuse for it. In some instances it may be due to the maker's ignorance of the correct dressing and since some trouble has been taken in this book to give the universally accepted ties of a large number of established patterns, I am hopeful that it may prove of assistance to amateur fly-tiers and also to professionals, not all of whom are altogether blameless in this matter. There are fly-dressers, I am sorry to say, who, lacking the correct materials, are inclined to substitute others with the hope, too often justified, that the user will not notice the difference.

It is almost impossible to lay too much stress on the necessity of tying standard flies in accordance with the proper dressing as laid down by the inventor or agreed upon by tradition or general consent. In the case of some patterns which demand feathers now almost unobtainable, some modification cannot be avoided but whenever some substitution becomes necessary it should be undertaken with understanding and care. Where common wing and body materials are concerned, the employment of any but the right ones is quite inexcusable. There can be little objection to properly dyed feathers, always with the important proviso that those used are of the right quality in the first place. Any fly-tier is open, of course, to alter a pattern in any way he thinks fit since there is no stud-book for artificial flies. He can wing a Red Quill with a teal wing if it so pleases him, but to call the resulting mongrel a Red Quill would be absurd. That may be an extreme example but nevertheless extraordinary looking flies masquerading under the names of well-known patterns may be purchased any day.

Wine growers jealously guard the reputation of their products by ensuring that they are correctly described. A good pattern of artificial fly is worthy of the same consideration and should be protected from the vandals who would turn it into something quite different.

I am speaking, of course, of standard flies which may be so incorrectly dressed as to be nothing more than travesties of the named patterns they are alleged to represent. No reflection is intended upon fly-dressers who vary the dressings of well-known patterns in order to make them effective for varying conditions. A Tup's Indispensable, for example, may be dubbed in several ways, any one of which will be effective for some particular occasion. Nevertheless there is only one Tup's Indispensable and any fly not tied in accordance with the recognized dressing should be designated "Tup's Indispensable (Variation)", or by some such label as will distinguish it from the standard dressing.

X. On Buying and Stocking Flies

One of the greatest troubles which faces every beginner when first he fishes alone is to know which pattern to use when so many are available. His tackle dealer may have advised him about the best flies, to buy but when he examines them at the riverside, he may find that he has three or four dozen from which he must choose one. Almost certainly he will wonder, as all of us must have done when we first started to fish, why it should be necessary to have such a vast number of artificials to cover relatively few insects.

The answer is that in the first place there are a goodly number of insects which provide food for trout, since in addition to duns, spinners, and sedges, there are all sorts of land flies which get carried on to the water at times, besides hosts of beetles, moths, shrimps, and so on. Many of these numerous insects have to be copied in the various stages of their existence, whilst in the case of the ephemerids, there are constant changes of colour in the sub-imago and spinner stages, each of which demands a slightly different treatment in the artificial.

Then again, there is another factor. Whereas half a dozen artists will paint the same scene in as many different ways, their pictures varying from the photographic effect to the impressionist, so does the work of fly-dressers vary in exactly the same manner. In consequence of this, it is not uncommon to find a number of different patterns all designed to imitate the same insect, none of which can be said to be more "correct" than the others. One may prove a sure killer on one day and another on the next, according to the conditions of water and weather. Experience alone can be the guide as to which is the most consistently effective pattern.

Lastly, for the average fisherman, the number of patterns will be almost doubled since the majority of them are tied in two styles—wet and dry.

In these circumstances, it is clear that to cover every eventuality, a great number of artificials will be required, although just how many is the minimum for the fly-fisher to carry, is a matter of opinion upon which few anglers will agree. Half a dozen different patterns, each in at least two sizes, will satisfy one man for the whole season. Others will say that even this small number is excessive and will tell you of those freak cases about anglers who fish year after year with one pattern only.

It is a point upon which it is difficult to offer advice but for myself, I prefer a wide choice because there can be nothing more exasperating than to find oneself without some particular pattern at the moment it is desperately required. With a collection of artificials, carefully selected to meet every possible emergency, this may still occur, although not quite so often! I must freely concede that it is not a difficult task to take a large number of fish on a small number of patterns, but I feel that by imposing a limit of this nature upon himself, the fly-fisher must rob himself of a great amount of pleasure. For that reason, I am always a little sorry for the "one-fly" man because he must lose some sport and a great deal of interest and fun.

A couple of medium-sized fly boxes of the usual design will accommodate over a hundred flies between them (exclusive of lake or extra-large patterns) which gives a choice of some forty different patterns in two or three sizes each. That may sound ample, but if one wishes to include wet and dry counterfeits of the commoner natural insects, together with examples representing nymphs, beetles, grubs, etc., plus a selection of popular fancy and general patterns for river and lake, and a small assortment of Mayflies,' then the number mentioned above will be greatly exceeded.

Most fishermen have a stock cabinet or stock boxes, in which they house their flies and from them, fill up the "working" fly boxes when they go a'fishing, according to the probable needs of the day. If one fishes the same water pretty regularly, this plan entails little trouble, but if one is travelling about, the selection needs careful consideration in relation to the type of rivers to be fished, the season of the year, and the probable state of the water.

The stock box holds a fascination of its own for any angler who can enjoy building up a collection of flies, just as did collecting stamps or birds' eggs in our boyhood. There are many worse ways of spending some of the long winter evenings than in arranging, re-arranging, and extending a collection of artificial trout flies. It is a pleasant task, besides being an essential one, for unless flies are examined regularly, they are bound to suffer from the ravages of moths. Some of the D.D.T. preparations now on the market will settle these little pests but even then only if the flies receive regular attention as, to the best of my knowledge, none of these substances will kill the eggs. Whatever form the stock container takes, it should be as moth-proof as possible, as if these creatures can get into a box, they will do so and their larvae will ruin the contents in an incredibly short space of time.

There are, of course, all sorts of ways of housing artificial flies and after testing many of them, I have come to the conclusion that there is nothing to beat an ordinary cigar box. It has several advantages besides being inexpensive. Being made of cedar, it repels moths, and as a rule the lids and joints fit so well that they cannot find a way in; but its greatest advantage is that those little cardboard boxes in which flies are generally sold, fit snugly inside it.

If these small containers are placed on edge, twenty of them can be comfortably housed in a cigar box measuring $8\frac{1}{2}$ x 5 x $2\frac{1}{4}$ inches, whilst if the exposed edges are marked with the name and sizes of the pattern it holds, a double advantage accrues. Firstly it provides a quick and simple method of learning the name and appearance of all flies in one's possession and secondly, shortages become apparent in time for replacements to be made. Some anglers find it convenient to arrange the small boxes with the fly names in alphabetical sequence, but in a matter of this sort, the most satisfactory arrangement is that which best suits the individual fisherman.

The lids of the cigar boxes should be marked with the type of flies they contain such as "Wet", "Dry", or "Mayflies". Six of these boxes will hold nearly 1,500 flies which, I imagine, must be as many as the most enthusiastic collector could ever want! They are made, of course, in several shapes and sizes, but a friendly tobacconist can generally produce some empty samples of the right dimensions to take the smaller containers.

Before leaving the subject, perhaps I may be permitted to offer a few words of advice to the tyro. When he first starts fly-fishing he will be wise to put himself in the hands of a friend or a reputable tackle dealer, who will be able to advise him about the patterns he will need. Nevertheless I would counsel him never to purchase a great number of flies until he has had at least a season's experience by which time he should be in a position to decide for himself the patterns he is most likely to want.

He will also, if he is wise, seek the advice of local fishermen, for on most rivers there are local patterns which are often highly successful, although they may be almost unknown and possibly useless on other waters.

And I would particularly advise him never to be afraid of "shop" flies, even though some angling writers are wont to be politely critical of them. They will not all be perfect, but the majority of these professionally tied specimens will be good enough to arouse the envy and respect of the most highly skilled amateur dresser. The latter, however, has one advantage over the commercial tier because he can (and should) buy the best quality hackles it is possible to obtain, and no others. The professional must needs purchase his feathers in bulk and the hackles will come in all qualities. The worst may be thrown out, but all the remainder must be used since he cannot afford to waste them. Should he do so, the price of flies would have to be considerably more than the average angler would care to pay. In spite of this the "shop" fly is nearly always beautifully tied and will stand up to wear and tear, although on account of the unavoidable variation in the quality of the hackles, and occasionally a departure from the standard dressing, it is as well, whenever possible, to examine all flies before buying them.

Every artificial fly should be true to pattern, firmly tied, with a neat and small head, and with the eye clear of wax. Trying to clear the eye of a hook which is clogged up with hard wax is one of the more annoying riverside pastimes because it invariably occurs to the pattern which is particularly wanted and only when it happens to be the last of its sort in one's possession.

A fly which proceeds to undress itself when first introduced to a trout is also a nuisance. Not only does it have to be "written-off" but it has to be changed for another, quite often just in the middle of the evening rise. (Perhaps in these circumstances it may be better to trim it up and continue. I recall an occasion when I fished for some time with a fly which had disintegrated and was sans wings, sans hackle, and had only half of its body left. Starting as a floater, it ended as a nymph, and was eminently successful—far more so than in its original form.)

In the case of a dry pattern, the wings should be firmly fixed and perfectly balanced so that the fly cocks properly on the water and does not lie flat on its side. The hackle should be full, stiff, and not bunched up; and it must be evenly spaced, save that some fishermen contend that a V-shaped piece cut from underneath is advantageous in that it will assist the fly to float on an even keel. The hackle should sparkle when held to the light and it should be stiff and steely since it represents the legs of the insect in a minor way only, its most important function being to ensure that the fly falls lightly on the water and then to support it on the surface.

The hackle of a wet fly may be softer, since it does not have to assist the fly to float; and it must be supple so that when sunk, the current may agitate it and thus give the fly the impression of life. Most hackle flies should be lightly dressed, and it is still a common fault to find them too heavily hackled.

And as a last piece of advice, I would add that like women and precious stones, artificial flies should always be chosen in the daylight.

XI. ON THE FLY-FISHER'S YEAR

March is a cold, uncharitable sort of month in which only hardy (or foolhardy) trout anglers venture forth. In April, there is often a dearth of fly on the water, although if a mild spell brings on a hatch, it can be a tolerably good fishing month—some will say one of the best. At this season, the trout will mostly be in the pools rather than in the fast runs, and if they take the fly at all, they do so in no uncertain manner, as if they welcomed a change of food after the long winter months of bottom feeding.

With the appearance of the alder in May, fishermen can look forward to the most favourable period of the season; the best of it starts with the alder and ends with the mayfly. There are "early" rivers and "late" rivers, but on the whole the majority of them fish better during May and the first fortnight in June than at any other time.

After the departure of the mayflies and the stone-flies, sport deteriorates rapidly and soon after the middle of June, the rot sets in. Trout then become shy and fastidious, and although their natural curiosity may cause them to follow an artificial fly, they quite often do so without any intention of taking it. This lack of co-operation lasts right through the dog-days of July, which enjoys the unenviable reputation of being probably the worst fishing month of all. So that, roughly speaking, the six outstanding weeks of the season are followed by a similar number during which the most skilful angler will find it difficult to kill fish. The best hope of taking trout will be on a small dry fly (or an equally small lightly hackled wet pattern) fished in the fast broken runs, and of all July flies, there are few better than the Pheasant Tail. Nevertheless on rivers and lakes July is a month when fish are much given to smutting and although trout may be breaking the surface in every direction, they are extraordinary difficult to catch. On most rivers, unless these conditions are in evidence, one may sometimes fish for days on end without seeing a single rise. On the chalk streams, the b.-w.o. and sedges help to save the situation although better sport may be expected in the evenings than during the day.

An improvement generally manifests itself in August, especially if there be a fair amount of rain; and with the coming of September, the angler will find much better conditions. By this time, the fish will be deserting the runs and will be returning to the deeper pools and they will generally take the artificial fly with the same zest as they display in the spring. Taken all round, September is one of the better months for the fly-fisherman.

By October, it is nearly all over, except for rainbow trout which spawn and come into condition later than brown trout, and the angler is thus free to turn his attention to that other sporting fish, the grayling.

From January to the end of March, there are many trout anglers who look to the salmon to provide sport. Sometimes I do so myself, although never with great enthusiasm, for as a sporting fish, I rank the salmon well below trout and sea-trout.

But although there is a close season for fish, there is none for the fisherman, for he will find plenty to occupy his leisure hours during the winter months. There are rods to be overhauled, reels to be cleaned, baits to be re-mounted, lines to be treated, casts to be tested, flies to be dressed, replacements to be bought, and a dozen or more other jobs demanding his attention. The fence months, in fact, provide him with a golden opportunity for examining and renewing his tackle in readiness for the approaching season; improvising, improving, mending, making, and generally renovating his equipment.

To the true disciple of Izaak Walton, no task could be more congenial. As he works, he will recall red-letter days of the past,

look forward to the not-so-distant days of spring, and in imagination, see the trout rising again in the old familiar spots; and all
of them will be monsters which will take his fly in no half-
hearted manner. That he will derive considerable satisfaction
from his reflections is not to be doubted, for as every angler
knows, of the many pleasures fishing provides, anticipation is
by no means the least.

PART II

A LIST OF
NATURAL AND ARTIFICIAL FLIES
Arranged in Alphabetical Order

"For the making of these flyes, the best way is to take the naturall flye and make one like it that you may have sport; for you must observe what flyes haunt the water for the seasons of the yeare, and to make the like with cottons, woole, silke, or feathers to resemble the like."—HENRY PEACHAM in *The Compleat Gentleman* (1634).

"I cannot now in honesty but frankly tell you, that many of those flies I have named, at least so made as we make them here, will peradventure do you no great service in your southern rivers and will not conceal from you, but that I have sent flies to several friends in London, that for ought I could ever hear never did any great feats with them. . . ." CHARLES COTTON in *The Compleat Angler*, Part 2 (1676).

PREFACE TO THE LIST OF FLIES

ARRANGEMENT

In the following pages I have endeavoured to compile a list of natural and artificial flies taken by trout, grayling, and sea-trout, in a form which should be useful to the reader. By turning to the name of any natural insect, he can ascertain at a glance which artificial patterns are used to imitate it, and, conversely, by looking up the name of any pattern, he can discover immediately which insects it is intended to represent and, in most cases, how, when, and where it should be used.

To accomplish this, it has seemed desirable to include both natural and artificial flies in one alphabetically arranged list, a method which allows of quick reference, but which also gives rise to certain difficulties.

As an example, under the Blue-Winged Olive heading, the reader might reasonably expect to find the dressing of the Orange Quill. This pattern is considered to be possibly the best imitation of the natural fly, most likely in its spinner dress. This method has something to recommend it, but a difficulty is encountered in dealing with some other patterns. How, for instance, should the Red Quill be treated? Without doubt, it is a pattern frequently used to represent the b.-w.o., but it is also equally as effective as a suggestion of several other insects: to include its dressing and method of use under the Blue-Winged Olive would be misleading and to repeat these particulars under every natural fly it is supposed to represent, would not, I imagine, meet with general approval.

Again, whereas the Greenwell's Glory is regularly employed as an effective suggestion of the b.-w.o., it is an even better pattern to imitate the dark olive dun. As a general rule, therefore, the dressings and details of patterns given under the heading of any natural insect are solely of those which bears its name. Flies which are copies or suggestions of any specific natural insect and have a recognized name of their own (e.g. Red Quill) are listed under that name, although, of course, reference is made to them under the names of any natural flies of which they are considered to be serviceable imitations. Exceptions have been made in a few cases, in which for some reason a separate heading appears to be unnecessary or undesirable.

Where there is any chance of confusion between the artificial and natural fly, the initial letters of the former are shown in capitals, viz. March Brown, whilst the latter is printed in "lower case", viz. march brown.

THE DRESSINGS

It must be emphasized that the dressings of the various patterns have been carefully selected. It would have been possible, and very much easier, to have given five or six times the number, but I venture to think that it would have been proportionately less helpful to readers. Wherever an original tie is quoted, it has been thought wise to give it, whenever possible, in the inventor's own words. Only in the matter of hook sizes has some liberty been taken. Where some of the older patterns are concerned, the sizes of hooks suggested by the originators would be considered too large for modern usage, and in other cases, the inventors failed to make any reference to this matter. All hook sizes in this book are in the nature of recommendations only and allow of some latitude for personal predilection.

ILLUSTRATIONS

Publisher's note: The current edition includes four new colour plates of 60 fly patterns, replacing the previous plates. We have tried to illustrate a good selection of flies from several categories: hackled dry flies, winged dry flies, hackled wet flies, winged wet flies, nymphs, sea-trout flies, and grayling flies. Although there could be many different criteria for choosing which patterns to illustrate, we decided that the most valid method of selection would be to pick the patterns we thought readers would most often want to tie. So most of the patterns shown were selected on the grounds of popularity.

All the patterns were tied in their correct sizes, using the materials specified in this book. However, in two of the plates the patterns are shown larger than life-size, for clarity. (Hackled dry flies and nymphs are shown at one-and-a-half times life-size; winged dry flies at one-and-a-third times.) We hope this will not cause readers any problems that are not outweighed by the extra clarity. In the two remaining plates, the patterns are shown approximately life-size.

Also in the interests of clarity, the photographs for this edition were shot against a white background. For the most part, this makes it easier to see the outline of the fly, and avoids having strong colours in the background detract from the natural colours in the patterns. However, in one or two instances pure white parts of the dressings may be difficult to see. Two examples are the white nylon wool in the Bowtie Buzzer and the white cock-hackle wings of the Red Ant. Again, we hope that the advantages of a simple white background outweigh the disadvantages.

The flies shown in the four colour plates were tied by Jacqueline Wakeford, and photographed by her husband, David Hawker.

CLASSIFICATION, ETC.

The scientific names of insects are, I am informed, in a state of temporary confusion due to a world effort to standardize them. In this book, the old nomenclature is used because I feel sure that fly-fishers will prefer the names made familiar to them by Halford and Mosely, at any rate until such time as the scientists have settled their differences of opinion.

However it may be as well to point out that entomologists have recently take to the practice (which I have not followed) of using the term Ephemeroptera to denote all those insects which were previously known to anglers as Ephemeridae, and applying the latter name solely to mayflies.

A LIST OF NATURAL AND ARTIFICIAL FLIES
Alphabetically Arranged

ADJUTANT BLUE

One of F. M. Halford's dry patterns designed to imitate the iron blue dun. I do not think that it is used as a trout fly to-day, least of all on the chalk streams where it originated. It owes its inclusion here to the fact that it is a very useful floating pattern for grayling, especially on cold days in the autumn, when the iron blue dun is on the water. Halford's tie was:

Body: A strand from the pinion or tail feather of an adjutant, stripped on the edge only by tearing down the longer flue, with finger and thumb.
Wings: Medium starling.
Hackle: Blue Andalusian.
Whisks: Three fibres of hackle.
Hook: 16 to 14.

Nowadays it is often seen dressed with a coot wing instead of starling; and to avoid any untoward incident and possible injury to some innocent officer of the Army or R.A.F., it may be as well to make it clear that the adjutant in this case is a different sort of bird. It is, in fact, a large Indian stork, and as the feathers are now almost unobtainable a peacock quill dyed blue is generally substituted.

ALDER (*Sialis lutaria, S. fuliginosa*)

The Alder, or Orl fly as it is called in some parts, is known to almost every fisherman because it is a common enough fly of which the larva thrives not only in pure rivers but also in water so highly polluted as to be deadly to other forms of insect life. There are actually two species in England, but the differences between them are small and anglers can reasonably treat them as one fly. The Alder is a distinctive insect with a large black head, a dark (nearly black) thorax, and turkey brown wings, heavily marked with dark brown nervures, but it is generally recognized more easily by the way in which it folds its wings over its back like a sloping roof and by what has been well described as its "hump-backed" appearance.

Conceivably it might be mistaken for a sedge, although its wings lack the hairs which are characteristic of the caddis flies, except for the difference between them when on the wing. The sedge's flight is a quick purposeful affair, whilst the alder flops along like some old lady. The fisherman is soon made aware of a hatch of alders because they are insects which persist in alighting on his hands and neck, although, unlike the mosquito, they are friendly and entirely harmless.

Although alders are found in tremendous numbers in the vicinity of rivers, lakes, and ponds, giving the impression that they must be on the water in strength, this is seldom the case for they never get there save by accident. But they are seldom far away from the water and will be found close to it, resting in trees, bushes, plants, buildings, etc., often in amazing numbers, and whilst it is true that they do not often get on to rivers save in small numbers (presumably because they can usually fly well enough to clear them), they sometimes get blown on to lochs in sufficient quantities to cause a big rise of fish. These occasions, however, are rare and since trout do not get many chances of feeding on the natural fly, it is rather a mystery why they should take the artificial so well.

Widely distributed throughout the country, the alder makes its annual appearance in May and June and although very much of a water-side insect, it is not a water-bred one. The eggs which number between two and three thousand are laid by the female on rushes, sedges, rocks, etc., overhanging the water in order to give the hatching larvae the chance of dropping straight into it. On a flat surface, the eggs are neatly arranged in rows, whilst on a round surface, such as a plant stem, in a spiral.

The brown patches of eggs must have been observed by most anglers as they can be seen on the sedges, etc., along the edges of rivers and lakes in great numbers during May and June. The female fly works backward over the egg patch which is covered with her body as she lays it. If removed from her eggs during the operation, and replaced at another point, she will return to the unfinished patch and complete it before commencing a fresh one. A most orderly creature, this old lady!

In about ten days' time, the eggs hatch out and the young larvae either fall direct into the water, or if as is sometimes the case, they hatch a little distance from it, they immediately take to it, for in their case it is a question of water or death. On reaching the river or lake, they proceed to bury themselves in the mud or silt.

The young larva is one of the commonest inhabitants of our waters and is a repulsive-looking creature with a broad head and body which tapers off rapidly to a very narrow tail. Below the three pairs of legs, are a number of attachments on each side of the body which look like smaller legs, although in reality, they are the larva's gills. I think that it is possible to confuse this brownish-coloured nymph with the larva of the whirligig beetle, another common water creature, and it should therefore be remembered that the latter has a long narrow body, which does not taper off towards the tail, and also an insignificant head.

Alder larvae are strong swimmers, particularly when young, and feed on small water insects having a special fondness for caddis larvae and the smaller Ephemeridae nymphs. After twelve months or so of aquatic life, during which time it grows and sheds its skin many times, the larva seeks dry land again. Crawling a short distance from the water (normally only a few yards) it finds a bank or some suitable patch of soft ground in which it quickly buries itself. Sometimes the hole may be a shallow one and in other cases it may be as much as eight inches deep and it is here that the creature sheds its last larval skin and becomes a pupa.

In about a fortnight's time, the adult fly emerges and digs its way out, leaving behind its cast skin which shows all the organs and the form of the pupa. Soon after this the insect takes wing and mating takes place on some plant, fence or building, but never in the air.

The Artificial Fly

The Alder is one of the oldest of patterns and, during the last three hundred years, the dressing has changed surprisingly little. As a dry fly, it is not successful on all rivers, which is indeed curious, for when trout get a chance to take the natural insect, it is invariably when it is struggling on the surface of the water. Fish can hardly take the winged pattern as a representation of the larva, since there is no resemblance between them, but the fact remains that when the Alder is fished either wet or semi-submerged, it often provides capital sport. It is one of those mysteries one so often finds in angling for which there would appear to be no logical explanation.

Personally I seldom use a wet fly after April and consequently my experience of the Alder is not great, although even in these circumstances, it has given me more than one red-letter day. For when trout are taking the artificial at all freely, there would seem to be no limit to the number of fish one can kill on it and for that reason, it is a fly which no fisherman can afford to ignore. It is as effective on lakes as on rivers and during the mayfly season when a Green or Spent Drake fails to interest trout, an Alder is considered to be the correct answer since, for some unknown reason, it may kill remarkably well at that period.

I am well aware that Halford seemed to be of the opinion that the alder was of little interest to anglers and that he suggested that many of them did not know an alder when they saw one, or to be more accurate, that when they observed the sedge, *Sericostoma personatum*, they thought that it was an alder. It has always surprised me to find these views emanating from such a reliable observer although a possible explanation of some of Halford's strange views is that he did not realize that the Alder is a pattern which will kill well on one river and is useless on another, in spite of the fact that the natural fly may occur in numbers on both. Yet there does not seem to be any doubt about that, although why it should be so I cannot explain.

Certainly the Alder is a favourite pattern with many fishermen, although it can never have had a greater admirer than Charles Kingsley who immortalized it in his *Chalk Stream Studies*. Since that work is not now easy to obtain, I cannot resist quoting from it at some length although aware that the passage will be well known to many readers:

"O thou beloved member of the brute creation," wrote Kingsley. "Songs have been written in praise of thee; statues would ere now have been erected to thee had that hunch-back and those flabby wings of thine been 'susceptible of artistic treatment'. But ugly thou art in the eyes of the uninitiated vulgar; a little stumpy old maid toddling about the world in a black bonnet and a brown cloak, laughed at by naughty boys but doing good wherever thou comest and leaving sweet memories behind thee; so sweet that the trout will rise at the ghost or sham of thee for pure love of thy kindness to them, months after thou hast departed from this sublunary sphere. What hours of bliss do I not owe to thee! ... Have I not seen, after a day in which the earth below was iron and the heavens above as brass, as the three-pounders would have thee and thee alone, in the purple duck, old Moody's face grow redder with excitement, half-proud at having advised me to 'put on' thee, half-fearful lest we should catch all my lady's pet trout in one evening? Beloved alder-fly! Would that I could give thee a soul (if indeed thou hast not one already, thou and all things which live), and make thee happy in all aeons to come! But as it is, such immortality as I can,

I bestow on thee here, in small return for all the pleasant days thou hast bestowed on me."

Most trout fishermen have some affection for the natural alder and her artificial for she is a herald of the best of the season's fishing.

March is a cold month and in April there is still a dearth of fly on the water. But with the departure of that month, a largish fly makes its seasonal appearance. In my own case, its identity generally puzzles me for a moment until it dawns upon me that it is none other than our dear old friend and staunch ally, the alder. There can be no reason, of course, why its advent should prove so unexpected (although somehow it usually does) but it is always pleasant to renew acquaintance with this old lady since her arrival denotes that the best fishing of the year should be close at hand, because, as I have already said, the cream of it starts with the alder and ends with the mayfly.

That Kingsley held such a high opinion of the insect was meet and proper, since he it was who invented the best dressing of it; the very same pattern on which Mr. Skues once took eighteen brace of trout in a day, only two of which were under a pound. And on the following day, he creeled sixteen and a half brace, nearly all of them on the same fly. Kingsley's tie for his pattern was:

Wings: Two pairs from secondary feathers of a dark, frackled game hen, dull side innermost, and sloping well over the body, with the hackle in front of them. The wings, in fact, should lie nearly flat.
Hackle: Black or dusky hen wound in front of the wings.
Body: Peacock herl dyed magenta.
Silk: Crimson.
Hook: 12 to 14.

This is the usual dressing of this famous pattern although some anglers prefer it with a body of dark floss silk, which may be a better tie for the chalk streams; but on other rivers, and on lakes, the original is preferable. In the smaller sizes, a single pair of wings will suffice and personally, I would never have a double wing even on the largest size.

Like most alder patterns, the above will continue to attract fish long after the natural insect has departed, for most of them are also quite effective as suggestions of the darker sedges.

There are a goodly number of other winged patterns to choose from and amongst the best of them is one known as the Crosbie Alder. It is well spoken of by some fishermen who should know, including Mr. Skues who has taken trout up to 4 lb. 6 oz. on it.

The Crosbie dressing is as follows:

Body: Rubber over claret silk showing through. *Hackle:* Darkish blue.
Wings: Peahen sloping well over the body. *Hook:* 12.

On the whole, in common with a great many others, I am not fond of winged imitations of any insect, but the Alder is an exception. Both the above patterns kill well but for the sake of those fishermen who prefer hackled flies, there are two patterns which can be safely recommended—the Herefordshire Alder and the following fly which I believe was evolved by Mr. Skues.

Tying silk: Claret waxed, clear wax.
Hackle: Dark blue feather from the breast of a blue cock or hen, woolly to the tip of each fibre.
Body: Peacock herl from stem of eyed feather, dyed magenta. *Hook:* 10 to 12.

For a variation, this pattern can be hackled with dark grouse. It serves quite well as a suggestion of many of the medium-sized dark sedges, especially at dusk.

The Herefordshire alder, by the way, is another hackled pattern which is more often fished dry than wet. A splendid killer, it is, nevertheless, one which I include under the Alder heading with some hesitation as I very much doubt whether fish take it for an alder at all. That it will take trout when the natural insect is on the water is true enough, but it is quite as effective before the alder makes its seasonal appearance and long after it has departed. And it loses none of its attractiveness when fished on waters where the natural fly has never been seen.

There was a time not many years ago, when the Herefordshire Alder was almost unknown outside the county which bears its name, although it soon established itself as a favourite on the Shropshire streams and on those along the Welsh border. Then it was looked upon as a good general fly; nowadays along the Clun, Onny, Teme, Lugg, Arrow, Ledwych, Rea, Corve, and Usk (or, at least, on certain parts of those rivers), it enjoys a great reputation and no pattern is more popular. Visiting some of those streams recently, I met a number of fishermen who use this pattern, and no other, the season through, fishing it in most cases as a floater. It should be mentioned that in the districts referred to, this fly is frequently spoken of merely as "the Alder" which is apt to confuse visitors from outside the county.

In recent seasons, its fame has spread farther afield and I have heard of good bags of fish having been made on it in Devon and Ireland. On

most of the rivers mentioned above a largish fly (on a size 12 or even a
10 hook) appears to be favoured.

Having said so much in commendation of this pattern, I must add
that in my experience, whereas it will kill exceptionally well at times,
I have found it more or less useless when trout are not in a taking mood
and need tempting; and even on its own "home waters" I do not find it
nearly as effective an all-round fly as the Grey Duster.

The dressing of the Herefordshire Alder is:

Tying silk: Yellow, well waxed to give it a brown colour.
Body: Centre tail feather from a cock pheasant.
Hackle: Medium blue dun or Andalusian cock.
Hook: 10 to 14.

That is the dressing in general use to-day, but Canon C. F. Eagles
had another which deserves mention because he used very few patterns
and caught a colossal number of trout on them, so that we can be sure
that all his flies were first-rate killers. Moreover, it was probably he who
originated the Herefordshire Alder. The dressing for the Canon's fly
(which he always fished wet) was:

Body: Pheasant tail fibres over purple floss, with the floss showing as alternate
rings.
Hackle: Weathered Andalusian (brown dun).   *Hook:* 10 to 12.

ALEXANDRA

Originally known as "The Lady of the Lake", this well-known fancy
pattern was renamed in honour of our Queen Alexandra, then H.R.H.
Princess Alexandra. It appears to have come into general use around
1860, but who invented it is uncertain. Most authorities attribute it to
W. G. Turle, of Newton Stacey, Stockbridge, although others give the
credit to Dr. Brunton, the creator of Brunton's Fancy.

There was a time when the use of the Alexandra was barred on some
waters on the grounds that it was too deadly, although it does not bear
that reputation to-day. How the myth arose is a subject for speculation
as none of the great fly-fishers of that time would appear to have had
any enthusiasm for it. I cannot remember one who has anything to
say in praise of it. Personally I have no faith in it at all as a trout fly for
rivers and I have met very few anglers who are not of the same opinion.
There may be something to be said for it as a lake fly and it is sometimes
used by Blagdon anglers; and it is said to be effective for sea-trout.
Always fished well-sunk, the Alexandra may possibly be taken for a

stickleback or a minnow in its mating livery of scarlet, green and silver. Without doubt it is a pattern which almost every angler can recognize at sight, although the reason for that is probably because it is shown in every tackle dealer's catalogue, due, I suspect, to the fact that it is one of the most satisfactory patterns to illustrate in colour.

Body: Flat silver tinsel.
Wings: Strands of green peacock herl, usually tied with a strip of ibis on each side.
Hackle: Black hen.   *Tail:* Red ibis feather, and/or peacock.   *Hook:* 10 to 12.

ANTS (*Lasius niger, Formica rufa, etc.*)

Ants are not, of course, aquatic insects, but in their brief winged state they often swarm near water in countless thousands so that inevitably large numbers fall on the surface. This occurs on hot days in August and September and when it does so, it causes great excitement amongst trout who will settle down to feed on the ants, whether they be black, red, or brown, to the exclusion of anything else. One may not be lucky enough to meet a migration of the winged ants like this more than once or twice in a lifetime for it only occurs on odd days each year. But when one comes across it, there is nothing more annoying than to find that one cannot take advantage of the opportunity through having no suitable pattern to offer the fish. I speak with some feeling because many years ago such an experience happened to me. The trout were gorging themselves on the ants and because there was nothing in my fly-box that remotely suggested these creatures, my creel remained devoid of occupants when it might so easily have been filled.

The insects are too well known to need any description and are of no great importance to fishermen except during their short annual migration in the winged state as mentioned above.

Of the large number of dressings designed to imitate the different species, the two following may be taken as fairly typical:

Black Ant

Wings: Pale starling.   *Hackle:* Two cock starling hackles.
Body: Peacock dyed black or quill from a chaffinch's tail feather, with a butt of black ostrich.   *Hook:* 14.

Red Ant

Wings: Medium starling wing feather.
Hackle: Blood-red cock.
Body: Crimson tying silk with a couple of turns of bronze peacock herl as tag nearest the bend of hook.   *Hook:* 14.

Mention must be made of Lunn's patterns for the red and dark ants.
I have not tried them myself, but friends who have done so, have told
me that they are capital flies. Writing of them in *River Keeper*, Major
J. W. Hills says: "They do not account for many fish in the season
because ants are only flying a short time, but after a flight has crossed,
which may be as early as July, do not forget to try an ant. I consider it
to be the surest take of any pattern of any insect." The dressing for the
red ant (dry) is as under:

RED ANT (LUNN's)

Body: Wind on deep orange silk at the end of the shank to form the body of the
insect; then give a few single turns to make the waist.
Wings: Strip enough fibres from a large white cock hackle and straighten. Tie
on slanting over the body. Trim off in front and cut the length required to
form the wings.
Hackle: Light bright red cock hackle.
Tying silk: Deep orange.
Hook: 15 to 17.

Mr. J. W. Dunne produced one of the best imitations of an ant, but
like certain other of his flies, I find it a little troublesome to tie. Mr.
Arthur Ransome's dressing is much simpler. He gives details of it in his
Rod and Line, a book, incidentally, which makes particularly pleasant
bedside reading. Actually the tie is almost the same as Lunn's, with
orange tying silk for the thorax and orange floss silk for the pear-shaped
body. Red cock's hackle are used for the legs. Perhaps it will be better to
let Mr. Ransome speak for himself. "The floss silk", he writes, "seems
extravagantly bright when dry, but when oiled . . . it darkens, like the
tying silk, to a deep ruddy chestnut. In the actual insect, the wings lie
flat over the tail and project a little beyond it. This impression can be
reproduced by tying in on the thorax a pair of hackle points. The tips
of the hackles are constricted in tying in and the effect is of narrow
glassy wings. I used the palest honey hackles I could find. The body is
more easily shaped if the floss silk is split, so as to have a narrow band to
wind in and so one that will not so readily become unmanageable. . . ."

With half a dozen of these impressionist ants, duly oiled, in a match-
box on a hot August day with fair water in the river, it was, of course,
impossible not to hurry off to show them to the trout. . . . My impressionist ant had hardly floated six inches before a trout had him. Twelve
fat little trout (a whole jury) mistakenly declared themselves satisfied
of the innocence of my impressionist ant, besides one or two that I
had missed or lost.

Their verdict is enough to justify me in offering this extremely simple dressing to those who one day or other are likely to need an ant or two in a hurry.

Mr. Ransome concludes with an observation or two, which deserve special attention: "With it should be a warning that on a dull day shortly afterwards, the fish would not look at the Ants, but came well to other flies. The Winged Ant is not a general utility fly, but when it is good, it is very good. That is when, and only when, the ants are on the river. That may happen any day at this time of the year (August), but it is likeliest to happen on a bright hot day."

It is, however, the wood ant (*Formica rufa*) which is the trout's favourite. And naturally so, because it is larger than the other species and along those river valleys where it is found its nests will be seen everywhere. Often it is present in such vast numbers that it is not only during its short winged state that it gets on the water. Swarming over trees and foliage along the banks, specimens are constantly falling into the river, where trout will be quick to snap them up. Nevertheless it is during the short annual migration of the winged ants (which occurs in July or August) when the real feast takes place. The fall of the insect on the river is apt to be very local, but wherever it occurs, great sport will be enjoyed if a suitable imitation is available.

The Welsh Partridge and the Claret and Mallard are both similar in colouring to the natural wood ant and either will serve as a killing imitation of it. Whether fished dry, semi-submerged, or sunk, they will give satisfactory results.

If you require a more exact imitation of the natural insect, Mr. Skues has evolved the following pattern. Wet or dry, it is an excellent fly and one which may also be used to represent the smaller varieties of ants. The dressing is:

DUSKY WOOD (SKUES)

Tying silk: Hot orange, waxed clear wax.
Body: Two round blobs of deep dusky red-brown pig's wool, trimmed to ant shape, and exposing tying silk between them as waist.
Hackle: Blood or mahogany red cock tied just behind the shoulders; two turns only.
Hook: 13 or 14.

Any reference to the life history of ants may seem to be out of place and for that reason I have left it until the end. Ants are not, of course, aquatic insects and consequently it is of no assistance to the angler to know details of their life and habits.

At the same time, I cannot recollect any occasion when a fall of ants has been under discussion amongst fishermen without one of them having raised the question as to the reason for this annual migration and generally as to how and why these apparently wingless creatures develop wings. Almost invariably these questions remain unanswered.

That being the case, and although the subject may seem irrelevant here, I believe that brief notes about the private lives of ants will be welcomed by most fishermen, who on the whole, are keenly interested in the birds, the beasts, the flowers, and the insects they come across when enjoying their sport. And the life history of the ant is in many respects remarkable, as befits an insect which is particularly highly developed and for its size possesses an exceptionally large brain.

Most of us know that some species of ants capture others and turn them into slaves and also that aphides (green-flies), of whose sweet secretions ants are very fond, are kept in specially constructed chambers and are guarded and "milked" by worker ants detailed for the job. Fewer know perhaps than an ants' nest is air-conditioned and that workers are posted at the doors to close them at night or during inclement or cold weather, and, conversely, to see that they are open during the day and on hot nights. Or that ants have two stomachs, one to provide sustenance for themselves and the other for the benefit of the community; from the latter are fed the queens, the young and the needy.

Anglers, however, are more interested in knowing a little about the great annual flights of ants which they are almost certain to observe at some time during their fishing expeditions, but to understand the reason for these, it is necessary to know something of the ant's community.

Each nest shelters three types of ant, the males, females, and a third sex, the workers, which in reality are incomplete females. Of these the first two are winged and the latter, wingless. The workers also vary in form and size according to the functions they have to perform. The winged females which are destined to become wingless queens, are then solely engaged in breeding and are fed and tended by their own retinue of workers. There may be several queens in a large nest, and strange as it may seem, they live together in perfect harmony.

Once every year, on a hot summer's day, the immature winged females, accompanied by the winged males, leave the nest on their first and last flight, whilst at the same time, those of neighbouring communities do the same. Modern scientific opinion tends to the view that the flight is planned and put into being by the worker ants, which prevent any attempts to make premature flights until the appointed day, when they all drive out the winged members of the nest.

The flight is in reality a nuptial one and not a migration, as anglers usually suppose. Mating takes place in the air, sometimes within a few yards of its origin, in which case the female will at once return to her old home or possibly to some neighbouring friendly nest. In each case she will be welcomed and received as an additional member of the breeding staff.

There is, however, always the possibility that she may not meet a suitable mate until she is a long way from her original nest. When this is the case, after rubbing and pulling off her wings which will not be required again, she may experience difficulty in finding the nest from which she started or any other friendly abode, and then nothing remains to her but to establish a nest of her own.

The winged males die after pairing, so that the queen proceeds to lay her eggs in solitary state. All her first-born will be worker ants, for without them the many functions to be undertaken in an organized community could not be carried out. It is they who look after and feed the queen and the next batch of young, and it is they who construct the intricate chambers and passages which form the nest.

The queen, when once mated, continues to lay eggs, at the rate of about half a dozen an hour, for the remainder of her life, which may be of six or seven years' duration or even longer. Compared to most insects, ants are long-lived, workers having been known to have survived as long as sixteen years, which enables them to instruct and teach their successors in a manner rare in the insect world. It is the workers who feed the larvae (which are incapable of feeding themselves) and who break open the pupal cases at the right moment to free the young ants, since they can seldom perform this act without assistance. The workers, too, are responsible for moving the larvae from one chamber to another so that they may enjoy exactly the right temperature, which must vary in different parts of the nest according to the vagaries of the weather. And, incidentally, it is the pupae which are erroneously called "ants' eggs" and which are sold dried as food for aquarium fish.

Scientists agree, I believe, that whereas man's ancestry goes back a mere million years or so, ants have inhabited this globe for between 40 and 50 million years. This should have given them ample time to develop, yet one must beware of thinking of an ants' nest as a perfect example of a socialistic state for, truth to tell, it is a community with a distinct air of "Alice in Wonderland" about it. Ants shelter and succour

numerous parasites, some of them beetles many times larger than themselves which in the end are their undoing, for eventually they will de-
stroy all the inhabitants of the nest, although even in these circumstances,
nests are known to have had a continuous existence of eighty years. John
Stewart Collis put it this way: " When we think of ants we generally
visualize extreme order and efficiency, but the oddity of the parasitic
intrusion undermines this idea. If we ourselves were to sit down to table
with porcupines, alligators, and lobsters, and to feed them at the expense
of our own children; if we were indifferent to crickets nearly as large
as ourselves; if our houses were inhabited, against our wills, by cock-
roaches the size of wolves, and flies the size of hens; if we fed monstrous
animals with our babies because they exuded whisky, we could hardly
stress the efficient ordering of our lives. Yet that is a fair comparison,
according to Wheeler and Huxley, with the habits of the ants."

APHIS

The aphis, or green-fly, is what scientists call "a form of homopterous
Hemiptera" which sounds very important for such a minute creature.
To ordinary folk it is the little insect which is such a pest to gardeners
and especially to rose growers.

From June until the end of July, it is common along the banks of most
waters, and in spite of its diminutive size, its bright delicate green colour
makes it conspicuous amongst the sober hues of the majority of insects.

Trout are quite inordinately fond of these small flies which are often
blown on to the water from nettle beds and other vegetation bordering
streams. A gust of wind will sometimes cause them to fall or be carried
on to the water in such numbers as to produce a rise of fish over a wide
area. That it must take thousands of these little flies to do this is obvious
but they are often present in the vicinity of rivers in millions. On the
Upper Onny, for example, marrow-spoon tests have shown that for
nearly two months they are more or less the main diet of the fish.

The aphis does not lay eggs, but produces her young alive and prolific breeders like rats and some fish cannot compete with her. It has
been computed that if all the descendants of one pair of these insects
reached maturity, in one season alone their total weight would be
greater than that of all the human beings in the world! This is not really
surprising because the young aphides themselves, commence breeding
when only a fortnight old.

Nevertheless, although both trout and grayling like these flies few
fly-fishers will think it worth while to carry any special patterns to

imitate them, if, indeed, it is possible to copy such an insignificant insect. Should the necessity arise, one could but try some small green pattern and probably a Blagdon Green Midge or an Arrow Fly would serve.

APPLE GREEN

One of the most popular grayling flies in all parts of the country and extensively used for trout in most European countries except Great Britain. As a grayling pattern, it is best liked as a summer and early autumn fly, being fished both wet and dry. There are several slightly different dressings, of which that given below is perhaps the most popular.

Body: Light-green floss.
Wings: Pale starling feather.
Hackle: Ginger cock.
Tail: Three whisks as hackle.
Hook: 14.

AQUATIC SPIDER

In many ways, this is an extraordinary fly, for it will cause more fish to rise than any other pattern with which I am acquainted. More than once I have fished up a stretch without moving a trout and then have fished it again with an Aquatic Spider and have immediately had half a dozen rises to it. The fault of this fly seems to be that the proportion of fish hooked to those risen is far less than one might reasonably expect: and the obvious course of changing to a smaller pattern does not overcome the trouble.

The method of using the fly is to retrieve it slowly in such a way as to cause the legs to work backwards and forwards, a movement which trout appear to find irresistible. It has been used with some success as a dry fly for salmon; it has killed a number of mahseer; it is a wonderful lure for big chub, and can be used as a floating pattern for trout on almost any type of river or loch.

Made with a solid (shaped) cork body, covered with peacock herl, and with peacock herl legs, it is not the easiest pattern for the amateur to tackle without tuition. It is a pattern I always have with me, not only because it will sometimes take trout when nothing else will, nor because it was invented by my father, but because there are times when one likes to know whether the fish are still there!

ARROW FLY

This pattern is rather similar to the Blagdon Green Midge. Feeling that the latter is often taken for those juicy little green caterpillars which, in summer, often swarm in thousands on the leaves of trees overhanging the water, I redesigned the Midge on caterpillar lines. The Arrow Fly was the result and since then it has provided me with some excellent sport on several occasions. It can be fished wet or dry but is most effective when fished under oak trees bordering a stream. There are times when the caterpillars fall into the water in a most regular manner, even in still weather, and there is nearly always a good trout waiting to receive them. Give him a fair imitation of the caterpillar and he is almost certain to take it without any hesitation at all. The Green Caterpillar is used for the same purpose. The tie for the Arrow Fly is:

Body: Emerald green silk body, hackled from tail to shoulder with a white hackle, grub-wise.
Hook: 12 to 14.

ATTRACTOR

A spider fly of the fancy type, which often proves a good killer on fast rocky rivers. The tie is:

Body: Light orange tying silk, well waxed.
Hackle: From a peacock's neck feather.
Hook: 14 to 16.

AUGUST DUN (*Ecdyurus longicauda*)

The August dun, or autumn dun as it is also called, has four wings and two setae, and is so like the march brown that for years anglers felt puzzled about it; they knew that it must be a separate species but it had no scientific name, and it is only in recent times that modern entomologists have afforded it recognition. Actually it was classified as a separate species by an English entomologist named Stevens, over a hundred years ago, but this had been overlooked until it was rediscovered by Mr. Martin Mosely when he was endeavouring to clear up the mystery of this insect in 1932. So for a long period *E. longicauda* had the unusual distinction of being a fly recognized as a species of its own by fishermen but not by scientists, and it was the latter who had lagged behind.

Although so very similar in appearance to the march brown, the duns show certain points of difference. For one thing the august dun is generally rather smaller, and for another, its wings lack the characteristic mottled markings of the march brown. The female spinners are almost indistinguishable but the male spinners of the august dun are most striking-looking creatures and have aptly been described as having the appearance of red-hot needles. Some I observed on a tributary of the Welsh Dee last September had bodies that were more pink than red although doubtless these would have become darker in the course of a day.

As far as fishermen are concerned, there is not much likelihood of confusion arising because it is safe to say that any fly looking almost exactly like a march brown, if seen in late summer or in autumn, is definitely an august dun. The march brown is seldom on the water after the first fortnight in July, whilst the august dun does not appear until the same month, does not hatch in any great numbers before August, and is still prevalent during September and October. Major John Evans has suggested that a better name for *E. longicauda* would be the Autumn Brown and I am sure that all anglers will agree with him.

The august dun is unknown on the chalk streams but is fairly widely distributed elsewhere, although like the march brown it prefers fast-running streams. Special patterns to imitate it do not appear to be necessary because the ordinary March Brown patterns will obviously serve the same purpose. Nevertheless, there are a number of patterns bearing the name August Dun, commencing with one given by Ronalds. Mr. Skues prefers a copy of the spinner and suggests the following dressing for use in July and September:

Hackle: Red cock.
Body: Flat tawsy gut ends, dyed red-orange, tied in at the shoulder and whipped over the bare hook to the tail and then back to the shoulder. He expresses the opinion that probably an orange-red seal's fur body would prove equally as effective.
Wing: The speckled part (from near the root) of the red feather from a partridge's tail.
Whisk: Honey dun cock.
Hook: 13 or 14.

Francis Walbran had a dressing (wet) which he called the August Brown, a good name for the natural fly, although I like Major Evans's better. Walbran had great faith in his pattern and when the natural insect was on the water in the late summer, he made some remarkable catches on it, including one or two dozen good trout from the Yore in three hours' fishing. His tie for this fly was:

Body: Light brown floss silk, ribbed with yellow.
Legs: Brown hackle.
Tail: Two rabbit's whiskers.
Wings: From a cock pheasant's wing feather.
Hook: 12 to 14.

During the autumn this fly is also useful for grayling.

AUSTIN'S GOLD
A wet pattern for large trout or night fishing and useful on lochs. The invention of Mr. G. Austin of Birmingham, whose tie for this fly is:

Body: Flat gold.
Hackle: Red cock's tied from tail to shoulder, palmer-wise, and then cut off level with the point of the hook.
Wings: Brown mallard tied "rough" and slightly longer than the hook.
Hook: 10 to 12.

BABY SUN-FLY
This is the Rev. Edward Powell's name for this pattern which he originated and which, fished dry, appears to be an excellent fly to imitate the black gnat in the early part of its season. Why this should be so is not easy to understand because a brown body and a coch-y-bondhu hackle—not to mention the whisks!—would hardly seem a good imitation of *Bibio johannis*. On the other hand, most patterns designed as copies of the black gnat are, in my opinion, too black and the body of Mr. Powell's fly is perhaps nearer that of the natural insect. But it is indisputable that when the black gnat first comes on (which is in April or May according to the locality) the Baby Sun-Fly will kill extraordinarily well for a while, although, for some unknown reason, it appears to lose its attractiveness later on. But for the first week or rather more, it is a pattern which is capable of great execution. The inventor's tie is:

Tying silk: Black.
Body: Rabbit's face ribbed with tying silk.
Hackle: Very small coch-y-bondhu cock.
Whisks: Three strands coch-y-bondhu or black.
Hook: 14 to 16.

If one analyses any of Mr. Powell's patterns, the pains he takes to obtain some particular colour or tint becomes evident, a fact which may well account for the success many of them enjoy. The "make-up" of the Baby Sun-Fly is no exception since the body is of a special colour and of the right consistency to make the fly float well. A rabbit's coat is brown on top and bluish next to the skin *except* in that small triangle between the eyes and the nose and it is from there that we must obtain the dubbing for the body of this pattern, because only at this spot is the colour sequence brown, black, blue.

Mr. Powell advises fly-dressers to sink their scissors into it to the proper depth to obtain an equal quantity of brown and black and then to rub it together. The result is a dark-brown felt-like substance full of short stiff fibres just right to stand up on the surface film but also having enough body to hold oil. This is the mixture required for the body of the Baby Sun-Fly and also for that of the Paragon—and none other will do.

BADGER HACKLE

Any fly hackled with a badger hackle can, I suppose, be called a Badger Hackle and however incorrect this may be, it is quite commonly done. Yet I have never met a fly-fisher who would not agree that there is a pattern of that name, although not one in fifty knows what it looks like. At first sight, this may seem strange but it is not really so because the Badger Hackle is a most elusive sort of fly. To the best of my knowledge, no dressing for it, under that name, is given in any angling book, ancient or modern. On this point I am open to correction, but a search has failed to reveal one.

It may be that there is no such fly for whereas there are ties for the Badger Quill, Badger Quill Hackle, Badger Red Tag, Barlow's Badger, Badger Variant and Detached Badger, there is never a mention of the Badger Hackle. But I think there is, for I have always understood that it is the same as the hackled Badger Quill but tied with a silk body. Because in the case of these two patterns it seems to me that the hackle is more important than the body, I never use either, much preferring the Grey Duster which is a near relative and a better all-round fly, or even a Grey Palmer.

However, for those who require it, the following is a useful dressing (by Hanna) of a "Badger Hackle".

Tail: Black cock hackle fibres.
Body: Black silk, usually ribbed with silver wire.
Hackle: Well-marked badger hackle, i.e. black centre with white list.
Hook: 14 to 16.

This pattern can be varied by using a hackle in which the list is not pure white but creamy or yellow. Fished wet or dry, it is often a success as a suggestion of the black gnat.

The Badger Quill Hackle is tied in several different ways of which one of the most usual is:

Tail: Black cock hackle fibres.
Body: From the stripped quill of a peacock's eye feather.
Hackle: Well-marked badger hackle.
Hook: 14 to 16.

The above, which should be fished as a floater, is preferable in my opinion to the winged pattern known as the Badger Quill, an old fly revived by Halford, but which never appears to have become very popular.

The grayling fisherman has the choice of a number of flies of the badger hackle variety of which the undermentioned are probably the most universally used.

BADGER RED TAG (Woolley)
Body: Bronze peacock herl, with tip of gold or silver under tag.
Tag: Red floss.
Hackle: Badger cock hackle.
Hook: 14 to 16.

RED BADGER
Body: Red floss, ribbed silver wire and silver tipped.
Hackle: Badger cock from shoulder to tail.
Hook: 14.

BLUE BADGER
Body: Blue floss, ribbed silver wire and silver tipped.
Hackle: Badger cock from shoulder to tail.
Hook: 14.

SILVER BADGER
Body: Silver tinsel, with red tag at head and tail.
Hackle: Badger hen.
Hook: 14.

BAIGENT'S BROWN

A pattern designed by the late Dr. Baigent of Northallerton, for all-round dry fly-fishing, and there can be no doubt that it is a first-class killer in most waters and under all sorts of conditions. The theory of this fly has been fully explained by Lieut.-Colonel Keith Rollo in *The Art of Fly-Fishing*. The dressing consists of a yellow floss silk body, wings of the fibres of a hen pheasant quill, with a large dark furnace hackle at the head. The tying silk is yellow and the hook size may vary between 11 and 16, according to local conditions.

BARM FLY

A pattern unknown to-day and one of which I have no personal knowledge. At one time, however, it was known as the "Knobbler" and enjoyed a great reputation. Francis Francis thought much of it and said that he had found it deadly on many streams, and for that reason alone it should be worth reviving. It was probably intended to represent one of the larger sedges.

Body: Large and fat, of any fur of a creamy colour.
Hackle: Red cock's.
Wings: From a dark speckled cock pheasant's wing feather.
Hook: 12.

BEAVERKILL

An American wet or dry pattern, discovered and named by Judge Fitzwilliam Fitch, the original being an unidentified pattern purchased in England in, or about, 1825. Writing of this fly, which is highly popular both in Canada and the States, that great American authority, the late Theodore Gordon, said: "The original patterns from which the so-called Beaverkill fly originated, were bought in England, and I fancy must have been imitations of sedge flies." This may be correct but if so, the original is scarcely likely to have been dressed with a tail. If it was a hackled pattern, it may well have been a Silver Sedge. There would seem to be no valid reason why the Beaverkill should not prove as attractive in this country as it does in North America.

There are two variations of the fly, dressed as below, both of which are normally fished dry.

Wings: Dun, light or darkish.
Hackle: Brown, head to tail.
Body: White floss silk.
Tail: Brown mallard.
Hook: 12.

The dressing of the second is:

Wings: Curlew, brown.
Hackle: Brown, shoulder only.
Body: White silk, ribbed flat gold.
Tail: Usually none; sometimes brown or grey mallard.
Hook: 12.

I think that the first is decidedly the better pattern, although the second is said to be nearer the original English fly, which possibly had landrail wings, for which curlew's are a good substitute.

BEE FLY

The several patterns bearing this name have been in existence for centuries, but nowadays they are not considered to be of much account in this country except for chub fishing, for which they are still popular. In Austria, Germany, and other countries, however, they are still well liked for trout fishing, and fished dry, in hot summer weather, they appear to take quite a number of good fish. The type illustrated is a typical one which has been tried with some success on English and Irish lakes. The dressing is:

Body: Alternate wrappings of black and orange chenille.
Wings: Pale starling wing feathers.
Hackle: Ginger cock sparsely tied.
Hook: 12.

BEETLES (*Coleoptera*)

The importance of beetles to the fly-fisherman is not as fully appreciated as it should be. It must be some thirty years since Leonard West pointed this out to me and since then I have been increasingly conscious that he was right.

All through this book I have endeavoured to emphasize that except on those few streams where the up-winged duns are of paramount importance, the food of trout is made up of a great variety of different sorts of insects and amongst them, the great Coleoptera order, which contains no less than eighty-six families of beetles and goodness knows how many thousands of species, cannot be ignored.

Beetles are present in tremendous numbers in almost every river, brook, lake, and pool, and there are hundreds of species of aquatic beetles which both in their adult and larval states are freely taken by trout and grayling, as is clear from the frequency in which they occur in autopsies.

In addition, there are, of course, scores of land beetles which accidentally get carried on to the water, where the buzzing disturbance they create serves to attract the attention of fish.

If a census were taken of the sub-surface insect population of any stream or loch, it would be found that Coleoptera constitute a major group. In view of all these circumstances, it is surprising that anglers as a whole trouble so little about imitating them. There is no particular difficulty about doing so, either by a hackled fly, fished on or below the surface, or by those "exact imitations" in size, shape, and colour, if not of some particular beetle, at least of a group of beetles. Because so many of the latter are beautiful examples of the fly-dresser's art, most fly-fishers like to carry a few patterns, although for some obscure reason they are apt to look upon them as being more decorative than useful. The result is that most close imitations of beetles become such permanent residents of the fly-box and are so seldom (if ever) allowed to leave it, that in course of time they qualify as its oldest inhabitants.

This is a mistake, for there is not the slightest reason why they should not kill just as well as any other type of artificial fly, but I am inclined to think that they would be more generally used were the patterns endowed with popular names. For the most part, they are seldom referred to except as "a beetle of some sort". Floating patterns often take well on hot sunny days in dead calm water when there are not many other flies about; in fact, just in those conditions when it is usually most difficult to find any fly to interest fish; and often when sunk, they will account for old and shy trout which would not easily be tempted by any other sort of artificial fly.

An example of the "exact-imitation" type is shown on Plate VIII, 2, whilst other flies which made good suggestions of beetles include such patterns as the Coch-y-bondhu, the Soldier and Sailor beetles. Water Cricket, Doctor, Devonshire Doctor, Explorer, Governor, Imp, Green Insect, Little Chap, March Brown, Marlow Buzz, Red-Eyed Beetle, and Simple Simon.

Since writing the above, another beetle pattern has come to my notice and is one for which space must be found. It came to light recently when I found a letter written to me by Mr. Leonard West a year or two before his death in 1925. Enclosed with it was a fly evolved and tied by himself as a general suggestion of many beetles. It is unlikely that details of this pattern can have been published before, since it must have been invented long after the appearance of his book, *The Natural Trout Fy and its Imitation*. Mr. West gives it no name, merely referring to it as his No. 3, and adding that it was principally a "sun" pattern which was his own "special medicine" for use on hot still sunny days. Since he devoted so much time to studying and imitating beetles, I am sure that this simple fly, evolved as it was after a lifetime's experience, should be well worth a trial. The dressing is:

Body: Peacock herl.
Wings: Golden pheasant tippet.
Hackle: Black cock's.
Hook: 14 to 12.

BI-VISIBLES

Bi-visibles were the invention of Mr. E. R. Hewitt, the American angler, who used them first in 1898 and who is well known in Great Britain as the author of *Telling on the Trout* and other fishing books. The forepart of the hackle is white and it is claimed that this enables the user to see the fly more easily at dusk or in a poor light.

Ray Bergman, the well-known American writer, in his book *Trout* gives a dressing for a badger Bi-visible followed by others for a Black, a Brown, a Brown and Grey, a Blue, a Grey, and a Pink Lady Bi-visible. The dressing, which is extremely simple, consists of a badger (or black, brown, grey, etc.) hackle tied Palmer-wise along the bare hook with whisks of the same colour, finished off with a white hackle at the eye. The Pink Lady, however, has the body modestly covered with gold tinsel, and in her case the Palmer hackle and whisks are ginger, plus the inevitable white hackle at the eye.

BLACK ANT. See ANTS

BLACK DRAKE. See MAYFLY

BLACK FURNACE

A dry fly for sea-trout in daytime, invented by the late Dr. J. C. Mottram.

His tie was:

Body: Black ostrich herl.
Wings: Short brown fibres from the tail of an English partridge, tied on either side like the points of a camel-hair brush. Two or three turns of black ostrich herl in front of the wings.
Hackle: Long glossy black, continued down body.
Hook: 10 to 12.

BLACK GNAT (*Bibio johannis*)

Actually this insect is not a gnat, but is a member of that great family of two-winged flies, the Diptera. In appearance it is much like a small house-fly about a quarter of an inch in length, although on the water it appears to be considerably smaller. Neither is it really black, although superficially it would seem to be so. Examined closely, it will be apparent that the female has a very dark brownish-olive body and brownish legs, whilst her wings, which lie flat on her back (house-fly fashion) have pale tips. The male has a much more slender body and is darker all over than the female, so that he looks as near black as no matter.

Although not water-bred insects, they spend most of their adult life in the vicinity of water. Widely distributed throughout the country, they are with us from April to September, being most prevalent around St. John's (Midsummer) Day, which gives rise to their Latin designation.

These little flies appear with great suddenness over the water, without being seen in flight and often in enormous numbers. Even in May I have seen myriads of them playing about over the river in swarms of such density as to create a haze sufficient to obscure the water, making it difficult to see the exact position of a rise. Like some other species of land-bred flies, including their near, but larger, relative, the hawthorn fly, they mate on or close to the surface of the stream.

There are times when trout will studiously ignore these flies but on many days they will take them in a voracious manner and I have opened many a trout which has been crammed full of them.

Most fishermen carry a pattern or two, although the natural fly is by no means an easy one to copy and the artificial is not always successful. On lakes and pools it is generally more reliable than on rivers. But if fishing with an artificial is often an unsatisfactory business, there is some consolation in the fact that when the black gnat is on the water some up-winged duns are usually present and trout will generally pick them out in preference to the more prevalent black gnat.

Personally I seldom trouble to carry an imitation of this insect because either a Williams's Favourite, with the whisks removed and tied on a small hook, or that other good fly, the Dogsbody, will kill fish quite as well as any pattern specifically designed to imitate the natural insect.

The best pattern I have ever used was given me many years ago by the late Mr. Leonard West, the author of *The Natural Trout Fly and its Imitation*; it was tied by himself and proved a wonderfully good killer on Yorkshire rivers and becks. There was nothing very unusual about the dressing and I could only think that the quality of the hackle was responsible for it being such an outstanding success.

As the male and female flies differ in shape and colour, quite different dressings are used to imitate the two sexes and there are several of each to choose from. As a rule, the Black Gnat is fished dry, but sometimes a wet fly, or even a deeply sunk one, attracts fish better.

My experience of Mr. Dunne's patterns is slight but some of them

bear a high reputation and none more so than his female Black Gnat
which he ties with an olive body made by winding medium coloured
silk over a plain bronzed hook and with the wings suggested by bright
hackle points dyed bottle-green and red-wine colour. The full dressing
will be found in *Sunshine and the Dry Fly*.

Halford's pattern for the male insect still remains popular. The dressing is:

Wings: Two pale blue dun cock hackles.
Hackle: Two black starling hackles.
Body: Undyed peacock quill with four turns of black horsehair at shoulder.
Head: Three turns of pale maroon horsehair.
Hook: 15.

Pritt recommended a wet pattern without wings or hackle; merely
an ostrich herl body tied on a size 15 hook. H. S. Hall devised a pike-
scale wing for his own dressing of the fly, but whenever I have tied
this pattern, trout have invariably ignored it. That, of course, may have
been the fault of the angler and not of the fly. There is a simple hackle
pattern to imitate the male insect which, I fancy, was invented by
Roger Woolley, with this tie:

Body: Black quill.
Hackle: Black cock's or starling's neck feather.
Hook: 16.

I do not know what colour tying silk he recommends but would
suggest nut brown.

E. M. Tod, who wrote *Wet Fly-Fishing*, and who was one of the
most accomplished Scottish trout fishermen of his generation, favoured
a wet pattern which he used with great success. He dressed it on a
small double hook and said that he found it a capital fly for the border
streams from April to June. It is an effective pattern even when the
natural insect is not on the water, although it does not seem to me to
bear much resemblance to the natural fly of either sex.

Tod's own dressing was:

Body: Black silk.
Tail: Two strands from a black hen's hackle.
Hackle: Small black hen's hackle.
Wings: From the feather of a starling.
Hook: 14 to 16.

Nowadays professional fly-dressers usually dispense with the tail
and there would seem to be no justification in retaining it on any wet
pattern designed to be a copy of a fly like the black gnat. The same is

true of a floating fly if exact imitation is aimed at, but in this case, buoyancy may be of more importance and there is no doubt that a tail helps a fly to float nicely.

Of all the wet patterns, I know of none better than that designed by Mr. Skues which serves all practical purposes. The dressing as given in *Minor Tactics* is:

Wing: Palest snipe rolled and reversed.
Body: Black tying silk with two turns of black ostrich or knob of black silk at shoulder.
Legs: Black hen or cock starling's crest, two turns at most.
Hook: 16.

Mr. Skues ties his pattern of the female with a wing (roofing the back) made of a darkish feather from the outside of a young starling's wing with a pale tip.

If, as often happens, black gnats fall on the water when pairing, tail to tail, trout are quick to seize the chance of securing a double mouthful. The standard pattern to imitate the coupled insects is known as the Knotted Midge. Any of the usual dressings can be used but with a hackle tied in near the tail as well as at the head in order to give the effect of two paired insects. It is a fly which floats really well and which, on occasions, is exceptionally effective. But of the many flies designed as imitations of the black gnat, I do not think that there are any better than Williams's Favourite, the Dogsbody, and the Rev. Edward Powell's Baby Sun-Fly, although these three are in reality general patterns. The Dogsbody does not bear any resemblance to the natural insect, but I have found it one of the most reliable patterns when black gnats are on the water, especially on warm sultry summer days. Of flies which bear an obviously closer likeness to the natural insect, that old pattern, the Tailey Tail has few equals.

If a good deal of space has been devoted to *B. johannis*, it is because I consider that outside the chalk streams it is one of the more important flies to bothe trout and grayling fishermen. It is found on or near the water throughout every month of the season and far more consistently than duns, sedges, or stone flies.

Because the artificial will not always kill, some anglers are willing to ignore it. This, I feel sure, is a mistake. Whilst it is true that only at times (usually on sultry days in summer) do fish settle down to feed on black gnats to the exclusion of everything else, they will always take them on and off when duns are not present in force and there is no doubt that black gnats form a considerable part of the trout's surface food. The regular presence of these insects in autopsies is sufficient proof of this.

BLACK NYMPH

Dr. R. C. Bridgett in his book on fly-fishing has provided a number of dressings for wet and dry patterns which include a Black Nymph, Brown Nymph, and Green Nymph. These, however, are hackled flies and bear little resemblance to patterns commonly known and sold as nymphs. That, of course, does not mean that they are not good suggestions of natural nymphs and they may prove quite as effective as any of the exact imitation type, although personally I feel that it would be better to apply the name of "artificial nymph" solely to the latter. The patterns referred to above are all useful and I have heard them praised by experienced anglers.

BLACK AND ORANGE

A sea-trout pattern reputed to be especially effective on hot sunny days when the water is low and clear. Originally a Galway fly, it is much used in Ireland and is generally, although not always, fished as a wet pattern.

The dressing is:

Body: Orange floss silk.
Wings: From the tail feather of a black cock.
Hackle: Black hen.
Tail: A few strands of golden pheasant tippet.
Hook: 6 to 10.

Other flies of the same genus are the Black and Silver, which has a flat tinsel body, and the Black and Claret, with a claret floss silk body. All are good sea-trout patterns.

BLACK QUILL

A popular Irish pattern, more especially in the south, which is often used to imitate the black gnat. Fished both wet and dry, but more often wet.

Body: Black quill.   *Wings:* Dark starling.
Hackle and Whisks: Black hen.   *Hook:* 14 to 16.

BLACK SILVERHORNS. See SILVERHORNS

BLACK SPIDER

The invention of one James Baillie, this fly is famous as being the favourite (wet) pattern of W. C. Stewart, the author of *The Practical Angler*, who killed an enormous number of trout on it. The old dressing is:

Body: Brown silk, waxed.
Wings: Hackled with the black and green glossy feather from the neck of a cock starling.
Hook: 12 to 14.

Like all spiders, it should be sparsely dressed and made with very soft feathers. Useful at any time of the season, it excels in the spring. Stewart said of it that it was the most killing artificial he knew and from the day he was first shown it, he was never without one on his cast; and probably Stewart killed more fish each season than any man has done since!

BLAE AND SILVER

The Blae and Silver and Blae and Black are standard Irish wet patterns for lake and sea-trout fishing. Others of the same genus are Blae and Blue, and Blae and Gold. In the smaller sizes, all are good grayling flies.

Dressings:

BLAE AND SILVER

Body: Flat silver tinsel.
Hackle: Pale badger.
Wings: Wild duck wing feather.
Tail: Fibres of golden pheasant tippet.
Hook: 10 to 14, larger for sea-trout.

The Blae and Black is similar but for a black seal's fur body and black hen for the hackle.

BLAGDON GREEN MIDGE ⎫
⎬ See CHIRONOMIDAE
BLAGDON OLIVE MIDGE ⎭

BLOODY BUTCHER. See BUTCHER

BLOODY MARY (Variation)

On dead calm waters on bright summer days, this pattern has served to take an odd fish or so, particularly from lakes. It is a useful fly to tempt fish when they are taking their siesta and one is at a loss to know what to offer them next. Definitely a fancy pattern, I believe fish take it only because they have never seen anything like it before! It is best fished well sunk. The dressing given below is said to have originated in Wales.

Body: Peacock herl.
Tip: Gold tinsel.
Hackle: Cuckoo dyed scarlet.
Tail: Red ibis feather (short) or tippet.
Hook: 10 to 12.

BLUEBOTTLE (*Cynomya mortuorum*)

Also known as the meat fly, blow fly, and shade fly, the bluebottle needs no description. It is one of the best flies for dapping for trout and chub and when it gets on to the water, as it often does, the buzzing disturbance it creates nearly always attracts fish. There is an artificial sometimes called the Blue and Black which is supposed to imitate the natural fly and which is said to take fish in August and September, but I have had no experience of it. The artificial is not of much importance and it is to be doubted whether many anglers ever carry one today, although in some parts of Ireland it is regularly used. Ronald's dressing given below is still as good as any:

Body: Bright blue floss silk tied with brown thread, showing the brown at the head.
Wings: Feather from a starling's wing.
Legs: Black hackle from a cock wrapped down the principal part of the body.
Hook: 12 to 14.

T. J. Hanna has designed a most attractive pattern which is normally fished on the surface but which, in Ireland, is also used for dapping ("shade-fishing") instead of the live insect.

His dressing is as follows:

Body: Cork covered with smoky blue balloon rubber which should be bound tightly in the middle with strong tying silk to give the fly a bulky abdomen and a thick but smaller thorax.
Hackle: Black.
Wings (if required): Blue Andalusian hackle tips made to lie flat over the body.
Head: Finished off with red celluloid varnish to imitate the reddish head of the natural fly.
Hook: 12.

Properly tied, this gives a most lifelike fly which should take fish. Even if it does not, it is a pattern which looks remarkably well in one's fly-box and which always attracts the attention of non-anglers and increases their respect for the fly-dresser's art! In Ireland the Bluebottle is as often as not called the Blue-Stare, stare being an old name for starling and having reference to the wing of the fly.

The natural insect is a loathsome dirty fly, but for the angler it has its uses. It is almost the best fly of all for dapping and its larva, the maggot, provides the coarse fisherman with his most popular bait. That it is sometimes used to catch trout is undeniable, although there is no surer way to ruin a trout water than by the regular use of a maggot or worm. In this connection I would like to quote some words written by my old friend, G. Scott Atkinson, Chairman of the Midland Fly Fishers. They have been published before, but cannot be repeated too often.

"The man who catches trout in coloured water on worm or gentle is greatly to be pitied; not only is he selfish towards his fellow anglers and unfair to a sporting fish but he, most foolishly, deprives himself of the greatest of all angling pleasures—that of striking a fish which he has seen rise to his fly. . . . That the practice is selfish to one's fellow anglers—and incidentally to oneself—cannot be denied, for small trout seize the bait so fiercely that they have almost always to be killed; we cannot expect to catch big trout if all the little fellows are slaughtered! The trout is a lovely fish which rises freely to the fly; why, then murder him by clumsy, ugly methods when he may be taken in an artistic manner which permits the return of undersized fish? And why, oh why! if you are lucky enough to have access to one of the loveliest things in the world, a river holding trout, deny yourself nine-tenths of the joy which it can give?"

BLUE DUN

An indispensable pattern used to imitate the dark olive and iron-blue duns. With suitable variations in the colour of the materials and in the appropriate sizes, it serves also as an effectual suggestion of the pale watery duns.

First mentioned in 1676 by Charles Cotton, it has never been satisfactorily settled as to which natural species he intended the name to refer and entomologists do not apply the name to any insect. It is, therefore, incorrect to talk of a natural blue dun, for there is no such creature.

Quite a number of fishermen, however, use the term to denote the natural olive dun. Perhaps they have reason on their side, for Ronalds gave a dressing of yellow silk dubbed with the fur from a hare's ear which, when wet, provides a clear olive shade, which certainly suggests that the old pattern was intended as a copy of the olive dun.

It is worth noting that the base of the fur taken from a hare has a
bluish tinge about it and the Blue Dun in any of its forms looks blue
enough. But directly it becomes wet or is touched with oil, it changes
to a definite olive of a shade closely akin to the colouring of the large
dark olive of spring.

No artificial fly is made in a greater variety of dressings and styles.
They differ in every part of the country. Devon, Hampshire, Yorkshire, Derbyshire, the Clyde, the Usk, Scotland and Ireland, all have
their own special ties and methods of dressing, but wherever it is used
the Blue Dun is a prime favourite for trout and grayling, especially
in the first part of the season, from March until the end of May.

Fished wet or dry, it proves more successful on most rivers as a
floater, although in some districts it is never used as anything but a wet
fly. Well sunk, it may be used to imitate a nymph. Half a century ago,
the Blue Quill was generally preferred to the Blue Dun as a dry fly, but
nowadays the majority of dry fly-fishermen seem well content with a
hackled Blue Dun.

To go back three hundred years, it is interesting to note that Charles
Cotton recommended the down from a greyhound for the body of the
fly.

"Take a small tooth-combe", he wrote, "and with it comb the neck
of a black greyhound; the down which sticks in the teeth will be the
finest blue you ever saw." Incidentally, had his spaniel known of this,
its doggy heart would have surely rejoiced, for in so many of his dressings for other flies, his master showed an inordinate liking for the fur
of a black spaniel.

There are so many ties for the Blue Dun that it is hard to say which
can be selected as being the most typical, but I should choose the following two. Both are suitable for trout and grayling.

Body: Yellow silk dubbed with mole or water-rat's fur.
Wings: Dark starling's wing feather.
Hackle: Pale-blue dun.
Whisks: Two fibres from a rabbit's whiskers.
Hook: 14.

Body: Water-rat, rabbit's belly fur or mole dubbing spun on primrose silk.
Wings: Snipe.   *Hackle:* Medium blue hen.
Whisks: Medium blue hen.   *Hook:* 14.

Mr. Eric Taverner in *Trout Fishing from All Angles,* mentions that
the latter dressing suggests the under-colour of the hatching nymph.

I do not think that it is necessary to give a great many more dressings, in spite of the large number from which a choice could be made; and it might only serve to confuse the reader. Those given below, with the two already mentioned, should provide an ample selection for any part of the country and all of them are good killers.

In *Minor Tactics of the Chalk Stream*, Mr. Skues gives the following dressing for a wet pattern:

Wings: Snipe.
Body: Water-rat on primrose or yellow tying silk. Vary body by dressing with undyed heron's herl from the wing, and ribbing with fine gold or silver wire.
Legs: Medium blue hen.   *Hook:* 14 or 15.

On the Don, when the dark olive is on, and conditions admit of a dry fly, a large-sized variant of the Blue Dun will often have some success. On the water, the finished fly should look rather like a bumble bee. I am indebted to Mr. D. A. Guild for the following dressing:

Body: Dark seal's fur over yellow silk.
Hackle: Very fuzzy honey dun hackle.   *Hook:* 12.

A tie popular in Scotland is:

Body: From the fur of a water-rat, ribbed with silver gimp or silver wire.
Hackle: Blue dun hen hackle.   *Hook:* 12 to 14.

In Ireland several different dressings are favoured. One of the most generally used for wet fly-fishing is the following.

Tag: Gold tinsel.
Tail: Two fibres mallard or rat's whiskers.
Body: Water-rat fur taken from the point of the ribs (tips cut off), mixed with a little golden olive mohair.
Legs: Water-rail, or the tips of the fur mixed with golden olive.
Wings: Bluish feather of the starling.
Hook: 12 to 14.

When I fished the Dove with the late Colonel Keith Rollo, he showed me a wet pattern which he called the Blue Dun Hackle and of which he was extremely fond. From his dressing for this pattern it will be seen that it is not unlike a Blue Upright.

Body: Peacock quill.
Hackle: Grizzly blue dun hackle with a nice sheen on it.
Tail: Two or three whisks of blue dun cock's hackles.
Hook: 13 or 14.

Since the Blue Dun is a copy of an Ephemerid, the body should
be kept slender according to one school of thought, although the usual
body dubbed with mole's fur or water-rat kills well enough for most
of us. Francis Francis was one of those who strongly disliked a bulky
body and he invented a good pattern which he called a Blue Dun.
For that reason alone I am including it here, although, in my opinion,
it has no more right to be called a Blue Dun than a Blue or Olive Quill
could be so termed. In reality, it is nothing more or less than an Olive
Dun. However, call it what you will, it is a good fly for which Francis
Francis gave this dressing:

Body: Light olive silk, waxed, and then partly untwisted to show the ribs when
  wrapped carefully on the hook.
Legs: Olive-stained hackle.
Tail: Two small hairs from a rabbit's whiskers.
Wing: Starling's quill feather stained in an onion dye.
Hook: 14.

The great Francis Walbran was a great admirer of the Blue Dun and
ranked it as No. 1 on the angler's list of wet flies. It has always been a
favourite pattern in the north and that ever-popular Yorkshire pattern,
the Waterhen Bloa, is only a variety of Blue Dun, tied to suit local
conditions, and probably serving to suggest the hatching nymph.

BLUE PARTRIDGE
An old pattern, this Yorkshire hackled fly is said to prove attractive
during the last fortnight in April and throughout May. It used to be
fished to represent the insect known as the gravel bed or gravel spider
and Pritt recommended it as being a first-class wet pattern for use in
a biggish water any time after the middle of May.
The dressing (Pritt) is:

Wings: Hackled with a feather from a partridge's back.
Body: Blue silk dubbed with a little lead-coloured lamb's wool.
Hook: 14.

BLUE QUILL
A chalk stream variation of the Devonshire Blue Upright. Fished
wet or dry, it often proves an effective copy of the pale watery duns,
and on some occasions, it would seem to suggest them better than any
other pattern. Nowadays it is generally tied as a hackled fly and fished
as a floater, although with a soft hen hackle, it makes a useful wet fly.

Like the Blue Upright, it is an excellent general pattern for lake fishing, especially when used as a floater. The dressing for the hackled fly is:

Tying silk: White or grey, waxed.
Whisk: Pale blue.
Body: Peacock quill, stripped and undyed, or sometimes dyed pale blue.
Hackle: Pale blue cock's.
Hook: 14 to 16.

This pattern may be tied pale, medium, or dark.

BLUE QUILL HACKLE

A variation of the above and, in reality, a pale edition of the Blue Upright. Halford gives a tie for this fly, but I should prefer Mr. Skues's more modern version of which the dressing is as follows:

Hackle: Pale honey dun cock.
Body: Undyed peacock quill.
Whisks: From honey dun cock's beard hackle.
Hook: 14 to 16.

BLUE UPRIGHT

One of the best of the west-country wet patterns, effective throughout the season. A general fly, it suggests equally well a dark olive, an iron-blue, or the willow fly.

The best pattern, I think, is that which was always used by Mr. R. S. Austin, the inventor of the Tup's Indispensable, to imitate the female willow fly and it was he who, I am told, originated it. Although this celebrated fly hailed from Devon, it proves a killing pattern all over the country, more especially perhaps on rough fast waters in the spring. And a friend of mine has used it, both wet and dry, as a lake pattern for many years now and does exceedingly well with it.

Austin's dressing was as follows:

Tying silk: Purple.
Body: Undyed peacock's herl, stripped, taken from the side of the long stalk of the eye feather, not in the eye. To suggest a tag like a bunch of eggs, use a herl that is cinnamon at the root.
Hackles: Steely blue game-cock's, sharp, bright, and nearly black, but with a definite blue centre. Wound on at the head or from head to shoulder.
Whisks: Ditto.
Hook: 10 to 14.

The Blue Uprights one gets in the shops are not always corretly tied

It is of the greatest importance that the steely blue game-cock's hackles are of the right colour and are stiff and sparkling.

As a grayling fly the Blue Upright is a great favourite with many anglers and is generally fished wet as a bob fly. Most effective in clear water in the autumn, it is a reliable pattern during a hatch of olives. A very experienced and particularly successful Lugg fisherman who takes a great number of grayling on this fly is convinced that it is more killing when tied with dyed instead of natural hackles.

BLUE-WINGED OLIVE (*Ephemerella ignita, E. notata*)

This well-known fly seldom makes an appearance before June and continues until October or November. On the Test and Itchen, it is essentially a summer and autumn insect, whilst on the Kennet, it may occur as early as April. Although abundant on the chalk streams during June and July, in other parts of the country, in spite of its wide distribution, the hatch is not often large enough to be of much interest to fishermen. In the South, however, it is an insect to be respected, for when it is on the water a suitable artificial copy is more likely to tempt heavy fish in goodly numbers than almost any other fly. The nymph is unmistakable: short and fat, dark olive in colour, it has three setae which are freckled, with black and white markings. One of the sluggish type, it is found amongst weeds and stones, depending upon a covering of mud for its protection. Present in most streams, it survives catastrophes such as floods and weed-cutting better than most other larvae, being highly adaptable.

The b.-w.o. is an easy insect to identify because (with the exception of the turkey brown to which it bears no resemblance and of the mayfly which is so much larger and caenis which are so much smaller) it is the only common Ephemerid to have three setae. Incidentally, when examining this species it is always as well to bear in mind the possibility of one of the tails having been broken off, although a microscope should reveal the broken stump.

It is a largish fly, the body of the dun being about five-sixteenths of an inch in length which is appreciably shorter than that of the march brown, but noticeably longer than that of the olive, the pale watery or the iron-blue. The four wings are slaty-blue in colour. The body of the female dun is greenish-olive and that of the male dun olive turning to a yellowish-brown. In the imago stage, both sexes have sherry-coloured bodies and are known to all fly-fishermen as sherry spinners.

The female spinner, before becoming darker with exposure to the air, is distinctly golden in appearance. She is the only spinner to carry her eggs in a little green ball at the end of her body and when doing so, her setae face forward, being bent round to hold the eggs in position until the spinner is ready to liberate them. When these sherry spinners are present in clouds, they may easily be mistaken for a flight of winged gnats, the resemblance to the shape of the latter insects being due to the egg sac of the b.-w.o.

E. notata is not, I fancy, found on the chalk streams and is uncommon elsewhere in England, although abundant on Irish waters. It may be distinguished from *E. ignita* by its colouring. The dun has whitish-grey wings with pale yellowish-green neuration and an olive-tinted abdomen. The wings of the male spinner are clear, faintly tinted with yellow, with greyish-green nervures and he has a greyish-green abdomen. The abdomen of the female imago is yellowish and both sexes have dark spots along each side.

The spent sherry spinner is almost unmistakable and in *Sunshine and the Dry Fly*, Mr. J. W. Dunne writes this of it: "Late in the evening, in the darkness, peering closely and intently at the water, you will see gliding swiftly by amid the hatching duns, a spinner with big flat-spread, whitish-looking wings, between which the red body looks stumpy and diminutive—yes, red as any lobster: there you have the Orange Quill."

Two unusual features about the b.-w.o. are worth noting. The hatch nearly always occurs in the late evening and trout take the insect, be it dun or spinner, with an unmistakable boil—a kidney-shaped boil with a whorl on either side. Secondly, the fly as a rule is not evenly distributed along a river but hatches in quantities only at certain favoured spots, so that it behoves the fisherman to obtain some knowledge of the position of these before the rise begins.

To ascertain this is well worth while because the b.-w.o. is quite capable of providing the angler with exceptional sport. It must be done in good time, because owing to the fading light the time available for the angler to take advantage of the rise is necessarily short and when it takes place he will have plenty to occupy his mind. Trout taking the b.-w.o. in the evening are generally fastidious and the chances of catching them are greatly lessened unless preparations are made in advance. Searching through a box to find the most likely patterns when the hatch is in progress is fatal. One must know just where they are as one cannot afford to waste any time: even when all is prepared, it will fre-

quently be found that the time available is all too short. When fish
are taking the b.-w.o. at dusk, every minute counts.

Halford was the first to use the modern name of the insect in his
Floating Flies (1886) and although he gave a dressing for an artificial
in that book and others in subsequent works, none of them are much
used to-day. It seems clear that he quite failed to appreciate the great
possibilities offered by a good imitation of the natural insect. This is
all the more strange since, of course, the fly was very well known to
him.

Unfortunately for the fly-fisher, the b.-w.o. is one of the most
difficult insects to copy successfully. Most fly-tiers have made attempts
to imitate it, but they are faced with the fact—for fact it is—that whereas
some particular dressing may kill quite well one evening, it may prove
useless on the next, or even at some later period of the same evening.

A number of established patterns are regularly used to suggest the
b.-w.o., including such well-known flies as Greenwell's Glory, Red
Quill, Indian Yellow, and Poult Bloa, but although all of them will
take fish on occasions, none are so regularly to be relied upon, in my
opinion, as those mentioned below.

First and foremost there is the Orange Quill. It is an outstanding
pattern and in my experience when duns are hatching towards night-
fall, it can seldom be bettered. All fly-fishermen have reason to be
grateful to Mr. Skues for this fly, as although it was not invented by
him, he was the first to appreciate, and call attention to, its efficacy.
The dressing of this great pattern will be found on page 272.

Although there must be some general measure of agreement that of
all flies designed to imitate the b.-w.o., the Orange Quill is almost
certainly the most reliable, not only on the chalk streams, but also on
every other river, there are times when the fish won't look at it and the
angler is then obliged to try something else. Luckily there are plenty
of alternatives, any of which may prove to be the best fly to suit some
particular occasion.

Dressings must naturally be varied to suit special conditions of light
and water and to imitate the shade of the natural fly at any given time.
The female spinner, for instance, changes colour several times before she
finally attains her sherry-like tint.

Mr. Skues has obviously paid a good deal of attention to copying
the b.-w.o. and has provided several attractive ties. Fishing on the
Itchen as he did for so many years, he had exceptional opportunities for
testing them. When trout are taking the dun and show no interest in

an Orange Quill, he suggests that the following pattern should be tried. It is normally fished wet.

Wings: Darkest starling or medium coot.
Body: Greenish-olive seal's fur.
Tag: Flat gold.
Whisks: Pale dun cock.
Hackle: Medium olive.
Hook: 14.

Other experienced chalk-stream anglers have produced notable imitations of the b.-w.o. and the late Dr. J. C. Mottram had great faith in one which he evolved and of which he wrote thus: "You can, with advantage, increase the fly's floating qualities by making it hackled all down the hook; indeed, the fly which I like most is built entirely for buoyance on a very light hook (Allcocks No. 1810) in three sizes. The fly has a cock hackle—point wings, set up, not flat like the wings of spinners. The body hackle is grey cock continued down the hook to the bend, and it has grey cock hackle whisks. It is not given any body at all. If you can manage to get this fly floating well up (and without any drag) over a rising fish, I will wager that the trout will take it."

Then there is a very good dressing of the dun evolved by Mr. G. C. Swayne, who claims that "fish will take it freely in the early season of the fly and that later on, it will be taken by some trout at some period of the day". His tie is:

Wings: Coot or water-rail.
Body: A brown drab or fawn wool with a slight olive tint, bound with gold tinsel.
Hackles: Light buff.
Whisks: Pale brown.
Hook: 14 to 16.

When fish are taking the male spinner of a dark-brown sherry colour, the orthodox answer will be found in a Skues pattern, his well-known Rusty Spinner of which the dressing will be found on page 301. For the female spinner, which perhaps is not so well liked by trout as the male, there are at least two useful patterns. The dressing of the first was published by Mr. Skues in his *Side-lines, Side-lights and Reflections* and will be found under Sherry Spinner on pages 304–5. The other is the Orange Spinner which I have found effective just before the b.-w.o. comes on in the evening. The liking trout have for orange in imitations of the b.-w.o. is rather puzzling since this colour is not found on the natural fly. Mr. D. Jacques has presented weighty evidence in favour of the theory that an orange bodied artificial is accepted by the fish only when spinners are on the water, and rejected decisively when they are absent. If this is not the case, I do not know how one can account for the effectiveness of either the Orange Quill or the Orange Spinner.

A dressing given by Mr. D. Jacques for the b.-w.o. is as follows:

Wings: Two pair from a wing feather of a coot.
Hackle and Whisks: Dark dirty olive cock.
Body: Plastic dyed olive over a grey ostrich herl dyed drab yellow.
Tying silk: Hot orange.
Hook: 14.

Lastly the Pheasant Tail, which Mr. J. W. Dunne thought so well of must not be overlooked as one of the best imitations of the female Sherry Spinner.

The artificial representation of the b.-w.o. is always likely to bring up big fish—trout which seldom take any fly off the surface and can only be tempted by a b.-w.o. or a mayfly. And when fish are feeding on the natural fly, they will take the artificial readily, although, as already mentioned, the exact pattern needed to deceive them will depend upon several factors and cannot be definitely predicted.

The hatch very seldom occurs before the late afternoon and more generally the fly does not come on in any force until nearly dark. As it is of short duration, there is no time to experiment with any great number of flies and for that reason I have contented myself with giving the names and dressings of only a few which experience suggests are likely to bring the best results. These remarks refer in the main to the chalk streams. On most other rivers, the b.-w.o. does not as a rule occur in sufficient quantities to be of any great interest to the fisherman; should it do so, I have found that the fish are generally quite content to take the Orange Quill or a Pheasant Tail.

As a grayling fly, the artificial b.-w.o. has its uses and is something of a favourite in the south. Where the natural insect occurs in the north, the Poult Bloa is generally used to imitate it. For southern grayling rivers Mr. Skues recommends a wet pattern which he terms "a sort of b.-w.o.", tied in this manner:

Body: Orange silk dubbed with fur of a blue cat, dyed greenish-olive in picric acid.
Hackle: A dark blue hen's neck feather.
Whisks: To match.
Hook: 14 to 16.

BORDERER

One of six patterns invented, for wet or dry fishing, by the well-known angler and author, the late W. M. Gallichan. The Borderer is perhaps the best of the series but all six are deadly on Welsh streams and lakes, for which most probably they were designed, since Mr. Gallichan's experience of Welsh waters was quite exceptional. The dressing of the Borderer is:

Body: Blue rabbit's fur with red silk tip.
Hackle and Whisks: Rusty dun hackle.
Hook: 14.

BOTTLE BRUSH

One of the late H. T. Sheringham's patterns. Writing in his own inimitable style about fishing with it in Wales, he said: "One or other of these monstrosities will sometimes, in the most insolent manner, prove itself capable of catching fish when other more respectable patterns have failed. One of the most scandalous instances of this occurred on the Penydwddwr some years ago. . . . Our united catches had for some days barely found us breakfast. . . . Then something induced me to put on the Bottle Brush. I have always thought of it as the Bottle Brush because it has no other name, and deserves none—had rather: it is now no more.

"The creature was two sizes larger than anything else in my book and was an unpleasing brown thing with an inordinate quantity of stiff stark hackle and no wings. Supposed to be a wet fly, it would have needed a paternoster-lead to sink it. I never met with a pattern I disliked more on sight. It was exactly like a bottle brush in shape.

"Well, I dragged this thing about the river in a half-hearted way, and presently a trout hurled himself upon it. I basketed him and soon afterwards another, and more followed until I had amassed sixteen of excellent size."

As has been stressed elsewhere in this book, when nothing else will take, a freak like the Bottle Brush will often do the trick.

Some years ago I fished a piece of water well stocked with trout averaging about a pound apiece. On this occasion I saw scarcely a rise all day, except for one trout which rose at the tail end of a weed-bed with some regularity. The most delicate and lifelike dry flies failed to interest him at all, although a good number of patterns were tried. Just before dusk, not having had a fish all day, I tried him again with a Red Quill and a Pheasant Tail, neither of which elicited the slightest response.

Becoming desperate, I put on an enormous Red Palmer, which might have been suitable for big chub but which should have terrified any self-respecting trout. Not a bit of it! He took it without hesitation: weight 2¼ lb.

BOTTLE IMP

A good pattern for grayling, usually fished as a floater.

Body: Blue-grey wool.
Hackle: Black cock's.
Tag: Scarlet ibis feather.
Hook: 14.

B.P. SPECIAL

The invention of the late Mr. Phil B. Bekeart, of San Francisco, a well-known angler on the Klamath River, from which in his time he took thousands of steelhead trout. His pattern, always fished wet, is well worth a trial for rainbow trout. The dressing is:

Tag: Gold tinsel.
Tail: Scarlet hackle.
Body: Red silk.
Butt: Peacock herl.
Throat: Peacock herl.
Hackle: Red hackle.
Wings: Brown speckled hen, with sides of jungle cock neck feathers.
Head: Ostrich herl, black.
Hook: 12 to 10.

BRADSHAW'S FANCY

Mr. Henry Bradshaw, of Bramley, Leeds, a celebrated Yorkshire angler towards the close of the last century, was a prolific inventor of fancy flies. Bradshaw's Adopted, a grayling fly, Bradshaw's Yellow, and Bradshaw's Fancy, are three which have survived and, of them, the Fancy is by far the best known.

There are few better patterns for grayling and in the autumn it is well worth trying for trout. The dressing is:

Tying silk: Dark purple.
Body: Copper-coloured peacock's herl.
Hackle: Feather from the neck of a Norwegian crow.
Tag: Bright crimson wool or floss silk, with a couple of turns at the head inter-
mingled with peacock herl.
Hook: 14.

BRADSHAW'S YELLOW

A useful sea-trout pattern especially for night-fishing. The usual dressing is:

Body: Yellow pig's wool ribbed with broad silver tinsel.
Legs: Coch-y-bondhu hackle.
Wings: Dark mallard.
Hook: 6 to 10.

BROOKES'S FANCY

A favourite Teme wet fly for both trout and grayling. It was invented by Mr. Brookes, a Ludlow postman, who died a few years ago. The dressing is as under:

Body: Purple silk ribbed with peacock herl.
Hackle: White.   *Hook:* 12 to 14.

BROUGHTON'S POINT

A famous northern wet fly for trout and grayling, invented in about 1830 by a Penrith shoemaker after whom it was named. He was a well-known angler on Ullswater and an accomplished fly-tier.

Dressing:

Body: Ruddy purple silk.
Wing: Starling under-wing.
Hackle: Black, with a few red strands intermingled.
Legs: Red hackle.   *Hook:* 12 to 14.

The above dressing is almost identical with that of the Dark Bloa, which is so well known in the north, and is the tie that is favoured to-day on the Ribble, Wharfe and Aire. It differs a little from the original dressing which had a light blue silk body.

BROWN MOTH (*Lepidoptera*)

There can never have been a time since artificial flies were first used that fishermen have not sought to copy moths, for when these insects happen to get on to river or lake, they create such a disturbance in their efforts to save themselves that their struggles can hardly fail to attract the attention of any fish in the vicinity.

The Brown Moth is an old aquaintance; one of those standard patterns which serve to represent all fairly large brown-coloured moths, and, like all artificials intended to suggest these insects, it proves most effective towards dusk or when nearly dark. Used at the right time, which is at the close of a hot summer's day, it may prove very killing. On a warm dry evening in August or September, a Brown Moth (or for that matter, any other moth pattern) if fished as a floater or in the surface film, will as likely as not attract a trout and frequently a large one. Therein lies, perhaps, the greatest merit of a pattern of this nature. It represents the largest insect normally taken by trout and because a large moth must be something of a mouthful for small fish, it is generally the larger specimens which are most prone to tackle it. At the same time every fly-fisherman knows the greedy little trout which will seize an artificial fly almost as big as itself, but it is the exception to the general rule.

As a lake fly, the Brown Moth is as good or better than on a river, although on any still water some movement must be imparted to this sort of pattern. No dead moth is of much interest to fish and it is the movement which attracts them. It should not be violent, but just enough to attract the trout's attention and to suggest that it is still alive. Any attempt to imitate the violent struggles of the natural insect may only serve to scare fish.

A useful dressing is:

Tying silk: Orange.
Body: Brown floss silk, rather thick.
Hackle: Dark red cock's from head to tail.
Wings: Dark owl.
Hook: 10 to 12.

BROWN OWL

A useful wet pattern for northern rivers, suggestive of many sedges. Most attractive during May and June, it is said to be taken freely when the willow fly is on the water. Pritt described it as a capital killer which could be used throughout the season. His tie was as under:

Wings: Hackled with a reddish feather from the outside of a brown owl's wing.
Body: Orange silk.
Head: Peacock herl.
Hook: 14.

Like all northern hackled flies, this pattern should be sparsely dressed.

BROWN SEDGE. See LITTLE BROWN SEDGE

BROWN SILVERHORNS. See SILVERHORNS

BROWN SPIDER

An old Yorkshire fly which was looked upon as an effective wet pattern from March to July.

Dressing:

Body: Dusky olive mohair, ribbed with gold twist or bright yellow tying silk.
Legs: A small mottled feather from the back of a partridge.
Hook: 12 to 14.

This, I think, is the oldest tie. Nowadays the fly is often dressed with a brown silk body and a long brown hackle.

BROWN WATCHET. See PARTRIDGE AND ORANGE

BRUNTON'S FANCY

The invention of Dr. John Brunton, who for many years was a well-known member of the Gresham Angling Society and who died in 1899. His fly is a popular grayling pattern and one of the better sea-trout flies, especially in late summer.

The original dressing was:

Body: One-third silver thread, two-thirds green peacock sword feather.
Hackle: Badger.
Tag: Red wool.
Hook: 14.

BUMBLES

The Bumbles are famous Derbyshire patterns of the wet palmer type which are deadly for grayling in any part of the country. As trout flies, they often kill well in hot weather, whilst in Ireland they are favoured for sea-trout fishing.

Halford gives some dressings for dry Bumbles and when he first introduced them they gained a great reputation as floating flies for both trout and grayling. Nowadays they appear to be almost invariably fished wet.

There are many varieties which include the Furnace Bumble, the Claret Bumble, the Red Bumble, the Orange Bumble, the Yellow Bumble, and the Honey Dun Bumble, etc.

I am not qualified to express any opinion as to which is the best pattern and, indeed, it would be difficult to do so since every fisherman has his own favourite and is fully convinced of its superiority.

Here are some of the dressings:

Claret (or Mulberry) Bumble

Body: Claret floss silk ribbed with a strand of peacock's sword feather.
Hackle: Medium blue dun cock from shoulder to tail.
Hook: 12 to 14.

Orange Bumble

Body: Orange floss silk, ribbed with a strand of peacock's sword feather and narrow gold tinsel.
Hackle: Honey-dun cock wrapped all down the body.
Hook: 12 to 14.

Honey Dun Bumble

Body: Salmon-coloured floss silk ribbed with a strand of peacock's sword feather.
Hackle: Honey dun hen's from tail to shoulder.
Hook: 12 to 14.

The above was one of David Foster's favourite grayling patterns for the Derbyshire rivers.

Steel-Blue Bumble

Body: Light orange, dark orange and cherry-coloured floss silk twisted together and laid on in alternate ribs with peacock herl between them.
Hackle: Steel-blue tied palmer-wise from head to tail.
Hook: 14.

Yellow Bumble

Body: Yellow floss silk ribbed with bronze peacock herl.
Hackle: Blue dun hen's from tail to shoulder.
Hook: 12 to 14.

BUSTARD

Bustard fishing is a method regularly practised in the north of England and on the Border rivers, especially the Eden. Unlike most fly-fishing, it is nearly always carried on at night, for Bustard flies can only be employed successfully after dark, when large catches of trout are regularly made on them.

The name Bustard (locally "Buzzard") has no connection with the bird of that name, being a north-country term for any large night-flying moth or, less frequently, for a big sedge; and there seems to be no doubt that the artificials are used to represent these insects.

There are numerous dressings, each designed to simulate some particular species of moth, but whatever the angling textbooks say to the contrary, I believe that nowadays experienced exponents of this form of fishing invariably rely on three patterns only, the brown, white, and yellow Bustards, with the following dressings:

BROWN BUSTARD
Body: Light tawny brown chenille.
Hackle: Buff.
Wings: Feather from the wing of a brown owl.
Hook: 10 to 12.ʼ

WHITE BUSTARD
Body: White chenille.
Hackle: Light buff.
Wings: Feather from a white pigeon.
Hook: 10 to 12.

YELLOW BUSTARD
Body: Yellow chenille ribbed with red silk.
Wings: A cream feather.
Hackle: Buff.
Tag: Strip of white kid.
Hook: 10 to 12.

Sometimes the wings are dispensed with and a light yellow hackle is used, tied palmer-fashion. In all three patterns, mohair is sometimes used in preference to chenille.

The older Bustard dressings are different from those favoured to-day. Pritt's tie for the White Bustard will serve as an example.

Wings: From a white owl's quill feather.
Body: White Berlin wool, ribbed with yellow silk or gold tinsel.
Head: Black ostrich herl, used sparingly.
Legs: From a white cock's hackle.
Hook: 10 to 12.

In parts of the country other than the north, a pattern known as the Bustard and Yellow is looked upon as being one of the best flies for night-fishing for both trout and sea-trout, whilst if there is a salmon about, there is always a fair chance that it will take. The usual dressing, which, it will be observed, is very different to that of the Border pattern, is:

Body: Yellow mohair, sometimes ribbed with oval gold.
Wings: Bustard's barred wing feather.
Hackle: Ginger.
Tail: Golden pheasant tippet.
Hook: 6 to 12.

This is a wet pattern but occasionally it is tied with a rolled wing and fished dry. The Bustard and Orange, similar to the above except for an orange body, is another good pattern after dark.

BUTCHER

The Butcher is said to have been invented by a Mr. Jewhurst of Tunbridge Wells, Kent, in association with a Mr. Moon, a butcher of that town. Originally known as "Moon's Fly", it received its present name in about 1838, probably on account of its connection with the "purveyor of meat" mentioned above and possibly also because of its colouring, the red tag suggesting raw beef and the wings the traditional blue apron of a butcher.

Of all wet flies, there are few more deadly in the early part of the season than a Butcher, whether it be used for river or loch, for brown trout, sea-trout, or rainbow trout. It is, too, a pattern which is known all over the world.

On Scottish lochs, it is probable that in one of its several forms, it takes more fish than any other fly, whilst it is almost as killing on rivers. It is generally supposed to be taken for a minnow or some other small fish.

Although it is customary to mount the Butcher as a top dropper, when three flies are used on a cast, I am quite sure that it kills equally as well when fished on the point. In the first few weeks of the season if the weather is cold and there is no fly at all on the water, silver-bodied flies like the Butcher and Peter Ross, fished deep, will often tempt fish better than any other patterns, whilst both are first-class sea-trout flies at any time of the year.

The Butcher must be regarded as a typical wet fly, but occasionally it is used as a floater for grayling and I have met one angler who always fishes it as a dry fly for trout both on river and lake and catches a great many fish on it! However, it is as a wet fly that it excels and the majority of fly-fishermen consider it to be an indispensable pattern. The correct tie is:

Tail: Red ibis.
Body: Flat silver ribbed with oval silver.
Hackle: Black.
Wings: Blue-black feather from a drake's wing.
Hook: 10 to 14; larger for sea-trout.

For lake fishing the fly is sometimes dressed with a black wing and some anglers swear by it but on the whole the blue-black drake's feather with a really bright steely sheen on it is far more popular.

The Butcher is often designated the Silver Butcher to distinguish it from its well-known variation, the Bloody Butcher. The latter pattern differs only from the Butcher in that it has a scarlet hackle instead of a black one. It is a showy sort of fly, favoured for loch fishing and for sea-trout.

Another variation well liked in Scotland, especially for loch fishing, is the Kingfisher Butcher which is tied as follows:

Wings: Blae.
Hackle: Orange.
Whisks: Fibres from the wing of a kingfisher.
Body: Flat gold ribbed with oval gold.
Hook: 10 to 12.

The Gold Butcher is the same fly as the Butcher except for the body which is of flat gold tinsel.

CADDIS FLIES
Life History

The caddis, or sedge, flies are of considerable importance to both fish and fishermen and are widely distributed throughout the British Isles. They belong to the Trichoptera order or, to give it an older name, the Phryganeidae, of which there are 188 British species.

Their life history is an interesting one and in some respects quite as enthralling as that of the Ephemeridae. The eggs hatch out in three to four weeks and from them emerge the caddis grubs, or cad-baits as some country folk call them, which are beloved by fish.

The larva is generally a dirty yellowish grub with a dark brown head and six legs and has rather the appearance of a large maggot. And it is this insignificant creature which is responsible for a wonderful piece of building.

Soon after it is hatched, it sets forth to construct its future domain, a portable dwelling, roomy, warm and silk-lined, with a camouflaged rough-cast exterior.

The interior is lined with soft smooth silk woven by the larva with its saliva glands as in the case of moths. The exterior is covered with local material and although different species use different materials the result is always the same, for as the case lies on the bottom of the river, lake, or pool, it becomes an inconspicuous natural-looking object which is not calculated to attract the attention of too inquisitive fish.

Minute stones and gravel, sand, pieces of stick and vegetable matter

are all pressed into service, sometimes alone and sometimes mixed together. In some instances when vegetable matter is used, the fragments
of weeds or bits of plants which cover the outside of the house are cut
into equal lengths and are neatly arranged in a regular spiral pattern,
the spiral always twisting to the left.

Experiments have shown that under artificial conditions, if a larva
is deprived of its case, it will build another, utilizing any material near
at hand. In this way grubs have been induced to make use of such unusual substances as coloured beads.

To my mind, however, it is not the exterior decoration of the caddis
case which is so amazing as that such a lowly insect is able to solve the
constructional problems which confront it. The house has to be made
of sufficient weight to remain on the bottom even in a heavy stream,
strong enough to withstand the pressure of the current, light enough
for the larva to move it about easily, yet not so buoyant that it will be
washed away with its occupant inside it. It will be appreciated, therefore, that some very delicate questions of balance are involved.

For about a year, the caddis larva lives in this house and wherever
he goes, the house goes with him. When the grub is walking about on
the bed of the river or lake, his head, thorax, and front legs protrude
out of the front end of the case, but by means of a couple of strong
hooks in his tail, he grips the far end of the house and is thus able to
drag it about with him. Should danger threaten he immediately retreats
to the comparative safety of its interior.

This protective casing is generally cone-like in shape, broad at the
head end and narrowing towards the other. As a rule, it is constructed
in such a way that the grub has ample room inside it, although as he
grows, additions and enlargements have to be carried out. When only
a question of length is involved, an additional piece is easily built on,
but when it is a matter of width a major operation becomes necessary.

This is accomplished by the larva cutting away as much as is needful
of the narrow tail portion and then building on a new and wider section at the other end. The new hole at the back door is then blocked up
and the exterior of all the new parts are rough-cast as originally.

Not all species of caddis grubs have portable mansions, for some make
similar cases which they anchor permanently to some heavy object
like a stone, although this, of course, entails their leaving their home
when they wish to feed. In some rare instances the larva does not build
any form of house and moves about freely, or as freely as is possible
in an element populated with enemies.

Larvae can easily be induced to leave their cases by poking them from the hind end. In the ordinary way the larva will come out of the front door and will crawl to the other, where after prising open the rear exit it will enters its house again. Should, however, it be made to repeat this action several times, it will frequently continue to crawl out and in, of its own accord!

For the most part, caddis larvae are vegetarians, feeding on the leaves of water-plants like water celery and crowfoot, although many are carnivorous, devouring molluscs and other water insects including the larvae of the ephemeridae, gnats, and diptera. Some are even addicted to attacking and eating their own close relatives.

After about a year under water, the grub is full grown and prepares for its next stage by blocking up the entrance to its house with a silken grating, which, whilst closing the orifice, allows water to percolate through it. Sometimes a few sticks or vegetable matter are added but never to the extent that they allow a free flow of water to pass into the case.

Grubs with portable cases take the precaution of anchoring them to a stone or rock to prevent the possibility of their being washed away during the larva's dormant state which is about to begin. In most instances, the grub now proceeds to build a silken cocoon inside its house and it is in this that the last change of skin is made and the larva becomes a pupa. Whilst it is in this torpid state of passive development, the wings, legs, and antennae are formed, although, of course, they have been developing for some time internally.

After a period of some weeks, or even the whole of the winter, the insect is ready to emerge in the spring. Finding itself provided with a most useful pair of large hook-shaped mandibles, it employs them to tear apart the grating and soon bites a way out of the case which has housed it for so long.

It immediately swims to the surface, using for this purpose its middle pair of legs, which are particularly strong and have swimming hairs attached to them. The final change from pupa to imago may take place on the surface, or on stones or rocks bordering the water.

First the head emerges, followed by antennae, legs and then the wings and in a very short space of time the insect is free of its pupal case and ready to fly. Generally speaking, larvae bred in fast-running water make the imago-change quickly; those which have spent their lives in still or slow-flowing water, in a more leisurely manner.

As in the case of all true aquatic insects, the ascent to the surface presents the most dangerous period, since fish are always ready to take advantage of it and seldom fail to make good use of the opportunity.

The newly hatched flies are pale and do not acquire their full colour until they have been exposed to the air for some hours. But they can fly well and mating soon takes place on reeds, bushes, walls, or hatches.

The eggs are deposited in various ways according to the species concerned. As a rule they are covered with a material which swells into a gelatinous mass on contact with the water or they may be laid in flat masses cemented together. Some species deposit their eggs on sedges and plants above or below the water. In others the female drops them as she flutters over the surface, and in some instances she walks down to the river beds and lays them in the mud or sand. After depositing her eggs she soon dies from exhaustion and the life of the male is equally short, seldom exceeding a fortnight.

The sedge is easily recognized from the way in which it folds its wings to form a gable, which gives the fly an elongated effect. The wings, it will be observed, are covered with small hairs. For the rest, the head is very small, the fly has four wings, six legs and prominent antennae which in some species are exceptionally long. The general colour of all sedges is some shade of brown. The fore-wings vary considerably, some being self-coloured, some speckled and some blotched.

The sedges are really nocturnal insects and during their very brief existence as winged flies their natural instinct is to remain hidden during the hours of daylight, emerging at dusk or after dark. There are, however, a number of day-flying sedges, of which the grannom is the best-known example, if one excepts the silverhorns, which are not of much interest to fishermen. But a number of sedges will be seen on the wing on most days during spring and summer, and these are the species which become best known to anglers. The most common are the caperer (*Halesus radiatus*), cinnamon sedge, silver sedge, the great red sedge, and *Anabolia nervosa*, sometimes called the brown sedge.

Many sedge flies, common enough in certain districts, have no popular names. On the Clun and Onny, for example, I have frequently observed a species, with antennae quite twice as long as its wings, which rejoices in the name of *Leptocerus nigronervosus*, whilst on the Welsh Dee and some of its tributaries, one of the most usual sedges is known as *Hydropsyche pellucidula*. Indeed on every river sedges may be seen in the day-time which, lacking English names, are not easily identified by the average fisherman. Not that this matters in the least, as far as the angler is concerned, for a few artificial patterns are sufficient to suggest the whole range of caddis flies.

The Artificial Fly

The many species of sedges differ in details which are of importance to the entomologist, although not to the fisherman, since in general form and colour there is no great amount of difference between them and consequently it is unnecessary for the angler to burden himself with a great number of patterns. Half a dozen, or less, in two or three sizes, and giving a range of colours from yellowish-brown to dark brown should be sufficient to meet every requirement.

A few patterns, however, the fly-fisher must carry, because there are few more genuinely useful flies than copies of sedges. They will take trout on almost every river and lake at any time of the day, although, as one would expect, they are generally most effective in the evening. Whether trout are smutting, or are not rising at all, seems to make very little difference to the success of a Sedge. Fish will often take one at the first time of offering, after they have refused to look at other artificial flies and a good sedge pattern is one of the best I know to tempt hefty old cannibals which can rarely be induced to take any sort of artificial fly. And a pattern like the Cinnamon or the Medium Sedge, or possibly Lunn's Caperer, will often kill well when the water is clear and like a sheet of glass, whilst, given a little ripple on the water, they can prove really deadly.

Most artificial sedges may be fished wet, dry, or semi-submerged, and curiously enough, the exact dressing does not seem to matter much as long as the general coloration and size is right. Perhaps this is not so curious, since when trout are feeding on the natural insects, they are unlikely to be over-fastidious as to its species. There are such an enormous number of different sorts of caddis flies, all very much alike in general appearance, that there must frequently be several species on the water at the same time.

And, needless to say, fish do not attempt to distinguish between them; all and sundry go the same way. For this reason, a general suggestion of a sedge is all that the angler requires.

Certainly some patterns are better than others, doubtless because they serve to imitate a greater variety of natural sedges, but even of the better patterns, there are several to choose from, and not much to choose between them, although most fishermen have their own special favourites.

Halford picked out three typical sedges (which he copied to suggest all of the rest) which were cinnamon, dark, and medium in colour, and presumably most anglers adopt this or some similar plan. Personally

I stick to a few well-tried patterns and carry each in at least two sizes. The best, I think, are the Little Brown Sedge, the Little Red Sedge, Lunn's Hackled Caperer, the Cinnamon Sedge and Hanna's Medium Sedge. Quite a formidable list, but in addition there are several others which are useful on occasions; and at least one pattern to suggest the hatching fly is very necessary.

My own method of fishing a Sedge is a little unusual, although quite successful. A start is made with a dry, but unoiled, fly and if fish take it on the surface, it is anointed with a drop of oil and fished as a floater in the ordinary way. If, on the other hand, trout fight shy of it after it has been tried for a reasonable time, the unoiled fly is allowed to sink, which it will do sooner or later. That is to say, it will first settle down in the surface film and later, a fraction under it, and it is when it is in one of these two positions, that the fly will often prove exceptionally deadly. Hence the success of Powell's Paragon, tied with hen hackles. If, however, the fish still ignore it, a complete change to normal wet-fly procedure may sometimes bring results.

Nevertheless, as a general rule, I find that most fish are taken when the fly is in the surface film or only just below it, when it is doubtless taken for a hatching larva; and I feel convinced that the larva which is about to hatch, or is in the act of doing so, is far more attractive to trout than the winged and perfect insect. For one thing, it is more easily secured at this stage and trout, like all other fish, do not expend any more of their energy than necessary.

Although, as will have already been noted, there are numerous useful patterns to suggest the imagos, it is a little strange that scant attention has been devoted to the insect in its pupal state just prior to hatching or to the state when it is actually changing from larva to fly. We know that this rather helpless larva makes its way to the surface and that it is at this particular period that it proves most attractive to trout and grayling. And as the pupa is not particularly difficult to imitate, it is clear that a suitable artificial must prove even better than a copy of the winged insect.

That the caddis at this time of its existence has not received greater attention from fly-dressers may be due to there being some doubt about the ethics of the case. Witness, for example, this passage from *Minor Tactics* on this subject: "I felt qualms in my mind as to whether it was quite the game to imitate the insect at this stage." Now, I must confess some amazement that anybody as "nymph-minded" as Mr. Skues, should have written that, because if it is considered quite permissible to copy an ephemerid in the immediate pre-winged stage, why should it be wrong to copy a sedge at the same period of its existence?

Not all fly-tiers suffer from this inhibition and, in recent times, quite a number of them have tackled the problem. The late Dr. J. C. Mottram, for one, provided a simple dressing as under:

Body: Light brown floss silk, the thorax of dark brown floss silk. Just behind the eye and pointing backwards, a few guinea-fowl hackle barbs are tied in, and on the other side, two long thin fibres from the sword feather of the peacock. These represent the long antennae, which at this stage are folded backwards, viz. from head to tail.
Hook: 12 or 14.

There is an imitation of the hatching sedge designed by Mr. John Hamp and used with great success in the summer months on both limestone and chalk streams. The natural insect from which this artificial was evolved was often found in trout caught in the middle afternoon.

The tie is as follows:

Hook 12.
Tying silk: Green.
Body: Dubbed with a mixture of fox fur and mole fur both dyed in picric acid, with a black rib, usually of two strands from the black part of a turkey tail feather.
Wing cases: Black wing feather, tied on the underside of the shank, facing backwards to reach almost to the hook point.
Legs: Two speckled black and white fibres from a guinea-fowl (or mallard) feather tied along each side, sloping backwards. Two cock pheasant tail fibres are tied in fairly short at either side of the thorax, the fine end pointing backwards. Then two of the same fibres are tied in on either side in the same way, but with the root end pointing backwards, also quite short. Finally, two more are tied in on either side in the same way, with the root end pointing backwards but this time extending the whole length of the hook.

Mr. Eric Taverner apparently believes that it is quite permissible to imitate the hatching sedge, for in *Trout Fishing from All Angles* he gives a dressing for a wet pattern which he has found of value. His tie is:

Silk: Dull green.
Body: Hare's poll, very warm and thickly dubbed.
Hackle: Medium blue hen or cock's hackle of poor quality.
Hook: 14 or 13.

This was especially designed to suggest a particular greenish-bodied sedge which is common on the Welsh Dee in May and June, the hare's poll representing the pupal shuck and the blue dun hackle the half-closed wings. Although the latter are greyish-brown when opened, they are much more of a blue slate colour when emerging from the pupa's wing sheaths.

That the fly-dressers of the past did not altogether fail to appreciate the importance to anglers of the caddis pupa in the act of hatching is possible, and, indeed, probable. It is likely that some of the old wet flies were designed with this in view, the well-known Devonshire fly, the Half-stone, for example, being an excellent suggestion of the hatching insect.

All artificial Sedges, winged or hackled, wet or dry, are effective for brown trout, rainbow trout, and grayling. And since they are as useful on the chalk streams as on fast rocky rivers, and are also sure killers on lakes and pools, no fly-fisher likes to be without a few patterns of these indispensable flies.

For particulars of the best-known patterns, see Barm Fly, Caperer, Cinnamon Sedge, Dark Sedge, Grannom, Invicta, Little Brown Sedge, Little Red Sedge, Medium Sedge, Paragon, Sand Fly, Silver Sedge, Silverhorns, and Welshman's Button.

CAENIS
The Natural Fly

The smallest of the Ephemeroptera, these are tiny little insects which hatch in great clouds at dawn or in the evening during the summer months, especially from June to August. There are actually four species, although anglers can treat them as one, for the general appearance of all of them is much the same. They are quite unmistakable, for, apart from their minute size, they have *three* setae and two wings. In appearance, they are white—a creamy white body, rich brown thorax, and milky white wings. Beautiful models in miniature of the larger ephemerids, they seem to be regarded as a delicacy by trout, which will take huge quantities of them. That caenis are seldom found in an autopsy is doubtless because fish digest them quickly so that all signs of the insect disappear except for the thorax, which on account of its diminutive size is easily missed.

The Caenidae. are widely distributed, being equally at home on rivers and lakes. The hatch which is often of tremendous dimensions is generally a local one, occurring on some stretches of a river and being entirely absent from others, although the spent spinners will float down and cause a general rise.

This rise is not as a rule of a type that gives much satisfaction to a fly-fisherman because the fly is a most difficult one to copy and well deserves the name of the White Curse, by which it is sometimes known. Nevertheless, no angler can afford to ignore any common insect which is so well liked by trout, and some study of it may repay the fly-fisher.

The life-cycle of the caenis species is unique in several respects, for alone amongst the Ephemeridae the metamorphosis from sub-imago to imago takes place in the air, and usually within fifteen minutes of the nymph hatching. In fact the life span of the winged insect is extraordinarily short, for it hatches, changes from dun to spinner, mates, lays its eggs, and falls on the water in a spent condition, to die, all within the space of about an hour and a half!

Mr. F. E. Sawyer has made a special study of this insect and I cannot do better than quote what he has written about them in the *Country Sportsman* (July 1947): "The hatch of duns is sometimes enormous, many thousand rising from the river in the short period of perhaps half an hour. Within a few moments these may be seen to cast their shucks, some flying about with the setae still imprisoned. Soon the air seems to be alive with glistening, miniature flies. The spinners have congregated. Both sexes dance and weave with the vagaries of air currents about ten or twelve feet above the surface of the water, looking much the same at a distance as a cloud of gnats on a late summer evening.

"In the short period of transposition, the setae, of which there are three, have grown from short long-haired stubs of one-eighth of an inch, to more than an inch in length. This is especially noticeable in the males.

"With the hatch of duns comes the rise of trout and what a rise! Every fish in the river seems eager to get his or her share and as the little flies hatch in such quantities as to be on every square foot of the river at once, this is not difficult. For a short period—ten minutes or so —the river boils with rising fish and then it stops as abruptly as it started as the last dun becomes airborne. Now comes a time of waiting with only an occasional rise to a damaged fly and then, as the spinners return to the water, so the fish start rising again. Often the fall of the spinners is immense and the big trout in good positions will lie so near to the surface of the water that the dorsal and tail fins continually break and show above it. In such cases, the actions of the trout cannot be termed a rise; the fish just stays in the surface and gobbles like a duck. Perhaps for an hour there is continual activity, then . . . the dawn rise is over."

The Artificial Fly

Often when trout are "smutting", it is likely that they are really feeding on spent caenis spinners, because even from a short distance, it is next to impossible for the fisherman to see these little insects. Even if he is wise to what is exciting the trout, it is rarely that he will be able to take full advantage of the rise because caenis, on account of their diminutive size, are most difficult insects to imitate. In fact, more often than not, a general rise to these flies proves merely an exasperating experience for the angler.

The fly-dresser should have no special difficulty in constructing a passable copy of a caenis but its size is apt to defeat him. A particularly small hook is essential; it should be no larger than a size 20 and although eyed hooks are made in that size, nothing smaller than an 18 is really practicable for fly tying—and even to dress a fly on that size hook will tax the powers of most experienced amateurs. The small hook demands the use of very fine gut (5x or 6x) which will call for great care in handling if used in conjunction with a fairly stiff dry fly rod. Nevertheless, these difficulties are not insuperable and although it can never be easy to construct and use an imitation of any fly as small as a caenis there are several dressings for those who wish to give one a trial. Mr. G. E. M. Skues, for instance, has taken fish on a pattern he tied with palest starling wing, a white silk body, and a tiny white cock's hackle, on a size 17 hook.

All patterns to imitate caenis must obviously be lightly dressed and always fished on the surface. Those mentioned below should prove efficacious, although personally I have only used the spent pattern which has accounted for a few trout on a lake where large hatches of caenis are a feature in June and July.

DUN (SAWYER)
Tying silk: Black.
Whisks: Three short fibres of a cream cock hackle.
Body: Mole's fur spun on the black silk.
Thorax: The centre stalk of a black ostrich herl tied in to form a hump-backed effect with the shiny side uppermost.
Hackle: Three turns of a tiny dull dark blue hackle.
Hook: 20.

SPINNER, FEMALE (SAWYER)
Tying silk: Black.
Whisks: Three blue cock hackle fibres, about twice the length of the hook.
Body: Cream-coloured dubbing on the black silk.
Thorax: As for the dun.
Hackle: A tiny bright blue cock hackle, wound three times round, finished off with black silk and a spot of varnish.
Hook: 20.

SPINNER, SPENT (TAVERNER)

Tying silk: White or palest primrose.

Whisks: Three fibres palest cream cock and a shoulder hackle of red ant colour.

Body: Three close turns of tying silk on tail to represent the last three segments, followed by silver mole spun rather thinly on white silk.

Hackle: Small white or cream cock as clear as possible.

Hook: 18.

The patterns with the above tie which I have used have all been dressed on larger hooks (size 16), but probably a smaller fly would have been advantageous. They produce a pattern nearer in size to the natural insect, although this advantage is rather offset by the fact that they make hooking fish more difficult. And there is little object in making fish rise to one's fly, unless one can hook them!

CAPERER (*Halesus radiatus, H. digitatus*)

The name Caperer is correctly used to designate two species of sedges, both of which are large and cinnamon coloured. In practice, the name is indiscriminately applied by fishermen to many other cinnamon sedges and on the Test it is sometimes used for *Sericostoma personatum*, which is Halford's "Welshman's Button".

The name is supposed to come from the habit of the female flies which dance over the water as they deposit their eggs, continually rising and dipping during the process. At dusk on fine evenings in August and September, very large numbers of these sedges may be seen thus engaged.

The caperer, whether it be *H. radiatus* or *H. digitatus*, is of a general cinnamon colour, rather more brown on the body and thorax, with brown-mottled yellowish wings, mottled with dark yellow and brown specks and streaks. Not that it is of any great importance that an angler should be able to recognize it, because, as already mentioned elsewhere, there are so many sedges, differing only in small details, that it is quite unnecessary for the fisherman to identify the actual species, except possibly in the case of a very few notable exceptions. The sedges can be more conveniently divided into a few groups according to size and colour, and this is, in fact, the only possible way of reducing their numbers to manageable proportions.

There are many good patterns which can be used to suggest the caperer, of which the Dark Sedge, Cinnamon Sedge, Medium Sedge, and the Little Red Sedge are probably the most usual.

The dressings for Lunn's Caperers will be found under Welshman's Button.

CATERPILLARS

To many fly-fishermen, the necessity for or desirability of using any imitation of a caterpillar would seem to be very slight. But there are times when an artificial can do great execution; and, of more frequent occurrence, times when one will collect a few fish which would be unlikely to fall to any other fly. Wherever trees, especially oaks, over-hang river or lake, caterpillars will be found and the observant angler will often see a disturbance going on under the trees caused by trout regularly taking some insect. No artificial fly, dry or wet, will interest them unless it is an imitation of a caterpillar, for it is on that the fish will be feeding to the exclusion of every other insect.

At any time in the summer, caterpillars are liable to fall into the water and trout will always snap them up, but it is in the hot weather that some species of caterpillars are obliged to seek the ground in order to pupate and they accomplish this by floating earthwards on fine silken threads. In even a light breeze, many will descend instead upon the stream or lake and when this happens every trout in the neighbourhood will get into position to enjoy the feast.

Dapping with a live caterpillar is often successful, but it is a tricky business and more fish will be lost than landed. On the whole, better results will be obtained by discovering the type and colour of the cater-pillar on which the fish are feeding, and mounting a suitable imitation. The caterpillars may be of different species but more often than not, they will be small, juicy, and yellowish-green, the larvae, I believe, of *arctia caja*.

Of the several patterns sold as copies of caterpillars, I like best the Green Caterpillar and the Arrow Fly, although flies in other colours may be required. The fault of most imitations is that they are alto-gether too big. It is the small short caterpillars which trout like best and no artificial of more than half an inch in length is likely to prove of much use.

The possibilities of this form of fishing should not be ignored because it will quite often be the means of taking a few trout, and usually good ones, when they will not look at anything else.

CELLULOID WINGED FLIES

Artificial flies with clear or veined transparent wings made of celluloid, or similar material, were introduced over thirty years ago and ever since they have been re-invented by enthusiastic but inexperienced fishermen.

To the human eye they obviously resemble the delicate wings of the natural insect more closely than do any feathered concoctions, but unfortunately for their creators, trout do not seem to hold the same views—in fact, they will have nothing to do with them. Flies tied with wings of this sort must also be terrible to cast. I have had no personal experience of them, but many years ago, at a dinner of the Fly-Fishers' Club, William Senior (then editor of the *Field*) described what happened when he and a friend tried one of these patterns—in this case a gauze-winged Mayfly. "It turned out to be a musical Mayfly," he said. "With a short and gentle cast there was a humming as of a line or two of the 'Old Hundredth'. The cast, extended at its full length, would bring forth a wild shriek behind one's back, and then it would go down with a sort or ripple of soft and yet softer music, and finally touch the water with a Wagnerian crash. The fly at last went off with a crack which exceeded the cry of a Jew's harp."

Flies have also been patented with wings made up of a number of thin celluloid fibres (or similar substances). These, I believe, have proved quite effective, more especially on lochs.

Patterns tied with natural wings have also been made, unless I am mistaken, for I have in my possession an artificial fly of which the wing has every appearance of being a natural one. It would seem impossible to copy the nervures and cross-nervures so closely, by artificial means, although how the wing was stiffened and affixed to the hook is quite beyond me. Neither have I any clue to the inventor, as I discovered the pattern in a box of mixed dry flies given to me by the late F. H. Heald, sometime clerk to the Trent Fishery Board. He was unable to say where it came from, as many of the flies concerned were passed on to him by an old angler and may have been tied fifty years before.

CHIRONOMIDAE (Midges)

At least three species of the non-biting midges are of interest to anglers, C. *viridis* (green midge), C. *tentans* (olive midge), and C. *plumosus*, the golden dun midge of Ronald's.

Of the latter, I know little, but the first two hatch in tremendous numbers, are quite large flies, and are well liked by trout. They appear early in June, last throughout the summer, and occur almost invariably on still water—on lakes, reservoirs and pools. All three are true water-bred insects (of which the larvae are the well-known blood-worms) and enjoy a wide distribution. Perhaps fishermen might not have paid much attention to them had not Hugh Sheringham pointed out that on many waters they form an important part of the trout's diet at certain times, and that they are not so small that useful artificials cannot be tied to simulate them.

The larvae and pupae of midges and gnats are found everywhere where there is a deposit of mud or sand. Their habitat is in sluggish or still water, and rainwater butts, for example, are often full of them. They form, perhaps, the basic food of lake and pool trout and con-sequently they must be of some interest to the angler. Many a time I have opened lake trout to find their stomachs packed full with these creatures which vary in size and colour, some being brown and others black, olive, or red. These larvae rest tail uppermost and head down (or in the case of the pupae, head up and tail down) and may be seen sus-pended vertically from the surface downwards. They do not possess legs, or to be correct, they only have unformed legs, but the tail of the larva and the head of the pupa is provided with distinctive hairy appen-dages. Of all of them, the larvae of the chironomidae, popularly known as blood-worms, are the biggest and most worth the consideration of fishermen. They are unique in the insect world as they contain red blood exactly as in human beings and other vertebrates.

Imitating them is not an easy matter and few dressings are therefore available. Dr. Mottram gave a good deal of thought to the question and eventually produced patterns which offer some hope of success. His method was to take a small wedge-shaped piece of cork and bind it on to the shank of a light hook with strong thread, the thicker end of the cork extended very slightly beyond the eye of the hook. Two or three grey barbs from an emu's feather are tied in near the hook eye. The thick end of the cork is dyed or inked black: the body can be left in the natural cork colour or coloured to choice. Cutting such a small piece of cork to the right wedge shape is not too easy, but if it is done correctly the finished fly should float vertically in the water, with, of course, the business end of the hook downwards and the eye on the surface. They are cast to a rising fish just like a dry fly but they should not be worked, although if a very slight movement is given to the fly occasionally, it will serve to attract a trout's attention. It is essential that the fly should float and to make sure of this it may be necessary to grease the last few feet of the cast as well as the fly itself.

C. *viridis*, which Sheringham called the Blagdon green midge, because it occurs in quantities on Blagdon reservoir, where even the larger trout take it freely, is a gnat-like insect with a bright emerald green body, nearly half an inch in length. Like all other chironomidae, the adult insects have two long hairy antennae, more hairy in the males than the females. Found on still waters throughout England and Wales, it may often be observed in warm weather on or near the water in swarms of such dimensions as to give the appearance of a rising ground mist. How greatly trout appreciate this fly is evident from the frequency with which it is found in autopsies.

C. *tentans*, Sheringham's Blagdon olive midge, is slightly larger with a body full half an inch long. This is generally of a pale olive-yellow colour with greyish-olive markings dividing the segments, but is subject to some variation. On hot sunny days, especially after sunset in August and September, it often appears in huge numbers. Like its green relative, it is greatly appreciated by fish.

C. *plumosus*, which Ronalds calls the golden dun midge, is a close relation of C. *tentans*. Another midge which may be C. *anthracinus* is common on some lakes in April and May. Rather smaller than C. *tentans* it is jet black, with whitish wings.

The artificial patterns to imitate these midges are described below. The first two, I believe, are the invention of the late Dr. J. C. Mottram, although I cannot be definite about this.

BLAGDON GREEN MIDGE

In my own experience, this is a particularly useful fly, not only as a copy of *C. viridis* for use (generally as a floater) on still waters, but also as a first-class dry pattern for rivers, especially those fringed by trees and bushes.

Chironomidae are not usually found on rivers, so that possibly trout take this fly for a small juicy green caterpillar, whilst it is quite effective as an imitation of the aphis. Over a number of years now, I have used it fairly regularly during hot summer evenings on both lakes and rivers and have found it a killing pattern, good enough to have a permanent place in my fly-box. The dressing is:

Body: Emerald green wool.
Wings: Stiff white hackle at shoulder.
Hook: 14 to 16.

The Blagdon Green Midge is not, of course, the only pattern which may be used to imitate *C. viridis* more or less effectively. The more recent dressing given below is worth particular attention because it was evolved by Mr. John Henderson, who besides being a very good fisherman and entomologist, has made a special study of the chironomids and can be regarded as an expert on them.

Body: Sisal fibre, or a strand from a swan's feather, dyed emerald green.
Legs: A cut grey-haired Plymouth Rock cock hackle tied in at tail, i.e. ribbed up the body and used also as hackle.
Wings: Light grey cock hackle points.
Hook: 14 to 16.

This pattern was unknown to me until this year and as yet no suitable opportunity of trying it has occurred, but it sounds to me as if it might be the answer to the lake fisherman's prayer. And he would welcome a reliable answer to it, because the green midge (also known as the grass-green midge) is of real importance to him, since it often appears, not in mere thousands, but literally in millions. On occasions too, it will invade a river in the same manner, although as already mentioned, it is far more of a still-water insect. On the whole it must be said that the green midge has never received from fly-dressers the attention it merits.

Blagdon Olive Midge

Designed as a dry fly for lake fishing, this is another effective summer pattern. Although many really big trout have been taken on it, personally I have never found it as attractive as the Green Midge. The dressing is:

Body: Heron's herl.
Hackle: Stiff olive hackle at shoulder.
Wings: Two blue dun cock hackles.
Hook: 14 to 16.

Golden Dun Midge

An old pattern of which Ronalds says that the natural prototype is *C. plumosus.* He recommends its employment up to the end of May and states that great sport may be had with it. His tie was as under:

Body: Olive floss silk ribbed with gold twist and tied with dun silk thread.
Wings: From the palest feather of a young starling.
Legs: A plain dun hackle.
Hook: 15 or 16.

CINNAMON AND GOLD

A favourite wet pattern for lake fishing in Scotland and Ireland and, in the larger sizes a most effective sea-trout fly. The dressing is subject to variations but that given below is fairly typical.

Body: Flat gold tinsel.
Wings: Brown owl or partridge.
Hackle: Light ginger.
Whisks: Tippet fibres or ibis.
Hook: 8 to 11.

CINNAMON QUILL

A dry fly, useful as a general imitation of any red spinner: not only of the imago of the March brown (the correct red spinner) but also of the spinners of the turkey brown, female pale watery dun, female olive dun, female iron-blue dun, and the female b.-w.o. (sherry spinner).

Dressing:

Wings: Pale starling.
Hackle: Two pale sandy ginger cock hackles.
Body: Pale cinnamon-coloured quill found at the root end of some peacock quills down the stem; or condor dyed a faint brown-red.
Whisks: Three strands as hackle.
Hook: 14 to 16.

A hackled version often proves successful and can be tied in the following manner:

Body: As for winged pattern.
Hackles: Pale sandy ginger cock and pale blue cock.
Whisks: Pale sandy ginger cock hackle fibres.
Hook: 14 to 16.

CINNAMON SEDGE (*Limnophilus lunatus*)

A medium-sized sedge with yellowish-cinnamon wings, marked with darker blotches and having a light-coloured crescent near the tip of each anterior wing. The body of the male is nearly green and that of the female, brown. Somewhere I have read that the name arose from a faint smell of cinnamon alleged to be given off by these insects, but if there is any truth in this, the scent must be faint indeed, and it would seem far more likely that the fly takes its name from its predominant colour.

The cinnamon sedge is widely distributed, being indigenous to the north, midlands, and south, and is abundant on many rivers and lakes from late June to September. The artificial patterns, of which there are a good many, may be used to simulate a number of sedges and in common with other artificial sedges, it is an effective evening fly on slow-flowing streams, especially in windy weather.

The Cinnamon Sedge is extensively used on the chalk streams in August and September, particularly towards dusk, and it is a general favourite on most rivers throughout Great Britain. A good autumn fly for grayling, in common with other sedge patterns, it is also a first-class lake fly for brown and rainbow trout, being especially useful on small sheets of water.

In July of this year, fishing on a weedy gin-clear pool of not more than half an acre in extent, I creeled several brown trout between two and three and a half pounds each, most of them being taken in the late afternoon between tea and dinner, and all either on the Cinnamon or Medium Sedge. The fish were able to get a very good view of the fly in the calm, clear water, but they were not once led into temptation by any of the many patterns of other dry flies which were offered them. They would come up from the depths, look at them and disappear. Yet when a Sedge was put over them, their suspicions appeared to vanish and they took it without hesitation. Recommended dressings are:

Dry (Woolley).

Body: A strand from a cinnamon turkey tail feather, ribbed gold wire.
Body Hackle: Ginger cock's.
Shoulder Hackle: Ginger cock's tied in front of wings.
Wings: Landrail wing feather.
Hook: 11 to 13.

Wet, the old tie suggested by Ronalds and still as good as any:

Body: Fawn-coloured silk, tied on with silk thread of the same colour.
Wings: Feather of a yellow brown hen's wing, rather darker than a landrail's wing feather.
Hackle: A ginger hackle.
Hook: 12.

Ronalds adds that it can be made buzz with a grouse feather and that in either form "very great diversion may be expected with it".

CLARET AND GOLD

An Irish wet pattern, used for lake and sea-trout. The usual tie is:

Body: Flat gold tinsel.
Wings: Goose quill feather dyed dark claret.
Hackle: Cock's hackle dyed to match the wings.
Tail: Tippet:
Hook: 10 to 12; larger for sea-trout.

The Claret and Silver is the same fly tied with a silver tinsel body.

CLARET AND MALLARD 141

CLARET AND MALLARD

A splendid pattern for river or lake and without any doubt at all, one of the most generally useful wet flies. Certainly for a general fly for any month of the year in fast rivers, for lake fishing, or for sea-trout, there can be few more universally popular flies, and it has long been one of my own personal favourites. And except for the chalk streams, beginners might do worse than follow the advice given to me by a well-known and most experienced wet fly-fisherman many years ago: "When in doubt, try a Claret and Mallard."

On lochs throughout Scotland, it is reputed to kill more trout than any other pattern, whilst the Irish boatmen swear by the "Claret". Excellent on lakes at any time of the day, it is particularly effective at dusk or after dark, when in contradiction of the generally accepted idea, it will often prove more successful if tied on a fairly small hook, say a 12 or 14.

For sea-trout, the Claret and Mallard is probably the most popular of all wet patterns, whether fished in the day or after dark. For rainbow trout, it is a reliable fly and I have taken many grayling on it, although it is not looked upon as a particularly good pattern for these fish.

As a trout fly, the Claret and Mallard is as useful on a big river as it is on a little mountain beck and there are few types of rivers on which it will not kill. In short, it is one of the best all-round general-utility patterns.

What trout take it for is a matter of opinion, although one would not be far wrong in calling it a "nymph-suggesting" fly. Of one thing I am certain, and that is that when trout are occupied in that most irritating diversion of routing amongst weed-beds to disturb and drive out shrimps and other aquatic larvae, a small Claret and Mallard, well sunk, will often cause their downfall. There is nothing gaudy about this famous pattern for, in fact, the gentleman wears a neat but rather drab suit with just a touch of colour in his socks and tie, but he is a great and efficient workman who is often worth more than his weight in gold. He may be used in any position on the cast although normally he does best as a tail fly.

Of the origin of the "Claret" there is some little doubt, but it is not a particularly old pattern. Generally is it attributed to William Murdoch, a one-time celebrated Aberdeen fisherman, who invented the Heckham Peckham and is said to have evolved many other first-class lake flies "with the help of some friends and gillies".

The standard dressing of the Claret and Mallard is:

Body: Claret seal's fur, ribbed with fine gold.
Wings: Dark bronze feathers from a mallard.
Hackle: Natural red cock's.
Tail: Tippet.
Hook: 10 to 14; larger for sea-trout.

A common mistake made in dressing this pattern is to use seal's fur too light in colour. The fly kills much better when tied with a dark claret body.

There are several other patterns in the mallard series, all of which are useful loch flies, but none of them quite equal to the "Claret". The best known are the Mallard and Green, Mallard and Silver, Mallard and Red, and Mallard and Yellow.

Mr. Skues informs me that there is a Norwegian mayfly which is well imitated in its spinner stage by the Claret and Mallard. Using this pattern to imitate the natural insect, he found that it killed well on lakes in southern Norway.

CLARET DUN (*Leptophlebia vespertina*)

Something like a small march brown but far more akin to a turkey brown, this ephemerid is found almost exclusively on still waters and is especially common in Ireland, particularly on Lough Arrow, where, at times, the artificial does great execution. It is not unknown on rivers and Mr. G. E. M. Skues tells me that although he only observed it once on his stretch of the Itchen, every patch of still or slow water was then littered with spent or dying flies.

The dun has smoky, blue-black wings with dark legs and both duns and spinners have deep claret bodies from the colour of which, the name of the fly is derived. The spinners are similar in appearance to the sherry spinner but their colouring is rather sharper. The fly appears first in late May and continues to August. Having four wings and *three* setae (tails), it cannot be easily confused with any other up-winged dun except possibly the turkey brown (*L. submarginata*). The latter, how-ever, is found on many rivers and is plentiful on the chalk streams where the claret dun is extremely rare.

Although the claret dun occurs spasmodically on some English and Welsh lakes and has been reported from a few slow-running streams in various parts of the country, it is not a fly to which the English angler need pay any attention and the artificial, except in Ireland, is of no account.

CLARET HACKLE

A New Zealand pattern, which will kill well on Scotch and Irish lakes.

Dressing:

Body: Peacock herl.
Hackle: Claret.
Wings: Starling.
Hook: 6 to 12.

CLARET SPINNER. See IRON-BLUE DUN

CLOËON

The genus cloëon may not be of any great significance to the ordinary trout fisher, unless he is interested in being able correctly to identify the various ephemerids, in which case he should note it well, for cloëon may easily upset his deductions.

There are three species of this insect, only one of which has a popular name—the Sail Wing (q.v.)—and that is of local application only, being used solely on a few Scottish lochs. Nevertheless, cloëon are very common on all still waters throughout Great Britain, and unless examined closely they can easily be mistaken for pale wateries or olives. That they are neither will be made evident when one notices the absence of the usual small hind wings. They are, in fact, the only members of the ephemeroptera to have *two* wings and *two* setae, although their nymphs have the usual three setae.

Cloëon appear from June to August on lakes and ponds, and there must be very few pools in which their larvae are not present.

COACHMAN

A standard artificial pattern which nears no particular resemblance to any natural insect, except possibly to some light-coloured moth. Used wet or dry, mostly as an evening fly, or after dark. There are fishermen who hold no great opinion of this pattern, except as an evening fly when its colour makes it easy to spot. For my own part, I look upon it as one of the better general flies. For river work, a small Coachman, used at any time of the day, will frequently tempt fish which fail to respond to other patterns, especially in the summer and autumn months. Although probably it is more usually fished wet, personally I have seldom used it except as a floater.

As a lake fly, the Coachman is generally conceded to be a highly effective pattern, but I would go further and say that when a dry fly is required for lake or pool fishing, a small floating Coachman is to the still-water angler what the Red Quill is to the river fisherman—one of the most likely patterns of all to provide sport. It has other merits too, which are not always recognized. When trout are smutting at dusk and persistently refuse to look at any artificial one offers them, it always pays to mount a dry Coachman, dressed on a 14 or 16 hook (preferably the latter), and not only because it is a fly which is easily seen by the angler. It also kills well as a wet fly, its best position being as a top dropper.

Many fishermen aver that the Coachman kills better when the wings have lost their original whiteness, and some go to the trouble of rubbing mud into them; others, like myself, prefer the fly with a claret seal's body, instead of the usual peacock's herl.

So far I have not mentioned the hackled Coachman. Although it is by no means so well known as the standard pattern, my own experience suggests that for dry fly-fishing, either in river or lake, it is the better killer. Nowadays I only use the winged fly at dusk or as a wet pattern. There are two or three other variations, such as the Gold Coachman and an orange-bodied type, besides one known as the Lead-Winged Coachman, which is not really a Coachman at all, being tied with a starling or landrail wing. None of them, I think, is greatly used.

The origin of the Coachman is generally ascribed to a Tom Bosworth, who was a coachman to three British sovereigns—George IV, William IV, and Queen Victoria. Another version was given by a correspondent in the *Field* in 1853, who wrote: "A brother of the Whip, who plied his art on the banks of the Cray in Kent, being at a loss for a fly, put together from some odds and ends, a nondescript fly. . . . This coachman's name was John Hughes and the fly was named after the inventor."

Either of these may have invented it, although the only reliable evidence extant is that the fly originated in the first half of the nineteenth century. Salter was the first to refer to a pattern of this name in his fifth edition of the *Angler's Guide*, in which he mentions the "Harding Fly or Coachman". Previously, in the third edition published in 1815, he had also referred to the "Harding Fly" but without the alternative name. The list of flies in March's *Young Anglers' Companion*, which was probably published between 1810 and 1825 also includes the "Harding Fly or Coachman". Who Harding was or whether the fly

invented by him was the same Coachman we know to-day has never
been ascertained. Possibly it was quite different for in 1839, T. C. Hofland, in his *Angler's Manual*, described the Coachman as having a copper-
coloured peacock herl body, with a red hackle and landrail wings, a
pattern which is now known as the Dark (or Lead-Winged) Coachman. A year later, however, Kirkbride in the *Northern Angler*, tells his
readers that the fly should be winged with "a white feather from the
underside of a duck's wing" and in 1847, Fitzgibbon, in his *Handbook
of Angling*, gave the tie as being "body, peacock's herl, full and short:
wings, fibres of any small white feather; legs, a turn or two of a red
hackle", which is the same dressing as used to-day.

It is clear, therefore, that the Coachman in its present-day livery is
over a hundred years old. Only a reliable pattern could have maintained its reputation for this length of time, a reputation too which
extends far beyond the shores of this island. There must be few, if
any, countries where anglers ply their art in which the Coachman is
not looked upon as a standard pattern. In U.S.A. and Canada it is
perhaps even more popular than in Great Britain and probably shares
with the Parmachenee Belle the honour of being the most universally
used wet fly.

The standard dressing is:

Wings: White swan.
Hackle: Red cock.
Body: Copper-coloured peacock herl.
Hook: 10 to 16; up to 8 for lake fishing.

That for the hackled pattern is:

Body: Copper-coloured peacock herl.
Hackle: White cock hackle with a shorter red one in front or the two mixed
together.
Hook: 12 to 16.

Reference has already been made to the Dark or Lead-Winged
Coachman, another pattern of great utility. Its invention is generally
attributed to H. R. Francis and the date about 1870, but from the notes
above it will be seen that it is almost certainly a much older fly.

COCH-Y-BONDHU (*Phyllopertha horticola*)
The Natural Beetle

It is extraordinary, but true, that the majority of fly-fishers have but
a hazy idea what the artificial Coch-y-bondhu is intended to represent.

A beetle of some sort is the extent of the knowledge of a great many and, stranger still, angling authors are equally as vague.

Some of the latter describe the insect as "a button-shaped beetle" (whatever that may mean) and the reader is generally informed that it hatches in thousands in June and July and that trout take it freely. From that they turn hurriedly, doubtless with relief, to firmer ground, with a description of the artificial and when to use it.

Alfred Ronalds, for instance, who calls it the Marlow Buzz, identifies it as *Chrysomela populi* and says that it is to be found in June flying amongst poplar trees. Halford has even less to say. Francis Francis mentions that the coch-y-bondhu is also called the Shorn Fly, Hazel Fly, Marlow Buzz, Fernwebb, Brackenclock, etc, and describes it as looking like a diminutive cockchafer; but that is all. Taverner in *Trout Fishing from All Angles*, tells us much the same.

Even Leonard West has little to say although he makes mention of the fact that there is confusion as to the prototype of the artificial fly. Some authorities, he says, claim that it is *Phyllopertha horticola*, but since this beetle is not definitely red and black, he thinks that the honour should go to the red cowdung beetle (*Aphodius foetens*) which was known around Bala and in the vale of Festiniog as the coch-y-bondhu. A famous entomologist has informed me that in his opinion the coch-y-bondhu beetle is undoubtedly *Telephorus lividus*, the common soldier beetle.

It is likely, even probable, that the name is applied to more than one species of beetle according to the locality, but since the name is as Welsh one, one may reasonably accept as the natural prototype of the coch-y-bondhu, the beetle known throughout Wales by that name, provided, of course, that there is general agreement as to what it is. And I think there is.

Some years ago, with the purpose of discovering whether there was such unanimity, I communicated with a number of fishermen in various parts of Wales and asked them to forward me specimens of the insect known to them as the coch-y-bondhu. When, in due course, these reached me, in each and every case they proved to be *P. horticola*.

This beetle is about half an inch, or a fraction less, in length. Whilst red and black would serve as a rough description of its general colouring, it is actually more of a reddish-brown with a dark peacock green thorax. The protruding portions of the body and legs are practically black, whilst the underside is similar in colour to the thorax, although somewhat darker.

It first appears in strength in June and is prevalent for about three weeks, although small hatches may occur later. As its natural habitat is amongst the bracken and heather of the mountains and moors, it is more common in Wales and Scotland than elsewhere, and it is found on some rivers and lakes in those countries in truly enormous numbers. Yet it is a land-bred insect, only getting on to the water by accident. On lakes, in particular, it will at times cause a big rise of fish, as anglers who fish the Welsh lakes, like Vyrnwy, can testify.

I have seen several hundred yards of the beach at Fairbourne, Merionethshire, so thickly carpeted with countless thousands of these beetles, that it was possible to scoop them up in handfuls and to fill a child's bucket with them in a few minutes.

A light breeze had carried them there from the bracken on the nearby hills, in spite of the fact that they appear to be strong flyers. It is not difficult to imagine what happens when similar conditions prevail near a river or lake, for trout are extremely fond of the coch-y-bondhu. I have never observed it in the Midlands or the south, although I have noted it in small numbers in Herefordshire, near the Welsh border.

Incidentally, whilst coch-y-bondhu is the customary spelling today, Welsh authorities maintain that coch-y-bonddu, which may be roughly translated as "red and black", is more correct and I doubt not that they are right. Nevertheless, I am of the opinion that it is more likely that the original name of the beetle was coch-y-boldu, meaning "red and black belly". Some old Welshmen spell it that way to-day and it is a pretty accurate description of the natural insect.

From the confusion which has arisen both as regards the prototype of the artificial pattern and the spelling of the name, readers may guess—and guess rightly—that the coch-y-bondhu is not a chalk-stream insect and consequently it has never been the subject of research and publicity as have been those flies which favour those southern waters. But the natural beetle is of importance to all who fish the lakes and rivers where it is found and the artificial is a standard pattern, known and used the world over.

The Artificial Fly

The artificial Coch-y-bondhu is a very well-known standard pattern and a close suggestion of the natural insect, although it is also effective when the beetle is not on the water and, in fact, on rivers and lakes where the natural coch-y-bondhu is never seen. This is quite under-standable, for although the ordinary pattern is an excellent impression of *P. horticola*, it also serves as a useful suggestion of many other beetles.

There are anglers who can see no resemblance at all between the hackled fly and any species of beetle, let alone a particular one. And it must be admitted that more than one angling authority (including that keen observer Leonard West) has taken the Coch-y-bondhu as being an example of an artificial fly which has no likeness at all to the insect of which it is supposed to be an imitation.

That is not my view and to any readers who may be sufficiently interested I would recommend a little experiment. Place half a dozen artificial Coch-y-bondhus in a box with an equal number of the natural beetle and then proceed to pick out the former. There can, of course, be very little difficulty about this, for a feathered imitation can easily be distinguished from a living insect, and from that point of view it is an unfair test. But it is one worth making because what will at once become apparent (and which will, I think, cause some surprise) is the manner in which the colouring of the artificial matches that of the natural beetle. It is amazingly close and this little test can be guaranteed to make any angler, who could see no resemblance between the artificial and natural, entirely revise his opinion.

For Welsh and Scottish streams and for small waters generally, there are few better all-round patterns than a Coch-y-bondhu, and few which are so foolishly neglected. Wet or dry, and at any time of the season, it is always a good pattern to try on a strange river. I have used it on rivers, becks, lakes, and pools, in many countries and it has invariably proved its worth as a most efficient general pattern, although there is possibly some truth in the accusation, sometimes made against it, that it tends to attract small trout. It kills quite as well fished dry as wet and, using it as a floater, I have found it especially effective on dykes and "feeders".

The old standard dressing, which admits of little variation, is:

Body: Two or three strands of copper-coloured peacock herl twisted together, tipped with flat gold.
Hackle: Coch-y-bondhu.
Hook: 14 to 12.

When used as one of a team of wet flies, the best position for the Coch-y-bondhu is as the top dropper and if it can be kept skimming along the surface, it can be deadly.

The natural beetle is often used for dapping in Wales and a great number of fish are taken on it every season.

A friend of mine was fishing at Abergwynolwyn some years ago, at a time when the "locals" were making big catches with the natural beetle and as he had been having indifferent sport, he bought a tin full of them from a lad.

Relating this to one of the local fishermen, he added that he would stick to the artificial fly for the rest of the morning but if he still failed to get any fish, he intended to try the naturals in the afternoon. The Welshman's reply was that he would do no good with them as the trout would only take the natural lure between 10 a.m. and 1 p.m.

With some experience of Welsh superstitions, my friend put this down as pure rubbish and soon after lunch commenced his nefarious work with the live beetles. Much to his surprise, the fish would have nothing to do with them. After that "as a matter of interest", which was as good excuse as any for a dry fly man who had thus fallen from grace, he pursued his experiments for several days. And as a result, he assures me that he satisfied himself that trout will not take the natural coch-y-bondhu much after midday.

This incident is curious and supports the theory that the artificial, which kills at any hour of the day, is not always, or indeed usually, taken for the natural insect.

On the other hand, the natural beetle sometimes gets carried on to lakes in large numbers and when this occurs, it creates a great furore amongst the trout which take it voraciously; and under these conditions, great sport is generally had with the artificial fly, when it is obviously take for the natural insect. On these occasions, a pattern known as "Kennedy's Coch-y-bondhu" often does great execution. Made of rubber, or some other composition which floats well, it is perhaps more of a lure than a fly, but it is a good copy of the live beetle.

Of the few variations of the standard fly, only three need be mentioned. The Red-Ribbed Coch-y-bondhu is useful on lakes and some fishermen prefer it to the established pattern.

Shrimpton's Coch-y-bondhu was the invention of Mr. S. A. Shrimpton who has found it deadly over a number of years on the Normandy rivers and especially on the Risle, a pure chalk stream. It is the standard pattern but with coch-y-bondhu hackle wings tied forward after the manner of a Mole fly. A grand floater, it should kill anywhere.

There is another pattern of special interest which is known as West's Coch-y-bondhu, which is seldom used for trout, but which is a first-class grayling pattern. Apparently its invention is attributed to the late Leonard West, although I have failed to find any mention of it in his *Natural Trout Fly and Its Imitation,* and in all the correspondence which passed between us I cannot recollect any reference having been made to it. Yet possibly it may be his, since in his book he pointed out that "the fact that nature provides so exact a counterpart of the elytra of this beetle in the tippet feather of the golden pheasant seems to have escaped the notice of most".

This feather may be useful to copy the wing-cases of the red cow-dung beetle, but it is a poor imitation of those of *P. horticola,* a point which must be borne in mind when copying the latter species. Certainly West would never have made a copy of this insect, or of the cowdung beetle, with the enormously long antennae which the pattern in question carries and which will be seen in the illustration of it on Plate VIII. If this fly was designed by him, I can only think that they have been added since by someone less well acquainted with natural beetles, most of which have but short antennae.

However, there is no doubt that it is a most attractive looking pattern and one which should serve as a general suggestion of many beetles; and there would appear to be no reason why, when divested of its long feelers, it should not prove an efficient trout fly. As a dry pattern for grayling, it enjoys a high reputation, and I am informed that on the Teme in particular, experts prefer it to most other flies for summer and early autumn use. It is tied in the usual beetle-fashion with the following dressing:

Body: Bronze peacock herl.
Elytra: Longish strands of golden pheasant tippet. The tying-in of these should be so judged that part of the black rib of the tippets shows on the top of the body, when the tippet fibres are being tied down.
Hackle: Coch-y-bondhu.
Hook: 14.

The antennae have been omitted as being superfluous.

CONNEMARA BLACK

A good wet pattern for trout, sea-trout, and lake fishing. Renowned in Ireland, the land of its origin, it is a favourite for sea-trout in every part of the United Kingdom. The dressing is:

Body: Black wool or seal's fur, ribbed with fine oval silver tinsel.
Wings: From the bronze shoulder feather of a mallard.
Tail: Small golden pheasant crest feather.
Hackle: Natural black cock with a hackle from the blue feather from a jay's wing in front.
Hook: 12 to 9 for lake fishing and larger for sea-trout.

COWDUNG (*Scatophaga stercoraria*)

This is a fly which is recognized by most fishermen for it is one of the commonest insects found near rivers, and is present throughout the season. It may appear as early as January and last until the first severe frosts arrive. Rather like a common house-fly, it has two clear wings with marked veinings and a small dark spot on each; a portly brownish-yellow (almost olive) body with a dark thorax and large head. The larvae feed upon the excrement of cattle and the females may be observed hovering near it preparatory to laying their eggs in it.

There is reason to doubt whether some land-bred flies which, according to many writers, are often blown on to the water are of any consequence to the fly-fisher, because in actual fact, the insects in question are so seldom seen on the water. This, however, does not apply to some flies, to take but two examples, the alder and the daddy-long-legs may often be observed struggling on the surface of both rivers and lakes. And it is certainly not applicable to the cowdung fly because whenever there is a breeze it gets carried on to the water in goodly numbers.

This may not be of much account in high summer, but on cold days in March and April, when there is often a complete absence of other fly life on or near the water, I have frequently seen cowdung flies driven on to the river in considerable quantities and such rises as there have been have been occasioned by the trout taking them. Once on the water, this fly appears to find it impossible to "take off" again, but it rides the surface well for a long time and in consequence offers a mark to any trout on the look-out for a meal.

All present-day authorities seem to be agreed that the artificial is "good medicine" whether there is any wind or not, which is in direct variance with the old tradition that it is only likely to prove successful in rough weather. This may be true, although personally I should never bother to use a Cowdung when other flies are hatching in any force;

but when the natural insect has the river more or less to itself, as it sometimes does, a suitable artificial copy is a most likely pattern to attract
the fish.

It is usual to imitate the male fly which wanders farther afield and has
a brighter-coloured body. There are several dressings to choose from
which can be fished wet or dry, although the latter are generally more
killing. Halford, who was one of those authors who rightly recommends the artificial for use in windy weather, gave one tie, but to my
mind it is not as good as the older one evolved by Ronalds which was
as under:

Body: Yellow worsted or mohair, mixed with a little dingy brown fur from a
bear, or left rough and spun on light brown silk.
Wings: From a landrail.
Legs: Of a ginger-coloured hackle.
Hook: 12 to 14.

Another popular and modern tie is given below. This was evolved
by Mr. T. J. Hanna to whom I am obliged for the correct dressing.

Body: French chenille dyed brownish-yellow.
Rib: Light green silk.
Hackle: Honey dun, darkish.
Wings: Darkish honey dun hackle tips tied flat in the manner of Diptera.
Hook: 12.

This body is made in two sections, the longer one towards the bend
of the hook. Hackle and wings are tied in in front of this section and
then a couple of turns of chenille will be sufficient to form a head in
front of the hackle and wings. The latter should lie flat like those of a
house-fly. The finished article approximates closely to the natural fly
in shape and colour.

It seems to me that it should not be too difficult to construct a better
pattern of the cowdung than any now extant, although it would have
to be more of the impressionistic order than an exact imitation.

If one picks one of these flies off the water (it is almost certain to be
a male), it will be noticed that the body is almost a pale olive colour,
although if the insect is placed in a box for an hour or two, this will
change, first to brownish-yellow and eventually to a dirty brown. So
let us have an olive body, although admittedly the light green silk used
by Hanna over the chenille is not far wrong. But I should prefer a
hackled fly with a mixed hackle with some colour in it because many
a time I have noticed how, in certain lights, the wings of the cowdung

appear to sparkle and glisten with iridescent tints—yellows, blues, reds, and green. My conviction is that the natural insect as seen by the fish must appear far more brilliantly coloured than any of the ordinary artificials which we offer them.

Perhaps I have written too much about the Cowdung, for it cannot be considered a pattern of any great importance to fly-fishermen. Nevertheless it has its uses, because, fished on the right occasion, it may quite possibly be the only fly which will take trout.

CRANE FLY. See DADDY-LONG-LEGS

CRIMSON TAG

A capital grayling pattern (wet) which was T. E. Pritt's favourite tail fly—in itself ample recommendation. It must not be confused with that other famous grayling fly, the Red Tag.

Dressing:

Body: Bright green peacock herl, dressed rather full.
Hackle: Bronze feather from a golden plover's breast when in full plumage.
Tag: Crimson wool.
Hook: 12 to 14.

DADDY-LONG-LEGS

There are a number of crane-flies (*Tipulidae*) of which the larger ones are known generally as Daddy-Long-Legs and colloquially as "Harries" or "daddies". The larvae are worm-like creatures well known to gardeners as being destructive to plants, roots, and grasses. Some are found in damp situations near rivers or among the mud in shallow streams and ponds, which doubtless accounts for the adult flies being so often found in the proximity of water.

The natural fly is an ungainly and poor flier which gets driven on to the water by even a light breeze. Of the liking trout have for it there can be no two opinions, for one has only to watch a daddy-long-legs on the water to see it disappear quickly in the jaws of some fish. Its gyrations on the surface create a disturbance large enough to attract any trout in the vicinity and it is nearly always the bigger fish which secure the prize. On the Irish lakes, and to a lesser extent in this country, the natural fly is a great favourite for dapping.

Considering all the circumstances, it is surprising that so many anglers neglect the artificial, for on lakes, pools, and slow-running streams one can hardly think of any artificial fly which is more likely to attract attention, whatever the conditions. It may be because the crane-fly has received but scant attention from fly-tiers, and more especially from angling authors, that few fly-fishermen ever give it much thought. I also suspect that there is a widespread impression that the copy can only be used effectively on lakes, although that is far from being the case. It will kill well on any sluggish stream whatever the conditions, and on every type of river, brook, or beck if the trout have not settled down to feeding exclusively on some species of fly.

The daddy-long-legs is not, of course, a pattern for regular or indiscriminate use, although it is a great one on the right occasion. On a hot summer's day, when the water is low and clear and there seems but little chance of rising a fish with any ordinary artificial fly, I can think of no pattern more likely to bring some reward than a copy of the daddy-long-legs, fished on the surface, with a little intelligence. It will be surprising if it fails to rise an odd fish or two and generally big ones at that.

The artificial is always fished dry and on lakes it should be jerked occasionally to make its behaviour consistent with the frantic struggles of the natural insect as it tries to save itself from drowning.

Some species of crane-flies appear in April and continue throughout the remainder of the fishing season. Their two brownish wings and six trailing legs make them quite unmistakable. An accident may result in the loss of a leg or two but this does not seem to inconvenience the insect in the least.

To construct a passable imitation should not be beyond the powers of any amateur fly-dresser and it will be a very poor imitation if it does not take fish. My own pet pattern is an Irish one tied by T. J. Hanna, although sometimes I vary his design by using undyed raffia for the body and find it is just as effective.

Hanna's method of making the fly is to obtain six fibres from a cock pheasant's centre tail feather and to tie a knot in each to represent the joints. Four of these legs are then tied on the bare hook, two on each side so that they point towards the head.

A piece of thin rubber is then cut from a bicycle tube and trimmed into a fine strip; it should be brownish in colour. Secure one end of this at the shoulder and wind between the legs to the bend of the hook and back again to the shoulder, overlapping slightly to give the effect of segments. Next bind the rubber securely and cut off the waste end. If this operation is carried out correctly a most natural-looking body will result.

Next, a natural red cock's hackle is selected and is wound in as on a dry fly. Two more jointed legs are now tied in to face backwards and lastly two brownish hackle tips to imitate wings. These are best tied on in spent style at right angles to the head. The hook should be size 10 or 12. The completed fly makes a realistic copy of the natural and although intended to be fished as a floater, it will serve quite well for dapping.

Leonard West used speckled cock for the wings, a brown ostrich thorax, with raffia for the body which he sometimes ribbed with fine gold wire. The legs were the same as on the Hanna pattern. It is hardly necessary to say that the fly should be tied to look thin and long.

DARK BLOA. See BROUGHTON'S POINT

DARK COACHMAN

In America the Coachman has fathered many offspring, even Fan Wing types. There is a Black Coachman, a Yellow Coachman, a Bucktail Coachman, a Carson Royal Coachman, and others too numerous to mention, including the Dark Coachman, which is also frequently used on this side of the Atlantic Ocean.

H. R. Francis and Cholmondeley-Pennell both recommend this pattern for west-country streams and it is still popular to-day for trout and grayling. Sometimes called the Lead-Wing Coachman, the tie is the same as that of the standard Coachman except that it is winged with a starling feather. It is a pattern of which I have had very little experience but many anglers I have met have spoken highly of it.

DARK SPANISH NEEDLE

Known also as the Dark Needle and the Needle Brown, this is a standard Yorkshire pattern for trout and grayling used to imitate the several needle flies. Invariably fished wet, it is said to kill best on damp close days in September, although it is fished throughout the season and has the reputation of often attracting trout when they will not look at other patterns. For particulars of the natural fly, see NEEDLE FLY.

Dressing (Pritt):

Wings: Hackled with a feather from the darkest part of a brown owl's wing.
Body: Orange silk.
Head: Peacock herl.
Hook: 14.

In another form the above pattern is known as the Light Spanish

Needle and it is considered a better fly for warm summer days. Pritt gives the following tie:

Wings: Hackled with a feather from inside a jack snipe's wing, or from the breast of a young starling.
Body: Crimson silk.
Head: Peacock herl.
Hook: 14

Both are serviceable flies for grayling right up to December. The rather unusual name of Spanish Needle probably arises from the peculiar steely shade of the wings of the natural insect and dates back to the time when Spanish-made needles were greatly favoured in this country.

DARK SEDGE (*Anabolia nervosa*)

This name is usually applied to one of the more common sedges, *Anabolia nervosa*, which is found in quantities in autumn along the edges of rivers and lakes. Dark-brownish in colour, it appears from July to October, both during the day and after dark. The various patterns designed to imitate it are all useful suggestions of any of the darker-coloured sedges. Effective for trout, most of them are also "good medicine" for grayling on the Itchen and other southern streams.

In *Floating Flies*, Halford gives a tie for a dark sedge which on the Test used to be known as "Hambrough's Sedge", and which is dressed as follows:

Wings: Cock pheasant's wing.
Hackle: Rusty coch-y-bondhu carried right down the body.
Body: Dubbing of white crewel ribbed with gold wire.
Hook: 14 to 12, and occasionally even larger.

In his *Modern Developments*, he provides another dressing which he calls the "Small Dark Sedge".

Wings: Landrail dyed dark chocolate brown.
Hackles: Two dark furnace cock hackles.
Ribbing Hackles: A dark furnace cock hackle.
Body: Stripped condor, dyed very dark maroon.
Hook: 14.

Then there is a wet pattern recommended by Mr. Skues, which he calls "Holmes' Dark Sedge". It was a favourite of Dr. Arthur Holmes who found it especially deadly when fished wet in the path of the moonlight. I believe that he attributed its invention to a friend of his, Major Fisher. The dressing is:

Tying silk: Crimson, waxed dark.
Hackle: Greasy-looking game-hen with a dark centre and pale ginger points, wound at the shoulder.
Ribbing Hackle: For sizes 11 and upwards, same.
Rib: Oval gold tinsel.
Body: Dark claret seal's fur, mixed with a dark fur such as bear's.
Wings: Cinder-coloured covert feather from peahen's wing or breast.
Hook: 13, 12, or larger.

These dark sedges are so useful to imitate a whole series of natural insects that space must be found for one more useful pattern. This is one of Lunn's dressings which he christened "Gilbey's Little Dark Sedge". Although it appears to be an ungainly looking creature, it is said to kill well in the daytime and to be especially good on a warm summer's evening.

The dressing is:

Body: Two or three fibres from turkey tail feathers dyed purple.
Wings: Rook's wing feather.
Hackle: One black and one dark red cock hackle.
Tying silk: Pearsall's gossamer, shade 13.
Hook: 14 or 13.

DARK WATCHET

Also known as the Little Dark Watchet, this is a northern standard pattern serving as a representation of the iron-blue dun. A hackled fly, it is always fished wet and kills well on bright cold days throughout the season although at its best from the middle of April until the end of May. A famous trout fly, and a serviceable wet pattern for grayling, it is known in different districts by various names such as Iron-Blue Dun, Little Iron Blue, Little Water-hen, and Little Dark Dun.

There are a number of dressings in common use and it is not easy to know which to recommend as the fly is generally a hackled version of the Iron-Blue Dun. Pritt gives no less than four dressings for it, but I think that the following old Eden tie is about the best.

Wings: From the breast of a water-hen.
Body: Orange silk dubbed with mole's fur.
Head: Orange.
Legs: A dirty whitish-brown from a hen's neck, or hair from a calf's tail, dyed yellow.
Hook: 14 or 15

Another popular dressing is that given by Edmonds and Lee. Their tie is as under:

Wings: Hackled with a dark smoky blue feather from a jackdaw's throat.
Body: Purple and orange silk twisted together, dubbed lightly with mole's fur and wound on the body so that the orange and purple show in alternate bands.
Hook: 14 or 15.

The curious term "watchet" is a northern one meaning pale blue.

DETACHED BADGER

A floating pattern which was at one time popular as a copy of the red spinner; in fact, Halford who was very successful with it, considered it the best imitation of the spinner ever produced. To-day one seldom hears anything of it although it is said to be effective on hot summer days and for lake fishing.

Halford's dressing was:

Hackle: Badger cock.
Body: White horsehair dyed brownish-red, worked on a foundation of double bristle also dyed the same colour, and the body ribbed with crimson tying silk.
Whisk: Pale cream colour.
Hook: 14 or 15.

DIPPER

It was not the intention that sea-trout flies should be dealt with in this work and as a general rule reference is only made to them when they happen also to be useful brown-trout patterns. But as the majority of fly anglers fish for sea-trout when an opportunity presents itself, I have thought it as well to include a few special patterns which are either so old or so new as to make it unlikely that the dressings will be well known.

Amongst modern flies which come into this category, the Dipper is one which is well worth noting. It was invented by Mr. C. V. Hancock, a past-chairman of the Midland Flyfishers and a highly gifted amateur fly-tier. The Dipper was designed as a salmon fly and for that purpose it has met with a great deal of success, but it is quite as effective for sea-trout when a sober-looking pattern is required. The inventor has kindly supplied the correct tie which is as under:

Tag: Oval silver tinsel.
Tail: Tippet.

Body: Two equal parts; firstly a turn or two of fiery brown floss and then fiery brown seal's fur, which is followed for the second part by black seal's fur, picked out.

Rib: Oval silver tinsel.

Throat: Gallina.

Wings: A few strands of bronze peacock herl under white-tipped black turkey, with a good bronze sheen.

Cheeks (not necessary for sea-trout fly): Jungle cock, short.

Hook (for sea-trout): 6 to 9.

DOCTOR

A hackled dry fly designed by the Rev. E. Powell and considered by many fishermen to be the best of his many good-killing patterns. A coch-y-bondhu-like fly, it serves to represent several beetles and is effective throughout the season both for river or lake. The name is derived from the better-known Devonshire Doctor, of which it is a modification.

Its fame as a trout pattern has spread in recent years and it is by no means to be despised as a dry fly for sea-trout. Some of those I have seen in shops have been incorrectly dressed and I am obliged to its inventor for letting me have the correct tie.

Hackle: One large coch-y-bondhu cock—ten or eleven turns.

Body: Black rabbit's flax; rear quarter, white rabbit dyed in picric acid, producing a yellowish to bright yellow colour. The body should be loose and bulky to suggest the stalwart build of a beetle.

Whisks: Coch-y-bondhu cock.

Hook: 12 to 14.

The Devonshire Doctor is rather different. Usually fished wet, with a body ribbed with flat gold and minus the yellowish portion near the tail of the fly, which is an important feature of Mr. Powell's pattern.

DOGSBODY

A hackled dry fly, which looks like a cross between a Gold-ribbed Hare's Ear, and Rough Olive, and a most effective general-purpose pattern.

For such a generally useful pattern, it is surprisingly little known especially in view of the fact that it was invented over twenty years ago by that famous Usk angler and fly-tier, the late Mr. Harry Powell. The story of its invention is told in the following letter which I received from Mr. William Hickey, who succeeded Mr. Powell, and is himself a skilful angler.

"I worked for the late Harry Powell from 1915 to 1927, when I bought the hairdressing business from him, so I think I can help you with regard to the Dogsbody. One afternoon in 1924 we were tying flies to pattern for a client who lived, I believe, in North Wales, and were puzzled over the body of one particular fly.

"After mixing various kinds of worsted, etc., we were still not satisfied, when into the saloon came a farmer with a mongrel sheep-dog, a rather foxy-looking animal. It was the answer to our problem. I set to work shearing the farmer, whilst Harry Powell sheared the dog.

"I enclose some of the hair for your inspection and also a couple of the original flies. Some of the present-day patterns have little or no likeness to the original one. Since the fly came to us without a name, we had to invent one for it and decided to call it the Dogsbody. I have always thought that trout take this pattern for the sand-fly. It seems to be an excellent pattern during April and May when there is no particular insect on the water and I find it equally as alluring for grayling. You mention that you have had good sport with it when the dark olive has been on. So have I and I think that if I had to choose only one fly, I should take the Dogsbody."

Possibly it kills best from April until mid-June and again in September on days when there is a scarcity of fly on the water. Its most striking feature, however, is that it often proves most effective when trout have settled down to feed resolutely on some definite insect but are disinclined to take conventional imitations of it. When fish have been giving their whole attention to such divers species as black gnats, olives, small perlidae, and iron-blue duns and have refused to be tempted by any ordinary patterns, I have found them take a Dogsbody with confidence. It is often particularly deadly when black gnats are on the water and will kill as well on lakes as on rivers.

By no means a "sheet-anchor" pattern, since often fish will have nothing to do with it, the Dogsbody is extremely useful on occasions and when more celebrated flies have failed, it will frequently deceive one fish after another. If trout are not taking the artificial fly as one would have them do, it is always worth a trial and it has given me many days' good sport.

I shall ever feel grateful to Miss Rudge, the well-known Birmingham fly-dresser, whose work cannot be too highly praised, for bringing this pattern to my notice.

Mr. Powell's original dressing, as confirmed both by Mr. Hickey and Miss Rudge, was as follows:

Body: Brown tying silk dubbed with camel-coloured dog's hair, ribbed with flat oval gold.
Hackle: Barred Plymouth Rock, with a red cock's hackle in front.
Whisks: Three strands from tail of a cock pheasant.
Hook: 14 to 16.

Dyed seal's fur can be used for the body but the dog's hair is preferred if one can get it of the right colour. A hackle of ginger cock and light Andalusian would make a useful variation.

DOTTEREL DUN
Fished wet or dry as a copy of the pale watery dun, although it is also a nymph-suggesting pattern. A good standard fly from the end of April onwards especially on cold days. Its name of course, is derived from the wing feather. The following is an old tie hailing from Cumberland where the Dotterel Dun has always been a great favourite:

Body: Brown fur from a hare's face.
Hackle: Feather from the outside of a male dotterel's wing. Or as a substitute, a feather from the inside of an old cock starling's wing.
Hook: 14.

In Yorkshire where the pattern is also very popular, the usual dressing is:

Body: Straw-coloured silk.
Wings: Hackled with a feather from the outside of a male dotterel's wing.
Head: Straw-coloured silk.
Hook: 14.

With an orange silk head and body, but otherwise tied as above, the fly is sometimes called the Dotterel and Orange and with this dressing is effective for grayling, as is also the Dotterel and Yellow.

Pritt, who had a very high opinion of the Dotterel Dun, said that a feather from a young curlew would do just as well as the dotterel.

The Yorkshire dressing is a useful one to suggest a hatching nymph as is also this Skues pattern:

Hackle: Tiniest dotterel hackle, not hackled at all at the head, but palmer-wise for halfway down the short body.
Body: Yellow tying silk.
Hook: 16.

DOWNLOOKER. See OAK FLY

DRAGON-FLIES (*Odonata*)

There are many species of dragon-flies in this country but it cannot be pretended that any of them are of great interest to either fish or fishermen (except, perhaps, in the naiad or nymph state), although on a few streams trout appear to have developed a liking for the smaller types, which they take off the surface with sufficient frequency to make the use of an artificial worth consideration. Nevertheless dragon-flies add interest and beauty to ponds, lakes, and rivers all over the British Isles and for that reason a few notes about them may not be out of place. There may be readers who will reasonably feel that no insect not regularly taken by fish should receive attention in a book devoted to fly-fishing. Being firmly of the opinion that there is much more in fishing than the mere catching of fish, I should disagree with anyone holding that view and I make no excuse for this digression into the habits of one of our most common aquatic insects. Dragon-flies form part of the anglers' world, that world which they share with river-side birds and beasts and insects, and in which most of them are interested, quite regardless of whether trout share their interest in the insects or not. And on the whole, fishermen are extraordinarily ignorant about dragon-flies, which is understandable, for there are over forty species found in the British Isles of which scarcely any have popular names. Of many colours (blue, green, red, brown, black, white, and purple), they vary in size from some fully three inches long to others of less than an inch.

There is no pupal stage, the imago or winged insect hatching directly from the naiad (or nymph). The nymphs naturally vary in size according to the species but those of the Damsel-flies (*Zygoptera*) are no larger than nymphs of the Ephemeridae and trout like them equally as well. The nymphal stage lasts about a year, although the temperature and food supply regulates this and in some instances, it may be prolonged for several years.

The larger nymphs are carnivorous, feeding on other larvae, although some of them are quite capable of attacking and eating tadpoles and other small fry. The amount of harm they do to a fishery in this respect must be exceedingly small since there are easier ways for a slow-moving nymph to obtain food than chasing fish: and dragon-fly nymphs crawl very slowly. When alarmed, however, they can shoot forward at some speed in a series of jerks, by bringing into action their emergency jet-propelled apparatus. Its working is simple enough. The abdomen is hollow and is expanded to its fullest extent; water is taken

in through the tail and by a contraction of the muscles, is suddenly and
forcibly ejected again, which results in the insect being propelled forward for a short distance at a rapid rate.

All dragon-fly nymphs, large and small, have one feature in common
which is unique in the insect world. This is a remarkable piece of
mechanism known as the "mask" .It is an extending arm terminating
in a pair of strong hooks, which is hinged to the nymph's lip, and it is
shot out when any suitable insect comes near; the victim is held firmly
in the hooks, is drawn to the nymph's mouth and is then devoured.
When not in use, this apparatus is folded away under the head and lies
flat between the forelegs.

When the nymph is fully grown, it climbs up some water-plant and
rests with its head above the surface for some hours, whilst certain
developments are taking place within its body. Then, generally at dusk,
it climbs to the top of the plant and remains there in an inverted position
for about an hour. When thoroughly dry it splits its skin and in a
period of about ten minutes, the winged insect will have completely
emerged. The insect holds on to its nymphal case for half an hour or
so whilst is rests after its struggles and then with a sudden movement, it
drags the rest of its body from the shuck.

Even now the fly is not perfect for the wings are small, soft, and useless, but they soon begin to expand as blood is pumped into them from
the insect's body. In ten minutes or a little more, they will have attained
their full size, although they are still too limp for flight and at least
two hours must elapse before the fly can use them. Generally the dragon-
fly will rest all night and when the morning sunshine appears, it will be
strong enough to take wing and commence the ceaseless search for food.

The dragon-fly is a tremendous eater, feeding mostly on gnats,
mosquitoes, flies, wasps, and moths, all of which are taken alive and
usually on the wing. The adult fly is quite harmless to human beings
and is, in fact, beneficial, for each fly must account for some thousands
of gnats and mosquitoes during the course of every day. Their eyesight is phenomenal for they can see objects up to ten yards away and
movements up to twenty yards. In consequence of this the larger
specimens are not easily caught for they have no difficulty in evading a
net. The big ones too are strong fliers and it has been computed that
one species can attain a speed of sixty miles an hour, although this is
far greater than the average speed of English specimens.

One type (*Anisoptera*) have the unusual power of being able to fly
backwards for a short distance. The smaller Damsel-flies are by no

means strong fliers but some of the larger species have been known to fly hundreds of miles and have been seen in swarms over the sea, by ships far from land. Little is known about these migrations, although it is believed that in some cases they are undertaken regularly. The life-span of the winged insect may not be more than a month, or possibly two, but here again not a great deal is known about it, although it is certain that no species survive a winter in Great Britain.

Mating takes place in the air, on reeds, or even above the treetops and soon afterwards the female proceeds to lay her eggs. These are of two main types, elongated and round. Those flies which produce the former place them carefully in the leaves and stems of water-plants or on float-ing vegetation. Round eggs are dropped direct into the water, gener-ally being washed off the female who dips the extremity of her body into the water, either when flying over the surface or when she has settled on some floating object.

Several species of the small Damsel-flies, which lay elongated eggs, crawl down water-plants to place their eggs in the stems beneath the surface. Sometimes, during this operation, a considerate husband will hold on to his wife and will assist her to regain the air.

Dragon-flies are found all over the British Isles on streams, lakes, and garden ponds, from late May until the end of August, being most abundant in June and July. On some lakes, they appear in considerable numbers and this June on the upper Lugg (a rapid river), I observed almost as many dragon-flies as mayflies.

From the fly-fisherman's point of view, dragon-flies cannot be considered of much importance, in spite of the fact, already mentioned above, that trout will very occasionally take small specimens off the water, or of Bowlker's dictum of a couple of centuries ago, that "the Dragon-Fly is only used for Salmon Fishing". Trout like the nymphs well enough, but the larger ones are far too big and solid to copy with any degree of success and there would not seem to be any necessity to imitate the smaller varieties because, almost everywhere, they must be greatly outnumbered by the larvae of other insects which fish like equally as well or better.

Dragon-flies have borne that name in England for over four hundred years and they come from one of the most ancient families, although in course of centuries, they have gradually decreased in size and now are far from being the "big bugs" they once were.

Time was—in the Palaeozoic age—when one species is known to have had a wingspread of no less than 2 ft. 3 in., a nasty sort of creature to have flying around one's bedroom at night and too big even for salmon!

DRIFFIELD DUN

The name of this pattern is rather misleading as it is more of a spider than a dun. An old north-country fly, it was named after the Driffield Beck, that rarety of the north, a pure chalk stream. The dressing is:

Body: Lead-coloured fur, ribbed with yellow silk.
Hackle: Ginger cock's hackle.
Whisks: Ditto.
Hook: 14 to 16.

It is sometimes tied with pale starling wings, well forward.

DUN SPIDER

One of Stewart's spiders and therefore a wet pattern which can be relied on as a general-purpose fly. Like all spiders, it should be sparsely dressed with a soft short hackle taken halfway down the body.

Body: Yellow tying silk, well waxed.
Hackle: Small dun feather from under-part of starling's wing.
Hook: 14.

EARLY BROWN

This name is applied by Halford to *Nemoura meyeri*, one of the minor perlidae (stone-flies), similar in appearance to the February red (*Taeniopteryx nebulosa*), but smaller. He points out, however, that the name is not exclusively used for this insect but is shared with several other species of perlidae which occur in the early spring. In fact, it seems to-day to be applied to almost any small member of the stone-fly family which the angler finds himself unable to identify with any degree of exactitude. The Nemoura family are very common and when a breeze carries them on to the water, fish take them readily. They are well suggested by several of the old-established northern wet patterns such as the Winter Brown, Light Woodcock, Dark Woodcock, and the Brown Owl.

EDMEAD

At one time, some fifty years ago, this was a popular pattern in the Midlands, but to-day it is scarcely known in this country. In many parts of the Continent, however, and throughout Scandinavia, it still enjoys a good reputation. It is a fly which I have never used myself, but a friend tells me that he has found it an effective lake pattern for trout, either with the original dressing as shown in the illustration, or with a red body which is now more generally preferred. The modern tie is:

Body: Red-brown floss silk, ribbed with fine gold wire.
Wings: Grey mallard breast feather.
Hackle: Light red cock's.
Hook: 12 to 10.

EDMONSON'S WELSH FLY

Another pattern which in the distant past was considered a first-class lake fly. Nowadays it seems to have become entirely forgotten, although its dressing sounds sufficiently attractive to warrant its revival. Invented, I believe, about a hundred years ago by a Mr. John Edmondson, who was in business as a tackle dealer in Basnett Street, Liverpool, it soon became a favourite on the Welsh lakes, especially in April and September and an effective pattern on Welsh streams towards the end of the season. Edmondson's own dressing was:

Body: Dirty yellow mohair, tipped at tail with gold tinsel.
Legs: A black-and-red hackle.
Wings: From a feather of the woodcock's wing.
Hook: 10.

EPHEMEROPTERA

A family of especial interest to fly-fishermen since it includes the mayfly, olive dun, iron-blue dun, blue-winged olive, pale watery dun and the march brown. The life history of a typical member of this family is related under the heading of "Mayfly".

ERMINE MOTH

This splendid dry pattern was devised by the Rev. Edward Powell, who called it the Ermine Moth or White Moth. As there is a well-known fly bearing the latter designation, I think it is as well to stick to the former name and thereby lessen any chance of confusion which might otherwise arise.

Originally tied to suggest various white or light-coloured moths, it is a great killer from June until the end of the season. It is a reliable floating pattern at any hour of the day for rough or coloured waters and is quite as effective on lakes, although as one would expect, it is particularly useful as an evening fly, since it shows up well in the half-

---

light. Judging by my own experience, I am of the opinion that it is a more deadly pattern than the standard White Moth.

Writing about it, its inventor says: "I find myself getting more and more dependent on this pattern from June onwards. I originally designed it to suggest the Ermine, the Gold Tip, the Magpie, and several other species of Lepidoptera, and that, no doubt, is the reason why it kills so well on many Welsh rivers where the mayfly is unknown, but perhaps its most spectacular successes have been won on English streams where the trout have retired to digest after a surfeit of Ephemera. Most of us have had the irritating experience of arriving at a river and finding the whole surface covered with mayfly but with the fish apparently so gorged that not a solitary rise is to be seen. Then is the time for the Ermine Moth. Its value as a pick-me-up for dyspeptic fario has to be experienced to be believed. I try to persuade myself that it is not because it reminds them of the spent gnat but . . . anyhow, I can vouch for the fact that I have many times tried a carefully and realistically tied Spent Gnat on such occasions without the slightest result and then begun catching fish straight away, directly I substituted the Ermine Moth.

"It is a marvellous fly all day sometimes and its colour gives one an extra half-hour's fishing at nightfall when other patterns are invisible.

"I have also found that in gin-clear stills when trout are rising to aphis and other tiny forms at short focus, a miniature edition of this fly tied on a No. 0 (15) or 00 (16) hook is sometimes deadly when anything bigger would cause a panic. The difficulty here is to get a grey partridge hackle small enough, but a careful search exactly in the centre of the bird's chest will disclose next to the skin a few that will serve."

In one way the Ermine Moth and the Grey Duster closely resemble each other for both kill really well when fished dry on rough streams and in neither case is it clear why trout should take them so freely. And why the former should attract fish gorged with mayfly defies any explanation.

The inventor has kindly provided me with the correct dressing for the Ermine Moth which is as follows:

Hackles: Two large grey speckled partridge.
Body: White rabbit ribbed with one strand of unravelled three-ply black knitting wool or coarse black thread.
Tag: A loop of two-ply orange wool tied in flat, protruding a quarter of an inch beyond the bend of the hook and then cut off so as to make a short fork. This wool should be a yellow and not a red-orange.
Hook: 14 to 12.

EXPLORER

Of the origin of this fly I know nothing, although many years ago I christened it the Explorer for my own convenience. As a hackled dry pattern of the general order suggesting a beetle, it sometimes proves very useful on rough mountain streams, whilst it is a likely sort of fly for use at dusk on any river or lake. To anglers who like patterns of the general utility order, the Explorer can be recommended for trout or grayling for it will take fish when many better-known flies prove unsuccessful.

The tie is:

Body: Peacock herl ribbed with gold tinsel.
Hackle: Dun cock's hackle carried down the body.
Hook: 14 to 12.

FEBRUARY RED (*Taeniopteryx nebulosa*)

Known also as the Red Fly and Old Joan, this medium-sized member of the perlidae family appears first in the month from which it takes its name and continues throughout the summer. It is the female which is known to fishermen as the February Red, the male being an insignificant insect with long legs and often aborted wings, which is seldom, if ever, taken by trout.

The female is about half an inch in length, with reddish-brown body, deep orange-red on the underside of the abdomen, and reddish-brown wings marked with two bands which make the fly easy to recognize.

Although absent from the chalk streams, the February Red is common in many other parts of the country, notably in the north, Midlands, Wales, and the west-country. It is also found in Ireland. The artificial, in one of its several forms, is a popular pattern for lake or river in the early part of the season and is a useful grayling fly. One of our oldest patterns, it is the Dun Fly of the *Treatise* (1496), wherein it is described as having a dun body and the wings from a partridge. In the 450 years which have passed since then, the dressing has remained much the same.

Aldam's tie is one of the best and is as follows:

Wings: From a centre feather of a partridge's tail.
Legs: Feather from a jenny wren's tail.
Body: Medium shade of orange tying silk and red-brown fur from the back of a fox's ear.
Hook: 14.

Along the Welsh Dee and its tributaries, a hackled fly is preferred tied thus:

Body: Orange mohair spun on claret silk.
Legs: Blue dun hen's hackle of a smoky tint.
Hook: 14.

In the north, the natural fly is well-imitated by that celebrated Yorkshire wet pattern, the Partridge and Orange, although northern grayling anglers still favour the old dressing given by Ronalds, which he called the Red Fly. His tie was:

Body: The dubbing is composed of the dark red part of a squrrel's fur, mixed with an equal quantity of claret-coloured mohair, showing the most claret colour at the tail. This is spun on brown silk thread to form the body.
Wings: From the softest quill feather of the peahen's wing which approaches the tint.
Legs: Of a claret-coloured stained hackle. No feather of its natural colour that I know of is of the proper shade. Clip some of the upper fibres off that the wings may lie flat.
Hook: 14.

In his remarks about this pattern, Ronalds says: "This is the earliest fly in north Derbyshire. The tint of the wings is that of a cake of glue held between the eye and the sun. It is best made hackle-way, with the under-covert feather of a woodcock's wing wound upon the above body. In Lancashire it is called 'Old Joan' and the body is made rough with claret-coloured wool. Thus made it kills well in the Derwent."

Ronalds' dressing is a little elaborate but it is obviously one over which he took a good deal of trouble.

My personal choice is for a hackled floater tied in this manner:

Body: A dark quill from the stem of a peacock's tail feather, dyed claret.
Hackle: A dark rusty blue cock.
Hook: 14.

FIERY BROWN

Although better known as a salmon fly, this is an excellent wet pattern for lake and sea-trout, being especially popular in Ireland and Canada. Michael Rogan (1833-1905) of Ballyshannon is generally credited with its invention, although I am inclined to thank that its origin is lost in antiquity, for there is some reason to believe that it is the same fly referred to by Charles Cotton as the "Bright Brown".

The correct fiery brown colouring is a peculiar and elusive one, and probably no two fishermen ever agree as to what it should be. The usual tie is:

Body: Reddish-brown seal's fur, ribbed with gold wire.
Wings: Bronze mallard feather.
Hackle: Red cock's hackle.
Tail: Tippet.
Hook: 6 to 10.

FISHERMAN'S CURSE

The curse, like the smut, is a generic name bestowed by fishermen upon a minute fly which hatches in immense numbers, creates a great furore amongst trout, but which unfortunately is too small to copy effectively or even reasonably closely. Found on rivers and lakes all over the British Isles during the greater part of the season, these little insects belong to many species. The smallest member of the Ephemeroptera, the caenis (of which there are six British species) is often referred to as the "white curse" and can be annoying enough, but the smut, sometimes called the "black curse" and which is generally some species of Simulium, can be even more exasperating. Whether fish are taking them off the surface or just below it, they prove a real curse to fly-fishers, quite apart from the fact that they can inflict an unpleasant bite on his person.

I have seen streams and lakes which appeared to be boiling with feeding fish and have been driven to the depths of despair when every pattern offered them has been most definitely and ignominiously rejected. This piscine activity which promises so well proves nothing but gall and wormwood to the angler when it is caused by fish devoting their whole attention either to smuts or a fall of caenis spinners. On these occasions, the presence of a fisherman will not easily scare fish or divert them from their purpose, but although they will continue to feed in an inexorable manner, they will entirely ignore all (or nearly all) artificial patterns.

In these circumstances authorities generally recommend a Knotted Midge, a Wickham, a tiny Black Gnat, or any really small black artificial. Any of them may account for an odd fish but the chances of them doing more are extremely slender. The fish just laugh at one's efforts and go on feeding. My own preference is for a Coachman tied on a 16 or 18 hook and although at first sight the choice of a white-winged fly to imitate a near-black insect may seem peculiar, I think it can be justified. But before enlarging upon that point, it will be necessary to consider the life cycle of the smuts and curses (about which the average fisherman is profoundly ignorant) as understanding it should assist in devising ways and means of getting the best of fish engaged in smutting, which without any doubt is one of their most irritating occupations.

The Simuliidae or black flies of which there are numerous species, are small greyish insects with exceptionally broad wings with a definite vein near the front edges. The eggs are laid on the vegetation fringing rivers in such a position that they may be washed by the water. On hatching, the larvae, which are mostly creamy white or grey in colour, with cylindrical caterpillar-like bodies, enter the water at once and attach themselves to the undersides of plants and stones situated in the fastest part of the stream. Sometimes the heavy current will dislodge the larva in which case it lets out a strand of silk as a "lifeline" and uses it to regain its original position.

After two to six months, depending upon the time of year at which the eggs were laid, the larvae are ready to pupate and so proceed to build a brown fibrous cocoon. After a brief period which would appear not to exceed three weeks in normal circumstances, the pupa will be ready to assume its imago state. The metamorphosis is a simple one as the insect merely breaks out of its case and in its winged form is carried to the surface in a bubble of air. It is during the course of this journey, which generally takes place in May and June, that trout take the heaviest toll of the insects.

What angler has not seen a stream or lake alive with fish busily engaged in taking insects just underneath the surface film? This is no bulging or tailing affair with violent rises here and there, but every trout in the area will be seen to be feeding quietly, but persistently and continuously. In these conditions, a close examination of the water will often show that the great activity is occasioned by fish feeding on tiny species of Diptera during their ascent. That they seldom take them off the surface may be because on reaching it, the insects fly off too quickly for fish to secure them. Probably too the fly proves more attractive when encased in its bubble, and if that is so, it provides a clue as to why a black or near-black pattern is not the best imitation of the insect at this particular period. Quite possibly a small Coachman or some similar artificial may prove a closer suggestion of a dark insect inside a glittering globule.

At times, however, fish will be discovered smutting on the surface, constantly breaking it as they suck in insects so small as to make them invisible to the angler, although he will realize that the phenomenon is connected with the myriads of tiny flies hovering and weaving over the water; and he will also realize that his hopes of making a large bag are very slight. Yet if he will watch the behaviour of the trout for a while, he may still discover a method of creeling an odd one or two.

When fish are thus preoccupied, it will often be found that they are taking different kinds of insects—the small blackish Simulidae (smuts and light-coloured flies, which a close examination will reveal as either spent spinners of Caenis (white curse) or some minute species of Chironomidae (midges). Close observation will show that whilst both types are being taken, it is a combination of the two which attracts most attention; and since this black-and-white dish is about double the size of either insect alone, it may be copied with more chance of success.

When this occurs (and it is a common happening), one can be pretty sure that the black curse concerned will be one of the many species of Hilara belonging to the Empidae family, of which the males hover over the water, picking up dead insects and other objects such as flower petals, buttercup stamens and so on, which are light enough for them to lift. More often they will swoop on the light-coloured spinners and midges, and if they use their victim as a raft for a few seconds whilst negotiating a safe hold, the chances are that a trout will be quick to seize both insects. If on the other hand the smut is able to carry off his prize, he will envelop it in a silken case before presenting it to his trusting wife. There is method in this procedure for the idea is that she shall be kept busy unravelling the silk during the act of mating, a most unusual and ungentlemanly habit, particularly when the gift turns out to be nothing more exciting than a flower petal.

In this instance again, it will be appreciated that some pattern like a Coachman is more likely to prove any acceptable copy of the light and dark insects than any of the all-black artificials which are generally tried. That even a small Coachman is likely to take a lot of fish is not suggested although in my own experience, I have seen an angler kill several on one when others fishing the same stretch with the conventional Black Gnat have failed to connect with a fish.

It must be admitted that smuts and midges are most abominally small and that many fishermen think that when trout are taking them, they are best left alone since the chances of doing any good are almost nil. But I must confess that when fish are feeding voraciously I hate having to admit to myself (or anybody else) that I cannot catch them. Even if one kills only an odd fish when they are smutting, it induces a pleasant feeling of achievement which is likely to be far greater than that which results from creeling a dozen when they are in a taking mood and no great amount of skill is required to catch them.

Trout engaged in feeding on smuts are a perpetual challenge to the fly-fisher. They openly defy him but they should not be allowed to do so without some attempt on his part to defeat them, and in any case does not much of the interest of angling come from trying to find solutions to little problems of this sort?

FITZGERALD

A forgotten pattern which once upon a time was considered a capital dry fly of the fancy variety. Altogether a colourful pattern which some angler who is fond of experiments may like to revive. The old dressing is as under:

Tag: Two turns of swan's feather dyed orange.
Body: Peacock herl dyed magenta.
Wings: Light widgeon.
Hackle: Badger dyed dark ruby.
Hook: 14 to 16.

I must confess that it is a fly which I have never tried and is included here with what may be deemed scant justification. The fact is that in some pencilled notes on flies made by an angler some thirty-five years ago, I came across the following laconic but intriguing entry: "Fitzgerald. Wonderful wonderful fly! three brace more to-day." On the strength of that, a friend of mine tested this pattern and on the first occasion he used it, landed a trout of nearly four pounds, a local record.

FLIGHT'S FANCY

Originated over seventy years ago by a Mr. Flight, of Winchester, to imitate an olive dun. Halford recommended it for use in hot weather and especially during a mayfly hatch, when, at times, he said, it would kill better than any specific copy of the mayfly itself. It should be noted that the primrose silk body when soaked, changes to green-olive. There are at least two dressings for this fly but I believe the following is the original:

Wings: Pale starling.
Hackles: Two pale buff Cochin cock hackles.
Body: Primrose floss silk, ribbed fine flat gold.
Whisk: Gallina dyed slightly olive green.
Hook: 14 to 16.

FLYING CADDIS

A modern American floating pattern which has been tried in this country with success. The dressing is:

Body: Mohair dyed yellow, ribbed gold tinsel.
Hackle: Red cock's.
Whisks: Three strands from a cock pheasant's tail.
Wings: Medium starling.
Hook: 12 to 14.

FOG BLACK

An old and almost forgotten Wharfedale pattern which was one of T. E. Pritt's favourites as an imitation of the black gnat. He recommended it for use from June to the end of the season, especially in warm dull weather in summer and autumn. It is also a capital fly for grayling during September and October.

Dressing:

Wings: From a bullfinch's wing.
Body: Dark purple silk, dubbed with heron's herl, or more sparingly with black ostrich herl.
Legs: Hackle from a starling's neck.
Hook: 14.

FORD'S FAVOURITE

Invented some sixty years ago by Thomas Ford of Caistor, a poet and angler. He claimed that it possesses the merit of attracting the larger fish only. It is still used in the north and is looked upon as an effective wet pattern. The old dressing is:

Body: Blue silk.
Legs: Black grizzly hackle.
Wings: Dark snipe.
Hook: 12.

FORE AND AFT FLY

A type of dry fly with a short stiff hackle, front and rear (the shoulder hackle being rather the longer), divided by a good-sized body, usually raffia. It was made popular by Mr. Horace Brown who was well known as a fly-fisher on the Kennet over a long period, although his name for it was the "fore-and-after" fly.

It is claimed for this method of construction that it makes a fly exceptionally buoyant, as indeed it must, although it seems to be more often applied to mayflies than to ordinary trout patterns. The colour of the hackles appears to make little or no difference to the effectiveness of the fly, and many anglers find it very effective. Generally hackles of different colours are preferred, although one of them is nearly always white, for it is as attractive to trout as any other colour and is easier seen by the angler. Olives or red are useful for the other, but a large number of fishermen like both hackles to be white.

That a pattern of this colour should prove so successful may seem at first sight to be a little surprising, but a possible explanation is that the two hackles assist the fly to stand high on the water, with only the tips of the hackles touching the surface. The result is that even shy and suspicious fish may be deceived because they get but a blurred and in-distinct view of the fly itself. In this respect a Fore and Aft must more closely resemble a natural dun than the usual type of artificial dry fly which sits, rather than stands, on the water.

I have been told that a Fore and Aft attracts trout because it represents a sub-imago in the act of emerging from its nymphal shuck, but that is a theory which nowadays is often advanced (on the most slender grounds) to account for the success of some pattern, when no better explanation can be found.

There are many methods of dressing a fly, all of which are really outside the scope of this book. I have thought fit to refer to the Fore and Aft (of which my own experience is negligible) because possibly it is a better way of imitating a natural insect, as seen by fish, than is obtainable by the orthodox method of tying a dry pattern.

FRANCIS FLY

Designed by Mr. Francis Francis in, or about, 1858, the appearance of this pattern was followed by a sharp controversy as to what it was intended to represent, a question which was never settled. Fish probably take it for some sort of caterpillar to which it bears more resemblance than to a fly, in spite of the wings.

If the inventor was not to be drawn as to the natural prototype of his fly, he had plenty to say about its advantages as the following will show: "It may seem egotism in me to place this fly first on the list; but since its invention, from the accounts I have had of its qualifications, from all parts of Great Britain, from various parts of Europe, and indeed from all quarters of the globe where salmonidae are found, it certainly appears to have gained, as I hope, a well-earned reputation. I first found it kill well on Welsh rivers, where I tested it severely against the far-famed coch-y-bondhu . . . and it killed above three fish for one killed by the coch-y-bondhu. I therefore brought it into public notice and it was greatly favoured . . . and wherever I have gone, I have found it an un-failing resource when many other favourites failed. I have killed well with it dressed on a No. 11 or 12 hook, and equally well (where it was suitable) on a 7, 8, or 9. It is an excellent evening and night fly dressed on a No. 7 or 8 hook, owing to the lively and attractive play of the hackle point wings. Dressed large it kills sea-trout well and it has even slaughtered many a lordly salmon, while I have seen large numbers of it, dressed like some huge moth, sent out to India to kill mahseer amongst the Himalayas."

Now Francis Francis was undoubtedly a first-class angler, with a great deal of experience, so that his words cannot lightly be disregarded. When first I read them many years ago, they impressed me to the ex-tent of giving the Francis Fly a prolonged trial, but with most disap-pointing results. In fact, I don't think I caught a single fish on it. Others cannot have fared much better for the passing of time has done nothing to add to its reputation, although up to a few years ago it was still used on northern waters, and possibly still is to-day. I am sorry that this pattern has not proved more of a success for Francis Francis must have been a real fisherman and a most likeable fellow.

The original dressing was:

Body: Copper-coloured peacock herl, ribbed distinctly with copper-red silk.
Hackle: Medium blue dun.
Wings: Two hackle points of a grizzly blue dun cock's hackle (not hen's), set well up.
Hook: 10 to 12.

FREEMAN'S FANCY

This wet pattern was invented around 1900 by Captain W. Freeman, who is known to shooting men as the founder of a well-known pheasant-rearing farm in Oxfordshire which, I believe, still exists.

It has always been a source of surprise to me that this fly has not be-come better known because at times (when a brightly coloured pattern is required) it is an effective lake fly and it is really first class for sea-trout. But it is as a lure for rainbow trout that it excels. In lakes, reser-voirs, and pools which are stocked with these fish, Freeman's Fancy is, in my opinion, not merely the best wet pattern, but no other fly can approach it. That has been my experience and also that of many friends who have tried it. Some years ago, a fisherman who used it on several Irish loughs and rivers, told me that he was amazed at the success it achieved. Some 90 per cent of all the trout he caught fell to a Freeman's Fancy and that old popular favourite, the Claret and Mallard, was quite outclassed.

It is not a fly which will always take on lakes, and on Loch Leven I have never caught a fish on it, although on some other lochs I have found it kill well, whilst both in Scotland and Wales, there are few better patterns for sea-trout.

The tie is:

Body: Flat gold tinsel.
Wings: Brown mallard with a small strip of jungle cock on each side.
Hackle: Bright magenta dyed hackle.
Tail: A small bunch of orange toucan.
Hook: 10 to 12; larger for sea-trout.

FRESHWATER LOUSE (*Asellus*)

Where this creature occurs, it may be of greater importance to the angler than he realizes for in such places it may possibly be the trout's chief article of food. Reference to autopsies which I have carried out certainly tends to suggest this, although it would be untrue to say that the louse is of much account in the majority of our rivers. In lakes, it is a different story and I have notes of trout which were full of these insects. In one case, the fish contained one beetle, three caddis pupae, and eighty-four freshwater lice. In another, three small water insects and no less than two hundred and thirty-four lice! It will be seen, therefore, that it is an insect which anglers cannot entirely ignore.

Mr. Martin Mosely has informed me that he has only found these creatures in muddy waters quite unsuitable for trout. This greatly surprises me, for in the Midlands at least, there must be few lakes, reservoirs, and pools in which the freshwater louse is not present, and often in tremendous numbers. Many of these waters are fed by strong streams, as was also a small lake in Wales I fished some years ago in which the weeds were swarming with these lice. It would therefore seem that whereas *Asellus* prefer still waters or slow-flowing streams, they can stand a fairly strong flow of water, although not so strong as to wash them out of the weed beds in which they crawl about and in which trout often search for them. To what extent they are found in rivers, I have no reliable data, although they are abundant in some of the limestone streams of southern Ireland.

The water louse is very much like the ordinary wood louse to look at but is more lightly built with longer legs and antennae. The colour varies a good deal but is generally a grey-brown with a dirty-white abdomen. The body is extraordinarily flat, so flat that one wonders how it can accommodate the internal organs. Young water lice are quite transparent and are excellent subjects in which to examine the blood circulating. The adults are fairly big, the larger ones being as much as three-quarters of an inch in length. As far as my observations go, they do not swim but crawl about in the weeds in which they make their home.

Anglers know so little of these small crustacea that it is unlikely that any special pattern to imitate them has been evolved but there is an effective copy to hand in the hackled March Brown. It should be dressed on a 14, or even a 16, hook and well sunk.

FRESHWATER SHRIMP (*Gammarus pulex*)

This small crustacean, which is widely distributed throughout Great Britain, is a favourite diet of trout, and when engaged in hunting shrimps, they will seldom allow their attention to be diverted to flies —natural or artificial. Found in the chalk streams, the shrimp has a preference for shallow running water although it is frequently present in shallow lakes and pools which have a stream running through them. Other species of gammarus of slightly different appearance are found in the brackish waters of river estuaries, whilst a somewhat similar, but smaller, amphipod (known as *Corophium lacustrae*) occurs in some of the Norfolk broads.

The importance of the freshwater shrimp to anglers is great for it is often found in rivers and lakes in enormous numbers—the whole bed of the stream being carpeted with them. It is not surprising that where these conditions obtain, shrimps become one of the trout's chief articles of food.

They are not difficult to recognize since their shape is not unlike that of the better-known sea-shrimp, although they seldom exceed 2 cm. in length. Their colour varies a little from a reddish-brown to a grey-brown.

In view of trout's liking for these crustaceans and the deliberate way in which they feed upon them, many attempts have been made to produce a satisfactory artificial copy. Some of these creations look wonderfully lifelike, but personally I have never enjoyed much success with any of them, nor do I know of any fishermen who have had better luck with them.

When trout are routing amongst the weeds for shrimps, a hackled March Brown will often tempt them, if it is fished well sunk, and for some reason, which is not clear to me, they will also fall sometimes to a sunken Claret and Mallard dressed on a 14 hook.

Mr. Skues recommends a fly (which I have not tried) tied palmer-fashion, with the hackle fibres cut off from the back of the hook, dressed in the following manner:

Hackle: Pale red, dyed olive.
Body: Seal's fur mixed pale orange and olive, tied to below the bend of the hook to suggest the curve of the shrimp's back.
Rib: Fine gold wire.
Hook: 16, t.d.e., Limerick.

Anglers who wish to dress their own imitations should not find it difficult to construct a reasonably lifelike pattern from many sorts of materials including silk, wool, raffia, rubber, and celluloid. The finished product may quite possibly fill the tier with a glow of pride but whether the fish will share his opinion is a different matter.

GINGER QUILL

A good floating variation of the Red Quill which is used to imitate the pale watery and light olive dun. Like all patterns with quill bodies, such as the Blue Quill, Iron-Blue Quill, Orange Quill, etc., it is effective on most dry-fly streams and is a useful pattern for west-country rivers in the early spring.

Hackled quill patterns sometimes prove more attractive than winged flies and grow in popularity every year. The usual tie for the Ginger Quill is:

Hackle and Whisks: Pale brown ginger.
Body: Peacock quill, pale.
Wings: Palest starling.
Hook: 16.

For a hackled pattern, this Halford pattern should fill most needs:

Head Hackle: Pale blue dun hen.
Shoulder Hackle: Pale ginger cock.
Body: Well-marked strand of peacock, undyed or dyed a faint brown-red.
Whisks: Gallina dyed a faint brown-red.
Hook: 14 to 16.

GINGER SPINNER

Either wet or dry, this is a most useful general fly to suggest a variety of spinners. I believe that it originated in Yorkshire but it has never become as popular as its utility warrants. A few years ago I gave it an extended trial during July and August on several rivers and found that it would frequently take trout which had steadfastly refused other flies. A very useful pattern which deserves to be better known. There are at least two dressings for both wet and dry varieties but they differ only slightly and those given by Edmonds and Lee in *Brook and River Trouting*, and which are given below, may be used with confidence.

The tie for the floating fly is:

Wings: Fibres of light-grizzled blue cock's hackle, dressed spent.
Body: Light cinnamon quill.
Tail: Two strands from a ginger cock's hackle.
Legs: Ginger cock's hackle, two turns at most, as this fly must be lightly dressed.
Head: Orange silk.
Hook: 14 or 15.

The wet pattern is dressed as under:

Wings: Fibres of light grizzled blue cock's hackle.
Body: Flat gold wire with a wrapping over it of orange silk, the silk to be untwisted and only one or two strands used.
Tail: Two strands from a ginger cock's hackle.
Legs: Ginger cock's hackle.
Head: Orange silk.
Hook: 14 or 15.

Mr. Skues has a pattern of his own creation with which he did very well on the Itchen at sunset. In appearance, it is a most attractive fly and I look forward to trying it at the first opportunity.

His dressing is:

Body: Hot orange tying silk dubbed with pale orange seal's fur and with a fine gold rib.
Hackle: Pale sandy dun cock.
Whisk: Ditto.
Hook: 15.

GNATS. See CHIRONOMIDAE

GOLDEN CROW

The invention of Mr. Henry Bradshaw, the famed Yorkshire angler, who was responsible for "Bradshaw's Fancy", and many other good flies. The Golden Crow is an effective grayling pattern (always fished wet) which was one of Mr. Carter Platt's favourites; and there were few men who knew more about the likes and dislikes of the grayling.

Dressing:

Body: Gold tinsel.
Hackle: A feather from the breast of a Norwegian crow or a young grouse.
Hook: 14.

GOLD RIBBED HARE'S EAR

Although classed as a fancy pattern, this fly is exceptionally attractive to trout and must always be the first choice of every fly-fisherman when the medium spring olive is on the water. An all-round killing pattern, it is always a favourite with those anglers who believe in using two or three patterns only right through the season, and it is one of the few patterns which is quite as effective on the chalk streams as on other rivers. In Halford's time it was considered as probably the most killing fly for the Test and similar rivers, and there is no part of England where it is anything but a renowned pattern, whether fished dry or wet, winged or hackled, for trout or for grayling.

The Gold-Ribbed Hare's Ear is a good example of an artificial which trout appear to take for some particular natural insect, to which, in our eyes, it would seem to bear no resemblance at all. As already mentioned, it is an infallible pattern when the medium olive of spring is being taken (and sometimes when the dark olive is on the water), yet the rough grey body of the G.-R.H.E., ribbed with gold, does not look to us in the least like the smooth-bodied olive dun, and it is almost certainly taken for the hatching nymph of the olive.

Many species of nymphs, when in that rather jumbled state of getting out of their shucks, must look not unlike a Gold-Ribbed Hare's Ear, when the pattern is correctly dressed, which is not always the case.

Nowadays there is a tendency to over-hackle this fly and make it resemble nothing at all, but forty or fifty years ago it was tied differently. Then it carried a very sparse hackle and was dubbed fully around the thorax, the fur being teased out with a dubbing needle to make it resemble legs, until the pattern really looked a good representation of a nymph in the process of shedding its shuck. That the modern pattern kills well is testimony to the intrinsic worth of this fly, but I feel sure that dressed as it used to be, it is even more effective.

In those days, the G.-R.H.E. was fished either wet or very slightly submerged. which is, in my opinion, how it should be fished, but alterations came about when dry fly-fishing became the accepted thing on the chalk streams. For the moment it will not be necessary to consider the several theories as to what the G.-R.H.E. is intended to represent although reference is made to them later for those who may be interested. All the ordinary fly-fisher will want to know is that it is a first-class pattern for trout when they are taking the medium olive in spring and for trout and grayling at any time of the season as a general nymph-suggesting fly. Halford afforded it a high place amongst the most generally useful flies and it was also the favourite pattern of several famous anglers including Thomas Tod Stoddart, the poet of Tweedside, and of H. S. Hall whose name is so closely associated with the introduction of the modern eyed hook. Writing of it he said: "There are times when every fish in the river seems to be bulging and ignoring flies on the surface, but I have had really good days on the Hare's Ear floated cockily over roving fish."

My favourite dressing for the wet pattern (below) is almost certainly the old standard tie. As a rule it kills best when fished in the surface film or just under it.

Body: Dark fur from the root of a hare's ear spun on yellow or primrose silk.
Ribbing: Flat gold tinsel.
Hackle: Long strands of the body dubbing picked out with a dubbing needle.
Whisks: Three strands as hackle.
Hook: 14 to 16.

Nowadays it is nearly always dressed as a wing pattern, the tie being as above except for the addition of wings which are made from medium or pale starling primary. For the floater double wings are sometimes preferred, and of the usual dry patterns, probably that below evolved by Ogden, the Cheltenham fly-dresser, well over half a century ago, is still the most popular.

Wings: Pale starling.
Body: Pale primrose silk.
Legs: The lightest fur from a hare's face spun on pale yellow tying-silk and
   worked as a hackle.
Whisk: Four or five strands of a ginger cock's-beard hackle.
Hook: 14 to 16.

For grayling fishing, wet or dry, a hackled fly is considered better
than the winged variety and hackled with rusty blue cock it is a valuable
pattern especially for the southern streams.

There are a number of other Hare's Ear patterns, but one seldom sees
much of them nowadays. Their use has gradually receded as the popularity of the Gold-Ribbed pattern has increased. Incidentally, it was or
a small dry Gold-Ribbed Hare's Ear, dressed on a size 15 hook, that in
1907 the Rev. S. E. V. Filleul, when fishing the Frome near Dorchester,
landed a trout of twelve and three-quarter pounds. A remarkable catch,
made even more so by the fact that the fish was too big for the landing-
net and was eventually landed in a wicker clothes basket, hurriedly
requisitioned from a nearby cottage.

Since looked at casually the G.R.H.E. does not appear to look like
any natural insect, although it is a most killing pattern, there has always
been rather an air of mystery about it and many opinions have been
expressed as to what trout take it for and how it should be fished. These
different theories are worth examining because it is peculiar why a
nymph-suggesting fly, as undoubtedly it is, should be tied with wings
more often than not and should generally be fished as a floater. The
only explanation I am able to advance is that the wings seem to have
been added some sixty to seventy years ago at a time when the dry fly
purist was coming into being and his narrow creed forced him to
convert many killing wet patterns into dry specimens so that they
might be fished on the chalk streams without tarnishing the user's
reputation, contaminating fellow-purists, or polluting the river. The
Gold-Ribbed Hare's Ear was far too good a fly to escape this purge
and although it was recognized as being an imitation of a hatching
nymph, wings were added for no other reason than that it might become a fit and respectable member of the select company of chalk-
stream dry flies.

Surprisingly enough Halford dressed it in this manner solely so that
it might comply with his conventional dry-fly theory and with a truly

magnificent disregard for what it was designed to represent. And ever since then the G.-R.H.E. has been commonly tied with wings and often with another abomination—a feathered hackle. Halford was not the only guilty party as other well-known fly-dressers of his day (including Holland of Winchester and Ogden of Cheltenham) followed his example. That their flies killed well enough it true for the Gold-Ribbed Hare's Ear seems to attract fish however it is tied, although I am tolerably certain that dressed with wings and used as a floater, it never kills so well as in its original hackled state.

That Halford was well aware that the old wet pattern was a most successful copy of a hatching nymph is beyond dispute for he said so again and again. In his *Dry Fly Fishing in Theory and Practice* (1889), for example, he refers to the hare's fur body as having the same fuzzy appearance as the gills which run along the sides of a nymph and in *Dry Fly Entomology* he says that "this pattern is placed first of the series as the most successful of modern times. From early spring to late autumn it is one of the most killing of all the duns and is, besides, pre-eminently the fly to be recommended for bulging and tailing fish. It is probably taken for the sub-imago emerging from the larval envelope of the nymph just risen to the surface". Time did nothing to make him alter his opinion for as late as 1913, writing about this pattern in the *Dry Fly Man's Handbook*, he said: "It has always been my theory that it is a fair representation of a dun in the act of disentangling itself from the nymphal shuck."

From the above quotations from his books, there can be no doubt that Halford looked upon the fly as a copy of the hatching nymph and quite obviously, therefore, it should never have been given wings. If he had thought that it represented the dun, then, of course, it would have been right and proper to provide the artificial not only with wings but also with a good stiff cock's hackle to imitate the legs and to permit the fly to stand on the water in the manner of the natural insect. If, however, we agree with Halford, as most fly-fishers must do, that the G.-R.H.E. was designed as a copy of the hatching dun when lying in the surface film in the act of freeing itself from its shuck, then it is surely clear that the artificial fly, whether wet or dry, should have neither wings nor, of course, a feathered hackle. A much closer likeness would be secured by the use of strands of fur which so admirably suggests the legs and branchial gills of the nymph and that, I surmise, is just how the pattern was originally dressed.

In many ways the employment of fur to imitate a nymph is preferable to a cock's hackle. To quote the late Colonel E. W. Harding on this subject "under the magnifying glass the chief characteristics of the hackle made of hare's fur fibres is that unlike the cock's hackle, the fibres point in all directions. Three or four of the stiffer ones would either penetrate or make fairly large points of light and the softer fibres, with bended ends pointing in all directions, would mark the water with irregular points and lines of light. The broad gold ribs force the fur of the body into little tufts which reinforce and break the out-lines of the light produced by the hackle fibres that are bent back under the body." Fur therefore seems particularly suitable for producing the effect of the widespread explosions of light caused by the splitting of the nymphal envelope and the struggles of the dun to free itself from it.

To return to Halford, we know, of course, that in the end he re-treated from his obviously illogical position by entirely discarding the Gold-Ribbed Hare's Ear (which it will have been noted he once placed as the first fly in his series!) together with many another good killing pattern, in favour of his imitations of a selected number of chalk-stream flies, all of which were naturally the driest of the dry. In doing so, since he had never been able to identify the G.-R.H.E. with a float-ing dun, he must have eased his conscience although only at the cost of depriving himself and his apostles of the assistance of a number of their most valuable patterns. And thus it was that the G.-R.H.E., a real thoroughbred, was expelled from the Halfordian Stud Book, although without any permanent harm to its reputation. This established favour-its is still popular today even if being winged and fished on the surface has somewhat impaired its old efficiency.

In referring to the original form of the Gold-Ribbed Hare's Ear, I must admit to standing on dangerous ground because nobody knows when or by whom it was invented. All we know is that the hare's fur for bodies has been used from time immemorial and utilizing the same material for the thorax and legs was a very early inspiration, but cer-tainly there is not the slightest reason to suspect that the original pattern was anything but wingless.

In recent years a novel theory has been advanced that the ordinary winged pattern as seen from below, may look to fish like a newly hatched dun standing upon its discarded shuck. It is an intriguing idea as it would provide some justification for turning this good old wet fly into a winged floater. If I do not find it altogether convincing it is chiefly because I have seldom seen a sub-imago standing on its shuck and using it as a raft to carry it downstream. Admittedly nearly all the up-winged duns, including the olives, stand on their nymphal skins whilst withdrawing from them during their metamorphosis but during that time only their wing-pads are visible. Directly the wings are freed sufficiently for them to be hoisted, the insect and its now empty shuck generally part immediately.

To sum up, the Gold-Ribbed Hare's Ear tied as a winged floater and fished on the surface is a passable copy of the olive dun, especially when tied in the Ogden manner with a sparsely dubbed body which gives the fly a slender apparance. Dressed as was the original pattern with a dubbed body and a thorax and hackle of fur, it is probably the best suggestion extant of an olive nymph in the act of hatching, and fished in this form either in the surface or a little below it, it is a fly which for this purpose has no equal.

GOLDEN OLIVE

An old renowned wet fly for sea-trout, perhaps more universally used in Ireland than elsewhere, but a killing pattern in any river. Mr. Roger Woolley gives the following dressing:

Body: Golden olive seal's fur, ribbed gold oval wire.
Tag: Orange floss.
Hackle: Golden olive.
Wings: Golden-pheasant tippet fibres and brown mallard over.
Hook: 7 to 12.

GOVERNOR

An old fancy pattern still favoured in some districts for use on hot summer days, either as a floater or sunk and in a wide range of sizes from 16 to 12.

T. C. Hofland held a high opinion of it and recommended the following dressing:

Body: Coppery-coloured peacock's herl, ribbed with gold twist and tipped with scarlet twist.
Legs: Red or ginger cock's hackle.
Wings: The light part of a pheasant's wing.
Hook: 14.

Halford gave a rather similar tie but with a woodcock wing and a butt of primrose silk or flat gold. Nowadays, the woodcock wing is generally utilized and with a bright orange floss tip instead of primrose, the fly is popular for trout and grayling, although less so in the north and west, than in other parts of the country. In U.S.A., where the Governor is a well-known pattern, still another variation is found, the orange floss giving place to bright red silk.

The illustration shows an effective variation of the ordinary English fly, which if, as is generally supposed, it was originally intended to be an imitation of a beetle, must be a better likeness than the standard dressing. This tie should serve as a suggestion also of several of the more brightly coloured diptera.

The dressing is:

Body: Peacock herl.
Tip: Gilt paint.
Wing: Old English starling with a nice green sheen.
Eyes: Two small gilt beads.
Hackle: Red cock's hackle.
Hook: 14.

Don't despise it because of the gilt and beads, as I did once, until I saw a brace of trout taken taken on it which between them weighed over six pounds. There are times when it will kill better than most patterns.

There is one other variation worth mentioning, the Orange Governor. It is a favourite wet pattern in U.S.A., although it originated in the south of England. The usual dressing is:

Body: Peacock eye, tipped with orange silk.
Hackle: Red or ginger cock's hackle.
Wings: Starling wing.
Hook: 12 to 14.

GRANNOM (*Brachycentrus subnubilus*)

The Natural Insect

Commonly known as the greentail, this little sedge appears in the south and Midlands in about the third week of April, and lasts from ten days to three weeks. In Scotland the hatch is generally later and may not occur in the Highlands before June. Common in some European countries (notably in Norway, although rare in France), it is found on a good many English rivers from Devon to the north of Scotland, but I have never observed it on any lake.

On the streams on which the grannom occurs, of which the Kennet is the classical example, it is usually found in countless millions and I have seen these insects in clouds of such density as to make it next to impossible to see across the river. Its occurrence on any river is apt to be erratic and sometimes it will disappear from a river, or from a certain part of a river, for several years, only to re-appear in its former strength. Why this should be so has not been determined, although as Mr. Martin Mosely has pointed out the grannom suffers more than most flies when weeds are severely cut as is a seasonal custom on some streams. The pupae are at that period in their cases, attached to weeds and are incapable of moving, with the result that they get carried away and much valuable trout food is lost. Seasonal and periodic variations apart, there is reason to think that on account of this intense and ill-timed weed cutting, the number of grannom has permanently diminished on many streams during recent years.

The grannom is of importance to anglers because it is a day-flying sedge which appears in the early spring; brings up the larger trout, and provides an ample food supply just when trout need one most, following the lean and hungry months of the winter. It is not surprising that trout take it with avidity and to the extent of gorging themselves.

The grannom is not difficult to identify, for where it is found, it is present in such tremendous numbers that it is unmistakable. It is the only sedge to appear in force in the early spring, and there is no doubt that fish take it most freely just when the pupa is hatching.

A sober-looking small sedge, with a body not exceeding half an inch in length, of a greyish colour, and with wings of yellowish-grey (marked with a few irregular yellow spots) which darken with exposure, the grannom would not be recognized by many anglers were it not for

the numbers in which it occurs in the spring. Except, of course, for
the female, which in the later stages of her existence is quite distinctive,
for beneath her body and at its extremity, she carries a large bunch of
bluish-green eggs which no angler could fail to see. These eggs are
enclosed in a gelatinous sac which is held in a cavity formed by the
last two or three segments of her body being turned inwards. It is, of
course, on account of this that the grannom is commonly called the
greentail, although strictly speaking, the name should only be applied
to the egg-carrying female imago. Fish certainly like the female better
than her spouse, although, as already mentioned, they much prefer the
hatching pupa to the perfect insect. Since almost every artificial copy
of the insect is supplied with a green tail, it should be noted that there
is no green on the body of either male or female imago when they are
first hatched, although there is a small green spot at the end of the
larva.

The Artificial Fly

Fly-dressers have always paid a good deal of attention to the grannom and especially to the female imago, so that there are many patterns
from which to choose. The artificial, however, is not always to be
relied upon, particularly when the insects are on the water in clouds,
but when fish are in the right frame of mind, great sport may sometimes be enjoyed.

Dressings vary in different parts of the country and with so many
variations, I hesitate to express an opinion as to which is the best, the
more so since my own experience of the grannom is a limited one.
Chetham, in 1681, gave a tie with a body of fur taken from a brown
spaniel's ear, with the tail-end of sea-green wool, and wings of a
starling's quill feather, but of the older dressings there is none better
than that evolved by Alfred Ronalds:

Body: Fur of hare's face left rough, spun on brown silk. A little green floss silk
may be worked in at the tail to represent the bunch of eggs there.
Wings: Feather from a partridge's wing, and made very full.
Legs: A pale ginger hen's hackle.
Hook: 14.

He adds that the fly may be made buzz (hackled) with a feather from
the back of a partridge's neck, wound upon the above body.

Compare this with a modern dressing (dry) designed to imitate the
female, thus:

Silk: Bright green.
Body: Greyish-brown hare's ear with green wool at tail.
Wings: Hen pheasant or feather from a partridge's wing.
Hackle: Rusty dun game-cock.
Hook: 14.

Most authorities suggest that grannom patterns should be tied on hooks of sizes 12 to 14, but personally I consider that the latter size should be quite large enough for an imitation of a small sedge such as this. It should therefore be noted that my recommendations in this respect do not agree with others who, I must admit, have had far more experience of the grannom than myself.

For a wet pattern (again of the female), Pritt gives the following:

Wings: Hackled with a feather from the inside of a woodcock's wing, or from a partridge's neck, or from under a hen pheasant's wing.
Body: Lead-coloured silk, twisted with a little fur from a hare's face.
Tail: Green silk wrapped over the lower part of the body.
Hook: 14.

Two patterns should be enough for an insect which makes but a brief annual appearance, but mention must be made of a dry fly designed by the Rev. E. Powell and also for what he has to say about it. Writing in *The Country Sportsman*, that most excellent monthly, he expresses the following views about the grannom with which all who have had any experience of this insect, must surely agree:

"A hatch of grannom is", he writes, "a sad affliction, for it is generally so brief that there is little time to think and the trout seem to find it so satisfying that they are difficult to stir for the rest of the day. One moment you are flogging an apparently troutless river, and the next the whole surface and the air above it look as if they were charged with bits of minutely chopped hay and the fish are flicking their tails in every direction. Speed is everything then. You must know what to do and do it at once. He who wavers is lost. It will be all over before he has begun. Personally I dreaded the sight of the little wretch till on a hint from the great Dai Lewis of the Teify, I evolved the following pattern:

Tying silk: Green.
Body: Mole dyed in picric acid.
Hackles: Two, partridge—yes, but *what* partridge? That is the point. At the top
  of his neck the feathers are grey: at the bottom, brown: but somewhere mid-
  way you will find about half a dozen which are neither—a kind of greyish-
  brown—and that is what both you and the trout need for the Grannom.
Hook: 14, or smaller.

"The queer thing about this pattern is that the fish will take it wet
or dry."

Those are the words of an enthusiast but as I have indicated elsewhere,
what Edward Powell does not know about catching fish is scarcely
worth knowing.

Halford observed that on the Test, trout fed upon the larvae of the
grannom (or upon the pupae just about to hatch) and neglected the
imago or fully developed fly. That would seem to be true of all rivers
where the insect occurs in quantities and a representation of the larvae
should therefore prove profitable. For this purpose, Halford suggested
the following:

Wing: A very small piece of the point of a brown partridge hackle.
Hackle: Rusty dun.
Body: Formed by working over the shank of the hook a foundation of pea-
  green floss silk and ribbing it with a strand of peacock quill dyed green.
Hook: 14.

For the same end, Mr. Skues has a useful pattern which may be fished
wet or dry, which he calls the Grannom Nymph. The dressing is:

Tying silk: Bright green waxed with clear wax.
Hackle: Rich brown partridge back.
Body: Bright green lamb's wool tapered.
Hook: 12 or 13.

How a green body can be justified in a copy of the larva is not clear
to me, although doubtless the answer is that it attracts fish better that
way; and admittedly there is a small green spot at the tail-end of the
nymph.

GRANT'S MURDERER

A dry pattern used on the Teme and the Shropshire streams, and considered deadly in May and June. It was the invention of Mr. Herbert Grant, the Ludlow tackle dealer, whose tie for it was as follows:

Body: Gold tinsel.   *Hackle:* Pale blue dun, long.
Wings: Starling wing, rolled and tied well forward in Mole Fly style.
Whisks: Pale blue dun.   *Hook:* 12 to 14.

GRASSHOPPER

When the natural grasshopper is prevalent in the meadow grass near river or lake, a good imitation will often account for fish and there is said to be nothing better for really big trout. There are many methods of dressing an artificial but all must be looked upon as lures rather than flies and as such they have never made much appeal to English fly-fishermen.

They are far more popular on the Continent and in America and Canada than in this country. There is, of course, the artificial grasshopper so popular amongst grayling anglers in Worcestershire, Shropshire, and Derbyshire, although it is not a grasshopper at all and I have no idea how that name was fastened on it. It is still a lure, however, and very much of a lure too, for in its commonest form, a lump of lead, tapered at each end, is moulded on the hook shank and is covered with dark green wool, with a strip of straw running along each side. The straw is held in position by a number of turns of straw-coloured whipping silk. The hook may be as large as a number 5, which seems enormous for a fish with a small mouth like a grayling. The whole contrivance is rather fearsome and I cannot help but feel that there must be more pleasant and more artistic ways of taking grayling than this!

GRAVEL BED (*Anisomera burmeisteri*)

Although found on comparatively few rivers, the gravel bed, or gravel spider, is of peculiar interest to the angling fraternity, since it is generally agreed that no other insect—not even the mayfly—is capable of producing so much excitement amongst trout. Nowadays anglers appear to be paying more attention to this fly than they used to do and I know of many who make a special point of visiting the river at such times as a hatch may be expected.

The gravel bed is a gnat-like insect, with two lead-coloured wings, a darkish body and six long, dark olive legs, which look more black than olive, until examined carefully. A member of the Tipulidae family, the gravel bed is related to the crane flies and looks much like a miniature daddy-long-legs, but with its wings lying flat along its back.

There is little doubt that the creature must be amphibious. The metamorphosis takes place on the dry gravel and as soon as the fly has emerged, it makes it way to the water, on the surface of which it is quite as much at home as any truly aquatic insect.

The gravel bed is found in abundance on the sand and gravel beds of the upper reaches of the Severn; on parts of the Vyrnwy, Wye, Usk, Welsh Dee, and their tributaries; on several minor Welsh rivers; on some of the Derbyshire streams, and on a number of the north country, border, and Scottish rivers. To the best of my knowledge, it is not found on any southern river and there are no records of it from any chalk stream. In most parts where it is found, it makes its first appearance during the third week in April, although the big hatches seldom occur before the first or second week in May. In Scotland, anglers expect to see the gravel bed on the first warm day in May after the beech has burst its buds. The hatch may vary by as much as a fortnight on different parts of a river, but certainly a warm day is necessary. Should a cool breeze spring up at any time, the insects will immediately seek shelter amongst the stones and gravel, appearing again with remarkable rapidity directly warmer conditions set in.

The insects hatch in countless thousands, and should the weather be hot enough they will soon be seen racing along the surface of the water in every direction, gyrating, buzzing and generally carrying out their extraordinary manœuvres at a speed which is quite astonishing. The effect this has on trout must be seen to be believed. The water fairly boils as the fish dash about hither and thither after the flies. It would seem as if they could never have too many and there is no doubt that they will continue to feed in this frenzied manner until they are absolutely gorged. One might imagine that in these conditions the right artificial would be deadly, but although the execution is unlikely to be as great as the uninitiated might reasonably expect, the angler will be unlucky if he does not creel a brace or two. The behaviour of the insects, and of the fish, will largely be determined by the weather. The gravel bed does not always dash about on the river and at times one may observe them floating down stream as sedately as any dun, generally to be picked off the surface by a waiting fish before they have gone many yards.

Some of my friends who have had far more experience of the insect than I have, hold the opinion that in spite of the avidity with which trout take it, even a heavy rise is apt to prove disappointing to the fly-fisher, because it is virtually impossible to tie a satisfactory imitation of any fly as active as the gravel bed. Hugh Sheringham must have been of their persuasion for he wrote, "The gravel bed is an inferior sort of fly which appears in vast numbers and makes the trout go half-mad—just not so mad as to take an artificial fly. Ap Evans has two counsels for coping with the gravel bed. One was to use something else, such as a March Brown, or Half-Stone; the other was to give the affair up as hopeless. My feeling is that he thought more highly of the second plan."

Not everyone is of that opinion, and to-day many anglers consider that this insect often provides them with the best fishing of the whole season. Neither will they subscribe to the theory that there is any great difficulty in finding an artificial pattern which will take trout when the gravel bed is on the water. At the same time most of them seem to agree that the artificial fly becomes less attractive as the rise continues and that no one pattern will kill well throughout the day. Should the weather be fine and warm, the natural insect may come on as early as eight o'clock in the morning, and from then to about midday is generally the best time for fishing. During that period an angler may creel a number of fish, only to find that after lunch the magic has gone out of his fly and he can do no good at all.

There was a time when the gravel bed seems to have been better known than it is to-day and most of the old sporting writers referred to it either by its correct name, or by a local designation such as gravel gnat, gravel spider, sand fly and sand gnat. Alfred Ronalds probably made the acquaintance of the insect when he was living in Wales, for he classified the fly correctly over a century and a quarter ago, and gave a good illustration of it in his *Fly-Fisher's Entomology*. For its imitation, he suggested the following:

Body: Dark dun, or lead-coloured silk thread dressed very fine.
Wings: From an under covert feather of the woodcock's wing.
Legs: A black cock's hackle rather long, wound twice only, round body.
Hook: 13 or 14.

He adds: "This fly kills well in May; weather bright, water clear, and when no other fly will raise fish. Some prefer the brightest outside (scapular) feather of a woodcock's wing; and use the same feather to make it buzz. The silk for the body should be of the most repulsive, ashy, liver hue you can find."

On the Clyde, the gravel bed is looked upon as a fly of importance but during its season, local fly-fishers kill a lot of trout on some of the imitations which they have evolved. Mr. Andrew Macqueen of Bearsden has kindly sent me a pattern which he states is "good medicine", and which is tied by Mr. John Veitch of Peebles. I make the dressing to be as follows:

Tying silk: Purple.

Body: Stripped quill of peacock sword feather with purple tying silk showing at shoulder.

Wings: Fibres from hen pheasant's centre tail feather, laid almost flat along the back.

Hackle: Natural black cock's hackle, long and stiff.

Hook: 12 or 13.

Mr. Thomas Clegg, well known to Clyde fly-anglers as an "amateur-professional" fly-dresser who turns out some beautiful work, has been good enough to send me another dressing of the gravel bed, known locally as the Clyde Sandfly, which is a little different to the above.

Body: Thin black silk ribbed with bright blue silk.

Wings: Hen pheasant tail, speckled or marked portions only, leave out all black bars, sloped well down hook.

Hackle: Large shiny black cock, dressed sparsly but long in fibre.

Hook: 14.

Both the patterns given above are always fished on the bob and more often wet than dry. As proved killers, they are worth noting.

Finally there is a useful dry hackled pattern invented by Dr. Pryce-Tannatt, who has kindly supplied the correct dressing given below.

Body: Cigar-ash colour blue wool, wound on and then lightly varnished with diluted Durafix.

Hackles: Two turns at most of natural black domestic cock's hackle, twice as long in the web as the length of the hook, with a greyish brown feather from the back of a partridge, wound round as a second hackle in front of the cock's hackle.

Hook: 12 or 13.

Many fly-fishermen have been defeated by the gravel bed, but possibly if they will experiment with one of the flies given above, it may fill them with fresh hope and their creels with good trout.

GRAYLING STEEL-BLUE

One of Mr. Roger Woolley's grayling patterns for which he gives this dressing:

Body: Thin peacock herl, ribbed with gold wire, with three turns of orange silk at the tail and beyond that a tiny tip of silver tinsel.

Hackle: Well-grizzled bright blue cock's from shoulder to tail.

Hook: 14.

GRAYLING WITCH. See WITCH.

GREAT RED SPINNER. See MARCH BROWN

GREEN CATERPILLAR.

More than one fly bears this name but the best, I consider, is that shown on Plate IV. This has an emerald wool body, with a very short stiff hackle of the same colour along the whole of its length. The hackle should be clipped with scissors until only bristles remain and consequently it does not show up clearly in the illustration.

Fished semi-wet, or on the surface, during spring, it will take fish but it is during the last half of August and throughout September that it proves most valuable. Like the Arrow Fly, it is very effective where trees overhang a river, and is quite as good for lake fishing if used near the edges in the vicinity of trees and bushes. There are times when it can be very killing indeed and will take one fish after another, and this applies to grayling as well as trout.

GREEN IMP

This pattern was the invention of the late Mr. Percy Wadham, of Newport, Isle of Wight, who died in 1945. He was a great naturalist and a great fisherman and having had the pleasure of knowing him personally for a great number of years, I can testify that his knowledge of fish and fish-life was in many respects unique, and nearly all of it was gained in the hard school of practical experience. That his exceptional knowledge of matters piscatorial was not recorded in book form was entirely due to his great modesty. His Green Imp is a fancy pattern which kills well in hot bright weather and was designed, I believe, to imitate a series of beetles. Mr. Wadham took trout on this fly and mostly from streams where there were more fishermen than fish.

He kindly sent me the dressing which I give in his own words:

"The body is dressed by winding on two hackles from the top of the head of an old-English starling. Next, two hackles taken from the neck of the same bird, just below the head. These are longer in the fibre. Lastly, two more feathers from the top of the starling's head are fixed on flat for wings. The finished fly is a beautiful bottle green."

Although nearly every fly-dresser of renown has a word of praise and thankfulness for the common starling, because for many generations it has provided us with feathers for a large number of useful patterns, it seems to have escaped the notice of modern authorities that it was our old-English starling which provided the lovely green feathers. To-day, unfortunately, this bird is a rarity, having been driven away from its old haunts by the more virile Russian starling, the purple feathers of which, are nothing like so useful, and are totally unsuitable for certain patterns for which starlings' feathers are specified.

GREEN INSECT

There can be but few better-known grayling flies, although it is also useful for trout, which probably take it for a small beetle or caterpillar. But its *forte* is as a wet pattern for grayling and it has long been popular for these fish in every part of Great Britain where they are found, being especially well thought of in Derbyshire and Herefordshire as a deadly autumn pattern.

It is subject to some variations in the dressing but the old Yorkshire tie is still the favourite.

Body: Bright green peacock's herl.
Hackle: Soft silver grey hen's hackle.
Hook: 14 to 16.

More often than not, a red tag is attached which is said to add to the attractiveness of the fly, although not all fishermen hold this opinion. It is suggested that when this tag is added, the fly may be taken for a member of the Hemiptera family, known as the green bug, and which is similar in appearance to the aphis except that it is tinged with red. Whether this is so or not, it is clear that trout will take the Green Insect, and that grayling really appreciate it. In fact, as a grayling lure, it probably ranks only second to the Red Tag.

GREEN OLIVE

This fly has nothing to do with the olive dun as might be supposed but is an old Irish wet pattern for lake and sea-trout. The tie is:

Tag: Flat gold.
Tail: Teal, or sometimes strands of golden pheasant topping.
Body: Seal's fur dyed olive or pig's wool, sometimes gold-ribbed very lightly.
Hackle: Black or deep olive dyed.
Wing: Brown or dark mallard, or black coot mixed with woodcock.
Hook: 9 to 4.

This is a rather similar pattern to the (Irish) Hawthorne.

GREENWELL'S GLORY

There can be no fly the name of which is better known to the general public than the great Greenwell's Glory which is as it should be, for a more generally useful wet fly has never been made.

It was invented by Canon William Greenwell, of Durham, when he was fishing the Tweed at Sprouston in May 1854, and was intended as a copy of a fly which he had noticed the trout were taking in preference to the march brown which was also on the water. I have told the full story of its invention in *Trout Flies,* but briefly, the Canon went to James Wright, the famous Tweedside fly-tier and told him the sort of dressing he required and which he thought should make up into a good imitation of the natural fly he had seen. Between them they succeeded in producing a pattern that is to-day known and used by anglers the world over. Canon Greenwell died in 1918, at the ripe old age of ninety-seven, and was catching trout on his fly till the last.

The Greenwell is a good floating pattern, but it is as a wet fly that it excels. There has always been a doubt what trout take it for, although possibly it kills best when the dark olive dun is on the water and most probably the original natural insect it was designed to imitate was one of the olive duns. It will, however, take fish which are feeding on the b.-w.o. or the iron-blue, whilst it is generally worth a trial when the mayfly is up and in hot weather it serves as a useful lake fly. For all-round use throughout the year, it must certainly be accounted one of the best general utility patterns. Vary the dressing slightly and it can be made to serve as a suggestion of a whole range of olive duns. As a nymph suggesting pattern it is valuable at all times, although for this purpose it should be sparsely dressed and the hackled type is better than the winged. With a well-waxed body it may be used to copy the willow fly.

The correct tie is now fairly well known although some authorities appear to have ideas of their own upon the subject. That the dressing given below is the right one is beyond dispute because I have a letter in my possession in the Canon's own handwriting, dated 1st June 1900, in which he refers to it as being "the original and best edition of Greenwell's Glory".

Wing: Inside of a blackbird's wing.
Body: Yellow silk.
Hackle: Coch-y-bondhu.
Hook: 14.

In the same letter he adds: "I heard yesterday that it has proved equally successful as a loch fly, of course, on a larger scale, as it has on rivers." In another letter to a friend he writes, when referring to the dressing: "Gold thread can be added if wished."

There is reason to believe that in the original version, the yellow tying silk was well waxed with cobbler's wax to impart to the body a greenish-olive hue and that the wings, tied in a bunch and split, were more or less upright and not sloped back over the body as is now customary.

E. M. Tod, who has been described as having been as great an artist with the wet fly as was G. S. Marryat with the dry, always stated that the Greenwell was his favourite pattern for all-round fishing. The dressing he used was, however, a little different from that of the original, and to quote his own picturesque description, his pattern was tied thus:

Waistcoat: Yellow tying silk, waxed with cobbler's wax to give it a yellow and slightly dingy hue, ribbed with very fine gold wire.
Trousers: Coch-y-bondhu hackle, with tips yellow or pale golden, and the part near the "pen" of the feather, quite black.

Nowadays a hackled version of the Greenwell is becoming increasingly used and I must confess to a great liking for it. As a general wet pattern it is to be doubted whether it is as good as the original winged fly, although it is quite useful to suggest a nymph. But as a floating fly on river or lake, it is excellent. The usual tie is:

Body: Yellow silk, well waxed, and ribbed closely with fine gold wire.
Hackle: Furnace cock and medium blue dun cock.
Whisks: A few fibres of furnace cock.
Hook: 14.

One of the better variations of the standard fly was invented by Mr. Skues and his dressing for this will be found under Olive Dun on page 270. In Scotland, a yellow tag is sometimes added to the standard Greenwell and in New Zealand, anglers favour a bright red tag.

GREY DUSTER

My first introduction to this most excellent fly was on the Alwen, a Welsh mountain stream running into the Dee. The "locals" said that it was the only pattern one needed and they were not far wrong for, on that visit, it accounted for nine out of every ten trout taken.

Since then this pattern, which is always fished dry, has given me some splendid sport on all sorts of rivers, at all times of the day, and at all times of the year, although it is probably most effective during May and June, and again in September. On the Test and Itchen, it was a failure but elsewhere it is a great fly and one which sometimes proves quite irresistible to both trout and grayling. The Duster is particularly useful just before mayfly time and when the first small numbers of those flies make their appearance. Trout do not settle down to taking them for the first few days and are not easily tempted by an artificial fly. Most fly-fishers put on a small Mayfly or possibly an Alder, generally with more optimism than any real conviction that it will produce any great response from the trout. They would do far better to put up a Grey Duster, for under those conditions it will take fish and will continue to do so even when the mayfly is on the water in force; in fact, a Duster tied on a large hook, say a 10 or 11, will sometimes take trout during a big hatch of mayfly even better than a copy of the natural insect.

Why this should be so I cannot explain, as like the Blue Upright, the Grey Duster is probably taken as a rough suggestion of the smaller perlidae—the early brown, the February red, the willow fly and the various needle flies. Dressed, as it is occasionally, with whisks, it serves to suggest the early spring olive. Be that as it may, there can be no doubt that on fast-flowing streams, and perhaps rather surprisingly on lakes, the Grey Duster can often give other floating flies several lengths and a beating, for it has the inestimable quality of bringing fish up.

Being very buoyant, it rides rough water nicely and that maybe a factor in attracting trout, but I have still to find a satisfactory explanation as to why it proves so effective. Its lightly coloured hackle makes it easy to see in any light, a blessing to anglers whose eyesight is not too keen.

As a general utility dry fly for trout and grayling, the Grey Duster is one of the best—perhaps *the* best—pattern known to me. Certainly it is the only fly which has nearly tempted me to become a "one-pattern" angler. It has not succeeded in doing that, but I did find myself using it for days on end, because it will tempt fish with such regularity that it is difficult to find anything better.

In my opinion this is a pattern which is destined to become one of the best known of all general dry flies, and to readers to whom it is unknown, I pass on the tie with my blessing and in the certainty that on most rivers the fly will prove of value.

The dressing is:

Tying silk: Brown.
Body: Dubbed with light rabbit's fur, sometimes mixed with a modicum of blue.
Hackle: Badger hackle, well-marked with a black centre and white list.
Hook: 12 to 14. Larger for lakes.

Since writing the above, a few days on the Test have caused me to revise my opinion of the value of this pattern on the chalk streams under certain conditions. My visit was made towards the close of the mayfly season when the hatch had been a sparse one and there were very few flies in evidence beyond an occasional dun and a few spinners, mostly spent. The fish took an artificial spent drake quite well, although certainly no better than they did the Grey Duster. Having discovered this, I used the latter pattern rather more than a Mayfly, mainly because of its greater buoyance and visibility and also because (probably on account of its smaller dimensions) it hooked fish more securely; in fact, whereas several trout were lost on the Mayfly through being lightly hooked, not a single fish was lost on the Duster. Trout and grayling rose to it freely and it accounted for a considerable number of both species.

As I have said, the mayfly was nearly over, but I believe that the Grey Duster would have achieved the same results had the hatch been at its height. Colour was lent to this view when on leaving the Test I motored to the Onny in Shropshire. There the mayfly was still well on and there, too, for three days, trout took the Duster as if it were the only fly of interest to them. But good as is this pattern just before, during, and immediately after the mayfly is on the water, I must repeat that it proves on most rivers just as killing at other periods of the season.

GRIZZLY DUN

One of the late Mr. Walter Gallichan's patterns, designed for use on the Welsh and Shropshire streams. Fished wet or dry, this is a useful fly throughout the season. Trout take it well when olives are on the water, although I am inclined to think that it also serves to suggest the willow fly, needle fly, etc., which are abundant on most of the rivers, streams, and lakes in Wales. The dressing is:

Body: Yellow silk, well waxed, giving an olive effect.
Hackle: Grizzle grey badger hackle.
Tail: Grizzle.
Hook: 14.

GROUSE HACKLE

Francis Francis called this pattern a capital hot-weather fly and added that it was one of three "which will fill a basket on any mountain beck or trout burn in heather districts". The other two were a Partridge Hackle and Black Gnat. To-day the Grouse Wing is more often used as a nymph, with a thickish body and sparse hackle. In this form, well sunk, it will often prove highly efficacious in hot weather.

Body: Yellow silk body, with one turn of flat gold tinsel at tail.
Hackle: Small hen grouse hackle.
Hook: 12 to 14.

GROUSE SERIES

Standard northern wet patterns, used mostly for loch fishing, comprising such well-known flies as Grouse and Black, Grouse and Brown,

Grouse and Green, Grouse and Orange, Grouse and Red, Grouse and Yellow, Grouse Silver and Magenta, Grouse and Claret, Grouse and Olive, Grouse and Purple.

The Grouse and Green is my own particular favourite for lakes, but it is impossible to say which is the most popular fly. Nearly all of them are widely used and are also reliable patterns for sea-trout.

The dressings of a few of the best are given below.

GROUSE AND GREEN
Tail: Brown mallard, or a few fibres of golden pheasant tippet.
Body: Green wool ribbed with gold or silver wire.
Hackle: Dark ginger.
Wings: Brown mottled feather from a grouse's tail.
Hook: 8 to 12.

GROUSE AND ORANGE
Tail: Three or four fibres of golden pheasant tippet.
Body: Orange wool ribbed with oval gold.
Hackle: Red.
Wings: Brown mottle feather from a grouse's tail.
Hook: 8 to 12.

GROUSE AND PURPLE
Tail: Three or four fibres of golden pheasant tippet.
Body: Purple wool ribbed with silver.
Hackle: Black.
Wings: Brown mottled feather from a grouse's tail.
Hook: 8 to 12.

This is the most modern fly of the series which, in recent years, has become popular in Scotland, where some large catches have been taken on it on the Tweed and from Loch Leven.

GROUSE WING (*Mystacides longicornis*)

A small sedge found mostly in lakes, canals, and similar still waters, frequently in very large numbers during July and August. In size, shape, and the manner in which it flies backwards and forwards in batches, it is reminiscent of its near relative, the silverhorns.

The brown mottled wings, however, are very different to those of the silverhorns, and bear a close resemblance to the wing feathers of the grouse. The antennae are exceptionally long—rather more than twice the length of the wings. Trout will take the natural insect when the chance presents itself, but few anglers trouble to carry any special imitation of this little sedge which cannot be considered of any great importance. One of the standard sedge patterns on a size 14 hook should suggest it well enough.

HALF STONE

One of the best patterns for the Devonshire streams and much used in the west during the early part of the season. It is usually considered to be a representation of a hatching nymph but Mr. Eric Taverner has expressed the opinion that it is a better suggestion of a pupa of a caddisfly in the act of emerging into an imago.

The name of the pattern provides no clue so its origin is doubtful. It may refer to the colour of the fly or it may have been used to indicate that half of the body is of the same colour as that of a stonefly.

Halford gives it only as a floating pattern which is a little curious, since in the county of its birth it is invariably fished wet. The tie is subject to some variation but a usual one is as under:

Hackle: Blue cock's as for the Blue Upright, but not so dark.
Body: Yellow or primrose floss silk for the lower half, with a pinch of mole's fur or water-rat spun on at the shoulder before winding the hackle.
Whisks: Three strands of blue hackle.
Hook: 12 to 14.

HAMMOND'S ADOPTED

Whether this pattern is used nowadays I do not know, but in Halford's time it was looked upon as a good evening dry fly to represent any small brown moth. It was the invention of John Hammond, the fly-dresser who was in business in Winchester from 1856 to 1879. His tie for it was:

Wings: Woodcock's wing feather.
Hackle: A rusty brown-red cock hackle from tail to head.
Body: Dubbing of ruddy brown crewel ribbed with fine gold wire.
Hook: 14 to 12.

Dark hare's ear and mole's fur probably makes a better body, and the fly was often preferred winged with a hen pheasant's wing feather.

HARDY'S FAVOURITE

A fancy pattern, the invention of the late Mr. J. J. Hardy, useful in

May or June for trout and a serviceable fly for lake fishing and for sea-trout. Fished wet or dry.

Tail: Fibres of brown mallard.
Body: Peacock herl, ribbed with red silk.
Hackle: Dark partridge.
Wings: Dark brown turkey's feather.
Hook: 10 to 14; larger sea-trout.

HARE'S EAR

Also known as the Hare's Lug and Hare's Fleck this fly is a variation of the Blue Dun, and there must be nearly as many different dressings for the former as there are for the latter.

Fished wet or dry, the Hare's Ear in any of its many disguises will kill fish on most rivers and under a wide range of conditions, but if one excepts the gold-ribbed fly, it is impossible to say which is the most popular dressing.

The following may be considered one of the best versions.

Body and Legs: From a hare's face with the blue roots carefully clipped off, spun on yellow silk, very full at the shoulder.
Tail: Two fibres red cock's hackle.
Wings: Pale starling, or may be varied with wings of woodcock, with the dubbing picked out for legs.
Hook: 14 to 16.

Halford gave a dressing for a dry fly which he described as being "Ogden's original pattern"—that Ogden the well-known Cheltenham tackle dealer and fly-tier of a generation ago, who was also responsible for the Invicta. The dressing is much the same as the above except for the body which is of pale primrose silk.

In Scotland, the dressing (for the wet pat . ·-·) is only slightly different from the f. :: given above. A popular Scottish tie is:

Body and Legs: From fur of a hare's ear, tied with yellow silk, the legs well-picked out.
Wings: Woodcock.
Tail: Two strands of mallard feathers, tipped with gold tinsel.
Hook: 14.

A particularly good tie hails from Ireland where it is favoured for spring fishing and is always used as a wet fly. The old dressing is as under:

Body: Withered part of a hare's ear, mixed with golden olive mohair.
Tag: Gold tinsel.
Tail: Two fibres of mallard.
Legs: Red cock's hackle, short in fibre and only under the shoulders. May be varied by using wren tail.
Wings: Landrail (of a dull colour, not red), or starling.
Hook: 14.

See also GOLD RIBBED HARE'S EAR

HASSAM'S PET

Of all the amateur fly-tiers of this century, none has been more gifted than the late C. A. Hassam, a member of the Fly-Fishers' Club, and a well-known angler on the Derwent and Derbyshire Wye. The dressing of his own favourite fly (which was christened by Mr. Skues) is given below for I feel sure that many fishermen will be glad to have it.

A good dry pattern on the limestone rivers, some notable bags have been also made on it on the chalk streams. One angler known to me had the Itchen limit of three brace of trout on it, all before twelve o'clock in the morning. The best brace weighed three pounds and two and three-quarter pounds respectively.

It is not clear what natural insect Hassam set out to imitate or whether he intended the pattern as a general representation of some of the duns, but I think it is taken for the small dark olive of April and early May.

Mr. Hassam's own dressing was:

Tying silk: Primrose, at shoulder only.
Hackle: Pale ginger cock, the colour of a grain of wheat.
Whisks: Pale ginger cock tied in at shoulder.
Body: A pale yellow floss which goes pale green when wet or oiled, tied in at shoulder with waste end towards bend of hook and wound over waste end to near bend; then passed under whisks and wound back to shoulder where it is secured and cut off.
Hook: 15 or 16.

HAWTHORNE FLY (*Bibio marci*)

A large-scale black gnat, about half an inch long, this insect is rather similar in appearance to the common house-fly, but jet black in colour and distinguished by long hairy legs which in flight trail behind it and which can be well represented by two tips of ostrich herl dyed black.

As its smaller relative, the black gnat (*B. johannis*) takes its Latin designation from St. John's Day, so is *B. marci* named after St. Mark's Day which falls on April 5th, and which is about the earliest date one is likely to see this fly. It is by no means common before the beginning of May or after June, its occurrence coinciding more or less with the time that the hawthorne is in blossom.

The natural insect was known to anglers some centuries ago and is mentioned both by Dame Juliana Berners (1486) and Izaak Walton. In some districts it is known as the black fly and in others as St. Mark's fly, whilst in the west-country it is frequently referred to as the May fly.

Personally I have never found it of much account as an angler's fly, although it sometimes gets blown on to the water and then, attracted by the considerable disturbance it makes, trout will take it. On occasions, during May and June, these flies will be seen pairing in the air above, or close to, the river. If, as sometimes happens, they then land on the surface of the stream, fish will seize them readily, for they appear to find a double-mouthful of this (or almost any other) insect, more than they can resist.

Another common fly which is prevalent at about the same period is often mistaken for the hawthorne, for it is almost exactly like it in appearance and has the same long hairy legs trailing behind; but it has red eyes which the hawthorne has not. It is probably *nematus niger*, although I am not sure of this and in any case it is of no consequence to the fly-fisher as the same artificial patterns should serve for both species. A third insect very like the hawthorne fly is the heather fly (*Bibio pomonae*) which does not appear before August.

However, even though trout may not be over-fond of the hawthorne fly, the artificial will at times kill well. It is a pattern which I never carry because when one is required, I have found that a Williams's Favourite on a No. 12 hook will serve well enough. The standard Hawthorne pattern is a popular trout fly, fished wet or dry, and on occcasions, is a splendid fly for sea-trout. The usual tie is:

Body: Black ostrich herl.
Wings: Palest starling wing feather.
Hackle: Black cock.
Hook: 12; larger for sea-trout.

This pattern is often fished wet but is probably more killing used as a floater.

A closer imitation of the natural insect is a dry pattern designed by Roger Woolley, whose tie for it is as under:

Body: Two black strands from a turkey tail feather, tied in so that the bright black quill of them shows up most. The ends of the two strands are tied back after forming the body to represent the two long trailing legs of the fly.
Hackle: Black cock.
Wings: Palest part of jay wing feather.
Hook: 13.

In Ireland, where the fly is usually fished wet, the following old dressing is popular.

Tail: Gold tinsel.
Body: Two-thirds black horse-hair, remainder black ostrich herl.
Legs: Black cock's hackle, or topping of largest green plover, two or three turns.
Wings: Palest starling wing feather.
Hook: 12; larger for sea-trout.

There is, however, another pattern in Ireland also known as the Hawthorne, which is quite a different "crature", being purely a sea-trout fly and a killing one too. The standard tie used throughout Mayo, where the pattern originated, is:

Tag: Flat gold or tinsel, or sometimes orange silk.
Tail: Teal, or strands of golden pheasant tippet.
Body: Black silk.
Hackle: Black or port-wine brown.
Wings: Brown or dark mallard.
Hook: 9 to 5.

Some Irish anglers think that the addition of a blue jay hackle at the throat is an improvement. When sea-trout are the quarry, fly-fishermen could do worse than give a trial to this excellent pattern.

HEATHER FLY (Bibio pomonae)

Known in parts of Scotland as "The Bloody Doctor", this insect is of some importance to lake fishermen, far more so, in fact, than its better known relative, the hawthorne fly. The two insects are very alike but whereas the hawthorne is a spring fly, the heather fly does not put in an appearance before August, and although at a distance they are indistinguishable, when closely examined there can be no mistake since the top part of each leg of *B. pomonae* is of a brilliant crimson colour. Wherever one finds a loch or a reservoir in heather-clad country (and there are numbers of them throughout Cambria and Caledonia) there also will be found the heather fly. A fall of them may reasonably be expected on any hot sunny day in August and when this occurs the subsequent rise is likely to be furious for these ungainly creatures are often carried on to the water in great quantities. In his *Angling Sketches*, Andrew Lang describes how a fall of these insects on a Scottish loch produced the greatest rise of trout he ever saw in his life as the flies "were blown across the loch, not singly but in populous groups".

Although it is many years since *B. pomonae* was first known to me, I did not know until recently that it had any popular name but in the *Salmon and Trout Magazine* (No. 123), Mr. John Henderson refers to it as the heather fly—a very apt designation. This writer also mentions that it can be well imitated by the Hawthorne Fly if a rich red coch-y-bondhu hackle is substituted for the black shoulder hackle.

HECKHAM PECKHAM

A good loch pattern and excellent for sea-trout. Always fished wet, it is popular throughout Great Britain and Canada, and is one of the several useful flies which were invented by Mr. William Murdoch of Aberdeen. The modern dressing is:

Tail: Three or four fibres of golden pheasant tippet.
Body: Red seal's fur, ribbed with silver.
Hackle: Red cock's at shoulder only.
Wings: White tipped mallard feather with a nice green sheen on it.
Hook: 10 to 14; larger for sea-trout.

This is a better tie than the original which had a body dubbed with hare's ear and it is my own favourite sea-trout fly for use after dark. There are several other patterns in the same series, none of which, I think, are as popular as they were twenty-five years ago. The same is true of the fly in America for at one time all the Heckhams were much used throughout the States but in recent times their popularity has much declined. Yet there can be no doubt that the Heckham Peckham is a great fly for certain conditions and personally, like many other anglers, I would never be without a Heckham and Black, which is much like the Peckham but with a black seal's fur body ribbed with gold wire. It is a highly effective pattern for sea-trout and often deadly on dull overcast days. The Heckham and Silver, with an all-silver body, is useful both for lake fishing and sea-trout in bright weather. The present-day neglect of these two old well-tried patterns is surprising although it is probable that some day they will come into their own again.

HEREFORDSHIRE ALDER. See ALDER

HOFLAND'S FANCY

Invented about 1830 by T. C. Hofland (author of *The British Angler's Manual*), who stated that it was tied in an attempt to imitate a small spinner he had seen on the water, and that it has proved itself a good all-round pattern which would kill trout after sunset, in any part of the kingdom, and in any season.

Doubtless his claim was justified for to-day it is still considered a good general-purpose fly, wet or dry, serving as a rough suggestion of several insects and especially of the sedges. Popular in the north, it is a reliable pattern from April to June for trout and sea-trout.

The original dressing, as given by the inventor, was:

Body: Reddish, dark brown silk.
Tail: Two or three strands of red hackle.
Hackle: Red Hackle.
Wings: Woodcock's wing.
Hook: 12 to 14.

HOUGHTON RUBY

One of the most successful patterns invented by W. J. Lunn, the river-keeper of the famous Houghton Club. It serves well as an imitation of the female spinner of the iron-blue and, in recent years, it has become one of the most popular dry flies used on the chalk streams.

Lunn's own dressing was:

Hackle: Bright Rhode Island red hackle.
Wings: Two light blue dun hen tips from the breast or back, set on flat.
Tail: Three fibres from white cock's hackle.
Body: Rhode Island hackle-stalk dyed with red and crimson.
Tying silk: Pearsall's gossamer, shade 13.
Hook: 16.

HYDRACARINA

Water-mites (of which there are over 200 species indigenous to British waters) are found for the most part in sluggish streams, in lakes, and in ponds, but they are also occasionally met with in fast-running rivers.

They have received but scant attention from the angling fraternity since they are not well known, they are difficult to imitate satisfactorily, and there is a general impression—erroneous, I believe—that they are of no importance as an article of the trout's diet. Admittedly they are seldom found in an autopsy but this would seem to be because they disintegrate very quickly and consequently their presence is seldom detected.

The Hydrarachna are true water insects, laying their eggs on water-plants in which they have previously bored a small hole. The adults are quite unmistakable, having the appearance of small waistless spiders with a round body and eight legs. Most abundant during August and September, they are easily seen in clear water owing to their bright colouring. Most of those I have observed were of a bright brick-red, but sometimes they are green, blue, or yellowish-green, the colour varying even in the same species.

As they float about, or propel themselves slowly from one weed to another, trout take them voraciously. When fish are thus engaged, they show no interest in anything else, and for that reason, I am of the opinion that these mites can be of definite importance to the angler. I have observed them in considerable numbers in the Barnt Green lakes, at Blagdon, in a Somersetshire brook, and in other waters.

Unfortunately, I know of no artificial copy, and forbear to mention my own efforts to imitate them for although they appeared satisfactory to the eye, the trout would have none of them.

ICHNEUMON FLY (*Pachymerus calcitrator*)

The common ichneumon is a curious dark orange insect, which has the habit of lifting the rear half of its body until it is raised like an inverted U. This gives the fly a fearsome appearance, although it is quite harmless. There are over two thousand species, all of which are members of the Hymenoptera order, which includes all the wasp-waisted flies. Whilst it is numerous in summer (especially in wooded districts), and trout take it eagerly when it is on to the water, it is of very little interest to fishermen.

Its inclusion here is solely because, on account of its rather peculiar appearance, anglers often wonder what it is and their interest increases if they see one taken by a trout.

The ichneumon is the Orange Fly of Ronalds, but in this instance, it is difficult to agree with that sound naturalist, that "it is one of the best flies to be used for trout and grayling", although the natural insects are frequently found in the stomachs of fish. If, however, any fisherman wants a copy of it, he will find a suitable tie on page 271.

IMP

A grayling pattern, invented by Mr. H. A. Rolt, used in autumn to suggest the black gnat.

The dressing is:

Body: Two or three strands of light heron herl, twisted.
Hackle: Black or from the Impeyan pheasant.
Tag: Ibis over two turns of flat gold tinsel.
Hook: 14.

INDIAN YELLOW

An old pattern, said to have been invented by a Thomas Smith, of Sharrow, near Sheffield, which does not seem to be used nowadays either for trout or grayling. Yet, at one time, it had a great reputation as a killing pattern for both these fish, and is interesting as being a forerunner of the Orange Quill.

Mentioned by Aldam, it was also described in the fifth edition of Ronalds's *Fly-Fisher's Entomology*. The former had a particular high opinion of this pattern for he says: "As a rule, I use no other for the point fly on any river from May to September and have had success with it both for trout and grayling in October."

It is certainly intended as a copy of the blue-winged olive and as such it earned Halford's praise, especially for use on the Itchen. Although he considered that there were better copies of the insect, he stated that the Indian Yellow was a celebrated pattern with a great reputation.

The dressing, for a floater, is:

Wings: Inside grouse wing from a young bird.
Hackles: Two buff cochin cock hackles.
Body: Floss silk about the colour of natural Russian leather, ribbed with bright lemon-coloured tying silk.
Whisk: Buff cochin cock hackle.
Head: Three or four turns of orange tying silk.
Hook: 16 to 14.

INVICTA

The invention of the late James Ogden, of Cheltenham, this celebrated wet pattern is one of the most reliable flies for lake fishing, being especially deadly in the spring. In the north of England, it is sometimes used as a river fly and, in fact, is a great favourite with some anglers who employ it to imitate a dark sedge. When used for this purpose, it will take fish right through the season.

The dressing is:

Body: Seal's fur, dyed yellow, ribbed with gold twist.
Body Hackle: Red cock's hackle carried down body, palmer-wise.
Shoulder Hackle: Red cock with a few turns of blue jay hackle.
Wings: Hen pheasant tail feather.
Tail: Golden pheasant crest feather.
Hook: 10 to 14.

A variation of the Invicta was designed by Mr. John Eastwood for sea-trout and he and his friends have found it highly successful for these fish on the Carmenthenshire rivers. Known as the Silver Knicker, the dressing (which has not previously been published) is as follows:

Body: Flat silver tinsel.
Hackle: Jay, rather long.
Wings: Hen pheasant tail feather.
Tail: Golden pheasant crest feather.
Hook: 7 to 10.

Anglers who have tried this wet pattern for sea-trout speak in the highest terms of it and I am confident that it should kill in any river in the British Isles.

INFALLIBLE

Many years ago, when fishing a Devonshire stream in the spring, an old farm labourer confided to me that the only fly on which I should catch any trout was the Infallible. And he whispered the name as though there were magic in it, as indeed there is, for it would be difficult to think of one more likely to instil confidence. Unfortunately I had no pattern with me and since then, there has never been an occasion to use this fly during my infrequent visits to Devon. But the Infallible is a well-known hackled pattern in the west-country where it is used to imitate the iron-blue, and is generally fished well sunk. The dressing is:

Body: Mole's fur on claret or crimson tying silk, which may be shown at the tip of the tail.
Hackle: Dark blue dun cock's.
Whisks: Ditto.
Hook: 14.

IRON-BLUE DUN (*Baetis pumilus: B. niger*)

This small member of the Ephemeridae is one of the more important to the fly-fisherman, which possibly accounts for the number of names it has been given in different localities. They include the Dark Watchet (Yorks), Little Dark Blue, Iron-Blue Drake, Little Dark Dun, Little Blue Dun, and on the Usk, the Little Purple.

There is no fly which trout like better and when it is on the water they will frequently pick it out from other up-winged duns which may be coming down in greater numbers. It is a cold-day insect which hatches in spring when the sky is leaden and there is a nip of east in the wind. There are two species, of which the larger is first seen in April and is on the water until the end of June. The smaller variety are found in August and September.

The iron-blue is an easy insect to identify, being small with a short stocky body, two setae and four wings, which in the case of the dun are unmistakably a slaty-blue or inky colour. It is an insect which when once recognized is not easily forgotten.

Although the iron-blue dun is one of the smaller ephemerids, and considerably smaller than the olive dun, there is some variation in the size of the insect even on the same river and as already mentioned above, the spring variety is rather larger than the summer one. Beyond that the fisherman need not trouble about the difference between the species as it is too slight to be of any consequence.

The male spinner is known as the Jenny spinner and is quite unmistakable. Apart from its shiny wings, brownish thorax and two long tails, it has an almost white body, tipped with red. This makes a particularly striking two-piece suiting, yet curiously enough trout do not find it at all attractive and consequently the artificial is seldom worth using.

I always feel that the old names bestowed on many flies by Theakston were better and more easily understood than those we use to-day. The Jenny spinner conveys nothing, but Theakston's name for the male imago was the Pearl spinner which well suggests the nearly transparent pearly appearance of this fly. The extreme delicacy of the wings is the despair of most fly-dressers who try to copy them. The usual method to overcome the difficulty is to tie the pattern "buzz" to give it a gauze wing effect, using for the purpose some tiny pale grey feather.

However, it is the female spinner which trout really like and it is surprising that anglers have not found a popular name for her, although sometimes she is known as the claret spinner. Her wings are much like those of the male spinner but her dress is a dark reddish-brown with a touch of claret in both thorax and body.

The iron-blue hatch usually lasts until late afternoon and often causes trout to rise in a peculiarly violent manner, which should provide the fisherman with a clue as to what they are taking.

In view of the fondness trout have for this insect, it is only natural to find that fly-tiers have long paid special attention to copying it, although it is by no means an easy fly to imitate satisfactorily. Chetham gave a dressing for it in 1681, as also did Bowlker (1747) who knew the fly well and was the first to point out that it was particularly abundant on cold stormy days. Ronalds, Jackson, and David Foster were others who provided dressings for it.

Apart from the patterns bearing the iron-blue name, there are many others designed to imitate the natural insect in one of its stages. Among the best-known patterns, wet and dry, there are the Blue Dun, Houghton Ruby, Dark Watchet, Snipe and Purple, Pheasant Tail, and Rusty Spinner.

We are indebted to Halford for a good imitation of the male fly for which he gave this tie:

Wings: Dark starling dyed blue-black.
Hackles: Two grizzly dun cock hackles.
Body: Stripped condor dyed dark olive green.
Whisk: Gallina to match body.
Head: Three turns of horsehair dyed dark Van Dyck brown.
Hook: 15.

Some anglers may like better a more modern floating fly dressed as follows:

Tying silk: Crimson or claret.
Wings: Starling dyed inky-blue.
Whisks: White or palest blue cock.
Body: Peacock quill from the eye, dyed inky-blue, or darkest heron herl from a big secondary, ribbed with fine gold wire.
Hackle: Rusty-blue dun cock, darkish.
Hook: 16.

Another favourite dressing for the dry fly is:

Wings: Tomtit's tail.
Body: Mole's fur dyed purple.
Hackle and Whisks: Honey dun.
Hook: 14 to 16.

Then there is an old Irish (wet) tie as under:

Body: Darkest mole's fur, mixed with a little fiery brown mohair, the last two
turns picked out for legs.
Wings: Swift's quill feather (second or third leader).
Tail: Two fibres of rat's whiskers.
Hook: 14.

In the west-country there is a hackled pattern which proves attractive in the spring, dressed as follows:

Body: Claret quill.
Hackle and Whisks: Almost black, with brown tips.
Hook: 14.

A pattern of the nymph type will often give excellent results and of the several available, all of which are, of course, fished wet, I should choose the following which was suggested by Mr. Skues:

Tying silk: Crimson, waxed with brow
Body: Mole's fur dubbed on tying silk, well waxed, the sun exposed for two
or three turns at tail and shoulder.
Whisks: Two or three strands of soft white hackle, short.
Legs: The very short, nearly black, hackle from the throat of a cock jackdaw,
not exceeding two turns.
Hook: 16, round bend.

The novelty of this pattern lies in the use of a hackle so small as to suggest legs only. In Yorkshire it appears to be employed to imitate the wings. This is a much better pattern than that given for the iron-blue in *Minor Tactics*, and one which from experience, I can recommend with great confidence.

Before leaving the Iron-Blue Dun, it may be of interest to recall that it was the favourite pattern of Harry Plunket Greene, the author of that delightful book, *Where the Bright Waters Meet*. Writing about the fly therein, he said: "If I was to be limited to one fly only for the rest of my life, I would scrap all the others and stick to the Iron-Blue Quill. It is not merely a Test fly, for I have caught a two-pound trout with it in a little Scottish burn, casting it dry on chance up-stream into a likely place. There used to be a superstition that the iron-blue was a bad-weather fly and only useful in a thunderstorm, but my experience is that it is the best of them all on glass-smooth water in bright sunshine. In fact, it is often the only fly they will take in such conditions, and it is certainly the only thing they will look at when they are smutting. . . . Everyone knows the 'fisherman's curse', which in spite of its diminutive size, monopolizes the whole attention of the fish when it is coming down. . . . The Iron-Blue is the only fly of regulation pattern which will take in these circumstances."

Only once, when I was still at school, did I meet the author of the above. He came to sing to us, and when the concert was over I had the privilege of a short talk with him, and well remember the advice which he then gave me; that wherever I fished, I should never go far wrong if I stuck to the Irón-Blue!

JANE CRAIG STREAMER

Streamer flies are great favourites in America, and are widely used for catching salmon, trout, bass, and many other types of fish. The Streamer effect is obtained by the long wing projecting well beyond the bend of the hook. The material for the wings may be hair, herls or long hackles, the latter usually tied back to back in pairs or bunches. The dressing given here is a typical example:

Body: Flat silver tinsel.
Throat: White cock hackle.
Wings: Six long white hackle feathers.
Topping: Bright green peacock herl.
Cheeks: Jungle cock.
Head: Black varnish.

JENNY SPINNER. See IRON-BLUE DUN

JERRY MA DIDDLER

As is evident from its name, this fancy (wet) pattern hails from the other side of the Atlantic—from Canada. It has proved a great success on Irish loughs.

Dressing:

Tag: Scarlet.
Body: Dark green wool.
Hackle: Claret.
Wings: Brown turkey with a strip of goose, dyed scarlet, on each side.
Hook: 8 to 12.

JULY DUN

The olive dun is a spring and autumn insect but in July and August, a smaller dun makes its appearance on most rivers. It has a dark greenish body and grey-blue wings. The female spinner's body is a dark olive colour tinged with gold, which when she is spent, turns to a rusty claret tint.

This olive-like fly, now identified as *Baetis scambus*, was not recognized by professional entomologists and for that reason, it was ignored by Halford. But it is well-known to anglers by two popular names—the summer olive and the July dun. It is the female spinner of this insect which so frequently makes her way to the river-bed (there to deposit her eggs) via the fisherman's waders.

Many artificial representations are available, and, in fact, most of the old authorities (except Halford) give ties for an artificial, usually with bodies dubbed with a mixture of blue fur and yellow wool, or with other furs.

There is no doubt that during the summer months, when the natural fly is on the water, the July Dun is a most useful pattern.

Skues's tie is one of the most popular. Rather like his olive variety of the Greenwell, it is dressed as follows:

Tying silk: Primrose or yellow, waxed with clear wax.
Rib: Fine gold wire.
Hackle: Greenish-yellow olive cock.
Body: Dubbed with two or three strands of pale herl from the breast of a heron, dyed yellow-olive in picric acid.
Whisks: As hackle.
Wings: Starling, from palest to dark.
Hook: 15.

When the dun is coming down on the surface in July, and trout are paying attention to its nymph, the best "medicine" is the July Dun Nymph—another Skues pattern—with this dressing:

Silk: Bright yellow, well waxed.
Whisks: Soft dark blue hen.
Body: Mixed dubbing of olive seal's fur and a small amount of bear's hair, dark brown and woolly, taken from close to the skin, and bunched at the shoulder to suggest wing-cases. The lower part of the body is ribbed with fine gold wire.
Legs: A couple of turns of dark rusty dun hackle, very short.
Hook: 15 or 16.

The spinner is well suggested by either Pheasant Tail or the Rusty Spinner.

KILL DEVIL

A general name for a series of long hackled patterns, invented, I believe, by the late David Foster of Ashbourne. They have stubby peacock herl bodies with hackles varying in colour, according to the pattern. Reference to the illustration will show the style of these flies which certainly kill on the Dove and other Derbyshire rivers, being suitable for both trout and grayling.

KNOTTED MIDGE. See BLACK GNAT

LAMPORT'S SPECIAL

An American pattern invented by Mr. E. Lamport, of Medford, Oregon. In spite of its unusual appearance, it is a definite attempt to imitate some natural insect and in this country, fished wet or dry, it is quite effective to suggest a sedge, or possibly the hatching pupa. We have such a tremendous number of patterns of our own that it is seldom worth persevering with American flies which, on the whole, are not suited to our rivers. Whether Lamport's Special would prove to be an exception I cannot say, but on the few occasions I have used it, trout have shown a definite liking for it. The dressing is:

Body: Quill dyed salmon pink.
Rib: Yellow Silk.
Hackle: Bright red cock.
Wings: Brown Drake.
Horns: Two strands of cock pheasant's tail feather, from in front of head to rear of body and tied in at the shoulder.
Hook: 12.

LARGE RED SEDGE (*Phryganea grandis, P. Striata*)

Known as the murragh in some districts of Ireland and the bustard in parts of northern England, this is the largest of our sedges, having a body about three-quarters of an inch in length and a wing spread of two inches, or a fraction more in the case of the female. The body is dark reddish-brown, with reddish-brown wings, flecked and mottled with lighter markings. The two setae are slightly longer than the body. There is not much likelihood of this fly being confused with other sedges as its size makes it conspicuous and almost unmistakable. Strictly speaking the name large red sedge is applied to two different species but they are so nearly alike that anglers find it convenient to treat them as one and the same insect.

This sedge is not uncommon on our southern streams and occurs in many other parts of the country, whilst it is also found on numerous Irish rivers and loughs, especially in Mayo and Galway, where the natural insect is a favourite lure for dapping.

Appearing first in May, it remains until the end of the season, but being one of the night-flying caddis flies, it is seldom seen by fishermen much before dusk. In fact, probably most anglers recognize it as being the very large sedge which appears towards dark on calm evenings in June and often during the mayfly hatch.

Too large to imitate conveniently, I know of no special pattern designed as a copy of it, neither does it occur in sufficient numbers to warrant one. If for any reason an imitation should be wanted, almost any of the patterns designed to imitate the smaller sedges should serve the purpose.

LEE'S FAVOURITE

A wet pattern, popular in Westmorland and Cumberland, and one on which Mr. Richard Clapham, the angling writer, kills a great many trout. He tells me that except for an occasional change to a Black Spider he seldom uses anything else for fishing becks, tarns, and lakes. I can well believe that it kills well for dressed as a hackled fly, it becomes a William's Favourite, and tied in that manner Mr. Clapham has found it just as effective. His dressing for Lee's Favourite is:

Body: Black silk, ribbed with silver.
Wings: Blae.
Hackle: Black.
Hook: 14.

The same fly proves attractive on lochs, tied with a jay wing.

LIGHT CAHILL

A standard and popular pattern in U.S.A. and Canada, usually fished as a floater. Its origin is attributed to a fly-dresser named Cahill, who was born in Dublin and emigrated to New York.

The original tie was:
Wings: From the flank feather of a male wood duck.
Hackle: Brownish grey or buff.
Body: Light creamy-grey crewel wool.
Tail: Cock's hackle.
Hook: 12 to 14.

LIGHT WOODCOCK

A standard north-country wet pattern to imitate the smaller perlidae. Sometimes called the Little Winter Brown. Pritt's tie was:

Wings: Hackled with a feather from the outside of a woodcock's wing.
Body: Orange silk with a spare dubbing of hare's ear.
Hook: 14.

Jackson recommends a feather from a hen pheasant's wing, but most anglers prefer the dressing given above.

LITTLE BROWN SEDGE

Since sedges of various species are found throughout the British Isles for the greater part of the season on almost every river and lake and are much loved by fish, the majority of anglers carry two or three patterns to imitate them. The artificial Sedge is at all times a most reliable evening fly and there is no better all-round pattern in my opinion than the Little Brown Sedge.

The name for this pattern is my own, designed to distinguish it from the better-known Brown Sedge. The latter is a standard pattern, tied with a brown floss silk body, whereas the fly under review has a body of mixed wool. The difference seems to be slight, but it was an inspiration on somebody's part for this little alteration greatly increases the attractiveness of the fly.

The Little Brown Sedge, fished wet or dry, will kill well on every type of river or loch from June to September. Always a useful evening fly, it will often prove quite as deadly in the day-time; is particularly effective for trout nosing amongst weed-beds, and is good medicine for rainbows. Who invented this pattern, I know not, but it may justly be ranked with the Little Red Sedge as one of the most effective suggestions of the natural insects.

The tie is:

Body: Orange tying silk, dubbed with a mixture of fawn and brown wool, ribbed with fine gold wire.
Hackle: Red cock's, carried down the body from shoulder to tail.
Wings: Red hen (Rhode Island).
Hook: 14.

The wings should be tied in to slope over the body. For the dry fly they can be bunched and rolled, or double split, as desired.

LITTLE CHAP

As I have said elsewhere, the aristocratic trout of the chalk streams with such an abundance of ephemerids at their disposal, find beetles and other plebeian insects of very little interest. In other rivers, they are of some importance, although anglers are inclined to neglect them.

Whilst engaged in compiling this book, I sought Mr. Skues's

opinion on the value of beetle-patterns, although aware, of course, that most of his fishing has been done on the southern streams. His reply shows that he has always been alive to their possibilities and I cannot do better than quote what he said.

"I was still a beginner at fly-dressing when I saw in the window of a small tackle shop facing the law courts (London), then building, an orange beetle with a yellow belly, both back and belly of floss, and legs of dyed gut, which I soon afterwards imitated. I lost the one copy I tied after catching with it a nice brace of trout on the Colne at Uxbridge. I tied other beetles with brown hen feather back, peacock herl body, and black hackles, after Hewitt Wheatley's illustrations in *Rod and Line* (1894), but did little good with them on the Tweed. While still contributing to the *Fishing Gazette* under the pen-name 'Val Conson', I received from a Welsh angler whose name I have ungratefully forgotten, the following dressing of the Little Chap, which is really good and has given me trout up to three pounds.

"*Tying silk:* Crimson.
Hackle: Hen with dark blue centre and ginger-red points.
Body: Peacock's herl body from stem of eye feathers dyed fully in magenta.
Hook: 16, round bend.

"Lightly dressed: useful on rough streams as well as on chalk streams. See *Side Lines*, page 160."

The reference in *Side Lines* relates to an olive-green beetle which had the effect of making the big Itchen trout move from under the banks and set them cruising in midstream. Mr. Skues devised a satisfactory copy of it, similar to the Little Chap, but with an olive hackle. The dressing given above is well worth a trial when trout are smutting in the spring.

In the north of England, the Little Chap, ribbed with silver, is sometimes called the Smoke Fly and is considered an effective grayling pattern.

LITTLE MARRYAT

A chalk stream dry fly to imitate the sub-imago of the pale watery, named after G. S. Marryat, who with H. S. Hall, did so much to develop the dry fly in its modern form. Dressed on a size 14 hook, it is known as the Whitchurch Dun, Mr. Marryat's improved version of this pattern is the Quill Marryat, but both flies are useful. The original dressing is:

Wings: Palest starling.
Body: Fur from the flank of the Australian opossum.
Hackles: Two pale Cochin cock hackles.
Whisk: Pale olive gallina.   *Hook:* 16.

The opossum body is unusual, although the fur should not be difficult to procure, for in parts of New Zealand the animal is now so
numerous as to be considered a pest by the farmers. Its use here is
accounted for by the fact that Marryat spent many years in Australia.
To-day peacock is often used for the body.

Mr. Skues has an excellent modification of this old pattern:

Tying silk: White or pale straw colour.
Hackle and Whisk: Cream dun cock.
Body: Fur from a baby seal.
Wing: Pale starling.
Hook: 16.

Both of the above dressings make first-class grayling flies, but a fur
body is preferable to one of peacock.

LITTLE PALE BLUE

In an article written many years ago, Mr. Skues gave the dressing
of this fly which he recommended as being a useful pattern for rough
streams. It is a variation of the Blue Dun.

Tying silk: Yellow.
Body: Dubbed with hare's pelt.
Whisks: Pale blue, soft.
Hackle: Pale honey dun hen.
Wings: Darkish part of a primary of the small black-headed gull.
Hook: 16.

LITTLE RED SEDGE

A capital pattern from May to September, serving as a general impression of many sedge flies. Designed by Mr. Skues, it will take trout
and grayling on most rivers all afternoon and up to the evening rise
whenever up-winged duns are not present in force, although it is
naturally as an evening fly that it really comes into its own.

It has an additional merit and an important one, for it is deadly for
trout which are nosing amongst weed-beds, showing their fins and
backs but not breaking the surface. At such times, they are most difficult to tempt but if one can attract their attention with this pattern,
they will take it, as like as not.

Mr. Skues's dressing for the Little Red Sedge is:

Tying silk: Hot orange, waxed with brown wax.
Body Hackle: Long deep-red cock with short fibres, tied in at the shoulder and carried down to the tail.
Rib: Fine gold wire binding down the body hackle.
Body: Darkest hare's ear.
Wings: Landrail wing, bunched and rolled, and tied on sloping well back over the tail.
Front Hackle: Like body hackle but larger, and long enough to tie five or six times in front of the wing.
Hook: 14.

This pattern may be varied by splitting the wings and though equally as effective, it results in the fly not wearing so well. It may also be winged with two single strands of the pinion feather of a capercailzie dyed hot orange.

LOCK'S FANCY

One of the best imitations of the pale wateries, this well-known pattern was invented by John Lock, of Andover. A good dry pattern for both trout and grayling. The tie is:

Body: Pale primrose silk (turning greenish when wet), ribbed with fine gold wire.
Hackle and Whisks: Pale honey dun cock.
Wings: Light starling.
Hook: 14 to 16.

Except that he liked a little fur dubbing on the body, this fly is almost exactly the same as Ronalds's Blue Dun as given in the later editions of his *Fly-Fisher's Entomology.*

LUNN'S HACKLED CAPERER. See CAPERER

LUNN'S PARTICULAR

Mr. W. J. Lunn, who was born in 1862, went to the Test as a river-keeper when he was twenty, and was given sole charge of the Houghton Club's waters on the 1st January 1887, a post which he retained for forty-five years. It was not until 1916, however, that he commenced fly-dressing, but in the next few years he produced a number of patterns which have since become well known to all dry fly-fishers, although the majority are more effective on the chalk streams than elsewhere. Probably his best-known flies are Lunn's Particular, the Houghton Ruby, and his Hackled Caperer, and all of them are first rate. To have invented so many famous patterns in so short a time was a remarkable feat, even for one who was a keen observer and who had unique opportunities of studying natural trout flies. The story of his life and work became the subject of a book, Major J. W. Hills' *River Keeper*.

The "Particular" was first tied in the spring of 1917 as a representation of the olive spinner and throughout the season it is a reliable pattern which is always worth trying on a strange river where the trout are inclined to be particular, since it is reputed to have the faculty of attracting shy feeders.

Whether this is so or not, I do not know, but there is no doubt that the pattern is one of the best dry flies for general use on chalk streams. Major Hills had a very high opinion of it as is shown by the following extract from his book on Lunn. "It kills well when fish are taking olives and is marvellously good when they are shy or are taking spinners. If I had to be limited to one fly, I should choose this."

Lunn's dressing was:

Hackle: Medium Rhode Island cock hackle.
Wings: Two medium blue cock hackle-points put on flat.
Tail: Four fibres of Rhode Island from large hackle.
Body: Undyed hackle stalk of Rhode Island cock hackle.
Tying silk: Pearsall's gossamer, shade 13.
Hook: 14.

McCASKIE'S GREEN CAT

Named after a cat (from which the fur was taken for the dressing) which belonged to Dr. Norman McCaskie, a member of the Flyfishers' Club, this pattern proved a great lure for both trout and grayling. The full story of the fly is recounted by Mr. Skues in his *Side-Lights, Side-Lines, and Reflections*, and I cannot do better than give an extract from what he writes there. "I have taken and lost a good many good fish by its agency—but I have never been able to reproduce with my hackle the action and appearance of a wet and disconsolate daddy-long-legs in the throes of dissolution, so I have never been as successful as McCaskie with this particular pattern.

"I have, however, found that when in the day time the trout are taking blue-winged olive nymphs (and they never, or almost never, take the blue-winged olive in sub-imago form during the day) a fly dressed on a No. 1 hook with pale orange silk dubbed lightly and loosely with McCaskie's Green Cat and hackled lightly with soft dark blue henny hackle and glycerined to sink properly is really very effective, even in the hands of an angler who has a prejudice in favour of thinking he knows why he uses any particular pattern rather than another."

The dressing is as follows:

Tying silk: Pale orange waxed with clear wax.
Hackle: Soft dark blue henny cockerel as blue as possible (like the blue wing of a b.-w.o.).
Whisks: Soft honey dun cock's shoulder hackle.
Body: Blue cat's fur, dyed for thirty-six hours in picric acid.
Hook: No. 14 or 13 t.d.e. round bend.

It will often be taken in the day-time when the b.-w.o. is hatching and again in the evening. Also a good grayling pattern.

MALLARD AND CLARET, etc. See CLARET AND MALLARD

MALLOCH'S FAVOURITE

There must be few fishermen who do not know "Mallochs of Perth", the old-established tackle dealers. For several generations the family have produced some of the finest loch anglers in Scotland, which is sufficient guarantee for the well-known lake fly which bears their name. The dressing is:

Body: Peacock quill from the eye, tipped with silver.
Hackle: Blue dun hen.
Wings: Woodcock wing feather.
Tail: Red cock hackle fibres.
Hook: 8 to 14.

MARCH BROWN (*Rhithrogena haarupi and Ecdyurus venosus*)

The Natural Insect

That two species of march brown exist has only been confirmed during the lifetime of most living anglers. Previously British fishermen had accepted Halford's classification and had looked upon *E. venosus* as being the only march brown. Now, thanks to Mr. Martin Mosely and Dr. Esben-Peterson, the Danish entomologist, we know that the insect which hatches in enormous quantities (usually about noon) during March and April is *R. haarupi*. This, the true march brown, is found on most rough rocky rivers in Great Britain, although it is seldom seen on slow-flowing waters and is unknown on the chalk streams. It has several local names including the brown drake, cob fly, dun drake, and caughlan (Ireland).

The march brown (*E. venosus*) which appears in May and June does not do so in anything like such great numbers and consequently trout do not show the same great enthusiasm about it.

A larger member of the Ephemeroptera, the march brown has four wings, two setae, a brownish body and mottled brown wings. This applies to both species but *E. venosus* is rather larger and hatches sparsely in May and June and occasionally in late April and early July. Its dun is altogether lighter than that of *R. haarupi* and its wings are marked with more definite brown blotches and smears. I have known anglers confuse a June march brown with a mayfly, doubtless on account of its size for there is very little similarity otherwise, and the march brown, as already mentioned, has only two setae. Any big specimen seen in June will belong to *E. venosus* species and will probably be a female, which, as in the case of the mayfly, is larger than the male, and nearly as large as a mayfly.

The duns of both species are almost exactly the same and it is in the nymphal and imago stages that the main differences are apparent.

The spinner of *R. haarupi* is seldom seen, but it is a dark-coloured insect, with no red about it, and which is neither of interest to fish nor fishermen. The spinner which has long been known to anglers as the great red spinner is the imago of *E. venosus* and is a large bright ruddy fly which is quite unmistakable. The nymphs I have left to the last for they are possibly of more importance to the fly-fisherman than are the duns or the spinners of either species. In both instances, the nymphs are large and flat with the body broad in proportion to its length and they are ideally built for clinging to stones and rocks or for sheltering underneath them. Their streamlined shape prevents them being greatly affected by the current and they can swim strongly since their flattened legs act as oars. There the similarity between the larvae of the two species ends, for those of *R. haarupi* are nearly black in colour, whilst those of *E. venosus* are of a definite dull brick-red.

Their habits and behaviour are much the same, although the latter crawl out to hatch on land. The *haarupi* nymphs, however, make their way to the surface some little time before hatching and then sink down again to the bed of the river. This process may be repeated several times during a period of half an hour or so before the metamorphosis takes place on the surface and frequently in the strongest current. That, at this time, trout take a heavy toll of them is not surprising for the insects being some distance from any shelter must be "easy meat" for the fish which doubtless relish a large and succulent nymph after the meagre rations of the winter months. Since fish like these larvae so much, and have so little difficulty in securing them, some form of imitation is essential to any angler who ever fishes an artificial nymph. Not for a minute do I believe that it must be a close copy of the natural larva (which is a most difficult insect to copy satisfactorily) and I am certain that some hackled patterns of wet flies will prove more effective.

There are other species of Ecdyurus, and therefore members of the march brown family, but they are less common and of little interest to fishermen. *E. insignis* is a small insect with light sepia-grey wings (without the characteristic blotches) and with black setae. Its male spinner has a very pale green abdomen with the last few segments of light brownish-yellow. *E. volitans* occurs on the Thames and another moderately common species, *E. lateralis*, is rather similar in appearance to an olive dun.

The march brown has one great peculiarity; whereas the artificial is known to every fishermen and is one of the oldest standard patterns, it is surprising how little knowledge the average angler has of the natural insect although in March and April it hatches out in countless thousands on northern streams and on Welsh rivers such as the Usk. That south-country authors have mostly ignored it is understandable since the march brown is of little interest to them, but that other writers should have given it such scant attention is difficult to understand. Very few writers of the past or present make more than an odd perfunctory remark about it, concentrating almost entirely on the artificial imitations. But the march brown is one of the most important angler's flies on any rocky fast river and a hatch will cause the water to boil as the trout take the fly. Doubtless the reason why so many fly-fishers are not better acquainted with these phenomenal rises is that they occur in the early part of the season before the majority of anglers have commenced to fish. Whether the artificial is much good during the time that the natural insect is on the water in great strength is a different matter. From my own experience, I rather doubt if it is, but as I seldom fish before the middle of April, I have had little opportunity of observing the really heavy hatches of *R. haarupi*.

The Artificial Fly

Without any shadow of doubt, the artificial March Brown is one of the most universally used flies and few patterns have maintained their popularity over such a lengthy period. Cotton gave a dressing for it and so did Chetham (1681) who called it the Moorish Brown. Bowlker in 1747 gave the tie as hare's fur ribbed with yellow silk and with a wing from either a partridge or a pheasant, so that the pattern has remained practically unaltered for two hundred years. Since the first mention of it, almost every angling author has made some reference to the fly and has recommended it as being one of the indispensable patterns.

Although some fly-fishermen, including myself, feel that its high reputation is not fully justified, there is no denying that the March Brown is one of the most regularly used patterns in the early part of the season or that it will take fish at almost any period of the year, since it attracts trout even when the natural insect is not on the water.

What trout take it for has long been a subject for speculation and argument. As a suggestion of some sedges, it serves a useful purpose and it is supposed also to represent the turkey brown and the brown silverhorns. That it is sometimes taken for a freshwater shrimp, I have no doubt; and with the whisks removed, it makes a reasonably good imitation of the grannom. It also imitates quite nicely those small brown grass-moths, which during the summer months, teem amongst the long meadow-grass and which sometimes get carried on to the water in great numbers. Mr. G. E. M. Skues probably hit the nail on the head when he wrote that the March Brown "is an excellent fly, and as generally tied, quite a poor imitation of the natural fly and quite a passable one of almost anything else".

Whatever trout may take it for, the March Brown is a pattern which, except on the southern streams, must always be one of the first choices of every fisherman during the early months of the season; and it often produces good sport whether fished wet or dry, as a winged fly, a hackled fly, or a nymph, and whether used on river, brook, lake, or pool. Of the many dressings, the following two may be taken as probably the most typical.

Male:

Body: Copper-coloured silk, dubbed with fur from a hare's ear, and yellow mohair mixed well together, and ribbed with yellow tying silk.
Legs: From the back of a partridge.
Tail: Two strands from a partridge tail.
Wings: From the inner quill feather of a hen pheasant's wing, or from a partridge tail.
Hook: 12.

Female:

As above, but the body ribbed with fine gold wire in place of the silk, and with the wings lighter in shade.

To-day a hackled pattern is more generally favoured and one of the best dressings of this type is that recommended by Mr. Skues. He tells me that it was given to him by a Yorkshire fly-fisherman, Mr. Raffit, who was the north-country expert mentioned by Halford in connection with the experiment of fishing northern wet flies on the Test. The tie is:

Tying silk: Hot orange.
Body: Dubbed with hare's poll, strongly dyed hot orange.
Hackle: Snipe rump feather finished off behind the shoulder.
Hook: 13.

It always seems to me that snipe rump is better for wing or hackle than the more usual partridge or pheasant since it is closer in colouring to the natural insect. It figures prominently in the following dressing which is that recommended by Messrs. Edmonds and Lee in *Brook and River Trouting.*

Wings: Hackled with a mottled brown feather from a snipe's rump.
Body: Orange silk, dubbed with fur from the nape of a rabbit's neck, which has been lightly tinged red with Crawshaw's Red Spinner dye, and ribbed with gold wire or tinsel.
Tail: Two strands from a feather from a snipe's rump, same feather as is used for the wings.
Head: Orange silk.
Hook: 12 and 13.

A good many fishermen have great faith in the March Brown Spider, which is normally, of course, fished wet, but which is occasionally used as a floater with good results. Like all northern "spider" flies, this pattern should be very lightly hackled. It is subject to some variation but the following may be taken as a typical dressing:

Whisks: Two strands from a mottled brown partridge's tail.
Body: Dark hare's ear mixed with a little claret wool and ribbed with yellow or primrose silk.
Hackle: A long-fibred feather from a partridge's back.
Hook: 12 to 14.

Except for those who are fortunate to do all their fishing on the chalk streams, where the natural fly is never seen, I suppose that the great majority of anglers would agree that the March Brown is deservedly a favourite pattern. That they would be correct, there cannot be much doubt, although it is not a fly in which I have ever had much faith, and that in spite of the fact that I have seen many wonderful catches of trout made upon it. But they have been made by others and not by myself, which makes a difference, for it is a fact that however killing it may be, one will never do much with any fly in which one lacks confidence.

My own experience is that whereas the artificial is an effective pattern during April and the first part of May just as long as there are very few march browns on the water, it loses most of its charm directly the natural insects commence to hatch in great numbers and fish start to pay serious attention to them.

As soon as that happens, it seems wise to discard the artificial and to resort to a Welsh Partridge, Williams's Favourite, or a Partridge and Orange. Fished either wet or slightly submerged, one or other of them will nearly always bring success, due, I suspect, to the fact that they are all nymph-suggesting patterns. And I am convinced that when fish are really taking the natural march brown freely, an imitation or suggestion of the nymph of that fly will produce better sport than any copy of the winged insect.

My own crude and lazy method of making a suitable nymph is to trim a March Brown with a pair of scissors, removing nine-tenths of the wings and cutting back the hackle, until it more or less resembles a nymph. Although this plan works admirably, it is not likely to appeal to everybody. There are men who are particular and who require a more natural-looking object and for these, the following Skues dressing for a march brown nymph can be recommended. It should satisfy the most fastidious.

Whisks: Two short strands of cock pheasant's tail.
Body: Herl of cock pheasant's tail.
Ribbing: Fine gold wire.
Thorax: Bunch of hare's ear at shoulder.
Legs: Partridge light brown feather.
Hook: 13.

That makes a very nice pattern and one which should deceive fish far better than my rough "cut-me-down", although, whether, in practice, it will kill more trout is another matter.

There is another most killing dressing for a nymph which proves effective in the early months of the season and which is a copy of the *R. haarupi* nymph just before ecdysis. It has been used with success on many rivers including the Scottish border streams. The tie was suggested (and invented, I believe) by Major J. D. D. Evans, who is a skilful angler and one of our foremost trout-fly entomologists. As he lives on the banks of the Usk, a river notable for its huge hatches of march browns, it may be safely assumed that any copy of that insect which he recommends is worth special attention. The method of dressing is as follows:

Setae: Three fibres of the biggest white gallina procurable, dyed dark sepia, or three brown turkey feathers. The former are better because the turkey feathers are inclined to stick together when wet.

Body and Hackle: Dub half the length of the hook shank with a mixed fur compound made up of black rabbit, seal's dyed black, seal's dyed claret, and a very small amount of fur dyed fiery-brown (crottle). Rib with fine gold wire and tie in about six fibres of any large dark feather such as turkey, so that the list or top-side is upwards and the fibres are facing tailwards. Dub a big hump for the thorax and then bring over the fibres and tie them down to represent the wing-cases. Cut off the top fibres. The effect will be improved by a coat of cellulose varnish over the wing-cases.

Hook: 11 or 12.

The March Brown is subject to a number of variations to meet local conditions, and on the right occasion, most of them will kill well. Some of the most generally used are listed below.

SILVER MARCH BROWN

A well-known and popular pattern with a flat silver tinsel body, ribbed with oval wire. In other respects it conforms to the conventional dressing. A favourite loch fly and an excellent sea-trout pattern in all parts of Great Britain.

GOLD MARCH BROWN

Similar to the above, but with gold substituted for silver. The same observations also apply.

CLARET MARCH BROWN

The ordinary pattern, but tied with a claret hackle. Useful as a lake fly and popular in Ireland and New Zealand.

RED-LEGGED MARCH BROWN

A favourite throughout Wales, both for lake and river fishing. It is the standard winged fly tied with a red cock's hackle and is fished wet or dry. Possibly it suggests a sedge and it is generally most effective in the evening. Although a useful pattern, I think that the Welsh Partridge is an improvement upon it.

PURPLE MARCH BROWN

A modern pattern used mostly in Scotland and usually fished wet. It differs from the standard fly in that the body is of purple wool, ribbed with yellow silk, or sometimes with fine gold wire.

GINGER MARCH BROWN

One of the most effective patterns for autumn use and which on occasions kills exceptionally well. The dressings vary as regards wings and body, but one which I have found satisfactory is dressed thus:

Wings: From the inner quill feather of a hen pheasant's wing.
Hackle: Ginger cock's.
Body: Hare's fur spun on yellow tying silk.
Tail: Two or three whisks of ginger cock.
Hook: 14.

This can be tied as a dry fly but is generally fished wet.

MARLOW BUZZ

This is a very old pattern suitable for suggesting a wide range of beetles. The dressing is almost exactly the same as that for the Coch-y-bondhu and only differs from it in being ribbed with gold all down the body instead of only at the tip. When used for grayling, a tag of red or white wool is sometimes added. If my recollection is not at fault, the Marlow Buzz is very like the Pupil-Teacher which used to be a wonderful killer on the streams in South Wales, save that the latter had a blue dun hackle. Marlow Buzz, like Bracken Clock and Fern-web, is a name occasionally used to denote the natural coch-y-bondhu beetle, *P. horticola.*

MARSTON'S FANCY

Although apparently out of favour to-day, this is a good general fly which deserves consideration. It was the invention of the late R. B. Marston, of the *Fishing Gazette,* who knew too much about artificial flies to allow his name to be associated with any pattern which he could not recommend to brother anglers.

A wet fly, it is tied as follows:

Body: Dark bronze peacock herl, with a tag of gold tinsel and a red silk head.
Wings: Dark wing feather of a starling.
Tail: Three strands of black bear.
Hook: 12 to 14.

This should also serve well as a lake pattern.

MASON

This pattern was designed by myself for presentation on a certain occasion to General Sir Francis Davies, K.C.B., K.C.M.G. It was made up in Masonic colours as a salmon fly and was never seriously intended as a fish lure but tied in trout sizes it has killed sea-trout and a goodly number of rainbows. Possibly it is taken for a small trout or salmon parr for most of the fish I have caught on it have seized it with a pronounced rush. The dressing is:

Body: White silk ribbed with a few turns of flat tinsel, with three turns of silver twist at the tail.
Tail: Swan feather dyed dark blue.
Hackle: Dark blue.
Wing: White swan dyed pale blue with a strip of dark blue and one of white on each side.
Hook: 12; larger for sea-trout.

MAXWELL BLUE

MAXWELL RED

These two hackled patterns are used extensively throughout the west-country, but are little known in other parts of England. Both are good wet flies for general use, the Blue being but a local variety of the Blue Dun, whilst the Red is very similar to that splendid Welsh pattern, the Red-Legged March Brown. The dressing in both cases varies a little according to the district, but the following are usual:

MAXWELL BLUE
Body: Hare's flax (or grey seal's fur), ribbed fine silver wire.
Hackle: Medium to dark blue dun cock's.
Whisks: Three strands as hackle.
Hook: 14.

MAXWELL RED
Body: Hare's flax (or rusty-red seal's fur), ribbed fine gold wire.
Hackle: Red cock's.
Whisks: Three strands as hackle.
Hook: 14.

MAYFLY (*Ephemera danica: E. vulgata: E. lineata*)

Life History

The mayfly egg incubates in about ten to twelve weeks, although the period is a variable one, probably depending upon the temperature of the water. In one stretch of the River Windrush known to me, mayflies hatch a full week earlier in the top part than they do half a mile farther down where the stream receives a number of icy-cold springs. The young larva is of a dingy colour, lighter on the underside, with six legs, each with a single claw at its extremity, and three setae or tails.

The sub-surface life of the nymph is a complex one as during the two (sometimes three) years it lives under water, it undergoes a number of changes.

Born without gills, the larva has to breathe through its skin until the first change takes place when it is about ten days old for then breathing apparatus commences to form and it becomes a nymph.

From the start, the young larva burrows in the mud, silt, sand or clay on the bed or edges of the river or lake and it is from this that it extracts much of its food consisting of organic matter and microscopic larvae, although all nymphs are scavengers and little comes amiss to them.

The nymph is well adapted for digging, which it accomplishes with remarkable speed, as it possesses a wedge-shaped head, two powerful mandibles and very strong legs. The tunnel it constructs, although made with a margin for growth, will not be sufficiently commodious to allow the nymph to attain its full growth in it, so that from time to time, it is obliged to build a new and bigger gallery. Even the short journey this entails is apt to be a fatal one for there is scarcely a single inhabitant of the river, which if larger than the nymph will not attack and devour it; and the population of a river is a large one.

For the most part, therefore, the nymph remains at home, moving about as little as possible. If danger threatens when it is on the move, it will "freeze" until it is past for it is a poor swimmer and cannot hope to escape by that means.

How necessary are mud and lack of light to its existence may be appreciated by placing a nymph in clean water in a glass jar when it will survive for a short time only, whilst if mud be added and the jar kept in semi-darkness, the larva can be reared to maturity.

As this nymph reaches its full development after a couple of years or more, rudimentary wings commence to form under its skin and soon its internal organs undergo a change so that eventually it finds itself no longer able to live under water and is forced to seek a new method of life. It therefore proceeds to the surface by alternately swimming and kicking, although perhaps floating would be a better word than swimming.

Up till now the nymph has been constantly growing but since its skin has failed to grow with it, it has been regularly discarded. When the old skin has become too tight, the inevitable has happened; it has split open and the nymph has walked out of it robed in an entirely new garment. This will have happened frequently in the past although less frequently as the larva will have grown older and another moult has been due to occur.

The nymph will be about one and a half inches long by now and will be fully grown. If it is examined at this period, the form of the sub-imago can be clearly discerned through and underneath the nymphal skin. Its limbs and other organs can be seen and all of them quite perceptibly smaller than the corresponding limbs of the nymph in which they are still enveloped. If the creature is destined to become a female, the eggs which she will eventually lay can be clearly seen under a microscope since they are all developed within the nymph.

Having ascended to the surface, the nymph generally has to remain there for twenty to thirty minutes before it is ready for its next change. As the air under its skin which has permitted it to rise, also prevents it sinking to the bottom again, it must remain in great peril for this lengthy period. Its chances of survival would be small indeed could the trout cope with the thousands of hatching nymphs about them, but even a trout's appetite is limited.

Should the nymph survive it now goes through a complete transformation which is accomplished within a matter of seconds and if everything goes according to nature's plan, that ugly insect which was a nymph will energe as a beautiful fly—the sub-imago (dun) of the mayfly. When this change is about to occur, the nymph's skin splits at the shoulders and along the back and allows it to push its thorax and head through the opening thus made. Next the legs are disengaged and then the wings are withdrawn one by one from their covering cases and are unfolded and hoisted into an erect position; and finally the abdomen and setae are set free.

This is the normal order followed when the metamorphosis is successfully accomplished but sometimes accidents occur and the insect is unable to divest itself of some part of its nymphal shuck in which case it dies. Not only does the sub-imago shed its nymphal skin but on this occasion, it also discards all those organs for which it will have no further use. Amongst these are the mandibles, the mouth and the complicated breathing apparatus which up till this time has enabled it to extract oxygen from the water.

At times mayflies can be seen hatching out on the water in many hundreds. When first seen, there is only a speck on the surface but this grows larger and larger as the dun gets free of its nymphal shell until the emergence is finally completed and the newly hatched sub-imago carried downstream whilst drying its wings. When this has been accomplished, the fly uses its wings for the first time making a clumsy hesitating flight of only a few feet or even inches before it settles again on the surface of the river. There it rests, floating along the current like some small sailing ship, sometimes being involuntarily "turned about" when a gust of wind happens to catch its wings.

Although the dun is full-sized when hatched, these early trial flights are uncertain affairs as though the insect was not too sure of its ability to manage its new form of progression. They are certainly made as short as possible with frequent periods of rest on the water, while the dun is carried along with her wings aloft like those of a butterfly when at rest, in the characteristic manner of all the Ephemeridae.

After a few such flights and apparently satisfied that a more ambitious one may safely be tried, the dun leaves the river and flies to land where it seeks shelter and rest in trees, bushes, or in the long meadow-grass. This is another danger period for the insect for trout and birds will be watching and waiting so that many a dun perishes in the time between hatching and reaching the land.

The sub-imago is greenish-yellow in colour with more or less opaque wings which are covered with small hairs although these can only be seen when examined under a microscope. Both sexes of duns are known to anglers as green drakes. The foliage and uncut grass near the river are often thick with these newly hatched insects and should a ground frost occur at this time the mortality amongst them is tremendous. All those in the grass are doomed to die, but others which have sought shelter in trees and bushes may survive since frosts at this time of the year seldom rise more than a few feet above the ground.

After a period varying from twelve to twenty-four hours, the dun is ready for its final metamorphosis. Of all the groups of insects, the

Ephemeroptera is the only one of which the members undergo another change after they have reached the adult state and have attained the power of flight. But now the dun is to become an imago (spinner) and this final transformation is perhaps the most wonderful of all.

Although it is a deliberate process which takes several minutes to complete, it is not as well known to fishermen as is the change from nymph to dun, because it usually occurs on the underside of a leaf, and is consequently hidden from view. Grasping the leaf firmly, the sub-imago pulls and kicks itself out of its body covering and also out of the very skin of its wings, when (if all goes well) it emerges as an imago or fully developed insect.

After it has emerged, the discarded shuck of the body and the coverings of the wings are left behind and momentarily retain their original shape, although the latter soon collapse. The newly hatched spinner remains for some time clinging to the leaf or foliage which affords it protection and shelter whilst it becomes accustomed to its new status. The insect is slightly smaller than the dun (as one would expect since it has been compressed inside the sub-imago skin) and is an even more beautiful fly with clear wings tinged with blue and green and with a body more strongly marked with dark circular bands. The male imago is known to anglers as the black drake and the female as the grey drake. As a fully developed and perfect insect, the spinner has but one func-tion left to it—that of reproducing its species. Although it has no real mouth or digestive organs and consequently is unable to feed, its flight is strong and controlled and it is well able to enjoy the rest of its short life. The merry and enchanting aerial dances of the male spinners are well known to all anglers. On a warm afternoon, vast clouds of these flies will dance ceaselessly above the trees, bushes and meadows border-ing the water, rising and falling, constantly sweeping upwards and downwards, as if glorying in their new-found strength, although we know that nature has ordained that this will be only sufficient to permit them to fulfil their natural function. This dance of the male imagines is a necessary prelude to a fall of "spent gnat" on the water.

Should the day be too cold or blustery, the spinners are unable to undertake their dance and remain under cover until a warmer or quieter period occurs. Sometimes they will be seen dancing in thousands when a cold breeze springs up and the whole lot will immediately disappear, having been driven to shelter. But in warm weather the merry dance goes on, and ever and anon, a female imago will leave her sheltering bower to join the throng of dancing males. As soon as she reaches them, she will be seized by one (sometimes two) of them and after mating has taken place in the air, she will shake him off and return to land. The male will rejoin his fellows in their ceaseless nuptial dance, although not being given to monogamy, he will take another mate if an opportunity arises before his strength fails him.

I suppose most of us would like to think that the song of the birds and the dance of the mayfly spinners were expressions of the joy of living, but as regards the latter at any rate, there is a more mundane explanation. The main eyes of the male spinner are placed on the top of its head and are focused upwards. When the insects are driven together by the breeze, they drop downwards in order not to miss seeing any female passing over them, but since the earth limits their descent and they are incapable of hovering, they must constantly rise and fall. By some instinct, the female spinners (whose eyes are on the sides of their heads) know that the males' eyesight is keenest when focused upwards and consequently they fly above them.

Soon the time arrives when, again by some extraordinary instinct, hordes of gravid females are prompted to fly simultaneously to the river where, gracefully rising and dipping over the water, they expel batches of eggs which slowly sink to the bottom. Often on a quiet evening, thousands of female spinners may be observed over the water thus engaged. Even this simple act is in some ways remarkable for the male sperm is stored in a reservoir immediately inside the female's oviduct (the opening through which all the eggs must pass) with the result that each individual egg is automatically fertilized as it leaves her body.

The process of depositing the eggs is a rapid one in spite of the fact that each female may carry over six thousand of them. And for many it is an operation which is never concluded because as the spinners touch the water, fish are waiting for them. Should the fly manage to conclude her allotted task, as soon as her last egg has been dropped, she falls exhausted on to the water, where in a spent condition, with limp waterlogged wings outstretched, she is carried downstream on her last journey, her life cycle ended. After mating, the strength of the male spinner soon evaporates, and he, too, falls exhausted although more often on land than on the water. At times he does collapse on the river but that only happens if his strength fails as he flies towards the land.

As the imagines of both sexes are not able to replenish their strength by taking food, their life span in the winged state is short enough, and although it is longer than the twenty-four hours it is popularly supposed to be by most non-fishermen, it may not exceed four or five days, with about ten days as the extreme limit.

Both sexes of spent spinners are known by fishermen as spent drakes or "spent gnats". The latter term is obviously incorrect since there is nothing gnat-like about a mayfly, whereas the name spent drake is associated with the mallard drake which, for generations, has been used to wing the artificial fly.

It should be noted that the size of the hatch in any one season must necessarily depend upon what happened two years previously. A cold or very windy season will probably mean that the hatch of fly two years later may be a light one, although to some extent nature takes care to minimize the effects of abnormal weather. As has already been mentioned, the majority of nymphs hatch out after two years of life under water, but a few mature in one year, and a number require three years. In this manner the risk of an almost complete loss of life is lessened and a breeding nucleus is ensured.

That a warm or cold spring affects the date on which the mayfly hatches, I do not believe for one minute. The actual date will vary with different rivers but on the whole it occurs year after year with surprising constancy.

The Natural Mayfly

The mayfly (*E. danica*) appears in most parts where it is found towards the end of May or more usually early in June and continues for about three weeks. Widely distributed throughout England and Ireland, it is seldom found in the north or in Scotland. But in spite of its wide distribution, comparatively few rivers or lakes are favoured with a heavy hatch and in many places, although the mayfly may appear every year, the hatch is so sparse as to be of no interest to fish or fishermen. In most districts the mayfly season probably reaches its zenith in the first fortnight in June although there is considerable variation in different localities and on some Irish loughs it is not unusual for the fly to be well "on" by the middle of May, or more rarely, for big hatches to occur as late as August. Nevertheless, it is more of a June insect than one of May and if the name appears somewhat of an anomaly, this is due to the fact that the calendar was altered by eleven days in the year 1732, by which time the mayfly had already received the name which it still bears.

Of the three species, E. *vulgata* differs from E. *danica* in a minor degree only; hatches about the same period and remains for a similar time but generally it is found only on slow-running streams and on lakes. The third species, E. *lineata*, is rarely encountered.

The male spinner is of little importance to the angler, since as already mentioned, it seldom gets on to the water except by accident.

To give detailed descriptions of all the species in the various phases of their existence will not be necessary as the appearance of both duns and spinners is so well known to fishermen. Brief notes will therefore suffice.

All mayflies have four wings and three setae, and since these insects are so much larger than any other ephemerids, they are virtually unmistakable. The females are a little larger than the males and consequently the latter are sometimes thought to be "half-grown" flies, although actually, in common with all members of the Ephemeroptera, they do not alter in size after hatching. Not every fisherman knows that mayflies can hear; or rather that they have hearing organs which are situated in the wings, antennae and abdomen. This is true even of their nymphs.

The difference between a dun and a spinner is not difficult to determine as, like all species in this family, the dun has dull lustreless wings, hairy on the lower edges, and is clumsy in flight. The imago's wings are clear and glossy and its flight is strong and controlled.

The distinguishing features between males and females are many. The males (duns and spinners) have large eyes placed on the top of their heads, two small pincers at the tail (known as abdominal forceps), their forelegs are twice as long as the others and their setae are twice the length of their bodies. Females, however, have small eyes on the side of their heads, no abdominal forceps, forelegs the same length as the others and setae not longer than their bodies.

It may be as well to point out that in Scotland, the border counties, and throughout Yorkshire and Lancashire, the name mayfly is commonly used for the stone-fly (*Perla maxima*), and in some rural parts of the "West Country", the same name is used to denote the Hawthorne fly. For reasons which are not clear to me, modern entomologists have taken to using the term "may flies" as a generic name for all flies of the Ephemeroptera family. This seems to be a most illogical procedure since some of the species are to be found on the water throughout every month of the year, whilst to anglers, who have made the name mayfly particularly their own, the practice is apt to be confusing and annoying.

The Artificial Fly

Mayfly fishing, which coincides with the height of the angler's year, can prove a most exciting interlude and it can also be thoroughly disappointing, even though there be a big hatch of fly. It is, however, something to which most of us always look forward, because if trout happen to be in a taking mood, quite exceptional sport may be anticipated. The "duffer's fortnight" often belies its name, but there are years when achievement surpasses expectation and great catches are recorded on the artificial fly.

Oft-times too, the mayfly gives fishermen an opportunity of creeling heavy and elusive fish whose presence in the stream has hitherto been more suspected than verified. Why, at other times, when there is a big hatch of fly and when all conditions appear to be entirely favourable, trout obstinately refuse to look at any imitation of the mayfly, is a thing which has never been satisfactorily explained. It is a mystery, although a no greater one than several others connected with this insect.

When the fly first makes its appearance, it is usually some days before trout begin to evince any interest in it. At this period, fish are notoriously difficult to tempt and the standard practice is to try an Alder, although my own experience is that the Grey Duster will provide better results. The fish will often take it freely up to the time that the mayfly is well on, and, in fact, if dressed on a large hook (size 10), this pattern will continue to kill through the height of the hatch, sometimes even better than the standard copies of the natural insect. After the fortnight or so, in which the trout have gorged themselves on mayflies and have feasted, not wisely but too well, as is their habit at this period, they are generally disinclined to rise at all freely for a few weeks. In consequence of this, there is a division of opinion amongst fishermen as to whether a mayfly hatch is beneficial or whether, taken by and large, a river is not better off without one.

My vote is for the mayfly for fishing during its season will often provide an intensity of excitement packed into a short period which is not likely to be equalled at any other time of the year. But the real joy of mayfly fishing lies in the opportunity it presents to fly-fishers of getting on to terms with the really big fish which only rise when the mayfly is on the water. No other fly causes them to forsake their natural caution as does this insect. To my mind that alone is well worth any temporary deterioration in sport which may be suffered afterwards.

Artificial mayflies are dressed in three different styles; hackled, winged and spent. Time was when winged patterns were the most popular but nowadays hackled flies are generally preferred. Nevertheless it would be the height of foolishness to rely on this type of fly alone, for at times fish show an unmistakable preference for a winged floater. Nymphs need not be taken into serious account in spite of those rare occasions when they will take a number of trout. On the whole the artificial nymph is seldom successful, possible because the natural mayfly nymph is too large and too solid an insect to imitate in a satisfactory manner. Spent patterns, too, are not generally popular with either fish or fishermen, although sometimes they can prove extremely useful and any angler who does not carry a selection of this type of fly is making a mistake. An example of the importance of the spent spinner was provided this year. During the last three weeks, I have fished three different rivers, and although the hatch of fly was most disappointing, there was always a sprinkling of drakes on the water. For the first week, the Grey Duster proved to be by far the most effective pattern, but for the remainder of the unusually short period which the hatch lasted, the trout concentrated their attentions on spent spinners, almost entirely ignoring the green drakes which floated past them with immunity. Even in these circumstances, not every spent artificial fly interested the fish and they ignored anything of a sombre colouring. What they wanted, and the only imitation which they took at all freely was a light coloured one with a white, or almost white, body. Incidentally this was not my experience alone; friends fishing on other streams (some over twenty-five miles away) made the same discovery. I quote this example to show that even when the mayfly is on, trout can be extraordinarily fastidious and that it is therefore a good policy to carry a number of assorted artificials. In most years, I suppose, fish take the mayfly as we hope (and expect) they will do, but sooner or later, the day comes when they are in a less accommodating frame of mind and something out of the ordinary is required to tempt them.

Most fishermen have their own special favourites upon which, under normal conditions, they feel they can rely. I have several myself, but I recognize that there are other patterns which will doubtless kill just as well. Neither is it wise to pin too much faith on two or three flies for there is no doubt that to make the most of the mayfly season, a wide variety of patterns is necessary. More than once in past years, I have thought that at last I had found a fly which would take fish under almost any conditions, only to discover in the following year (or even on the next day!) that the trout would have nothing to do with it.

Artificial mayfly patterns run into many dozens and it would be impracticable to give particulars of all of them or even of those which are in regular use to-day; consequently I shall only attempt to provide a small selection of those which are known to be good killers. All of them are well-tried patterns which can be recommended with confidence, although I must again emphasize that there are many other excellent dressings which I have been obliged to omit. The best imitation will vary from day to day and can only be determined by observation, experience, or by a process of trial and error. It is quite possible that the degree and intensity of the light may make the difference between the success or failure of any pattern. Because of this, a particular artificial fly may prove highly effective at one period of the day and not at another, so that frequent changes of pattern may sometimes become unavoidable. On the other hand, there are seasons when the same fly will continue to attract trout day after day, so that one can only be guided by the circumstances of the moment. Generally speaking, an idea as to which pattern is likely to be most effective can best be gained by carefully observing the insect which the fish are taking and making sure whether it is a male or female sub-imago or imago, or a hatching dun. A few minutes' study of this sort will prove well worth while.

One difficulty arises in relation to nomenclature because comparatively few Mayfly patterns possess names which have received general recognition. Every professional tier appears to use his own, with the result that one may find several flies all bearing entirely different names, but of which the dressing is exactly the same in each case. Some makers dispense with names altogether and use code numbers for their mayfly patterns which does not lessen the difficulty mentioned.

Perhaps it is of no real importance, as most fishermen arm themselves with a goodly selection of patterns and as a rule, they are able to pick out one which will approximately match the natural fly on which the fish are feeding. In the case of the mayfly this does not present much of a problem since, owing to its size, it is generally easy enough to determine whether the trout are taking hatching nymphs, duns, spinners, or spent drakes.

In common with many other anglers, I hold the view that a winged artificial rather smaller than a natural fly will generally kill better than one of life-size. And it should not be too pale in colour. The living insect looks very light in the air but dark on the water, whilst the exact opposite is the case where the artificial is concerned. A pattern which when held in the hand appears to match the colour of the mayflies on the water will look much too light when it joins them and its artificiality must be transparent to the fish.

Winged Patterns

Of the many winged flies, the two most popular have well-established names. They are the two "Champions" invented some eighty years ago by John Hammond, the Winchester fly-dresser. They have a fine reputation and Halford had a high opinion of both of them. The dressings are as under:

GREEN CHAMPION

Wings: Rouen drake dyed a green-brown (Halford's No. VII dye). If the colour is not green enough, the feathers can be dyed again in a very weak solution of indigo.
Hackles: A grey partridge dyed in strong tea and a pale ginger cock hackle.
Body: Raffia grass over white quill, ribbed with fine flat gold and red silk.
Whisk: Gallina dyed in "Diamond" dark brown dye.
Hook: 12 or 13.

This pattern is sometimes very successful tied with a yellow chenille body.

Brown Champion
Wings: Rouen drake dyed a dark brown olive tint (Halford's No. VI).
Hackles, Body and Whisk: As for Green Champion.
Hook: 12 or 13.

In *Modern Development of the Dry Fly*, Halford gave six Mayfly dressings (two spent and four winged) of which I have selected the following:

Green Mayfly (Female) (Halford)
Wings: Mallard dyed a pale grey-green shade.
Head Hackle: Golden pheasant hen from neck.
Shoulder Hackles: Two pale cream cock hackles.
Body: Undyed raffia with six turns at tail end, and five turns ribbing body of medium cinnamon horsehair.
Whisk: Gallina dyed a dark chocolate brown.
Hook: 13.

The other winged tie I propose to give is chosen as being one of the most killing for the Irish loughs, although it will take fish anywhere.

Irish Mayfly
Wings: Yellow upright wings not less than half an inch high.
Hackle: Ginger.
Body: Yellow silk ribbed black.
Whisks: Three strands golden pheasant or brown mallard.
Hook: 8 to 11.

There are dozens of other winged patterns with bodies of silk, rubber, herl, cork, etc., but the two above should meet most requirements.

Hackled Patterns
Probably hackled Mayflies are more generally used nowadays than winged ones. Fish like them quite as well or better, and they are less troublesome to cast.

Again there are numbers to choose from, of which the dressing below is typical of the majority.

French Partridge

Body: Cream floss silk, cross-ribbed with fine gold wire and crimson tying silk.
Hackles: Inner, natural red cocks. Outer, feather from the back of a French partridge.
Tail: Three whisks red cock.
Hook: 12.

The above is a thoroughly reliable pattern, although personally I should place Goulden's Favourite at the top of the list. A modern creation, it is a splendid killer.

Goulden's Favourite

Tail: Three strands from a cock pheasant's tail feather.
Body: Translucent yellow-olive thin rubber sheeting; dyed raffia may be substituted if desired, although I do not think that it is as good as the rubber.
Hackles: First hackle, large red cock; Second, hot orange. Grey mallard, dyed greenish-olive is wound at the head in front of the other hackles.
Hook: 10, long shank.

The above fly takes its name from a sergeant of the Royal Irish Constabulary, who is a well-known Irish dry fly-fisherman. After trying out a number of conventional patterns, he suggested the use of a bright orange hackle and Mr. T. J. Hanna then designed the pattern for him. From the start, it proved a great success, often bringing up trout which were letting the too-plentiful naturals pass by. It will not always kill but when it does, I know of no fly to equal it. The method of making the rubber body translucent is the inventor's secret and is used on all his "True-Form" flies, but even with ordinary thin sheet rubber, the fly is quite effective, as in this case, I believe it is the hackles which account for most of its attractiveness. Hanna produced this pattern in about 1935 and had he never given us another, he would still have deserved the thanks of the angling fraternity, for it is a brilliant creation.

Amongst the more unorthodox hackled flies, the "fore and aft" patterns cannot be disregarded because many anglers have great faith in them and will use nothing else. The idea was developed a long while ago by the late Mr. Horace Brown, who for a great number of years was well known on the Kennet. Briefly, the principle is to have a hackle at each end of the fly, divided by a good thick body. Brown applied the same idea to smaller flies but it was as a Mayfly that it proved most successful. Although for this purpose he varied his hackles, his favourite dressing was:

FORE AND AFT
Head Hackle: Red cock's hackle.
Tail Hackle: Light badger.
Body: Undyed raffia.
Hook: 11 or 12.

The small thick piece at the very end of the feather was left standing out over the bend of the hook as a sort of tag or whisk and no other tail was used.

Sir Gerald Burrard, a particularly sound authority on all matters pertaining to flies, writing in *Game and Gun*, a journal which he founded, eulogized this pattern in these words: "The success of this fly is really amazing. It floats well, but rather low in the water, and time and again, I have had one taken by a trout which was rising steadily but which I could tempt with nothing else. I have little doubt that the trout take it for a nymph which has just reached the surface, or possibly for an empty nymph husk which is floating down just in the surface. But the fly is essentially a true dry fly and floats; my experience is that it is useless when fished wet. . . . The fly appears so unorthodox that a certain amount of courage is needed to make a start of using it; but once a start has been made, I am sure that confidence will be established very quickly."

Only on one occasion have I tried this pattern myself and I cannot pretend that it achieved outstanding success; rather the reverse in fact! Nevertheless many friends assure me that they have never found any type of Mayfly to touch a "Fore and Aft".

Another excellent Mayfly type is that known as a Straddle-bug, or Straggle-bug. On the whole, I am inclined to think that this form of fly gives more consistently good results than any other sort of Mayfly, whether hackled, winged, or spent.

A fly with long straggling hackles, it may be fished wet, semi-submerged, or dry, although it is normally used wet and probably kills best when so fished. Personally I have always used it as a floater and have had no reason to be dissatisfied with the results, although logically it should be fished below the surface.

There are several dressings, most of the patterns being hackled with a breast feather of a Summer duck or Canadian wood-duck; or rather, they used to be for these feathers are now almost unprocurable in this country and their importation is forbidden. The breast feather of a French partridge is generally used as a substitute and makes quite an efficient one.

The best tie in my experience is one of many known as the "Summer Duck", the name being applied to more than one pattern with very similar dressings and between which there is not much to choose. I have heard of some remarkable catches having been made on this fly including one bag of ninety-three trout which was made last year by a Builth Wells angler who never once changed his pattern.

STRADDLE-BUG (Summer Duck)
Tip: Very small gold twist.
Tail: Two or three fibres from a black cock's hackle.
Body: Raffia, ribbed with brown silk.
Hackles: Summer duck (or breast feather from a French partridge), long with a short and slight second hackle of bright orange.
Head: Peacock herl.
Hook: 10 to 12.

Another pattern of the Straddle-bug variety is one which Mr. Skues once told me that he had found attractive, and on its day, almost irresistible, was tied thus:

STRADDLE-BUG (Skues)
Whisks: Brown mallard.
Hackle: A ginger cock's hackle wound over the body.
Body: Raffia.
Ribbing: Fine gold wire.
Hook: 11.

Having stated what I believe most fly-fishers understand by a Straddle-bug, it becomes necessary to add that some anglers seem to reserve that name for a rather similar type of fly which is tied back to front. There is no doubt that dressed in this manner, it kills well and those who favour this style of fly are convinced that it is much more deadly than any more orthodox pattern. A back-to-front pattern is always fished well sunk, the theory being that the current of the stream, working against the set of the hackles, imparts to the fly an exceptional amount of kick and life.

Mr. J. R. Harris in *An Angler's Entomology* gives the following excellent dressing for the greendrake:

Shoulder Hackles: French partridge; blue-grey side feather dyed in picric acid and wound in front of a stiff white cock's hackle, also dyed in picric.
Rib Hackle: Light badger cock with grey or brown centre.
Body: Raffia dyed yellow.
Rib: Gold wire.
Tail: Cock pheasant centre tail fibres.
Tying silk: Light-coloured, waxed with white wax.
Hook: 5, 6, or 7.

Spent Patterns

A selection of patterns to imitate the spent spinners is quite indispensable for there are occasions when trout will take nothing else. Naturally these spent patterns prove most effective towards the end of the mayfly season when trout have become well accustomed to the natural spent insect, but it is worth noting that often they will kill well when there is scarcely a spent drake to be seen on the water.

There are so many spent patterns and so many of them are good that it is not easy to know which to recommend. The Moneymore is one of those which I regularly use myself and which is a good reliable pattern. It is an adaptation of Goulden's Favourite tied in a style which its designer, T. J. Hanna, calls "half-spent", and may be fished dry or very slightly submerged. The dressing is:

MONEYMORE
Tail: Three strands from centre feather of a cock pheasant's tail.
Body: Translucent yellowish-olive thin rubber sheeting.
Hackles: First hackle, red cock; second, hot orange.
Wings: Two grey mallard feathers dyed green-olive, tied in to lie flat and mixed with the hackles.
Hook: 10 or 11.

An alternative tie for the wings is barred grey partridge, dyed greenish-yellow.

Another of Hanna's spent patterns, his Spent Black Drake, I like even better. Tied to imitate the spent male spinner, it is a grand fly which has given me some great sport, and is a pattern which I would never be without. Dressing:

SPENT BLACK DRAKE (Hanna)

Tail: Three strands from centre feather of a cock pheasant's tail.
Body: Translucent white rubber sheeting.
Hackle: Badger hackle with a good dark centre.
Wings: White cock, cut to shape and tied in at right angles to hook, spent style.
Hook: 10 or 11.

The inventor gets a wonderfully translucent body, but how this is done, is a secret, but transparent plastic sheeting will do equally as well. Also clear sheet rubber wrapped over white silk gives a satisfactory result and failing this, the fly will still kill better than most, with a raffia body, painted white. This pattern is another of the "half-spent" type and is generally fished as a floater or just in the surface film. Some anglers have objections to cut wings, but Mr. Hanna uses them in several of his patterns and I cannot say that I have ever found any disadvantage in them.

Incidentally, Irish fly-dressers have long favoured rubber for the bodies of flies and were certainly making use of it in 1880, and probably long before. At the same period, cork was popular for Mayfly bodies both in England and Ireland and although it is still used to-day, few fishermen like it.

The two patterns above are almost the only spent mayflies that I personally use, but there are dozens of orthodox spent patterns, which are generally fished wet, and many of which are most effective at times. Probably Marryat's old dressing is as good as any and writing of it Halford said: "This, the late Mr. Marryat's last improved dressing of his well-known pattern, is the only imitation of the spent gnat, or imago of the mayfly, worthy of notice."

It is unlikely that many fly-fishers to-day would agree that this is the only spent fly worth consideration, although it is still amongst the best. The tie is:

SPENT DRAKE (Marryat)

Wings: Four dark grizzled blue dun cock hackle points set in horizontally.
Ribbing Hackle: A badger cock hackle.
Hackles: A grey partridge in front and a badger cock hackle close behind it.
Body: A strand of condor quill, dark at point and white at root, the white part worked in at the shoulder to show two or three turns of the dark colour at the tail end of the body. The body is ribbed with fine silver wire.
Whisk: Gallina, dyed in "Diamond" dark brown dye.
Hook: 12, long shank.

If condor cannot be obtained, dyed peacock quill will prove a suitable substitute.

A more modern dressing, of which I have heard enthusiastic reports, is as under. It was invented by Mr. W. J. Lunn, so bears the right hall-mark.

LITTLE SPENT GNAT (Lunn)

Hackles: One black cock hackle, one red cock hackle, and one grouse hackle.
Wings: Two feathers from the breast or back of a medium blue dun hen put on flat. Tie in a piece of fairly thick black silk and "figure 8" it to form a thorax.
Tail: Two fibres from tip of cock pheasant's tail feather.
Body: Raffia which has been painted white on the underside, ribbed with fine copper wire.
Tying silk: Olive, Pearsall's gossamer, No. 16.
Hook: 10 or 11.

There is one more pattern which must be mentioned. I know of no name for it, but many fishermen will recognize it as an old and popular fly.

SPENT DRAKE

Body: Raffia, painted white underside, ribbed fine copper wire.
Whisks: Three black cock hackle fibres.
Hackle: Well-marked badger cock at shoulder and carried down body.
Wings: Dark or medium blue dun cock hackle fibres, tied in spent fashion.
Hook: 11 or 12, long shank.

Miscellaneous Notes

The flies of which the dressings are given above may all be looked upon as thoroughly reliable patterns, although it must be admitted that when trout are really "on" the mayfly, almost any recognized artificial will prove effective and the fish then will take even flies which bear very little resemblance to the natural insects.

Some few years ago, the late Mr. Clarence Cole, a noted American angler and amateur fly-tier was good enough to send me a number of flies of his own dressing. They were certainly like our standard winged Mayflies in shape and structure, although in point of fact they were not imitations of the natural insect, nor were they intended to be, but were designed as ordinary floating flies for use on the great lakes of U.S.A. Actually they were identical in appearance with our standard types of winged Mayflies, except for the bizarre colouring of their wings, hackles and whisks.

As a matter of interest, I tested all Mr. Cole's peculiar coloured patterns when fish were taking the natural mayfly and was not a little astonished that trout took them quite as well as they did our conventional types. So much for the theory of exact imitation!

Perhaps I ought not to have been so surprised for it is generally known that very similar experiments have been undertaken many times before. To take but one example, Francis Francis in his *Book on Angling* made the following observations: "In 1897, as an experiment on the colour sense of fish, I had some Mayflies dyed bright scarlet and sky-blue. On June 2nd, I landed 31 trout and 2 chub on the Glade at Cassionbury with these unorthodox flies. Only one of the trout weighed less than a pound. On June 15th, using similar flies, I landed 11 trout in the Bean at Woodhall Park, Hertford. I kept four brace of these fish weighing 16 lb."

In the above instances, the trout must obviously have taken these baroque flies for copies of the natural drakes. That they do not always do so is clear from the fact that an artificial Mayfly will take odd fish at any time of the season and when everything else fails, one can do worse than try one. I have accounted for quite a number of trout both on lake and river when the natural fly has not been seen for many months or even where it has never been seen at all. Presumably in such cases, it has been taken for a moth.

During the mayfly season proper, it is seldom worth while mounting an artificial until the trout have settled down to feed on the natural insect in earnest. At first fish appear to be nervous of these large creatures and whenever the duns are coming down the stream in small numbers and fish are ignoring them or are taking only an odd specimen here and there, better sport will be had with a Grey Duster, an Alder, or a Herefordshire Alder than with any imitation of the mayfly. At the other end of the hatch, when trout are satiated with mayflies and disinclined to rise to an artificial of any sort, one can do worse than try an Ermine Moth. Sometimes it works wonders!

Although in England, mayflies sometimes hatch in hundreds of thousands and the air is full of them, we cannot compete with America in that direction. We are apt to be a little cynical about the immense scale in which so many things are done in U.S.A., but there is no gainsaying their mayfly hatch. Around the great lakes of America and Canada, these insects appear not in thousands, but literally in millions. The air is thick with vast clouds of them; they cover windows which have constantly to be swept clear to allow some light to pass through them. Pedestrians can distinctly hear a definite crunch as they walk along the footpaths and streets on a deep solid mass of mayflies. Eventually the insects have to be swept into large heaps where they soon decompose and set up a most unpleasant fishy smell and, in consequence, are known as "fish flies". In these circumstances, it is not surprising that in North America and Canada, the artificial Green Drake, used as such, is not the killing pattern it can be in this country. Even trout can have too much of a good thing!

MEDIUM OLIVE. See OLIVE DUN

MEDIUM SEDGE

A standard pattern used to suggest several sedges and a first-class fly for most rivers and lakes, whether fished wet or dry. The biggest fish are mostly taken in the later afternoon and up to dark, and they will often be tempted by a Medium or a Cinnamon Sedge when no other pattern will attract them. There is not much difference between the two patterns mentioned and both are equally good for brown and rainbow trout.

Halford gave the following tie for the dry fly:

Wings: Landrail, selecting full-coloured feathers.
Hackles: Two ginger cock hackles.
Ribbing Hackle: A ginger cock hackle.
Body: Unstripped condor dyed medium cinnamon.
Hook: 11.

T. J. Hanna has a Medium Sedge dressing in his "True-Form" series. At times it has provided me with wonderful sport and has been one of my favourite patterns since one hot sunny afternoon in August, when I took two and a half brace of rainbows on it, the best just over three pounds and the smallest two and a half pounds—not a bad average weight. The fly was fished semi-submerged in gin-clear water and the fish had previously disdained every floating pattern offered them, but when the Medium Sedge was put on, they took it without any hesitation at all. Out of consideration for the friend who had invited me to fish his well-stocked water, I stopped fishing, although the trout were still taking well and had I continued, my catch must have been very much greater.

That is not the only occasion on which Hanna's Medium Sedge has

served me well. I have had reason to bless it many times since and I
look upon it as an indispensable pattern.

The dressing is:

Body: Semi-translucent sheet rubber over cinnamon-coloured silk.
Hackles: Natural red cock's hackles.
Wings: Red hen.
Hook: 12.

MIDGES. See CHIRONOMIDAE

MISSIONARY

Invented by Captain J. J. Dunn, particularly for use on Blagdon and
similar lakes stocked with big trout. It was on a variation of this pattern
(tied with an orange hackle, instead of a white one) that Mr. C. G.
Heywood made a wonderful catch on the Tongariro River in New
Zealand, consisting of seven trout averaging twelve pounds each, all
taken during one morning's fishing. The two largest scaled sixteen
pounds each. Mr. Heywood kindly sent me a copy of the Missionary
from which I make the dressing to be:

Body: White wool, pulled, and spun on.
Tail: White cock's hackle.
Wings: A few fibres of black turkey tail feather, with strips of dark teal on each
   side. The wings extend well beyond the bend of the hook.
Hackle: White cock's.
Hook: 8 to 10.

MOLE FLY

A popular pattern throughout Europe and especially on the clear
streams of Normandy, some of which, such as the Risle, are pure chalk
streams. Nevertheless it is an English fly, taking its name from the
River Mole, in Surrey, and why it is less used in the land of its origin
than in many other countries is something of a mystery. As a floating
fly, it is effective on all gently flowing rivers and, owing to the style of
winging which balances the fly so well, it cocks better than most. The

Exactly what insect was the natural prototype of the Mole fly has
never been satisfactorily settled. One expert entomologist informs me
that it was originally tied as an imitation of the oak fly (*Leptis scolopacea*),
whilst when I put the same question to Mr. Martin Mosely, he expressed the opinion that it was probably intended to represent the olives
and possibly the yellow upright. This tallies with my own experience

that the pattern is most effective when olives are on the water in strength, although, for some unknown reason, the Mole fly is apt to prove killing during a mayfly hatch, when trout are not taking the natural insect too freely.

Nowadays this fly must be regarded as more of a French pattern than an English one, and it is therefore interesting to find that in *Les Mouches du Pecheur de Truites* (published in Paris, 1939) that the author states that it is an imitation of a sedge, one of the *"grands sedges roux du soir"*.

The reader must, therefore, decide for himself what natural fly this pattern is supposed to represent, although it is possible that all the authorities mentioned above may be right, because the Mole fly is subjected to many variations; in fact there are a number of widely differing dressings, although all conform to the same style of winging. The ordinary tie used in England is:

Body: Dark olive tying silk, ribbed with gold wire.
Hackle: Red cock with black base, tied from shoulder to tail.
Wings: Mottled hen pheasant wing feather, tied well forward.
Hook: 14 to 16.

This, however, is not the dressing most favoured in France. In Normandy, the most popular pattern is the President Billard; from the tie of this pattern, given below it would appear to be a definite attempt to copy the oak fly.

Body: Mustard-yellow floss silk.
Hackle: Coch-y-bondhu, ribbed down body.
Wing: Grey speckled hen, tied well forward.
Whisks: Coch-y-bondhu.
Hook: 14.

The whisks are definitely optional and are only used to balance the fly and to assist it to float.

MOSQUITO

A modern American pattern. Fished dry on a small-sized hook, it has proved itself an attractive fly on English rivers and lakes. I have never determined what trout take it for, but at times it kills well. The dressing is:

Body: Grey wool, ribbed with orange silk.
Hackle: Cuckoo.
Wings: Grey turkey.
Whisks: A few strands as hackle.
Hook: 14 to 16.

MOTHS. See BROWN MOTH, BUSTARD, ERMINE MOTH, WHITE
MOTH, HAMMOND'S ADOPTED

MYSTIC

Having largely resisted the temptation to include in this book any
patterns of which the ancestry is open to any doubt; having deleted
several which have gained local popularity in recent years, solely on
the grounds that time alone can prove their true worth, there seems
very little excuse for including the Mystic which neither I, nor anybody
else, has ever used. Nevertheless, it is a close relation of an excellent
pattern and there can be very little doubt that it will prove effective
for sea-trout and salmon.

Like the Mason, it is perhaps worth including merely to illustrate
the queer ways in which artificial flies are sometimes born.

For many years now I have maintained and hunted a pack of beagles
and on one recent occasion, a normally steady old hound named Mystic,
so far forgot himself as to chase a cockerel which crossed his path when
he was in a hurry to get on terms with a hare. In the ordinary way
this hound would have taken no notice of poultry but this time he
showed his disapproval of birds which get in the way of old gentlemen
engaged on urgent business, by removing the larger portion of the
cockerel's tail feathers.

Alas! The little hound had never a dog's chance of retaining his ill-
gotten gains (even if he had wanted to) for close on his heels was a
rather breathless amateur fly-dresser in the person of the assistant editor
of the *Birmingham Post*. The sequel was that a week later the gentleman
in question was good enough to send me a beautifully tied fly with the
following inscription attached: "To the Master of the Warwickshire
Beagles—the Mystic Fly or Cockerel's Brush—wishing him good
sport."

The fly is a variation of the same inventor's "Dipper", and if the
pattern is as good as the hound which provided the material, and of the
fisherman who fashioned it, there can be no possible doubt that it will
prove to be a grand fly. When next I have a rendezvous with sea-trout,
it will be the first pattern I shall try. The dressing is the same as for the
Dipper, except for the wing, which comes from a cockerel's tail and is
as near a small white-tipped turkey feather as any rooster's brush is
likely to provide, viz., black with a pronounced bronze sheen and a
pale (though not really white) edge.

NEEDLE BROWN. See DARK SPANISH NEEDLE AND WILLOW FLY

NEEDLE FLY (*Nemoura cinerea: etc.*)

Strictly speaking, this name should be applied, I believe, only to three species of the Leuctra family, although in practice, it is used by anglers to denote any of those small thin brown flies, with long narrow flat wings, which are so typical of the smaller perlidae. The needle flies are the smallest members of this family, seldom exceeding three-quarters of an inch in length and are widely distributed throughout the country on fast-running waters on which they will be found from March to September.

In common with the alder and the willow fly, these little insects have the habit of alighting on one's neck, face and hands, so that a hatch soon becomes obvious to fishermen. Like all species of the perlidae, they are appreciated by trout, and are imitated by many artificial patterns. The Dark Spanish Needle is one of the most frequently employed but there are several other north-country flies which will prove equally as good.

NYMPHS (*Ephemeridae*)
The Natural Insect

Every fishing book which touches upon entomology is almost certain to make some reference to the four types of nymphs of the Ephemeridae family, and most of them give neat little illustrations of each class.

If my suspicions are correct, more often than not the average reader is inclined to skip this section as being of little interest and less importance. Yet I would venture to suggest that the life history of the nymph is far from being the dry subject some imagine it to be and consequently I have dealt at some length with the life cycle of one species which may be considered typical of the rest. It will be found on page 235, under the heading of "Mayfly", and even though my pen cannot do justice to it, I trust that some readers will agree that the story of the nymph is not without interest.

But the habits of the mayfly nymph are different in some respects from those of his relatives in the other groups, so that a brief reference to the four classes becomes necessary if one is to understand in what manner they are dissimilar.

First of all, it will be as well to decide what is meant by the term "nymph". One definition is that it is a sub-aqueous insect, the larva of the order Neuroptera (nerved-winged flies) of which the Ephmeridae are of chief interest to anglers. Strictly speaking, the immature ephemerids are called larvae and only become nymphs when their rudimentary wings become visible, but since the difference in appearance between these two stages of the insects' existence is so slight, fishermen have long found it more convenient to use the term nymph to designate all the sub-surface stages of its life.

The four types of nymphs are known as the (a) digging; (b) flat; (c) crawling, and (d) swimming. The first group make their homes in burrows in the sand, mud, and silt, on the beds or margins of rivers and lakes. The mayfly nymph is of this type. The flat nymphs are found for the most part in swift-flowing rocky rivers where they will be found clinging to the underside of stones. Broad and very flat, they have a streamlined contour which, together with their strong clawed legs, enables them to keep their position in a heavy current. All swim fairly well and are said to be carnivorous. The outstanding example of this group is the march brown nymph.

Of the crawling type, it might be said that "they swim not, neither do they burrow", at least not to any noticeable extent. Slow in their movements, they are but poorly protected against the attacks of their enemies and have to overcome this deficiency by natural cunning.

Preferring gravelly streams and slack water, they manage to cover themselves with a thin layer of mud which serves a double purpose; it renders them invisible to marauding fish and at the same time provides them with a good tactical position for securing the small insects on which they feed. The most prominent representative of the crawling class is the blue-winged olive nymph, which is distinguished by the dark black and white markings of its setae.

The swimming group form an important one as far as anglers are concerned, because, included amongst them, are the nymphs of such well-known flies as the olive duns, iron-blue duns and the pale wateries. All of them have slender and more or less cylindrical-shaped bodies and prefer slow-running rivers and lakes, being especially prevalent in the chalk streams where they live amongst the weeds or move about over the stones and gravel. Their legs are too weak to permit them to move about quickly but they can swim and steer themselves fairly well. Out of water, they can do little else but wriggle.

Far more exposed to the attacks of fish and other underwater enemies than any of the preceding classes, the swimming nymphs are those which mostly cause trout to bulge and tail.

The majority of nymphs swim to the surface when the time comes for them to change to a sub-imago, but the metamorphosis of others, including some of the flat larvae, takes place on the stones, rocks, or shingle bordering the water. The underwater life of all nymphs, except that of the mayfly, probably lasts a year, from egg to dun. In the case of the mayfly, the period extends to two years and sometimes three.

The Artificial Nymph

It is not my intention to deal with the many patterns of nymphs which are now more or less firmly established, as the subject would need a whole book to itself and, in fact, two are already available, in *Nymph Fishing for Chalk Stream Trout*, by G. E. M. Skues, and *The Rough Stream Nymph*, by W. H. Lawrie.

Thanks largely to Mr. Skues, the shape and build of the modern artificial nymph has become pretty well standardized—a slim body, a few short whisks for the tail, a large thorax and a short hackle representing the legs.

Most of the smaller nymphs of the Ephemeridae can be quite well imitated but that of the mayfly has never, I believe, proved of much worth. Possibly the natural insect is too large and solid to be copied with much hope of success.

However, for those who wish to try, the following pattern, which is thought to imitate the emerging dun, is as good as any:

Hook: No. 10 down-eyed.
Silk: Pearsall's No. 16 (olive).
Body and Thorax: Cream-coloured seal's fur, or natural raffia.
Ribbing: Gold twist.
Whisks: Cock pheasant tail, tied short.
Wing cases: A strip from a brown game hen wing feather.
Wings: A few green-olive large hackle fibres.
Legs: Small grouse hackle or fibres at the throat.

Wind the silk to the bend, tie in whisks and ribbing, then form the body nice and fat. Bring the rib to shoulder. Tie in wing-cases feather sloping backwards, then wing fibres standing well up, then the legs and, finally, split the wing-cases feather and bring the two halves forward to the eye on either side of the wing fibres. Whip off.

It is a pattern well worth trying when the trout refuse to look at dun or spinner imitations.

Skues designed his patterns for chalk-stream fishing, although they will often do great execution on other types of rivers. Yet, I am inclined to the belief, that on rough fast streams when fish are definitely feeding on nymphs, certain wet flies will do just as well as any meticulous copy of a nymph.

Although, I believe, that Mr. Skues has rejected the theory, there is a strong opinion amongst many others who have given some thought to the subject, that the success of the north-country spider patterns is due to their likeness to aquatic larvae. In the fly-box, the resemblance is not evident, but in the water, they present a very different appearance. The long soft hackles cling closely to the hook and tapering from head to tail, the shape of the fly is not unlike that of a nymph. The effect is heightened by the longer hackles projecting beyond the bend of the hook for they quiver in the water and suggest quite well the movement of a swimming larva.

Although Halford gave a tie for the grannom nymph, he had no faith in this type of artificial. "How is it to be expected", he wrote, "that a timid, shy fish like a trout, should mistake that motionless supine compound of dubbing, silk, quill, and hackle, drifting helplessly and lifelessly like a log downstream, for the active ever-moving larva sparkling in the sunshine and varying colour at every motion as the rays of light strike it at different angles?"

In other words, whilst one can copy a nymph, one cannot give it "life". Many fishermen have held that Halford was wrong because fishermen have been catching trout on these defunct-looking nymphs for over half a century. Some anglers also believe that little would be gained by giving more vitality to the artificial on the grounds that when the natural insect is ascending to the surface, it floats upwards in a completely inert fashion. I must confess that when I have seen nymphs rising to the surface, they have had every appearance of life and movement which they seem to obtain from rapid vibrations of the tail.

As that great authority, Mr. Martin Mosely has said, the usual progress of the hatching nymph towards the surface is undertaken "in alternate bursts of extreme energy and inertness".

Because I feel that any improvement in the counterfeit insect must develop in the direction of imparting "more life", I am giving details of an experimental type of nymph which Mr. T. J. Hanna was good enough to send to me towards the end of last season. As the manner of tying a nymph with a detached body may be of interest to some readers who tie their own flies, I asked Mr. Hanna if he would let me know how he dresses his patterns and he kindly supplied the following in response to my request:

"My method of tying this nymph is to tie in a nylon or gut foundation, whisks and sheet rubber, about a quarter of an inch behind the eye of the hook. The nylon and whisks are kept stretched out and the rubber is wound over both of them and over the hook shank for a number of turns. Then nylon and whisks are held away from the shank, the end of the rubber is caught up with a pair of hackle pliers and one commences to wind over the nylon and whisks only.

"It is at this point that one makes the discovery that another pair of hands would be useful, for it is a tricky little operation at first. Having made the body of the requisite length one begins to wind back the rubber, continuing the process until the point is reached where the body leaves the shank. An extra turn or two is required here in order to obtain greater thickness and to counteract the disparity in size between the portion which has the hook shank running through it and the detached part. Next, continue winding over the shank again, tie in and cut off the waste where one commenced. A few strands from a centre tail feather of a cock pheasant are now tied in and my ordinary method of making a nymph (as described in *Fly-Fishing in Ireland*) is continued. All this may sound more difficult than it really is but if one can master the first part and make a detached body, the subsequent procedure is easy enough."

The usual method of fishing an artificial nymph is to cast upstream or up and across, allowing it to sink to a depth varying from 1 to 6 inches. It can be assisted to do this by moistening the last two feet of the cast as well as the nymph itself with saliva, glycerine, clay, or river mud. But there are other methods of fishing the nymph to suit various types of water and the different methods naturally give rise to different patterns, each adapted to meet the demands of deception and water conditions.

The secret of effective design of nymph patterns is a thorough knowledge of the appearance and habits of the natural insects. Mr. Frank Sawyer comes to the root of the matter in his book *Nymphs and the Trout* when he states: "Other patterns have been described from time to time which represent many of the small Ephemeroptera and I feel sure, if one could make these exactly as they have been evolved by those who have discovered the dressings, they would be successful." He then goes on to say that such patterns have been evolved only after their designers have spent much time studying the natural insects, and he, very sensibly, recommends the fly-tier first to devote himself to a similar study before attempting to make nymphs either to his own, or to anybody else's design.

The majority of fishermen probably support the theory that the artificial nymph must be given "life" but there are, undoubtedly, a number who fish the more placid chalk streams who are not so convinced.

Any angler who has fished the same length of the Itchen as Skues will doubt the necessity for "life", as most nymphs on rising to the surface immediately prior to their emergence as a dun seem to have long periods of inactivity during which they are exposed to mortal danger from the trout. These nymphs can be clearly observed trying to emerge on stretches where the river is glassy and unbroken and there appears to be a barrier at the surface which makes it difficult for the insect to push its way through to the air. On these occasions, the nymphs drift along for considerable distances in an inert fashion, but with brief periods of wriggling as though trying to pierce the surface barrier. The quiet drifting periods are probably only for resting purposes during which the insect gathers strength for another attempt at penetration.

That the nymphs are easily secured under these circumstances is indicated by the lazy roll with which the trout take them, just as when they are feeding on spent flies, which, like the nymphs, cannot possibly escape.

It was under these conditions that Skues developed his patterns and, thus, anglers who fish the Itchen and similar rivers are convinced that these patterns, if tied correctly with economy of material, are very effective as, indeed, are some more recent patterns designed on the same lines. One of the best of his patterns is his imitation of the medium olive, which is tied with a stripped peacock quill (from the eye feather) body, a wad of dark hare's ear for the thorax, a small dark blue dun hen hackle and dark unspeckled cock guinea-fowl whisks. His other patterns, as has previously been stated, will be found in his book *Nymph Fishing for Chalk Stream Trout*.

Mr. Frank Sawyer who made a careful study of the habits of nymphs, noticed, as too did Mr. J. R. Harris, that some nymphs of the swimming type made exploratory journeys to the surface, and show generally a restless sub-surface activity some little time before they are due to hatch out. This restlessness far below the surface attracts fish which take advantage of it by indulging their appetites at the nymph's expense. As a result of this observation, Mr. Sawyer designed certain nymphs in which fine copper wire replaced tying silk, thus enabling him to sink his artificials well below the surface without difficulty. That these nymphs are most effective cannot be disputed.

The method used by Mr. Sawyer for his favourite olive pattern is ingenious and can be described briefly as follows: First, he builds up the shape of the body and thorax with fine red copper wire, and then ties in four centre fibres of a brown-red cock pheasant tail feather at the hook end. He leaves the fine points protruding as tails, and then winds the remainder of the fibres and the wire to the eye. Then, leaving the fibres where they are, he winds the wire back to the rear of the thorax and bends the fibres back and fastens them in. Finally, he brings the wire forward to the eye and laps the fibres back to it again. He then cuts off any spare fibres and finishes off.

It will be noted that no hackle is provided as Mr. Sawyer has found that there is no need to include in the dressing anything to suggest legs. He stresses, however, and this is important, that the fly should have a very pronounced thorax and a body which tapers neatly to the tail. The thorax, which really represents the wing-cases, should be much darker than the rest of the body and this is achieved by the lapping of the butt ends of the fibres backward and forward.

Some doubt has been expressed at the use of a reddish-brown body to imitate the nymph of the olive dun, and it is possible that the trout take it for a drowned spinner, or even for the pupae of some summer sedges, which have a ruddy brown body and which are often found in autopsies during the bright days of July and August. This, however, does not alter the fact that the pattern is a first-class killer.

A pattern of the blue-winged olive nymph devised by Mr. John Hamp which has been extraordinarily successful on the Itchen when the naturals are hatching out during the daytime, is tied with a body dubbed with fox's fur dyed in picric acid mixed with hare's ear and a little hare's poll. A short hackle (one turn only) of a dark blue dun hen or very small partridge, and whisks from a speckled guinea fowl or mallard tied short. A gold rib is optional. Tying silk, pale orange. Hook, number 13 or 14.

I will not, however, pursue the subject further as this book is not intended in any way to instruct the reader how to fish.

In reference to the ethics of fishing an artificial nymph, my own view is that since the natural insect forms such a large and important part of the trout's diet, it is perfectly reasonable and legitimate for anglers to practise this form of fishing. Why it should ever be looked upon in any other light amazes me, for it is a normal form of wet fly-fishing, and it is generally agreed that many (possibly most) north country hackled flies are most probably taken for nymphs so that there is nothing exactly new in the idea! That it is a method of wet fly-fishing can hardly be disputed and consequently it must be agreed that it should not be employed on any water where "dry fly only" is a rule.

Beyond that I can see no reason why the use of an artificial nymph should be condemned as it sometimes is. The argument that too many undersized fish are hooked on Nymphs need not be seriously considered because, as Mr. Skues advocates, the artificial Nymph should be cast only over selected feeding fish, the operative word being "selected". When this is done, it is usually (not always) possible to pick out sizable trout.

That Nymph-fishing calls for any greater degree of skill than ordinary wet fly-fishing, I do not believe; in fact, the reverse may be the case. Nor does it seem to me to be in any way an unsporting or an over-deadly method of angling as is sometimes suggested. If I do not practise it myself more often, it is only because like so many others, I find that the use of a dry fly is more pleasurable, more interesting, probably easier, and possibly more profitable. Even on what are known as typical wet-fly streams, my conviction is that, taking the season through, the floating fly can generally hold its own against the wet patterns—or the Nymph.

Nevertheless it is a fact that a great number of fishermen have tremendous faith in the artificial nymph and maintain that no angler's education is complete until he has mastered the art of using it correctly. This is quite true, but this digression is occasioned by the attitude of some of them towards the dry fly. They point out that to try to catch fish on a floater when they are engaged in feeding on nymphs is extremely foolish, and, furthermore, that trout devote far more of their time to nymphs than ever they do to surface insects. And, therefore, they maintain that it must always be more profitable to fish a Nymph than a dry fly.

With much of this, one can but agree, although I think that the answer is that the real pleasure we get from fishing is not wholly derived from the number of fish we catch. The method of catching them is at least of equal importance. If that is agreed, I would venture to suggest that although both have their uses, the dry fly has more to commend it than the artificial nymph.

In conclusion, I cannot resist quoting from the leading article in *The Field* of 2nd October 1937, although I will do so without making a comment of any sort. It ended thus: "Does the maggot, with its sinuous attraction for fish, offend? Surely, after all, it is own brother to a nymph."

OAK FLY (*Leptis scolopacea: L. lineola*)

A large fly, nearly a third of an inch in length, with an orange and brown striped body. It is found in the early part of the season, usually on tree trunks, and from its characteristic attitude of resting with its head downwards, it is commonly known as the "down-looker". Other local names are Ash fly, Woodcock fly and Cannon fly.

The small oak fly (*L. lineola*) is similar in appearance to the oak fly but about half its size.

In *The Compleat Angler* we are told that it is a most excellent fly and that "you may make the Oak Flie with an orange, tawny, and black ground; and the brown of a mallard's feather for the wings".

In spite of the fact that most ancient angling authors mention the oak fly as one which is of interest to fishermen, I shall need a lot of convincing that as an article of a trout's diet it is of the least importance. It is a very strong flyer which must seldom get carried on to the water and I have very seldom seen one in an autopsy. Nevertheless, for some reason, the artificial pattern appears to be quite attractive to trout from April until June.

A typical modern dressing is:

Body: Orange floss silk.
Tail: Two strands of red hackle.
Hackle: Coch-y-bondhu hackle.
Wings: Woodcock wing feather.
Hook: 12 to 14.

That most ingenious fly-dresser, Mr. T. J. Hanna, has recently been experimenting with a new body material, or rather one which I do not remember seeing before. This is ordinary parchment which can easily be cut to any desired shape and can also be dyed. That does not exhaust its merits, for it is fairly translucent and becomes beautifully soft when wet, without becoming too limp. Readers will appreciate the possibilities it offers for bodies and wings of several insects and beetles.

OLD JOAN. See FEBRUARY RED

OLIVE DUN (*Baetis rhodani, B. vernus,* etc.)

The olive dun must be considered as one of the most important trout flies for several reasons. It is the best known and most common of the Ephemeridae; it is found on the water in every month of the year; it is widely distributed; and it is well-liked by trout and grayling.

There are few rivers and brooks in Great Britain on which it is not found and it is common throughout most European countries. Whereas other insects are seasonal, the olive is more or less always with us and wherever there is water, it is seldom far away.

The name is applied to two common and three rare species of the Baetis genus, but the differences between them are so small that anglers may conveniently treat them as one species. The natural insect hatches in every month of the year, although only abundantly so in spring and autumn. The big hatches decrease towards the end of May and, in any case, trout transfer their affections to the iron-blue dun directly that fly makes its appearance. By mid-June, the olive ceases to show in any strength, although it appears in large numbers again towards the end of August or early in September.

The large olive of spring is often known as the blue dun, although this is purely the angler's name for it and one which is not recognized by entomologists. As the season advances, the olive dun has a tendency to become lighter and smaller and the autumn insects do not compare in size with those of spring. The difference is so marked as to suggest that they are of a different species but there is no scientific proof that this is so. The hatch usually starts up suddenly about midday and is generally over by the late afternoon.

There cannot be many fishermen who are unable to identify the olive dun because constant contact with it has made most of us familiar with its appearance, but in view of its importance, a brief description is appended for beginners.

The dun is a little smaller than the b.-w.o., but half as large again as a pale watery or iron-blue dun. It has four wings and two setae, the hind wings being noticeably small with oval tips. The wings of the sub-imago are brownish-grey, although in cold weather, they take on a lead-blue tint. The setae are of about the same length as the body, which is olive in colour.

The male spinner has transparent glassy wings, turbinate eyes of a brownish-red colour, and a pale translucent olive-green body of which the last four segments are of a rich brownish tint. Except for its larger size, it could easily be mistaken for the male spinner of the iron-blue dun or that of a pale watery.

The female imago of the olive has transparent wings like those of the male and dead-gold body, which after exposure to the air becomes darker and eventually, when the insect is spent, a dead-leaf colour. She is then known to fishermen as a red spinner, although it should be noted that this term is loosely, and less correctly, applied to the spinners of several other Ephemerids.

The olive dun is not particularly difficult to identify, although one must beware of a small march brown (*Ecdyurus lateralis*) which appears from April to October and superficially looks far more like an olive than a march brown.

Fly-fishermen recognize two shades of olives and have named them the dark and medium olives. The latter is certainly considerably lighter in colour and is possibly a different species, although whether this is so or not, has yet to be determined. The necessity of observing the colour of fly which fish are taking will be appreciated as it will be a decisive factor when selecting an artificial pattern.

No fisherman would wish to be without a number of patterns to imitate the olive dun and for reasons which will be obvious, these should be in different sizes and in various shades with the darker ones predominating. As is only to be expected where such a useful and widely distributed fly is concerned, there are any amount of patterns from which to choose both in wet and dry. In fact, the number is so great that it is by no means easy to know which patterns to recommend, but one must certainly not forget such well-known flies as the Blue Dun, Blue Upright, Waterhen Bloa, Rough Olive, Olive Quill, Olive Upright, Gold-Ribbed Hare's Ear, Willow and Greenwell's Glory. For the spinners too there are several excellent patterns including the Red Spinner, Lunn's Particular and Pheasant Tail.

Of the patterns bearing the Olive Dun name, the following can be regarded as a typical tie for the dry fly:

Body: Medium olive seal's fur.
Wings: Starling's wing feather, primary.
Hackle: Cock's hackle dyed same shade of olive as body.
Tail: Three whisks, same colour as body.
Hook: 14.

For a wet winged pattern, that below is one of the most usual:

Body: Yellow tying silk, well waxed, and sometimes ribbed with fine gold wire.
Hackle and Whisks: Olive hen.
Wings: Snipe or starling wing feather, secondary.
Hook: 14.

Mr. Woolley recommends the addition of a gold tip to the bodies of all wet Olive Duns and there is no doubt that this makes them more attractive.

For the large early olive, Mr. Skues has a hackle dressing which is excellent. His tie is:

Tying silk: Yellow.
Hackle: Sharp darkish blue cock.
Whisks: Ditto, from spade feather.
Rib: Fine gold wire.
Body: A rainbow mixture of seal's fur, comprising yellow, orange, green, and olive, with a dash of crimson and a little hare's poll to bind the mixture.
Hook: 14.

For later in the season, there is another good hackled pattern, a Medium Olive, which is tied thus:

Body: Pale yellow horse-hair over the bare hook.
Hackle: Light natural honey dun.
Whisks: Ditto.
Hook: 14.

In his *Modern Development of the Dry Fly*, Halford gave a series of dry patterns for use on the chalk streams, many of which have retained their original popularity. All have condor quill bodies, a material which is not easy to obtain. Dyed peacock quill can be utilized as a substitute, but although it is easier to strip, it lacks the strength of condor. I like particularly Halford's dressing for the female dark olive dun, possibly because I have used it more often than any of his others. The dressing is:

Wings: Coot.
Hackles: Two cock hackles dyed pale olive-green.
Body: Stripped condor dyed pale olive-green.
Whisks: Gallina dyed pale olive-green.
Hook: 15.

Whilst there is no doubt that a quill body has a most natural appearance, on the whole I prefer fur of some sort, because it is a much better material for absorbing oil; and buoyancy is of great importance.

Of all flies tied to imitate the olive dun, it is probable that the most generally useful wet pattern is the Rough Olive of which the dressing will be found on page 299. Nevertheless as a general pattern wet or dry, it is likely that most fishermen would cast their vote for Greenwell's Glory. By slight changes in the colour and size, it can be used to imitate all the olives in their different colourings and consequently it is subject to many variations. The best of these is, I think, that first class dry pattern designed by Mr. Skues. Effective from April until the end of September, it may be tied in different shades to suit different conditions. The basic tie is as under:

Tying silk: Primrose or yellow, waxed with clear wax.
Rib: Fine gold wire.
Hackle: Greenish yellow-olive cock.
Whisks: Ditto, sharp and bright.
Wings: Starling, from palest to dark.
Hook: 15 or 16.

OLIVE QUILL

Fished wet or dry, this is a useful pattern for either river or lake and serves as an imitation of the natural olive dun. The colour of the wing is better on the dark side and in commercial patterns it is often far too light. The usual tie is:

Body: Peacock quill, dyed olive.
Wings: Medium or dark starling's wing feather.
Hackle: Dyed medium or dark olive cock's.
Tail: Three whisks as hackle.
Hook: 14 to 16.

Nowadays hackled patterns are often preferred and Halford's tie for the Hackle Dark Olive Quill can be recommended.

Head Hackle: Medium or dark blue dun hen.
Shoulder Hackle: Dyed green olive.
Body: Peacock (or condor) quill, dyed green olive.
Whisk: Gallina, dyed green olive.
Hook: 16 to 14.

Another good hackled variation is dressed as follows:

Hackle: Pale silvery dun cock.
Body: Peacock quill dyed canary yellow.
Whisk: White cock's beard hackle, dyed medium olive.
Hook: 14 to 16.

This pattern is usually tied buzz.

OLIVE UPRIGHT

A west-country pattern, fished both wet and dry, to imitate the olive dun. The tie for the wet fly is:

Body: Peacock quill from the eye, dyed yellow.
Hackle: Olive cock.
Whisks: Ditto.
Hook: 14.

ORANGE DUN

An old Yorkshire wet pattern for trout and grayling, especially useful in August and September in high coloured water.
Dressing:

Body: Orange silk.
Legs: Furnace hackle.
Wings: Dark part of starling's wing.
Hook: 14

ORANGE FLY

One of the oldest patterns but seldom used nowadays. According to Ronalds, it represents one of the ichneumon flies, those curious-looking insects, which in spite of their fearsome appearance, receive a hearty welcome from trout. According again to Ronalds, these flies are frequently found in the stomachs of trout, a statement which I can confirm. That ichneumonoids get carried on to the water in such numbers must be because there are so many of them—well over two thousand British species!

Whatever its natural prototype, the Orange fly is an excellent grayling pattern, and a better trout fly for rough streams than is generally supposed. At least one fisherman of my acquaintance, whose greatest pleasure in life is grayling fishing, is of the opinion that the Orange Fly is the most deadly grayling pattern ever invented. Ronalds's original dressing has never been bettered. It is:

Body: Orange floss silk tied on with black silk thread.
Wings: Dark part of a starling's wing or feather of a hen blackbird.
Legs: A very dark furnace hackle.
Hook: 14.

ORANGE GOVERNOR. See GOVERNOR

ORANGE OTTER

An astonishingly good dry pattern for grayling, invented by that well-known fly-tier and expert fisherman, the Rev. Edward Powell, of Munslow, Shropshire. The "O.O." is a fly over which even staid and sedate grayling anglers find it difficult to restrain their enthusiasm. I have heard it described as "phenomenal" and "devastating", and an American, who had enjoyed much sport with it in this country, told me that it was "one hell of a fly". Its inventor says that it is the only fly he knows which will bring up grayling from the bottom when they are not on the feed.

I can well believe this, for it is an unusual and most attractive-looking pattern which will take grayling from August to November. Incidentally, towards the end of the season—in August and September—it is well worth a trial for trout. At times they will ignore it entirely, but if they take it at all, it is deadly. But it is as a grayling fly that the "O.O." is pre-eminent, although why this should be so is not easy to understand since it is a fly which would appear to bear no resemblance to anything in heaven or on earth.

The dressing is:

Hackle: Very small red cock, tied nearly in centre of body.
Body: (In two parts, thorax and abdomen, divided by the hackle.) Pale biscuit-coloured underpart of an otter's throat, soaked overnight in picric acid solution, and then boiled for a few minutes in the same solution, plus an equal volume of red ink, plus an equal amount of water.
Whisks: Red cock.
Hook: 16.

The biggest difficulty in tying this fly correctly is to get hold of the right part of an otter's skin, for it is an area which measures a few square inches only. Most of the under-pelt of an otter is dark grey in colour and only on the throat and face is it of the required pale buff biscuit colour.

ORANGE QUILL

Under certain conditions of light, particularly in the late evening, this fly is the best representation of the blue-winged olive ever devised. For that reason, it is a pattern which no dry fly angler can afford to be without from June onwards, wherever the natural insect is found.

It was a pattern which was apparently unknown to Halford, although except for the colour of the body, it is the same as the Red Quill, and for the b-w.o. it is dressed on a rather larger hook than is usual for that fly. The Orange Quill is always associated with Mr. G. E. M. Skues, for although he did not invent it, it was he who discovered the pattern and, more important still, its great value when the b.-w.o. is hatching at dusk.

It was in the early 'nineties of the last century that Mr. Skues found a solitary specimen of this fly, dressed on a largish hook, among the stock of James Currel, the tackle dealer in Parchment Street, Winchester, and shortly afterwards when wanting a rather large fly to imitate some duns than any he customarily used, he tried the orange-bodied specimen. It did not take him long to find out that it was a pattern which was quite exceptionally efficacious when the b.-w.o. was hatching at dusk.

When trout or grayling are taking the natural insect and can be induced to look at the Orange Quill, they will take it freely and what is more, they will go on taking it, so that one can be almost certain of creeling a number of fish. There are very few patterns of which that can be said with equal truth.

Mr. Skues himself enjoyed some wonderful catches with this fly on the Itchen and in his *Minor Tactics* he says of it: "Patterns are tied which will kill an occasional trout, but the Orange Quill, if the river be anything like a good one, means three or four brace and probably all big fish." By some odd chance the dressing of this celebrated pattern has never been given in any of his books, although, I believe, he has given it in the *Journal of the Fly-Fishers' Club*. His tie is as under:

Tying silk: Hot orange.
Wings: Pale starling, rather full, as the natural insect has wings longer than the ordinary olive duns.
Hackle: Bright red cock.
Whisks: Same colour, or paler, from spade feather of cock.
Body: Pale condor quill, stripped, so as to show no dark edge, and dyed hot orange.
Hook: 14, occasionally 13.

Since the dun hatch and the fall of spinners is usually going on simultaneously, it becomes a matter of opinion as to whether trout take the Orange Quill for the male dun, or for the sherry spinner. Statements to the contrary notwithstanding, Mr. Skues himself has an open mind on the subject, as he has confirmed in a recent letter to me.

Whichever the fish take it for is not a matter of any consequence, and the Orange Quill must be regarded as one of the most satisfactory representations of the b.-w.o. It is a great mistake to think that it is purely a chalk-stream pattern. Nothing is further from the truth, and on rivers differing in character as widely as the Test and the Onny it has provided me with some of the best sport it has been my lot to experience. When conditions are right for its employment, I can think of no artificial fly which can fill the dry fly angler with a greater degree of confidence. Truly a great pattern!

ORANGE SPINNER

This pattern is recommended by Mr. Skues as being sometimes very deadly on an evening just before the blue-winged olive comes on. It is possibly taken for the female imago—the Sherry Spinner.

His dressing is:

Tying silk: Ordinary orange.
Body: Bright medium orange seal's fur.
Hackle: Rusty dun cock.
Rib: Fine gold wire.
Whisks: Three strands of spade feather from shoulder of honey dun cock.
Hook: 14 or 15.

ORANGE TAG. See RED TAG

ORL FLY. See ALDER

PALE AUTUMN DUN

This pattern was devised (for dry fly-fishing) as a representation of the autumn pale wateries, by F. M. Walbran, when he was fishing on the Wharfe in 1888. To-day it is used mostly as a grayling fly, but it bears no great reputation. This is a little surprising since F. M. Walbran placed it first on his list of grayling dry patterns, and he was one of the greatest grayling fishermen of all time. Doubtless, since he invented it, he had particular faith in its killing powers, but there is evidence to show that many other anglers of his generation, both in Yorkshire and Derbyshire, were equally convinced of its especial merits.

Walbran's dressing was:

Body: Pale yellow silk, dubbed with rust-coloured fur from a red squirrel.
Legs: Pale honey dun.
Wings: The slaty-blue feather from a tern's wing, set well up.
Hook: 14.

This pattern has no resemblance to Halford's Autumn Dun.

PALE WATERY DUN (*Centroptilum luteolum, C. pennulatum, Baetis biocu-latus, Procloëon rufulum*) (Plate V, 2)

For the last seventy years or so, the name "pale watery" has been used amongst anglers to denote any and all of the above four species which differ so slightly that to the average fisherman, they have the appearance of being one and the same fly. Modern opinion, however, decrees that it would be better for the two Centroptilum species to be treated separately and to have a nomenclature of their own. Accordingly they are treated in this manner below.

The pale watery dun is one of the smaller members of the Ephemeroptera, being about the same size as the iron-blue dun and consequently considerably smaller than the olives. It first appears in May and lasts through the season, although on northern rivers, I have no record of having observed it before June.

The dun has very pale greyish wings, a light (almost colourless) body, pale green legs and two setae. The colouring of both duns and spinners is subject to a certain amount of variation, but the duns, at least, are scarcely likely to be confused with any other flies except the olives. As a rough guide, it can be said that the wings of the pale watery dun are generally pale grey, whilst those of the olive dun appear to be of a darker colour with a touch of brown in them. As already mentioned, the pale watery dun is also smaller and a comparison of sizes alone should be sufficient to prevent confusion.

The spinners present a more difficult problem. The pale watery spinners are beautiful little insects with clear glassy wings and brightly coloured eyes, but the males are almost indistinguishable from the male spinners of the olive. Since trout cannot apparently differentiate between them, the matter is of no great consequence. However, in both cases, the last few segments of the body are of a different colour to the remainder; in the pale watery, they are dark orange, and in the olive they are more of a rich brown. The female pale watery spinner is very similar to the spinner of the female iron blue.

As I have already indicated above, the Centroptilum species have certain small points of difference to those of the Baetis family, and modern entomologists therefore hold that they should not be designated pale wateries. Although it cannot be of much importance to the average fly-fisher (who need not, therefore, trouble to read the next few paragraphs), it may be said that *C. pennulatum*, which is the real nigger in the wood-pile, is definitely rather larger than the other flies in the group and its wings cannot be termed pale; a better description of them would be slaty-blue, although they are not as dark as those of the iron-blue dun. Its season is from July until the end of September.

Mr. H. D. Turing, the editor of the *Salmon and Trout Magazine*, has suggested in that journal that the greater spur wing would be a suitable name for *C. pennulatum*, whilst *C. luteolum* might be called the lesser spur wing. This seems to be a sensible arrangement, although I am not sure that the possibility of there being a smaller type of *C. pennulatum* can be altogether ruled out, in which case I suppose it would have to be designated the not-so-great spur wing! The suggested names come from the characteristic spur found on the hind wings of both species of Centroptilum, an unmistakable feature, although one which cannot be detected with the naked eye. Incidentally, there was a time when *C. pennulatum* used to be known to anglers as the large blue-winged pale watery, and this name appears to be coming in favour again.

Both male and female duns of the greater spur wing are about the size of the b-w.o. duns, with wings of the same dark blue colour, plus a couple of very long setae. The body, however, is distinctive. Long and tapered and so light in colour as to be almost white, it is flat on the underside with faint brown markings on the last two or three segments of the rounded upper side. The duns and spinners of the b.-w.o. have, of course, three setae and those of the Centroptilum two.

The lesser spur wing (*C. luteolum*) is a useful fly to the angler, but like the rest of the pale watery family, it is too small and too fragile to be copied easily. The Poult Bloa would be quite a fair imitation were the wings not so dark. Mr. Turing has suggested that it might be worth trying a hackle fly with a pale blue hackle and a rather reddish-yellow body.

Intermittently found on many rivers, this species has been reported from the Test, Itchen, Nadder, Kennet, Usk, Upper Avon (Wilts), Dee (Wales), and from many other localities, including Lancashire and Yorkshire.

All the fuss about separating Centroptilum and Baetis is caused because modern opinion suggests that the spur wing is of much greater interest to trout than the pale watery, in spite of the fact that to our eyes they look so alike. Although the appearance of *C. pennulatum* is very spasmodic, no less an authority that Mr. Skues has said that when it appears on the water in any force, it is an insect of outstanding attractiveness to trout. In fact, this greater spur wing is now known to be one

of those flies which trout will often pick out from a mass of other up-
winged duns and consequently if an angler is lucky enough to detect
its presence on the river, he may enjoy great sport with a suitable
artificial copy. Mr. George Monkhouse, who has made a special study
of the spur wings, evolved the following dressing to represent the
female spent spinner:

Tying silk: Hot orange.
Body: Cream ram's wool mixed with a very little red seal's fur (a sort of Tup
mixture).
Hackle: Four turns of bright medium honey dun cock.
Whisks: Cream.
Hook: 14.

Mr. Martin Mosely has pointed out that the turbinate (viz. shaped
like a top) eyes of the male spinners of the two species are of different
colours, those of *C. pennulatum* being of a light cadmium orange and
those of *luteolum*, the lesser spur wing, being light red. This is worth
noting by those who are entomologically minded, for when the spinners are seen in the air or on the water, their brightly coloured eyes
form a most distinctive feature.

The pale watery dun is imitated by numerous well-known dressings,
of which that evolved by Mr. Skues is one of the most effective. He
terms it an improvement upon the Little Marryat and states that it
should be tied 'Hassam-wise', a method of dressing described in his
book *Side-Lines, Side-Lights, and Reflections*, on pages 231 to 234. The
tie is:

Tying silk: Cream waxed with clear wax.
Hackle: Cream dun cock.
Whisks: To match.
Body: Finest cream-coloured fur from seal's cub, close to skin.
Wings: Young starling.
Hook: 15.

Mr. Skues also recommends this spent pattern as being useful for afternoon or evening fishing:

Tying silk: Palest faded orange.
Hackle: Large pale blue cock, spun, and then fixed to right and left sides by figure of eight and cut down to the woolly centre of feather.
Whisks: Pale honey dun cockerel.
Body: Pale lamb's wool or baby seal.
Hook: 16.

Most artificial patterns, such as the Little Marryat, are fished dry. This is one of the most widely used, but several others can be recommended and are equally popular. These include the Blue Quill, Ginger Quill, Autumn Dun, Dotterel Dun, and Lock's Fancy, whilst to imitate the spinners there are the Pheasant Tail and Lunn's Particular.

The Little Marryat tied on a 14 hook is called the Whitchurch Dun, but it is then too large to serve as a copy of a pale watery dun. Mr. Taverner may perhaps be right when he suggests that it is taken for *C. pennulatum*.

Lastly, Tup's Indispensable must not be forgotten, for it is one of the best patterns to imitate the pale watery in its dun stage.

PALMERS

There are many sorts of Palmers, such as the red, black, grey, brown, gold, grizzle, white, red tag, and soldier. According to old authorities like Ronalds, all of them represent hairy caterpillars, especially those of the Tiger moth (*Arctia caja*), Ermine moth (*Spilosoma lubricepeda*) and the Fox moth (*Lasiocampa rubi*), all of which are better known by the schoolboy's name of "woolly bears".

This theory seems to be somewhat far-fetched, for one seldom sees any of these caterpillars and the number which fall into the water must surely be negligible. But whatever they take them for, fish will sometimes rise freely to any of the numerous palmer flies.

The present-day dressings differ to some extent from those used in Ronalds's days, and it seems feasible that in the smaller sizes, when fished wet, they may be taken for freshwater shrimps, nymphs, or the larvae of many aquatic insects. Larger Palmers, when used on the surface, are almost certainly taken for moths struggling on the water, for they must suggest these reasonably well.

Certainly as general flies, they prove quite tempting to trout in all sorts of waters and, towards dusk, I have known many a big fish fall to a judiciously placed Palmer after some of these fish had resisted the temptation to rise at small delicately tied patterns designed to imitate the fly on the water.

Thames trout are popularly supposed (probably quite erroneously) to find a Red Tag Palmer attractive, whilst the Soldier Palmer in a suitable size is a reliable pattern for sea-trout, and all Palmers are quite excellent for chub. Fifty or sixty years ago the Palmers, especially the red variety, were favourites for trout, but to-day they are more frequently used for chub and dace.

The Palmer is almost the oldest British fly and Izaak Walton refers to it in the following manner: "Mr. Barker commends several sorts of Palmer flies, not only those ribbed with silver and gold, but others that have their bodies all made black, or some with red and a red hackle."

The name Palmer arises from the days of the crusades when it was the term used for warriors who had returned from the Holy Land, since it was their custom to bring back branches of palm. It then became applied to the woolly caterpillars from their nomadic habits and subsequently to describe the artificial flies which they were supposed to represent.

The usual dressings of the more popular patterns are appended below. All nowadays are fished wet or dry.

Red Palmer

Body: Seal's fur or wool dyed red and ribbed with flat gold tinsel. Often peacock herl is preferred to the seal's fur.
Hackle: Red cock's hackle, tied palmer-wise.
Hook: 12 to 9.

Black Palmer

Body: Seal's fur or wool dyed brown and ribbed with flat gold tinsel.
Hackle: Black cock's, tied palmer-wise.
Hook: 12 to 9.

Grey Palmer

Body: Seal's fur or wool dyed grey and ribbed with flat gold tinsel.
Hackle: Badger, white with dark centre, tied palmer-wise.
Hook: 12 to 9.

Soldier Palmer

Body: Scarlet seal's fur or wool ribbed with flat gold tinsel.
Hackle: Bright chestnut cock, wound palmer-wise and held down by gold wire.
Hook: 12 to 9.
This pattern is often used to represent the soldier beetle.

The Blue Palmer and the Claret Palmer are Irish salmon patterns, quite unlike the flies known elsewhere as Palmers.

PARACHUTE FLIES

A type of fly in which the hackle is tied round a piece of gut or other projection affixed to the top of the hook shank near the eye so that the hackle lies horizontally across the hook which it covers in the manner of an open umbrella. The weight of the hook underneath the expanded circular hackle balances the fly which falls lightly on the water in parachute fashion. Mr. T. J. Hanna winds the hackles round their own stems instead of round some extraneous projection which makes the fly lighter, although probably with some loss of strength. Various patterns are made in parachute style which has long been the speciality of a well-known Scottish tackle firm but whether they invented it I am unable to say. An American account states that it was originated by Mr. William Brush, of Detroit, who applied for a patent for the idea in 1931 and this was granted in 1934. In this instance, the patent related, of course, to a projection on the hook and not to the fly itself.

A great many anglers are enthusiastic about this type of lure and maintain that not only does it fall more lightly on the water than any other form of artificial but also that it floats better. This may be true where placid streams are concerned and would account for the fact that parachute flies are said to be especially killing on dead calm water; but in rough fast rivers, their performance does not seem to me to be so convincing. When once a ripple or two has broken over them, my experience is that they soon become waterlogged. For lake fishing I have found them far better.

Perhaps being at heart something of a purist in that I prefer, whenever possible, to use a copy, or at least a suggestion, of the fly on the water, my enthusiasm for the parachute type of fly (which is definitely a nondescript) has never been great. On the other hand, there is no doubt that there are plenty of fly-fishers who swear by them and believe that they will often tempt fish when no other form of artificial is any good at all.

Of the several patterns of flies made up in this manner, the favourite would appear to be that known as the "Greenwell", although its resemblance to Greenwell's Glory is not too obvious.

PARAGON

One of the Rev. Edward Powell's patterns designed to suggest any dark sedge. Always fished dry, it proves deadly on some rivers although useless on others. On the whole, I think that it may be considered as one of the very best sedge patterns and it is well worth a trial at any time from June onwards.

Dressing:

Hackle: Two Rhode Island hen; not orange or red, but a cold purplish chocolate. About ten turns in all, well-pressed together.
Body: Rabbit's face, very full.
Whisk: Three or four fibres from the spade feather of a dark red cock.
Hook: 12 to 14.

Of the dressing, the inventor says: "This is a modification of one of Dai Lewis's patterns and is tied with hen hackles. The reason for this is that hen's feathers being fluffier and less sparkling than cock's, make a better suggestion of the wings of the Trichoptera family whose great characteristic is their hairiness."

The addition of the whisk is, of course, a departure from nature, but that does not seem to worry the trout and it makes the fly float better.

PARMACHENEE BELLE

Probably the most killing trout fly throughout the New World, it is by no means worthless in Great Britain. In spite of its appearance, which bears no resemblance to any living creature, as a wet fly for rivers and lakes in this country, it deserves consideration, whilst on Devonshire streams it is looked upon as a first-class pattern for sea-trout. I have killed a few trout on it and on each occasion have been filled with surprise that fish could be deceived by a lure of such fantastic appearance.

The Parmachenee Belle was invented a few years before 1880 by the great American fisherman, the late Henry P. Wells, or rather it was the joint creation of himself and a friend. The dressing seems to have been largely the outcome of pure chance, although Wells expressed the opinion that his pattern possibly imitated the ventral fin of a trout. I have also seen it suggested that it is intended to represent the February red, an idea which seems just as far fetched as the previous one.

Of this fly's enormous popularity in the States and Canada, where it is employed both wet and dry, there can be no two opinions, but even in those countries, anglers appear to have no definite idea as to why it proves so deadly.

Writing of this pattern Wells said: "Unless I am deceived, these large trout take the fly, not as an insect, but as some form of live bait. If this be true, an imitation of some favourite form of food is in itself sufficient in all circumstances, provided it is so conspicuous as to be readily seen. To test this theory, the fly in question was made, imitating in colour the belly-fin of the trout itself. Place the whole catalogue of known flies in one hand and this single fly on the other, and force me to choose and confine myself to that choice, and for fishing those waters, I would choose the Parmachenee Belle every time. I have tried it in sunshine and rain, at noonday and in the gloaming, and at all times it has proved successful."

"Those waters" were the Maine lakes and it was after one of them—the Parmachenee Lake—that the fly was named.

The correct dressing of this pattern, in the inventor's own words, is as follows:

Body: Lemon-yellow mohair, wrapped with silver tinsel.
Tail: Two to four strands of white and scarlet.
Hackle: White and scarlet. (I have sometimes wound both hackles on at the same time, and sometimes the white first and the scarlet afterwards and over the white, capping it as it were; the latter is the better.)
Wings: White striped with scarlet, the white decidedly predominating.
Hook: For Great Britain, 10 to 14.

Normally scarlet ibis mixed with white goose is used for the tail, and mixed scarlet ibis and white for the wings.

PARTRIDGE AND ORANGE

One of the standard north-country flies for trout and grayling, the Orange Partridge, as it is also called, is an indispensable pattern for fast rocky rivers and is almost as effective as a general lake fly.

With the Partridge and Yellow, a similar pattern but with a yellow silk body, it shares the name of the Partridge Hackle and both are sometimes known as the Partridge Spider. There are other patterns in the Partridge series with bodies of black, claret, green and other colours, but the two mentioned above are by far the most used.

There is some diversity of opinion as to what the Partridge and Orange is intended to represent; some anglers say a spent spinner, others a nymph, and still others, a freshwater shrimp. But all agree that it serves well as a copy of the February red.

The Orange Partridge is, in fact, a modern version of an old dressing of the February red, the orange silk body when wet, turning to a rich mahogany colour. The Turkey Brown of Ronalds is the same fly and is almost identical with another Yorkshire pattern, the Brown Watchet, except that the latter has a peacock herl head.

The Partridge and Orange is a first-class killer from April to the end of the season in most rivers and lakes, although, of course, it is on the northern rivers that it is most regularly used. Some years ago, when stationed in Yorkshire, I managed to fish the Swale and other rivers for a few hours each day on six days a week for the whole of one season. My diary shows that during that period about 85 per cent of all the trout I caught were taken on three patterns—Orange Partridge, Snipe and Purple, and Williams's Favourite. And of these three, the first named was the most successful and markedly so in the first part of the season.

Like all other northern spider flies, it is invariably fished wet and when in a team of three, as the centre dropper. The dressing is not subject to any serious variations, although E. M. Tod, after referring to the Partridge and Orange as being a fly "of the greatest importance", stated that one of the best bodies was one of stripped peacock quill. The standard tie is:

Body: Orange silk.
Wings: Hackled with a well-dappled feather from a partridge's back.
Hook: 14.
   The body is sometimes ribbed with fine gold wire.

Lunn designed a fly for use on the Test which he called "The Big Orange Partridge Hackle". The late Major Hills considered it invaluable for trout and grayling in all waters and weathers, especially for smutting fish, besides being very effective for any trout which has risen to some copy of the olive, as long as it has not been pricked. The dressing is:

Hackle: Feather from the back of a partridge, cut or pinched off so that the fibres are a little longer than the hook.
Tail: Pale buff.
Body: Two strands of Salome brilliant artificial silk, shade 403 (orange), ribbed with plain round gold wire.
Tying silk: Pearsall's gossamer, shade 13.
Hook: 14 to 12.

See also BLUE PARTRIDGE

PARTRIDGE AND YELLOW

Another old standard Yorkshire pattern, also known as the Yellow Partridge. During April and May, this is a useful wet fly in most rivers. Widely known as a trout pattern, it does not seem to be generally known that it is an even better fly for grayling, although it proves deadly for these fish both on northern rivers and on the southern streams. The fly shown in the illustration was tied by Mr. Skues and exemplifies his idea of the "set" and amount of hackle suitable for this class of fly. Few will disagree with him and to my mind it is a perfect example of what a "spider" fly should be. One sees too many on which the hackle is far too full and is set on at the wrong angle, with the result that they are far less effective in use.

   The dressing is:

Body: Yellow tying silk, ribbed with oval gold twist.
Hackle: Hackled with a light feather from a partridge's back.
Hook: 14.

PET

It is a little strange but none the less true, that out of the hundreds of new patterns which must be produced each year by ordinary amateur fly tiers, very few ever become known outside a small local area. Yet, amongst them, there surely must be some good enough to kill on any river. One such which I have in mind is the Pet which was created some years ago by Mr. C. V. Hancock. Fished wet as a bob fly in sizes rather small for the prevailing conditions, this simple pattern has proved itself highly attractive to river trout in rough streams, loch trout, grayling, and sea-trout. And dressed on a size 8 hook, still fished as a bob, it has accounted for salmon in low water rippled by the breeze. Sparsely tied, it should prove an effective pattern for greased-line work.

Not many fishermen can know of this first-rate fly, but if they will give it a trial when conditions are suitable, I am confident that the results will prove satisfactory.

The dressing is:

Tail: None.
Body: Half narrow oval silver tinsel; half scarlet seal, ribbed ditto.
Hackle: Black, not too soft. The scarlet seal should be pricked out to mingle with the hackle.
Hook: 14.

PETER ROSS

The dressing of this celebrated pattern was evolved by Peter Ross (1873–1923), who kept a small general store in Killin, Perthshire. Although a keen angler, he never tied his own flies, and when he suggested this variation of the standard Teal and Red, he could little have thought that it would bring him everlasting fame amongst his brother anglers. The Teal and Red is a first class lake fly, and it would appear to be almost impossible that some very slight alteration in the tie should improve it tremendously. Yet, such is the case. Ross's inspiration turned a good fly into a much better one, and from the day on which he first used it, the pattern has grown in popularity until today it is generally regarded as the most killing lake fly throughout the British Isles.

As a sea-trout pattern it has few equals, and is a great favourite in Scotland, Wales, and Ireland, whilst in England it seems to be the inevitable first choice of nearly everyone who fishes for sea-trout.

As a river pattern for brown trout, its reputation is not so great. Some anglers have great faith in it, whilst others say that they have never taken a fish on it. Personally, I have had very little success with this pattern on any river, but I have seen at least one very large catch of trout taken on a small Peter Ross in dead low water in the middle of a hot August. There is no doubt that it is taken for a small fish and it is, of course, always fished wet.

The dressing is:

Tail: Golden Pheasant tippet.
Body: Halved—the tail end of flat silver tinsel; the remainder of red seal's fur. The whole is ribbed with fine oval silver wire.
Hackle: Black.
Wing: From the breast feather of a teal.
Hook: 10 to 14. For sea-trout, up to size 8.

PHEASANT AND DRAKE

The invention of that famous northern fisherman, "Dicky" Routledge. Although he died over sixty years ago, tales of his prowess with the rod are still related. Of the capabilities of this pattern I have no personal knowledge, but its pedigree is ample recommendation. His dressing was:

Body: Orange floss silk ribbed with silver wire.
Hackle: Furnace.
Wings: Teal and a brown feather from a pheasant's back.
Hook: 12.

This fly was fished wet and dressed spider fashion. Routledge was a great believer in varying the body colouring of a fly to suit special conditions. The above pattern was sometimes tied with a yellow silk body and also with claret and purple silk.

PHEASANT TAIL

One of the greatest patterns for all-round fishing and possibly the most useful all-purpose fly extant. Fished wet or dry, it is an effective representation of a number of flies, although it is as a suggestion of the spinner, rather than the dun, that it excels and more especially of the imagines of the b.-w.o., pale wateries, iron-blue and medium olives. It may also be taken as a march brown nymph.

Originally a Devonshire pattern, the Pheasant Tail is now used on almost every river in England, Wales and Ireland: it will kill brown trout, grayling, rainbows and is a first-class lake pattern. Every fly-fisherman finds a place for it in his box, for there are few days from May onwards when it will not prove its worth. Yet as flies go it is by no means an old pattern, for it was only invented in or about 1901, by Mr. Payne Collier. His own dressing was as under:

Hackle: Honey dun, called in the West Country, "brassy".
Body: A very dark herl of a cock pheasant's tail feather, with four turns of gold twist.
Tail: Three long herls from a saddle hackle.
Hook: 14.

It is important that the centre feather of a cock pheasant's tail should be used. No other will do as well. When the fly is used to imitate the iron-blue, a blue dun hackle cannot be bettered.

There are a number of slightly different dressings, although for general use I doubt if any are as good as the original. Nevertheless, there is a very killing pattern favoured by Mr. Skues which is tied as follows:

Tying silk: Hot orange.
Hackle: Rusty or sandy dun cock, bright and sharp.
Whisks: Two or three strands of honey dun cock spade feather.
Rib: Fine gold wire.
Body: Two or three strands of rich-coloured ruddy fibres from the centre feather of a cock pheasant's tail.
Hook: 16 to 13.

PINK LADY

A standard American dry pattern with the following dressing:

Body: Pink floss, ribbed gold oval tinsel.
Wings: From the quill feather of a starling.
Hackle: Pale ginger cock's.   *Tail:* As hackle, or tippet.

Little known in this country, the Pink Lady has come into some prominence in Northern Ireland in the last few years, in connection with a rather unusual method of taking large trout.

Mr. T. J. Hanna, the well-known fly dresser, author, and angler, has broadcast on this subject, and in answer to my request for information he has kindly sent me the following notes.

"For the past few seasons, very big trout (up to 10 lbs.) have been killed at night on the Ballinderry, by using large flies such as the Pink Lady and other dry flies such as are used for salmon. The usual procedure is to cast over a rising fish and then to move the fly by a few turns of the reel; then a pause for a few seconds before winding in again. This is looked upon as dry fly fishing, although the fly is dragging most of the time. However, the fish will sometimes make a rush at a fly being pulled across them in this manner, although on the whole, it is an irritating sort of business, because the fish may ignore the lure for long periods, although they will continue to indulge in splashing 'rises' apparently at nothing.

"These fish are lough trout (or 'dollaghans' as they are known locally), which move up river before spawning and, in my opinion, are rarely feeding fish. When the water falls, all the fish fall back to the deeper pools, and although at night they will roll and splash about a great deal, I do not think that it can be considered a true rise; it is more like the play of a salmon or sea-trout. These big trout will take a large wet fly in high water, but they have never been known to take a floating fly until the new method was introduced.

"One of the first fishermen to experiment with it caught so many big fish that he became rather scared lest it should be thought that he had been poaching them, so he sent for the Inspector of Fisheries, Mr. W. D. Duff, himself an angler. That night, he caught over 30 lbs. of trout, the largest fish being one of 8 lbs. Mr. Duff had over 20 lbs. made up of four fish only.

"Large-hackled flies are favoured. They float well and when dragged in make a well defined wake in the water. In my view, it is this which attracts fish to take these monstrosities, which may have the appearance of a struggling insect. We know little about what induces predatory fish of this type to take flies at night, although I believe that it is largely a matter of water temperature, and also possibly, sheer caprice on the part of the fish."

The Pink Lady was the invention of Mr. George LaBranche, an American dry fly angler, well known in this country.

PINK WICKHAM. See WICKHAM'S FANCY

POOLE'S LONG HACKLE. See VARIANTS

POPE'S GREEN NONDESCRIPT

Whether fished dry or wet, this is a splendid pattern and is generally regarded as the standard fly for dealing with "tailers". When trout are engaged in this annoying topsy-turvy occupation, one may cast over them repeatedly without gaining their interest, even if one succeeds in attracting their attention. The Pink Wickham, Red Quill, and Green Midge are good flies for "tailing" fish, but none of them equal the Nondescript tied in a very small size.

Why this pattern should interest them on these occasions has never been satisfactorily explained, but as Mr. Skues has pointed out, if it does not work for a "tailer" when fished floating, it is quite likely to attract him if it is sunk.

A useful chalk-stream fly, it is sometimes very effective in taking fish which are rising amongst weed-beds. It was the invention of Mr. W. H. Pope of Dorchester, who throughout his life was a familiar figure on the Hampshire and Dorset rivers.

The dressing is:

Wings: Light starling.
Body: Light green floss silk ribbed with rather broad flat gold.
Hackle and Whisk: Bright red cock.   *Hook:* 16 to 18.

This pattern must always be tied on a small hook. In New Zealand, it is generally dressed with red tying silk showing at the tail and thorax. Tied thus, it proves good medicine on warm sunny days, although it should not be called—as it usually is—a Pope's Nondescript.

POULT BLOA

A standard northern wet pattern to imitate the pale watery and also an effective suggestion of the nymph of the blue-winged olive. It will take trout right through the season, especially on cold dull days, but it is perhaps a better fly for grayling than for trout. The dressing is as below.

Body: Yellow silk, dubbed with red fur from a squirrel.
Hackle: Hackled with the slaty-blue feather from under the wing of a young
    grouse.   *Hook:* 16.

It is varied sometimes by dressing it with a plain yellow silk body, with or without a few turns of fine gold wire. There are only a few suitable feathers in a wing and they can only be obtained from a very young bird. In an older bird, they are too dark in colour. Like most Yorkshire flies, this pattern must be hackled very lightly.

Poult, of course, is a term for a young bird or pullet. Bloa is a curious term and purely of dalesman origin. In John Swarbrick's list of Wharf-dale flies (1807), it is also spelt blo and bloo, but that may be because the gentleman of Austby was somewhat illiterate. Its meaning is by no means clear and north countrymen explain it in many divers ways, no two of which appear to agree. When I asked the late J. H. R. Bazley, he replied: "It refers, I think, to the cold cloudy bleak sort of weather feather, used frequently with a yellow or partially yellow body. This is my conception of it and I may be wrong, but I don't think so. The word may possibly include a natural fly which hatches in the conditions indicated, but I hardly think this is so."

PRIEST

More of a grayling fly than a trout fly, it is to-day used fairly extensively by Midland and southern grayling anglers, and is always fished sunk.

The dressing is:

Body: Flat silver tinsel, ribbed with fine oval silver wire.
Hackle: Badger cock.
Tail: A few strands of red ibis.
Hook: 12 to 14.

PROFESSOR

This famous pattern was named after Professor John Wilson ("Christopher North", the author) sometime after he was appointed to the seat of Professor of Philosophy at Edinburgh University in the year 1820. It is considered a great fly for sea-trout and big brown trout and has long been popular in all European countries, whilst in America, with some slight variations in the dressing, it is a tremendous favourite. Although a typical wet pattern, in both U.S.A. and Canada, it is often tied as a floater.

Stoddart in his *Scottish Angler* wrote of it: "Foremost is the fly called the Professor. The wings are formed of a mottled feather taken from the mallard or wild drake; the body is of yellow floss silk, rather longish (the body, not the silk, which is trig and tightly wimpled) and wound close to the head with a fine red or black hackle; tails are often used but we think them unnecessary. Instead of a yellow silk body, we sometimes adopt one of pale green, especially in loch fishing."

The modern dressing, which differs slightly from that given by Stoddart (which was almost certainly the original), is as under:

Body: Primrose yellow silk ribbed with flat gold tinsel.
Wings: Mottled grey mallard.
Hackle: Ginger cock's.
Tail: Two or three long fibres of red ibis feather.
Hook: 12 to 6.

There is a story told of the origin of this fly, which you can believe or not, although the story is almost as old as the fly and is not as impossible as it might at first sound. According to the old account, Professor John Wilson was fishing a loch on which trout were rising well when he ran out of flies. Having some hooks and silk with him, he decided to see what he could do with the only materials which were conveniently available. These were not too promising and he could do no better than use buttercups for the body and leaves and bits of dried grass for the wings and hackle. To his surprise, he caught a number of fish on this improvised pattern and so, on returning home, he tied it again in more durable form. I have suggested that this story may not be altogether true, although I like to think it is. In his book, *The Rod and Gun*, published in 1840, Professor James Wilson, the brother of the originator of the Professor, described the fly as having wings "usually of mallard wing, barred by nature in the usual way and varied in the ground-colour by being dyed by art, lighter or darker as may be deemed advisable. His body is formed of Paisley yellow floss silk, its texture rather tight and slim in form. It is not always advisable to hackle him, although he may sometimes be so slightly either with red or black about the shoulders, but his prevailing character is that of clearness, quietness, loveliness and originality of composition with a good deal of sarcastic sharpness about the barb."

QUILL GORDON

An American dry pattern invented by Theodore Gordon who might be called the Halford of U.S.A. A highly popular fly in the land of its birth, there seems to be no valid reason why it should not kill well on English rivers. At a poll held some years ago at the Anglers' Club of New York, it shared, with the Whirling Dun, the first place as the most successful dry pattern. Gordon's own tie for his fly was:

Body: A strip of bi-coloured peacock quill, ribbed with fine gold wire.
Tail: Three or four fibres from wood-duck feathers.
Hackle: Smoke grey.
Wings: The unbarred feather of a summer duck.
Hook: 12 to 14.

As the summer (or wood) duck feather for the wings is now almost impossible to obtain, the flank feather of a mallard can be used as a substitute. Sometimes the fly is seen tied with an Andalusian cock hackle but this is totally incorrect.

Dr. Burke of Jersey City, N.J., the author of *American Dry Flies and*

How to Tie Them, has a great liking for Gordon's fly, although he prefers it wet. He has said that he needs only two patterns for the season, of which one is the Quill Gordon. He uses it for the first few weeks and then changes to the dry Hendrickson. He has also pointed out that the bi-coloured peacock quill required for the Quill Gordon presents a difficulty to the fly dresser for it can only be secured by stripping off the bluish-green herl from a barbule cut from the eye portion of a pea-cock's shoulder plume, commonly miscalled a tail feather. As only about one out of every twenty-five feathers will yield this two-coloured quill (the rest being brown), the strictly correct dressing is seldom seen on commercial flies.

I have dealt with the dressing of this pattern at some length because, although it is not an English fly, thousands of Quill Gordons are tied each year in our English factories for export to U.S.A. and some I have seen bear very little likeness to the original.

Theodore Gordon (1854–1915) tied his first dry flies when he received a comprehensive collection of chalk-stream patterns which were sent to him by F. M. Halford at his request. Thereafter Gordon set to work to imitate American insects and the Quill Gordon is obviously intended as a definite copy of some natural fly, apparently an up-winged dun of some sort. That he eschewed the use of split-wings is accounted for by the fact that he disliked them and tied very few of his patterns in that fashion.

QUILL MARRYAT

One of Mr. G. S. Marryat's favourite patterns and described by Halford as "the late Mr. Marryat's improvement of the celebrated Little Marryat named after him".

I do not know whether Marryat was responsible for the Quill Marryat, although from Halford's comment this would seem likely. But it was George Holland, the Winchester fly-dresser, who first tied this pattern, although probably he did so to Marryat's instructions.

It is a chalk-stream dry fly of which my own experience is nil, but it is looked upon as being a great little fly on a pale watery dun day.

Halford gives the following dressing:

Wings: Palest starling.
Body: A strand of peacock eye slightly bleached in hydrogen peroxide until it is the *café au lait* colour of the opossum fur.
Hackles: Two pale buff Cochin cock hackles.
Whisk: Pale olive Gallina.
Hook: 17 to 15.

It will be seen that this pattern is the same as the Little Marryat except for the body, which should be tied with a quill so bleached as to be nearly white with the rib a pale brownish yellow. Holland told Mr. Skues that he used to bleach the starling wing by exposing it to sunlight in a window for a few days.

RAIL FLIES

Quite unknown to the majority of anglers who fish only in England, the Rails, like the Wrens, are considered standard wet patterns throughout Eire. There is no doubt that on Irish rivers they prove first-rate killers, being especially effective for evening fishing, which is understandable since they are useful suggestions of many sedges. There are numerous flies in this series, of which the best known are the Black Rail, Green Rail, Yellow Rail, Orange Rail, Silver Rail, Brown Rail, and Claret Rail. Examples of the dressings of three of them will probably suffice.

BLACK RAIL

Tail: Two strands of guinea-fowl or teal.
Body: Black silk.
Hackle: Black.
Wings: From the black rail mixed with guinea-fowl so that the spots can be seen.
Hook: 10 to 14.

RED RAIL

Tail: Rat's whiskers, or a few strands of golden pheasant tippet.
Body: Orange or cardinal red silk, sometimes ribbed with black silk or gold, very lightly.
Hackle: Cock's hackle dyed blood-red.
Wing: Landrail.
Hook: 10 to 14.

YELLOW RAIL

Body: Lemon-coloured floss silk.
Hackle: Outside wing of landrail, slightly trimmed.
Wings: The ruddy-coloured feather of a landrail's pinion, dressed rather long and full. A turn of gold tinsel at the tail.
Hook: 10 to 14.

The Red Rail is known in some districts of Ireland as the Red Hackle.

Natural landrail is now virtually unobtainable and some substitute must be found. The most usual is starling dyed landrail colour.

A DICTIONARY OF TROUT FLIES

RAILBIRD

An American pattern invented will over a century ago by John Benn, an Irish fly-dresser who settled in San Francisco in about 1855. This fly is regarded as a standard wet pattern in the Western states where it is exceedingly popular. It is effective for rainbow and sea-trout. The dressing is:

Body: Crimson hackle, ribbed with oval silver.
Wings: Teal with a strip of jungle cock on each side.
Hackle: Crimson and gold.
Head: Black ostrich.
Tail: Gold hackle.
Hook: 10 to 12; larger for sea-trout.

RAMSBOTTOM'S FAVOURITE

For lake or sea-trout, this is a splendid wet fly which deserves to be better known than it is. The inventor was the late Mr. Robert Ramsbottom, of Clithero, who had a lifetime's experience of fishing in Scotland and Wales and caught great quantities of sea-trout on his special pattern.

Body: Yellow seal's fur, ribbed with gold twist.
Tail: Red ibis feather.
Hackle: Coch-y-bondhu.
Wings: Mixed red, yellow, and blue dyed swan feathers mallard over.
Hook: 6 to 12.

The inventor recommended that the wing should be broken up between the finger and thumb so that the brighter feathers are perceptible through the mallard.

RECKLESS WILLIAM

One of Captain Dunn's Blagdon patterns which has proved very successful for large lake trout in this country, as also in the Tongariro and other New Zealand rivers.

The dressing is:

Tip: Round gold, four turns.
Body: One-third flat silver, followed by four turns flat gold and then by white floss.
Head: Green paint.
Hackle: Orange.
Wing: Pheasant tail dyed dark olive green, with a strip of dark green swan under crest over back.
Hook: 7.

RECKLESS WILLIAM'S MATE

Another pattern of the same ilk as the above, dressed as below. The general style of the tie of these two flies is shown in the illustration.

Tip: Oval gold.
Tail: Golden Pheasant crest.
Body: One-third flat silver followed by flat gold and then by white floss.
Hackle: Orange.
Wing: Silver Amherst pheasant, dyed light olive, with a strip of yellow swan under.
Hook: 7.

RED ANT. See ANTS

RED-EYED BEETLE

This name serves to denote a rather unusual pattern since it is adorned with two glass beads as eyes, which incidentally should be at the top of the head and not as in the illustration. Who originated this pattern is unknown to me and it is one which I should never have tried had not a very well-known angler told me that, notwithstanding its rather curious appearance, it would entice large trout in river or loch, just on those occasions when they need most tempting. It is, of course, intended to be fished wet, but if one can keep it floating, I believe that it is even more attractive. My own affection for this beetle dates back to a time, many years ago, when I had tried to tempt a particularly well-educated trout for several weeks with a varied selection of small dry flies, all of which it spurned. A day came when, in desperation, I fell so low as to mount this be-spectacled lure which had been so well recommended to me for large "difficult" fish. That trout took it first time and as he was the heaviest fish taken from that water for several seasons, the memory has remained with me. He scaled just three pounds.

The dressing is:

Body: Bronze peacock herl.
Head: Two red glass beads.
Hackle: Black cock's, long.
Hook: 12.

RED HACKLE

To the Red Hackle belongs the honour of being the earliest artificial fly of which any description exists. Aelian (A.D. 170–230) in his *Natural History* describes the Macedonian method of fishing and ends with the following words, as translated by Mr. William Radcliffe in his book, *Fishing from the Earliest Times*. "Now although the fishermen know of this, they do not use these flies at all for bait for fish, for if a man's hand touch them, they lose their natural colour, their wings wither and they become unfit food for the fish. . . . They get the better of them by their fisherman's craft. They fasten red (crimson red) wool round a hook, and fix on to the wool two feathers which grow under a cock's wattles, and which in colour are like wax. Their rod is six feet long, and their line is the same length. Then they throw their snare, and the fish, attracted and maddened by the colour, comes straight at it."

Dame Juliana Berners, in the second edition of the *Boke of St. Albans* (1496) says, "In the begynninge of May a good flye, the body of roddyd wull, and lapped abowte wyth blacke sylke, the wynges of the drake & of the redde capons hakyll." Izaak Walton also refers to "The ruddy fly, the body made of red wool wrapt about with black silk and the feathers are the wings of the drake, with the feathers of the red capon also, which hang dangling on its side next to the tail." Cotton mentions the Red Hackle by the name of the "Plain or Palmer Hackle".

To-day there exists some confusion as to what is a Red Hackle, but on the whole it has not changed so greatly in the last seven hundred years for one of the standard methods of tying it to-day is with a red wool body and a red cock's hackle. More commonly it is dressed as is the specimen illustrated, in this manner:

Body: Bronze peacock herl.
Hackle: Red cock's.
Hook: 12 to 14.

Very like the Red Palmer, it is used for the same purpose and can be considered a useful all-round pattern for trout, although a much better one for chub and dace. The Red Hackle is not a fly which I use myself, and I doubt whether many anglers trouble much about it, but it is sometimes a good pattern to tempt big old trout which appear to be too lazy to rise to a small lightly dressed fly. It can be fished wet or dry but both for trout and chub a floating pattern is likely to produce better results.

RED PALMER. See PALMERS

RED QUILL

"The Red Quill is one of the sheet anchors of the dry fly-fisherman on a strange river, when in doubt." Thus wrote Halford, and if to-day

the fly-fisher has not quite so much need for sheet-anchors, the Red
Quill still remains an invaluable fly. It will kill on all rivers and is an
effective floating pattern for still waters; it is a good fly for trout which
are "tailing" or "bulging"; for some obscure reason it will attract
fish which are feeding on iron blues; and perhaps more curious still,
although it is far more like a spinner than a dun, it will take trout
during a hatch of duns, perhaps better than an imitation of the dun
itself. It has no counterpart in nature, although it has been identified
with several duns and spinners and more especially the sherry spinner.
Enough to know that it is a pattern of great general utility, fished wet
or dry. I suppose most anglers think of it as a floating pattern only, but
it is almost as effective fished wet.

The standard dressing is:

Body: Stripped peacock herl from the eye feather.
Hackle: Bright red cock.
Wings: Pale or medium starling primary.
Whisks: Three fibres red cock.
Hook: 16 to 14.

As Mr. Eric Taverner has pointed out, the peacock quill body should
be made with a quill chosen to produce the effect of well-marked, alternate light and dark bands.

A good hackled pattern can be made with body, hackle, and whisks
as above, with a shoulder hackle of pale blue dun cock.

RED SPIDER

One of W. C. Stewart's favourite three patterns. Like all Stewart's
type of spiders, it should be tied with a soft mobile short-fibred hackle
to half-way down the body, and is always fished sunk.

Body: Yellow waxed tying silk.
Hackle: Small feather from the outside of a landrail's wing or small red hen.
Hook: 14.

RED SPINNER

This name is loosely applied by anglers to many spinners of the up-
winged duns but, correctly speaking, it should be used only for the
female spinner of the olive dun. The artificial pattern dates back some
hundreds of years and is one of the standard patterns carried by every
trout fisherman. Age has done nothing to diminish its popularity and,
fished wet or dry, there can be no doubt that it is a most useful pattern,

although personally I never use it, preferring other patterns (such as the Pheasant Tail) which seem to me to be closer imitations of the natural insect.

The usual dressing, which may be fished wet or dry, is as follows:

Whisks: Red cock.
Body: Red silk ribbed with fine gold wire.
Legs: Red cock, or hen.
Wings: Starling.
Hook: 14 to 12.

This pattern may also be tied as a hackled fly and is then hackled with a pale blue dun cock's hackle.

Mr. Skues provides a good seal's fur dressing, which like that given above, is equally as suitable for grayling.

Tying silk: Hot orange.
Hackle: Bright steely blue dun cock.
Whisk: Three strands from spade feather of same.
Rib: Fine gold wire.
Body: Crimson seal tied rather loosely.
Hook: 16 to 14.

As Major Hills has pointed out, the Red Quill is a modern version of the Red Spinner.

RED TAG

Although pre-eminently a grayling fly, this pattern is more useful for trout than is generally thought. I have used it in July for smutting fish with some success and throughout Australia it is looked upon as a regular trout pattern. As a grayling fly, it is the best of all of the fancy patterns. It originated in Worcestershire and was probably the invention of a Mr. Flynn, a Teme angler, around 1850. At that period it was known as the Worcester Gem.

In the year 1878, when it was still little used outside the county of its birth, a Worcester gentleman (possibly the inventor) gave a copy of the fly to F. M. Walbran who introduced it into the Yorkshire rivers, where it met with immediate success and soon became a leading favourite amongst all northern grayling anglers. The first time Walbran tested it on the Yore, he killed no less than twenty-five grayling on it. Presumably it was he who gave it the name by which it is now known.

The Red Tag is fished dry or wet, but more frequently the latter. When more than one fly is used, it is always fished on the tail. The original dressing, which is subject to very few variations, is as under:

Body: Bright green peacock's herl from the moon feather.
Hackle: Bright red cock's.
Tag: Bright red wool, or scarlet ibis.   *Hook:* 14.

It is believed that in the original fly the tag was made from strands taken from a green woodpecker's crest. Sometimes a turn of gold or silver tinsel is added under the tag. On the Eden, a tag made with a scarlet feather, such as ibis, is preferred to the wool. With a tag of Indian crow it is known as the Orange Tag, and is a favourite grayling fly for the southern streams. In the north it is known in some districts as the Treacle Parkin. A favourite fly for southern streams, it is a most effective pattern for trout on many rivers where the willow fly is of importance.

RED VARIANT

One of the series of floating flies designed by Dr. Baigent. It has a body of undyed peacock quill from the eye, light furnace hackle and a woodcock (or starling) wing sloping well forward. See also Variants.

ROUGH OLIVE

A favourite pattern on southern and Derbyshire rivers and a good imitation of the large dark olive of spring. A most useful fly from the opening of the season onwards, it is fished wet and dry, but more often as a floater.

There are several dressings. Halford gave one—No. 1 on his list of patterns in *Floating Flies*—and a rather similar tie is recommended by Skues, as under:

Wings: Darkest starling.
Body: Heron herl from wing covert, dyed brown olive, and ribbed with fine gold wire.
Legs: Dirty brown-olive hen hackle with dark centre and yellowish-brown points.   *Hook:* 14.

A good hackled pattern is made with the same body, and is hackled with medium or darkish blue dun cock's hackles, with a small dark olive hackle to represent legs. The whisks are fibres of dark olive cock. In Devon and the West, anglers favour a hackled fly tied as follows:

Body: Three strands of heron herl, first strand dyed brown-olive, other strands dyed greenish-olive.   *Rib:* Yellow silk.
Hackle: Green-olive, with a brownish tinge.   *Hook:* 14.

ROYAL COACHMAN

A great American and Canadian, sometimes fished dry but more often sunk. It will kill on lakes in this country, especially at dusk on a hot day, although, personally, I prefer the more democratic pattern.

The Royal Coachman was the invention of a New York professional —John Haily—who first introduced it in 1878. He remarked to a friend, "Here is a fly which is intended to be a Coachman, but it is not a true Coachman. What can I call it?" Mr. L. C. Orvis, who was present, immediately suggested that it should be called the Royal Coachman because of its fine garments, and it is by this name that it has been known ever since. Originally purely a wet fly, it is only in recent years that it has been successfully exploited as a floater. I have heard of it killing a number of trout on some Scottish and border rivers on bright sunny days.

The dressing is:

Body: Divided into three equal parts, the extremities of bronze peacock herl and the middle portion of scarlet floss silk.
Wings: White swan or goose.
Hackle: Red cock's.
Whisks: Two or three strands of golden pheasant tippet.
Hook: 12.

RUBY-TAILED WASP OR FIREFLY (*Chrysis ignita, C. ruddii*)

This insect is not a trout fly, although it might be called an angler's fly because it is so often seen resting on rocks, walls and stones near the water, where its brilliant colouring is almost bound to attract the attention of any passing fisherman. It owes its inclusion in this book to the fact that it is one of those insects which few people can see without wanting to know its name. How many specimens have been sent to me by angling friends for identification I do not know, but the number must be quite a large one. The Firefly is generally conceded to be one of our most beautiful insects and is mostly seen on hot sunny days, when its bright bottle-green head and thorax and its glistening ruby-coloured body scintillate in the sun and catch the eye some distance away.

There are two species, both fairly common. The larger, *Chrysis ignita* is nearly as big as a blue-bottle, although built on more slender lines, whilst *C. rubii* is a very similar fly about half this size. They are said to prey on the larvae of the common wasp, but in spite of their name, they are quite harmless to human beings. I have seen these flies on the water more than once, but they get there by accident only and it must happen so seldom that it is unlikely that fish ever see enough to get interested in them.

RUSTY SPINNER

This first-class pattern, designed by Mr. Skues, is one of the best imitations of the male spinner of the blue-winged olive—the beautiful little sherry spinner. In a smaller size, it often proves deadly during a fall of female pale watery spinners, especially at or after sunset, from towards the end of May onwards; whilst it is also a rational pattern to imitate the spinners of the July dun and the iron-blue dun. Normally fished dry, it will also kill well wet or semi-submerged.

Altogether the Rusty Spinner must be considered an exceptionally useful chalk-stream pattern, particularly during a fall of spinners in the evening. The tie, as given by Mr. Skues, is:

Tying silk: Hot orange, waxed with clear wax.
Hackle: Rusty dun cock.
Body: Chestnut-coloured pig's wool or seal's fur.
Rib: Fine gold wire.
Whisks: Three strands of spade feather from shoulder of honey dun cock, sharp and bright.
Hook: 14 (for sherry spinner); 15 (for pale watery spinner).

RUSTY RED

A wet hackled pattern hailing from Devon, which serves as a maid-of-all-work on most streams and is a useful variation to use in place of the Blue Dun.

Body: Hare's flax, ribbed flat gold.
Hackle: Rusty blue cock.
Whisks: A few fibres of above.
Hook: 14.

SAGAR'S FANCY

A Yorkshire fancy pattern, recommended by Mr. W. G. Bainbridge, the author of *The Fly-Fisher's Guide to Aquatic Flies*, who holds a high opinion of its merits as a spring fly. He gives the following dressing:

Hackle: Medium brown partridge back or shoulder feather.
Body: Bronze peacock herl, ribbed sky blue.
Hook: 15.

SAIL WING (*Cloëon*)

On many lochs, heavy hatches sometimes occur of flies which superficially look like large olives. That they are not olives will be evident if they are examined, when it will be seen that they have no hind wings, which shows them to be one of the three species of cloëon, the only ephemerids to have but two wings and two setae. These duns inhabit lochs and still waters, and are abundant upon Loch Leven where the boatmen call them "sail wings".

When trout are feeding on these insects, any of the standard imitations of the olive dun can be used, but the most likely way to secure a bag is to mount an Olive Nymph. There is always some period during a hatch when fish will take the nymph, and on lakes and pools the artificial nymph will generally give better results than any fly. "Sail wings" may appear early in the year, although personally I do not recollect having seen them except during July and August.

SALMON FLIES (Miniature)

Although salmon patterns, *per se*, do not come within the scope of this book, some reference to them is necessary because in small sizes they are often used for sea-trout, lake trout, and river trout, especially after dark. They are also highly popular for trout in the big lakes of Canada and are much used in New Zealand. Standard patterns like the Silver Doctor, Durham Ranger, Silver Grey and Jock Scott are normally favoured, tied on sizes 4 to 8 hooks and with dressings far less elaborate than those considered necessary for salmon. In fact, compared with true salmon flies, these trout patterns generally have the appearance of poor relations.

SALTOUN

An old pattern and a one-time favourite on the chalk streams. After falling into disuse, it has been revived in recent years as a lake fly and as a grayling pattern. The tie is:

Wings: Palest starling.
Hackle: Two pale ginger cock hackles.
Body: Black silk, ribbed with fine silver wire.
Whisk: Gallina dyed a faint brown red.
Hook: 16 to 14.

The fly is generally fished dry and if it is required as a wet pattern for trout, sea-trout, or grayling, it is better ribbed with silver tinsel and hackled with black cock hackles. For sea-trout a size 8 hook is not too large.

SANCTUARY

The invention of Dr. Thomas Sanctuary, one-time of Salisbury, who designed it some fifty years before his death (at Scarborough) in 1931. The doctor was a well-known angler on the chalk streams both for trout and grayling, and the fly which bears his name owes its survival to its effectiveness as a grayling pattern. The dressing is:

Hackle: Coch-y-bondhu.
Body: Dark hare's ear ribbed with flat gold.
Hook: 14.

SAND FLY (*Rhyacophila dorsalis*)

The scientific name of the Sand Fly described and illustrated by Ronalds is *Rhyacophila dorsalis*, a day-flying caddis fly of medium size. The brownish wings are generally blotched, although not always so, whilst occasionally males are found with green bodies. It is common from April to November on most rivers and I have noted it on the Test, Blythe, Dove, Swale and many Welsh streams. Naturally this sedge is most conspicuous in September and October when few other insects are on the wing and when it often hatches in fair numbers. The gravel-bed (*Anisomera burmeisteri*) is also known in some parts as the sand fly or the sand gnat.

The artificial, which seems to be a copy of the sedge, is reputed to be a useful pattern for wet fly fishing in April and May. I do not think that it is used much nowadays except in the north, where it is considered quite a fair fly for both trout and grayling. There are several dressings of which two should suffice. The old tie given by Ronalds is:

Body: Of the sandy-coloured fur from the hare's neck, spun on silk of the same colour.
Wings: From the landrail's wing, made full.
Legs: From a light ginger feather from the neck of a hen. The fly is made buzz with a feather from the underside of the wing of a throstle wound upon the above body.
Hook: 14.

Starling dyed landrail colour is nowadays usually substituted for the landrail which is almost unobtainable.

F. M. Walbran varies this slightly, as under:

Body: Red fur from a hare's neck ribbed with light brown silk.
Legs: Ginger-coloured hackle.
Wings: Ruddy mottled feather from inside of a hen pheasant's wing.
Hook: 14.

SANDERS' SPECIAL

Also known as the "Walter Sanders Special", this pattern originated, I believe, on the Teme. It is a favourite fly with many anglers both for trout and grayling.

The dressing is:

Body: White floss silk closely ribbed with silver twist.
Hackle: Cinnamon hackle.
Wings: Starling wing.
Hook: 14.

SEA SWALLOW

A grayling pattern, it is a popular wet fly in the north and was a favourite choice of F. M. Walbran who liked it as his first dropper, with the Red Tag on the tail. I doubt whether it is ever used by trout anglers to-day, but fifty years ago the Sea Swallow was considered as being quite a useful trout fly for the late evening.

The dressing recommended by Pritt was:

Wings: From a very light feather from the outside of a sea swallow's wing.
Body: White silk.
Legs: Fibres from the wing feather of the sea swallow.
Hook: 14.

Nowadays the body is usually made of peacock quill, stripped, and dyed yellow. The sea swallow is an old name for the tern.

SEDGE FLIES. See CADDIS FLIES

SHRIMP. See FRESHWATER SHRIMP

SHERRY SPINNER (*Ephemerella ignita*)

This name well describes the colour of the female spinner of the blue-winged olive which is so abundant on many streams in June and July and again in the autumn. The fall of spinners usually occurs towards dark and is a thrilling experience for the fisherman, since no insect is taken by trout with more relish.

There are many patterns available to imitate or suggest this spinner, including the Orange Quill, Pheasant Tail, and the Rusty Spinner. These make a popular and formidable trio as all of them are good killers, especially the first named. There is also another excellent dressing for the sherry spinner, which was evolved by Mr. Skues and is well worth attention. His tie for this pattern is:

Hackle: Palest honey dun with a fine dark centre.
Body: A mixture of seal's fur, orange, yellow-orange, and green, all softened with a small fine admixture of hare's poll, the whole producing rather nicely the amber hue of the natural insect.
Rib: Fine gold wire.
Whisk: Cock's shoulder hackle to match the hackle at the shoulder, three strands.
Hook: 14.

SILVER DOCTOR

Well known as a salmon fly, this pattern in plainer clothing and smaller sizes, is one of the best wet flies for big lake trout and for sea-trout. In Canada and U.S.A., few patterns are more popular for river or lake.

A suitable tie (for trout and sea-trout) is:

Body: Flat silver tinsel, ribbed fine silver oval.
Wings: Strips of swan or goose dyed red, yellow and green, covered on each side with a strip of a mallard's breast feather.
Hackle: Bright blue cock's.
Tail: Golden pheasant tippet.
Hook: 6 to 10.

A favourite dressing for America, and one which is just as useful in this country, is as follows:

Wing: Mixed yellow, white, scarlet and mallard; not one in which turkey brown predominates.
Body: All silver.
Hackle: Blue capped with guinea-fowl.
Tail: Golden pheasant tippet.
Hook: 6 to 10.

SILVERHORNS, BLACK (*Mystacides nigra, M. azurea, Leptocerus aterrimus*)

SILVERHORNS, BROWN (*Leptocerus cinereus, L. albifrons*)

These small sedges are recognized by their habit of flying round and round each other, over and above the surface of the water, sometimes rapidly approaching the bank and as rapidly retreating from it. Their exceptionally long antennae also form a notable feature of these flies, although there are other sedges with very long antennae, such as *Leptocerus nigronervosus* which in June is. common on the Welsh Dee and many other rivers. This species, however, is considerably larger and less common than the silverhorns, which are widely distributed on rivers and lakes all over the country.

Black silverhorns are of three species, all of which are black in colour and are not much liked by trout. A curious and interesting feature of these flies is that hooks are attached to the top edge of the hind wings which fit into grooves in the anterior wings. It is thought that the function of these hooks is to lock together the front and rear wings when the insect is in flight and thus give it greater stability and endurance.

The brown silverhorns, which are of a general brown colour, are very similar to the black, but possibly trout like them rather better. There is another species known as *Leptocerus albifrons* which is found on the chalk streams and which is chocolate in colour with white markings. This is also called brown silverhorns by anglers.

A little caddis fly which might easily be mistaken for the brown silverhorns is *Mystacides longicornus*, known in the north as the grouse wing, since the wings, which are brown with darker brown markings, are very like some feathers of the grouse. It is about the same size as the silverhorns with equally long antennae and is abundant on still waters during August and September (see GROUSE WING).

Trout certainly take silverhorns on occasions when there is nothing better offering, more so, perhaps, on lakes than on rivers. I have at times used artificial patterns of both the brown and black varieties, but on the whole they have not proved satisfactory and I do not consider them worth troubling about.

Perhaps the most remarkable thing in connection with silverhorns is that any species of sedge which hovers over the water in such vast numbers should be so little liked by trout.

SILVER SEDGE (*Odontocerum albicorne*)

Also known as the grey sedge, this is a large greyish fly found on the southern and midland rivers from June to September and, in some parts, in great numbers. It is identified by its silver-grey wings and its peculiar white-toothed antennae. Halford remarks that the artificial will kill well during the afternoon in hot weather, and more especially when the fish are smutting. This is worth noting, for although I cannot recall any other authority having recommended the use of a sedge in these circumstances, I am sure that Halford was correct. From my own experience, I look upon a sedge pattern as being one of the most likely to tempt trout when they are smutting, even in crystal clear water.

The artificial Silver Sedge is an effective floater to suggest various light-coloured caddis flies either on river or lake and is a popular pattern throughout Europe for trout and grayling.

A usual dressing is:

Hackle: Pale sandy ginger cock's hackle, from shoulder to tail.
Body: White floss silk, ribbed with fine silver wire.
Wings: From a landrail's wing feather.
Hook: 10 to 14.

SILVER TWIST

A member of the great Blue Dun tribe, this is a very killing grayling pattern, especially in clear water in autumn and, like the Blue Upright, it is particularly effective when a midday hatch of olives is on. Almost always fished wet, generally as the top dropper, it is also useful as a floater. When used as a tail fly, it is often deadly when tied in nymph fashion with a fraction of lead wire added at the thorax.

The standard dressing is:

Body: Blue rabbit's fur, ribbed silver twist.
Hackle: Medium natural blue dun hen, from shoulder to tail.
Hook: 14.

SIMPLE SIMON

A general utility pattern, wet or dry, and a cross between a Coachman and a Coch-y-bondhu. I first tried it many years ago and have used it with success on many occasions since. Quite effective as a suggestion of a shrimp and many sorts of beetles, it kills well whenever there is an absence of natural fly on the water. Dressing:

Body: Bronze peacock herl tipped with a turn of gold tinsel.
Hackle: Red and not too long, with a very short, sparse white hackle behind it.
Hook: 10 to 12.

SKINNUM

A popular American wet pattern sometimes finished dry.
Dressing:

Tail: Fibres from blue dun cock hackle.
Body: Stripped peacock quill, or grey floss with a black silk rib.
Hackle: Pale blue dun, very sparse.
Wing: From woodcock wing quill.
Hook: 10 to 12.

SKY BLUE

Also known as the Little Blue. Probably designed to represent an olive dun, this old pattern deserves to be better known than it is. The dressing is given by Ronalds, but to-day the fly is little used in England, although popular in France and other countries. Dressing:

Hackle: Yellow.
Whisks: To match.
Body: Pale ginger mohair mixed with light blue fur.
Wings: From the body of a sea swallow or of a very light blue dun hen.
Hook: 15.

SNIPE BLOA. See SNIPE AND YELLOW

SNIPE AND PURPLE

A wet fly said to represent the iron-blue dun, although about that theory I have my doubts. In Yorkshire and the north country generally, it is a standard pattern and one on which I have killed a great number of trout. Yet, strangely enough, except in the north, I have never done any good with it except on lakes, for which it is a most reliable pattern.

Throughout the north of England it is a sure killer in April and March and again in September, but only if the right dressing is used. Commercial flies are not always correctly tied. The Snipe and Purple should be hackled only with a feather from the outside of a snipe's wing, a dark feather, nearly black, found near the joint which corresponds to the elbow of a human being. It is also an excellent grayling pattern for spring and autumn on cold days. The Dark Snipe and Purple is the same fly but with a body of darker purple silk, well waxed.

The standard dressing is:

Body: Purple floss silk.
Hackle: Small feather from outside of a jack snipe's wing.
Hook: 14.

SNIPE AND YELLOW

Another of the Snipe series of spider flies, used for the same purpose and at the same season as the Snipe and Purple. Although not quite as popular as the latter, it sometimes proves infallible on wild cold days. Also known as the Snipe Bloa and Light Snipe and Yellow.

Dressing (Pritt):

Body: Straw-coloured silk.
Wings: Small feather from outside of a jack snipe's wing.
Hook: 14.

Tied with an orange silk body, it becomes a Snipe and Orange, and is a useful wet pattern for trout and grayling.

SOLDIER BEETLE (*Telephorus rusticus*)

SAILOR BEETLE (*Telephorus lividus*)

These two beetles appear in the meadows in thousands during July and August and there must be few anglers who do not know them. The soldier, also known as the fernweb, is the commoner of the two, and is of a dull yellowish colour with the elytra (wing-cases) tipped with dark blue. The sailor is of the same general outline and differs only in colour. It has blue elytra, a blue and yellow thorax, and an orange-red belly. The Soldier Palmer is said to be a representation of the former and the Fern Fly of the latter.

Fly dressers in all ages have paid some attention to these two insects, which is a little surprising as they are of no real interest to fly-fishermen. Like other beetles, they get carried on to the water in windy weather and, since trout then take them freely, it may be worth trying an artificial on hot breezy days in summer when the natural beetles are about. And it must be agreed that the artificial sometimes proves most effective for no very clear reason.

In 1940, Mr. G. E. M. Skues, finding the need for a copy of the soldier beetle on the Nadder, evolved a new pattern of which recently he has been good enough to send me the dressing and also a copy of a fly tied by himself, from which it is evident that he has lost none of his fly-tying skill in his eighty-seventh year. This is the best copy I have seen and is a most attractive-looking fly, of which the inventor says that it should be used in July "when the natural beetle swarms on the small thistle which has pink flowers". To the best of my knowledge, the dressing has not been published elsewhere and I feel sure that many fly-fishers will be pleased to have it and to try it out as a general beetle pattern. Mr. Skues's tie is:

Silk: Hot orange.
Body: Bright red–orange seal's fur.
Hackle: Red cock, sparse.
Elytra: Fibres from the breast of a cock pheasant.
Hook: 14, turned-down eye.

The cock pheasant fibres, tipped with blue-black, are extraordinarily suggestive of the wing-cases of the soldier beetle and the whole effect is exceptionally good. It is a pattern which, I feel sure, will account for a lot of fish.

SPENT GNAT. See MAYFLY

SPIDERS (*Araneidae*)

Several insects receive less attention from anglers than they deserve and none more so than spiders. Numerous sorts are to be found throughout the summer on the foliage and undergrowth near streams and lakes and occasionally one will get blown on to the water. Of those found near rivers, *Agelina labyrinthica* is perhaps the most common species and it may often be observed in considerable numbers especially amongst gorse bushes, although probably the true water spider is of more interest to fish. This creature (*Argyroneta aquatica*) lives entirely below the surface, generally showing a preference for still waters or sluggish streams. But of all spiders, the big wolf spiders (*Lycosidae*) are of most value for there are no less than thirty-seven species of them in Great Britain and they hunt their prey on land or on the surface of the water with equal facility.

Now since it will be agreed that spiders are easily imitated and trout feed readily on the natural insects, there must be some reason why anglers as a whole ignore the artificial. The cause, I would suggest, is solely because one so seldom sees a spider on the water and they are rarely found in autopsies with the result that they are dismissed as being of no importance at all.

That reasoning, in my opinion, is faulty for it is beyond dispute that when a spider gets on to the water, rare as that occurrence may be, it never progresses far before a fish takes it. It is, I believe, one of the very few insects which will attract a trout's attention when he has settled down to feeding exclusively on some particular fly.

My flybox always houses one or two copies of spiders although somehow or other I always forget to try them; or at least nearly always, for only a few days ago their utility was brought home to me in a rather striking manner. A very good trout was discovered rising persistently under the roots of an ash tree which ran down into the river. He was surface feeding but what he was taking was far from evident. Whatever it was it was too small for me to see, but since the fish was not easily put down, half a dozen different floaters were put over him and all of them were treated with contempt. In fact, more than once he rose within an inch of my fly, although not at it. Having wasted half an hour on this annoying customer, there seemed to be nothing for it but to give him best, and I was just about to move on when I thought of a spider, because even when a trout ignores every pattern offered him, he will sometimes find an artificial spider quite irresistible. And so it proved to be on this occasion for he took it without any hesitation at all!

I have related that incident because it may show better than in any other manner why, in my opinion, a copy of a spider should not be despised. It will not always be successful—in fact, the next fish to which I showed mine stopped rising immediately—but there is always a chance that it will account for a trout when nothing else will.

There are, of course, many patterns of spiders but as long as they are buoyant and are approximately the shape and size of the natural insect, the actual dressing does not appear to be of much importance.

SPINNING FLIES

There are several types of artificial flies fitted with metal spinning heads, and I believe that, under some conditions, they prove very attractive in lochs and deep river pools. It would be difficult to justify them on "fly only" waters, but they may be useful in removing old cannibals.

SPLIT WILLOW

A thoroughly sensible dry fly designed by the Rev. E. Powell to suggest small Perlidae, needle flies, etc., and particularly valuable for grayling during October and November.

The dressing is:

Hackle: Dark olive, very small.
Body: Peacock quill, dyed in picric acid.
Wings: A bunch of thrush primary (the part of the web above the yellow) rolled and then split to lie horizontally by figure-of-eight lashing.
Whisks: A few strands dark olive cock, or alternatively, a minute scrap of palest primrose wool as a tag, to represent an egg-bag.
Hook: 16.

SPUR WING. See PALE WATERY DUN

STONE FLY (*Perla maxima: P. cephalotes, etc.*)

The stone fly is a member of the Perlidae family, which includes a number of large and small species of importance to the fly-fisher.

Amongst them are the willow fly, yellow sally, early brown, February red, and the many needle flies.

Of those generally known as stone flies, there are several species, differing but slightly except in the matter of size. They are easy enough to identify (as far as the family goes) so that no detailed description will be required if the reader will glance at the photographs on Plate XII,

In Great Britain, their natural habitat is in the fast rocky rivers of the North, where the best-known member of the family, *Perla maxima*, appears in April and lasts until June, although rarely seen after the middle of that month. The same insect is abundant on the Usk, whilst smaller species are found on other rivers such as the Herefordshire Wye. The stone fly of the chalk streams, *Perlodes microcephala*, is appreciably smaller than its northern relative and is not considered of much interest to anglers.

The Perlidae are also present in rivers in France, Belgium, and Switzerland, and indeed, in most European countries. A very similar fly is indigenous to North America, it is very much larger than any British species.

As their name denotes, stone flies are found amongst the stones and gravel on the edge of rivers. The nymphs are true aquatic creatures which spend the winter in mud, silt, or gravel on river beds, preferring the deep water where the temperature is likely to be higher and less variable and where, of course, there is less chance of being frozen up. In the early spring, they move to shallows and later crawl to dry land. The adult nymphs are ugly insects which look ferocious enough to inflict a bite or sting, although, as a matter of fact, they are shy and harmless. Quite unlike nymphs of the Ephemeridae, they are considerable in size and possess two setae (tails) instead of the usual three.

Whilst living and growing in the river, they are a menace to other water insects, feeding on many of them, including caddis larvae, and with a special fondness for nymphs of the Ephemeridae.

When the final metamorphosis is due, the stone fly nymph crawls to the shore, where often thousands of them may be discovered beneath the stones and boulders along the river's edge. At this stage, the nymphs are known to fishermen as creepers. Extraordinarily quick in their movements, the adult nymphs are by no means easy to capture, although in the north at any rate, they are often sought after, since the creeper, fished like a wasp grub, is an exceptionally deadly bait and will often account for heavy trout which have long since ceased to rise to surface flies, whether natural or artificial.

Having found a suitable spot, such as a rock or a tree, the nymph blows out her body with air, the skin splits, and the final moult occurs which results in the insect emerging from its shuck as an imago. A few hours after reaching the adult state, the stone flies having become stronger and darker in colour, proceed to mate, usually on the stones and never in the air as is the habit of so many insects.

The female then flies to the river and, fluttering a few feet above it, drops her eggs *en masse*. On reaching the water, these separate and each becomes attached to a stone or plant by means of a length of thread which is provided by nature. In the case of *P. maxima*, the bundle of eggs can be seen at the rear end of the female's body. They are oval in shape and black in colour, and normally hatch in six to eight weeks.

After disposing of her eggs, the female lives but a short time and seldom does the life of either sex in the imago state last more than three to four days, since, as in the case of the Ephemeridae, the stone flies cannot eat after they have reached the winged stage. The life cycle from egg to imago is roughly one year.

The female *P. maxima* is over one and a half inches in length, and throughout the north of England is known as the May fly, whilst her husband is known to fishermen as the Jack, or Jack May fly—all of which is apt to be a little confusing to anglers from other parts of the country.

In spite of her large wings, which as in the case of all Perlidae, are folded flat on the back, the female imago is a very poor flyer, although in this respect she is better off than her husband. Those of the male *P. maxima* are so small as to prove functionless. The male is altogether a smaller and inferior insect and even the trout have little use for him.

The adults of both sexes have brownish wings with strongly marked nervures, and dirty yellowish bodies. They possess two tails and two antennae.

The Artificial Fly

Although on the chalk streams the stone fly may be of little account to anglers, the same is not true of many other rivers. In the north especially, the hatch is a large and regular one and trout take the natural insect (creeper and female imago) in a ravenous manner. There is, in fact, no other fly which they appreciate so well, and even confirmed bottom feeders and old cannibals are apt to forget themselves when the stone fly is hatching, and will take it voraciously. Unfortunately for the fly-fisher, it is one of the most impossible insects to imitate satisfactorily, although for hundreds of years fly-dressers have attempted copies.

As long ago as 1496, Dame Juliana Berners in her famous *Treatise*, made reference to an artificial stone fly. "The body of black wool and yellow under the wing and under the tail, and the wings of a drake," was her solution of the problem. Then in 1590, Leonard Mascall gave a dressing, as did Markham in 1614. Charles Cotton and Alfred Ronalds also published ties and since then scores of other patterns have been invented. Yet, I would venture to say, without much fear of contradiction, that not a single one of them has proved really satisfactory and to-day there is no such thing as a standard pattern of the stone fly.

I cannot pretend that it has ever given me much sport and for that reason I will refrain from giving the dressing. There is a more cogent reason why I do not give any at all and that is because I have never forgotten the remark made to me, more years ago than I care to remember, by a grand old Yorkshire angler who had lived on the banks of the Swale all his life. His advice was, "Never waste time with artificial copies of the stone fly. The very best of them are as near useless as dammit is to swearing." I can only concur.

That trout can be taken with a "copy" of the stone fly is true enough. For those interested in trying, the dressing given by Ronalds is:

Body: Fur of hare's ear mixed with yellow worsted or camlet, ribbed over with yellow silk, leaving most yellow at the tail.
Tail: A mottled strand or two of a partridge feather.
Wings: Feather from the pheasant's wing.
Legs: A hackle stained greenish-brown.
Horns: Two rabbit's whiskers.

A more modern dressing by Mr. John Veniard is:

Body: Hare's fur and yellow seal's fur mixed, ribbed yellow silk.
Wings: Hen pheasant wing, or four dark blue dun cock hackles tied low over back.
Hackle: Dark grizzle cock.

STRADDLE-BUG. See MAYFLY

SUTTON'S SPECIAL

The invention of Mr. John Sutton of Toronto, this is a great pattern for Canadian rivers. In this country it has proved effective on lakes and for sea-trout. A pattern little known to English anglers, it is worthy of attention.

Dressing:

Body: Slate-blue silk ribbed with gold tinsel, with a butt of peacock immediately behind the wing.
Tip: Gold tinsel.
Tail: Red hackle.
Hackle: Red cock's hackle.
Wings: Turkey.
Hook: 10 to 12.

TAILEY TAIL

The Tailey Tail (or Tail-to-Tail) is an old wet pattern which originated in Derbyshire and imitates the female black gnat. Used on the right occasion, it can be extraordinarily effective.

In the *Quaint Treatise on Flies and Fly Making* we are told that the tailey tail "comes about 25 May and continues until the Beginning of August. It is the Shee flee to the Black Gnat and of the same nature, but of a different colour".

Aldam commenting upon this pattern says that he killed thousands of trout upon it, including twenty-six brace during one day's fishing on the Derwent when three other anglers using different patterns creeled only five fish between them.

This "she-fly" is not, I think, much used to-day, although it is a most attractive and likely-looking fly which deserves to be resuscitated. Any fly-dresser who ties a pattern will, I am certain, fully agree with me.

Body: Herl from a brown turkey tail, ribbed with flesh-coloured silk.
Hackle: Sooty black hen's.
Hook: 14 to 16.

This is the dressing from the *Quaint Treatise,* but the fly kills just as well hackled with a feather from a moor-hen's wing.

TEAL SERIES

Standard wet patterns for lake and sea-trout and useful stream flies. They rank with the Grouse, Mallard, and Woodcock series and are possibly more widely used than any of them. Amongst the many combinations the best known are the Teal and Red, Teal and Silver, Teal and Black, Teal and Mixed, Teal and Green, Teal and Olive, Teal and Yellow, Teal and Orange, Teal and Claret, Teal Silver Blue, etc. The dressings of the first four are given as, on the whole, they are probably the most popular. The red and green types are wonderful loch flies, whilst the silver Teal is a deadly pattern for sea-trout.

TEAL AND RED

Tail: A few fibres of the yellow back feathers from a golden pheasant.
Body: Red seal's fur, ribbed with silver.
Hackle: Black and red.
Wings: From the breast feather of a teal.
Hooks: 8 to 14.

TEAL AND SILVER

Tail: A few strands of golden pheasant tippet.
Body: Flat silver tinsel, ribbed fine silver oval.
Hackle: Bright blue.
Wings: From the breast feather of a teal.
Hook: 8 to 14.

TEAL AND BLACK

Tail: Fibres of black cock's hackle.
Body: Black wool, ribbed with silver.
Hackle: Black.
Wings: From the breast feather of a teal.
Hooks: 8 to 14.

TEAL AND MIXED

Body: One-third each of yellow, red, and blue dubbing, ribbed oval silver.
Hackle: Black.
Tail: A few fibres of golden-pheasant tippet.
Wings: Teal.
Hook: 8 to 14.

TIPPET AND RED

The Tippet flies—Tippet and Red, Tippet and Black, Tippet and Silver—are favoured throughout Scotland and Ireland as wet patterns for sea-trout (especially in low water) and lake fishing.

The dressing of the fly is:

Body: Red seal's fur ribbed with fine silver oval wire.
Wings: From the tippet feathers of a golden pheasant.
Hackle: Red cock's.
Tail: A few strands as wing.
Hook: 10 to 12.

THOMPSON'S MOTH

Much used in some rivers and lakes in New Zealand, where it is
also known as the Mammoth, this pattern was invented, I believe,
by the Hon. G. M. Thompson, a one-time South Island M.P. It will
kill in our rivers and on the first occasion I used it, I grassed a
trout of 2½ lb. Further tests have convinced me of its effectiveness, especially at dusk. Some anglers consider that it kills better
when tied with a natural red hackle and a tail of fibres of the
same.

Dressing:

Body: Cream chenille.
Hackle: Mottled brown partridge.
Wing: Owl.
Hook: 12 to 14.

TOD FLY

The invention of E. M. Tod, one of the greatest authorities of his
day on wet fly-fishing and one of the finest exponents of its use. I doubt
if his pattern is much used to-day, but at one time it had a great reputation. His dressing was:

Body: Stripped quill from the moon-feather of the peacock.
Tail: Two strands of game-cock's hackle.
Hackle: A soft and somewhat mottled feather taken from the inside of the wing
of a woodcock.
Wing: Mavis (thrush) wing, inside of feather.
Hook: 14.

I prefer the wings tied in a bunch and divided (that is split) by the
tying silk; or else dressed with one wing only tied in a bunch and
placed upright. This fly can hardly be too sparsely tied.

TUP'S INDISPENSABLE

The dressing of this deservedly popular fly was the invention of a
professionsl fly-tier, R. S. Austin, who first produced it in about the
year 1900. He was a tobacconist at Tiverton and only dressed and sold
flies as a sideline. The creation of this pattern was his greatest achievement and even before his death in 1911 it had gained a great reputation
in this country.

The credit of naming the fly so aptly must be given to Mr. G. E. M.
Skues, who was one of the two individuals to whom the inventor con-

fided the secret of the dressing; the other was Mr. C. A. Hassam, a keen amateur fly-dresser who produced some beautiful work.

The Tup is fished wet or dry as an imitation of the smaller pale wateries, although, with slight modifications in the tie, it may be used throughout the season to simulate a number of duns, spinners, and nymphs. Fished sunk, it is useful for tempting bulging trout, whilst as a floater it is equally good on rough mountain streams as on clear placid rivers.

In fairness to Mr. Austin and later to his daughter (who carried on the fly-tying side of his business after his death, dressing nothing but the Tup) the original dressing of the fly was kept secret by those to whom it had been entrusted, for many years. A few years ago, on her retirement, Miss Austin gave Mr. Skues permission to publish the correct dressing, Mr. Hassam having died a little time before.

In the intervening years (although naturally experienced fly-tiers were able to make a fairly good guess about the ingredients of the fly), all sorts of weird creations were made and sold as Tup's Indispensable in order to meet the ever-increasing demand for this fly, which rumour had it was something out of the ordinary. As the correct dressing is still not widely known, the position is much the same to-day and some most extraordinary patterns masquerade under the Tup marque. They range from the quite unbelievable to the totally impossible.

As a matter of interest, I have looked up the dressing of this fly in half a dozen modern books and no two agree as to what it is. Add to this the facts that some of the material is not altogether easy to obtain and that the pattern is not one of the easiest to tie, and one finds the reason why so many monstrosities are still on the market.

I have thought it as well to treat this matter at some length, because some of the T.I.'s offered by makers are so unlike the genuine article, that they may cause disappointment to the user and give him a false impression of the fly's killing possibilities.

By the kindness of Mr. Skues, I am able to quote from Austin's original notes about his pattern.

In the first of these, dated 1900, he says that the fly "is dressed with full yellow silk, buzz, on an oo (16) Pennell hook, with a blue hackle of a lighter colour and freckled thickly with gold. Body of a mixture of ram's wool, cream coloured seal's fur, lemon spaniel's fur, and a few pinches of yellow mohair."

Mr. Skues suggested the use of crimson seal's fur instead of mohair, and from then onwards it was adopted by Austin. It will be observed that the tail is not mentioned in the above note, but I understand that it should be honey dun or bright light blue spade feather.

In a subsequent letter, we find Austin answering a question about the tag. Of this he writes: "The small yellow tip is conspicuous in the natural fly and I have regarded it as a very desirable feature in the imitation." And again, a little later, he says: "I do not call the yellow at the end of the Tup, a tag. It is hardly big enough for that."

The ram's wool used in this pattern is taken from the underparts of a ram or tup, and writing of it in 1908, Austin states: "I always wash the wool from a tup as it is almost invariably unfit unless you do. The floating power of the fly is not injured by this process if it be dressed with a good hackle and touched slightly with paraffin. I do not think that the addition you mention"—viz. an application of goose grease— "is desirable; indeed, I fancy that it would take a vast amount of washing to get all the natural grease out of the wool."

The ram's wool which is a feature of this pattern certainly contains much natural oil which is believed to shine in the water. Austin, however, was not the first to discover the useful properties of this wool as is generally supposed, since on page 160 of *The Driffield Angler*, which was published in 1806, it is given as a body for a Green Drake.

In another letter Austin says that the "Tup is about the best pattern that can be put up early in the year, say from the middle of April till towards the end of June". He made some great catches on his own fly as his letters clearly show. Writing in 1900 he says: "The first evening I used this fly, I got six fish, weighing 4¾ lb. in the pool at the top of the Kag; biggest fish 1 lb. 7 oz. The next night I had four weighing 5 lb., biggest fish 3 lb. ½ oz." Presumably these notes refer to the Exe at Tiverton.

It has often been stated in fishing books that the Tup was originally tied to imitate a "red spinner". That statement is, in my opinion, open to some doubt, although I am aware that it is in accordance with what the inventor wrote. The yellow tip is certainly not a conspicuous feature of the female olive imago (even when carrying a bunch of eggs), although this is the insect which is known to anglers as the "red spinner". In spite of what has been written about him, there is reason to believe that Austin was not a great entomologist and it appears to me far more likely that when he used the term "red spinner", he had no intention of applying it to the female olive spinner, but used it as a general term for several spinners as is quite customary. From his insistence upon the yellow tip, I think that it is more probable that

Austin's "red spinner" was the male pale watery spinner, a fly with a whitish body of which the last three segments are of a pronounced yellowish-orange colour, although that, of course, is purely surmise.

The Tup is effective throughout the season and the shades may be varied to imitate a number of nymphs, duns, and spinners. As a nymph, it is especially attractive since it bears a close resemblance to those which have the appearance of bleeding at the thorax.

When used to imitate the nymph of the pale watery, it should have scarcely any red in it, except at the head, and the dubbing should be carried down to the tail, whilst the hackles should embrace the shoulder. A soft and short blue hackle is recommended and it is best left un-trimmed.

In a letter to me about Tup's Indispensable, Mr. Skues, writing in his characteristic style, says: "The fly became so popular that Austin became utterly sick of tying it, and one of his customers said that the Dorsetshire Frome stank of Tup's Indispensables from Maiden Newton to the sea! . . . I vary the proportions of the materials from time to time to represent several different spinners, pale watery duns (floating), and nymphs of the pale watery, but Austin, and after his death his daughter, stuck to the original dressing as amended with seal's fur in place of mohair."

The Tup is not a reliable pattern in the sense that a Red Quill, a Greenwell's Glory, or the Grey Duster merit this term. Often it will prove useless, but used on the right occasion it can be a most exceptionally effective fly. Wet or dry, it will take fish on all sorts of rivers, it is a good lake fly, one of the best for grayling, and a standard pattern for trout feeding under the surface on nymphs, shrimps, water-lice and such like. In one of his books, Mr. Skues says that for these underwater feeders, he seldom requires any other fly than a Tup, although for this purpose he likes one dressed with a very short henny hackle, instead of the bright honey or rusty dun used for the floating pattern. I have found that this is a tip worth remembering.

TURKEY BROWN (*Leptophlebia submarginata*)

A largish dun, appearing on many rivers (including the Test) from May to August. .Very similar in general appearance to the march brown, it may easily be distinguished from that insect by being rather smaller and having three setae against the two of the march brown.

Sometimes, too, it is confused with the blue-winged olive, but whereas the wings of the b.-w.o. are of a slate-blue colour, those of the turkey brown are definitely brownish and heavily veined.

It is of little interest to the trout-fisher because fish do not appear to like it. They show no appreciation of the duns (although they look so like march browns) and they eschew the male spinner, in spite of the fact that it is so similar in appearance to the male spinner of the b.-w.o.

More than once I have watched turkey browns coming down a stream, and have been surprised how completely trout have ignored them.

VARIANTS

This name is generally used to denote nondescript long-hackled dry flies, although when and by whom the term was originated is not certain.

Round about 1900, Dr. Baigent of Northallerton was dressing long-hackled sparsely dressed floating flies which were then a novelty, and at some later date they became known as Variants since they were looked upon as being just variations of known patterns. This, of course, they were, but with certain points of difference in their structure.

However, it seems probable that, although they did not appear until many years later, it was Poole's flies which were chiefly responsible for popularizing the name. Either in 1910 or 1911, Mr. A. C. Poole and Mr. Martin Mosely shared a fishing on the Test and during that period, the former received from Messrs. Wyers Frères, Redditch, samples of longish-hackled flies tied on bare hooks. At Mr. Poole's request, Mr. Mosely tied a few similar flies but with a body of stripped peacock quill and, in some cases, a whisk. They proved to be wonderfully good light floaters, and anglers soon came to know this type of fly as a "Poole's Long Hackle".

That great fisherman, Mr. Horace Brown, thought a lot of them and suggested to Mosely that he should tie a few samples with wings. This he did and Brown immediately christened the result a "Variant", that is to say, a variant of the Long Hackle. The name stuck and before very long this type of fly became popular amongst southern fly fishermen.

Mr. Mosely's original dressing was:

Body: Stripped undyed peacock quill.
Hackle: Two or at the most three turns of a rusty-blue cock hackle with fibres at least twice as long as the hook, wound so as to stand well away from the shank like a thistledown.
Wings: Starling, tied as single wings.
Whisk: A few fibres of the rusty-blue hackle.
Hook: 13.

Mr. Mosely himself prefers the wingless fly, the original Poole's Long Hackle, but tied with an unstripped condor body, dyed olive, instead of the peacock quill which will not stand up so well to hard fishing.

Variants are exceptionally useful at times and I still cherish a pleasant memory of an experience on the Test many years ago. The trout could be seen taking something just under the surface, but I could not discover what it was and neither apparently could any of the three rods on the opposite bank, for not one of us could rise a single fish. After an hour, in sheer desperation, I mounted a Variant (one of T. J. Hanna's experimental patterns) and the first fish I put it over took it without any hesitation. That afternoon I creeled two brace of good trout and another brace in the evening, all on the Variant, whilst the anglers on the other bank failed to take a fish between them.

Although I have often tried Variants since, they have never brought me quite the same amount of luck again, although they will sometimes tempt a trout which has ignored other patterns and many fishermen have great faith in them.

There are many patterns such as the Red Variant, Brown Variant, Badger Variant, besides several which take their names from the well-known flies of which they are a hackled modification. Amongst the most useful of the latter is the Wickham Variant, which is a really excellent dry fly for general purposes. The dressing is:

Body: Flat gold tinsel.
Hackle: Red cock, long, bright, and stiff.
Hook: 14.

WASP FLY

Whereas trout may obviously appreciate a wasp grub, I cannot believe that they can have much liking for wasps. Yet copies of this insect are used in many countries, although in England, they are seldom, if ever, employed except for chub.

Some loch patterns known as the Black and Yellow Wasp, the Orange and Yellow Wasp, etc., are quite popular in Scotland, but as will be seen from the dressing given below, their name would seem to be about the only connection they have with the natural insect. Purely wet patterns, they are effective during August and September.

ORANGE AND YELLOW WASP
Tail: Golden pheasant tippet.
Body: Half yellow and half red-orange seal's fur, ribbed with silver.
Hackle: Red.
Wings: Dark teal.
Hook: 10 to 12.

WATCHET. See DARK WATCHET

WATER BOATMAN (*Corixa*, etc.) (Plate IX, 19, Plate VIII, 4)

This name is used by anglers to denote two water-beetles, rather similar in appearance. One belongs to the genus Notonecta, and is easily recognized by its habit of swimming on its back; and the other, a common species of the Corixae, which swim more normally and of which there are some thirty species.

Corixae are of interest to fishermen because autopsies show that they are found more often in trout than any other water-bugs. Largish beetles, attaining a length of three-quarters of an inch, they are brownhis in colour. Actually they "come in all sizes" for the newly-hatched youngsters are perfect miniature editions of their parents and as might be expected, it is the immature specimens which trout take most freely.

The boatmen are strong swimmers, possessing three pairs of legs and four wings of which the forewings are of a horny substance and the hind ones large and transparent.

Corixae are found in the quiet parts of many rivers, although they are really still-water insects and are nearly always present in great numbers on lakes, reservoirs, pools, and ponds. Most of their time is spent amongst the vegetation on the beds of rivers and lochs, but they are obliged to surface frequently in order to replenish their air supply. It is during the journeys to and from the surface that they fall a prey to trout.

In several respects they are queer creatures, for they are able to leave the water and fly whenever they feel so disposed. Then again, the air which permits them to live under water has to be stored in a hollow situated between the wings and abdomen. And they do not eat in the manner of other water insects, but secure their food, which consists mostly of decaying vegetation, etc., by sucking it up through the proboscis which they use like a vacuum cleaner. Stranger still, these beetles can produce a shrill penetrating noise by rubbing the teeth of one leg against a row of small pegs on another.

There are few dressings of these creatures; Leonard West gives one, but I do not care for it much and should put more faith in a sunken March Brown. Probably few fly-fishers think it worth while to attempt a copy of these boatmen, although on lakes it should be worth while since they form a by no means negligible proportion of the trout's diet.

Some little time ago, I asked Mr. T. J. Hanna for his ideas and he kindly sent me a pattern. When doing so he explained that it was a fancy creation not intended to be an exact imitation of any one species but that it would serve to illustrate his method of suggesting water beetles in general. As I feel sure that it will be of real interest to many readers who like to experiment in tying all sorts of flies, here is my interpretation of the dressing:

Body: Plymouth Rock hackle from shoulder to half-way down the hook, remainder left bare. The hackle is partly spread on each side of the body in semi-spent fashion.

Legs: Formed from stripped hackle stems, dyed orange-red and bent to represent the joints of the insect.

Wings: Cut from point of speckled hen wing with centre rib of feather left in and tied on flat. The wing is then varnished with shellac or cellulose varnish.

Hook: 12 to 10.

WATER CRICKET

The natural insect, *Velia currens*, is a small water-beetle rather smaller than the other pond-skaters and fatter in the body. Dark brown in colour, the adult has two orange stripes down its back, running from the thorax to the tail. The underside of the body of both the adult and nymph is also orange.

Although most common on lakes and pools, it is found on many rivers, where it prefers the back-waters away from the current. There is a winged type but it is the wingless form which is usually seen. Trout do not appear to be very fond of them, although there is no doubt that they will take them when other food is scarce and there is nothing more tempting within range.

Whatever opinion trout have of the natural insect, the artificial, although by no means a popular pattern to-day, is a first-rate fly for small lakes and sometimes on rivers. On some Welsh lakes, fish at times take it freely and I have had some good fish on it.

A few years ago, a keen fisherman wrote to me about a fly he had invented with which he had done tremendous execution amongst the grayling in a southern stream. He said that he had never met a fly to equal it and he must have been a little disappointed when I had to tell him that the pattern of which he was so proud to have been the inventor, differed in no respect from the dressing given by Ronalds for the Water Cricket.

Ronalds's dressing was:

Body: Orange floss silk, tied on with black silk thread.
Legs: Are best made of one of the two longest feathers of a peewit's topping. If this cannot be easily procured, a black cock's hackle will answer the purpose. Either of these must be wound all down the body, and the fibres then snipped off part way.
Hook: 14.
The shoulder should be left fairly thick.

Pritt states that the artificial is supposed to imitate "a spider which runs over the surface of the water" and gives this dressing.

Wings: Hackled with a feather from the golden plover's breast in its summer plumage; or the wing or back of a starling.
Body: Yellow or orange silk, sometimes ribbed with black silk. Sparsely dressed.
Hook: 14.

The Water Cricket is always fished wet.

WATER-HEN BLOA

This famous fly, known in Scotland as the Water-hen Blae, is one of the standard north-country patterns for trout and grayling. An old favourite, it still retains its popularity as a spring and autumn fly to imitate the dark olive and iron-blue duns, whilst there are few better nymph-suggesting patterns.

Invariably fished wet, its use is by no means confined to the north for everywhere it is known as an effective fly, especially on brooks and small waters generally. A first-class loch pattern, it is also one of the best grayling flies for the winter months. The old standard dressing as given by Pritt is:

Wings: Hackled feather from the inside of a water-hen's wing.
Body: Yellow silk, dubbed with the fur of a water-rat.
Hook: 14.

Great care must be taken with the dressing of this fly if it is to give its maximum efficiency. When fishing in Yorkshire, where I took a great number of trout and grayling on the water-hen bloa, I was very impressed at the insistence of experienced northern anglers upon the necessity of the dressing being just right. They would examine my fly with a critical eye and it was not long before I learnt their views on the materials which should be used. Particular care is always taken with the hackle. The feathers for this are taken from the second row from the top edge of the underwing of a moorhen; and it is considered essential that they should be spoon-shaped and glossy on the underside. No other feather will fill the bill.

Equal care is accorded the body. That great fly-fisherman, E. M. Tod, who preferred the water-hen bloa to any other hackled fly, wrote this about it: "The body is tied with yellow tying silk, waxed with colourless wax, dubbed very sparingly with fur from the water-rat or the water-mouse. Even the fur of the mole may be used when the other is not procurable. The two main points are to lay on the fur with a very sparing hand and if you do this the second point almost follows as a natural consequence; that you can always see plainly the yellow tying silk running in ribs down the body of the fly. It makes a unique and splendid body; in fact, without this body I should regard the fly itself as being less worthy of the high place I have accorded it in my list of hackled flies, misnamed spiders in Scotland."

Another great northern angler, Francis Walbran, recommended the Pritt dressing but with the body dubbed with mole's fur. He also varied the dressing at times by wrapping the hackle on a smooth body of yellow silk and was inclined to the opinion that this was possibly a better tie than the original.

Water-hen is, of course, another name for the moorhen and a water-mouse is a water-shrew. For the meaning of bloa, see Poult Bloa.

WATER-RAT

The invention of Mr. G. Austin (Birmingham), this is quite a useful hackled pattern, dry or wet, for rivers or lakes. The late Mr. Will Fyffe, the famous Scottish comedian, who was an angler of skill and experience, told me that he found it a good fly for Blagdon.

Dressing:

Body: Yellow silk with water-rat's fur spun thinly on the silk just to show the yellow rib.
Hackle: Blue Andalusian.
Whisks: As hackle.
Hook: 12 to 14.

WATSON'S FANCY

An old loch pattern still favoured in Scotland and a really useful sea-trout fly.

Dressing:

Body: Tail half of red, and rest of black seal's fur. The whole body ribbed with fine gold wire.
Wings: From the tail of a blackcock, with a jungle-cock feather on each side of wing.
Hackle: Black.
Tail: Golden pheasant crest feather.
Hook: 10 to 12; larger for sea-trout.

WELSHMAN'S BUTTON

There can be no doubt that this name really belongs to a beetle, although Halford, for some reason, chose to apply it to a sedge, *Sericostoma personatum,* and since then, southern anglers have followed his example. Why he did so is not easy to understand, because this well-known caddis fly had been known as the dun cut for over four hundred years.

Halford's fly is one of the day-flying sedges which appears in numbers at about the same time as the mayfly. It measures about half an inch in length and when first on the surface (after having risen from the bed of the river to hatch), its general colouring is similar to red-mahogany. This quickly darkens with exposure and when the insect reaches the river-side vegetation, the colour has usually changed to a dark chestnut-brown. The female—and the female only—is subject to some variation and may often be found with white patches on the wings.

The fly first occurs towards the end of May or early in June, sometimes in great numbers. Its appearance frequently coincides with that of the mayfly and when the latter is scarce, an imitation of the sedge should bring good results. *S. personatum* is not seen much after July and seldom in any abundance after June.

Halford's tie for the female is one of his most successful experiments and is a splendid imitation of the natural insect. The dressing (given in his *Modern Development of the Dry Fly*) is:

Wings: Pale brown hen.
Hackles: Two furnace cock hackles.
Body: Four turns of unstripped condor dyed dark cinnamon at tail end and for remainder of body, a thin strip from central quill of a brown hen wing-feather, dyed dark chocolate-brown, with glossy side outwards and ribbed with pale maroon horsehair.
Hook: 13.

There are two other patterns which I consider excellent. Skues's Little Red Sedge is the best known, but Lunn's pattern, which he calls the Caperer or Welshman's Button is also very good indeed.

In recent years, it has gained a great reputation on most rivers in the south and appears to take fish equally as well on rough northern and midland streams, and without any doubt it must now be ranked as one of the very best of all sedge patterns. It is often as effective in the day as it is in the evening, and even on a chalk stream, tied on a fairly large hook, say a No. 12, it kills as well as when dressed on a hook two sizes smaller. This is one of those patterns which every dry-fly angler, wherever he fishes, should carry and which he should never be shy of trying whenever there are any sedges on the water; or in fact even when they are not. Fished during the summer months on any river or lake where sedges are found (and there are few where they are not), it will often produce surprisingly gratifying results.

Lunn's original dressing was:

Body: Four or five strands from turkey tail feather with a ring in the centre of two strands of yellow-dyed swan's feather.
Hackle: One black cock hackle followed by one of medium Rhode Island.
Tying silk: Pearsall's gossamer, No. 13.
Hook: 14 to 12.

For his winged version, Lunn made the wings of coot bleached in peroxide and dyed chocolate-brown.

Mr. R. G. B. Gardner, of the Fly-fishers' Club, varies this fly slightly by using condor instead of swan, and dark condor instead of brown turkey, a tie which some anglers like better. There would also seem to be no reason why a coch-y-bondhu hackle should not be substituted for the double red and black hackles suggested by Lunn.

The true Welshman's button is a bettle found through Cambria, although it is not common, and although rather like a coch-y-bondhu it is certainly not button-shaped. Welshmen always refer to it as the "Welshman's butty", and this, one must conclude, is almost surely the original and correct name for the beetle.

Butty, of course, is a term for a friend or pal, and is a word still regularly used by the coal workers in South Wales, where the miner's mate is invariably known as his butty.

The only dressing I know to imitate this beetle is one given by Mr. Eric Taverner and is as follows:

Silk: Crimson.
Body: Greenish-bronze peacock herl.
Hackle: Black cock.
Wing-cases: Red feather from a partridge tail.
Hook: 13.

This is a good general utility beetle pattern for all rivers and lakes.

WELSH PARTRIDGE

Like every other fisherman who attempts to imitate natural insects, from time to time I have designed patterns, some of which have not proved unsuccessful. If reference is made to only two or three of them in this book, it is because I have seen so many "infallible" flies which have soon faded into oblivion that I hesitate to pass on any of my own dressings lest they should share the same fate. But I feel no hesitation about recommending the Welsh Partridge, which has provided me with some excellent sport for several years and which I think can be called a reliable pattern which will kill on any river except the chalk streams.

As a lake fly too, it is, on its day, the equal of any other dry fly known to me. During April and May and again in September it will take trout on almost every river and lake and on occasions it proves irresistible, taking one fish after another. In fact when first I tried it, it provided me with a red-letter day, for I creeled five brace of fish in an hour's fishing.

What fish take it for is difficult to determine, because, however much I try to persuade myself that they take it for some particular insect, the more I use it, the less support is forthcoming for this theory. Trout will take the Welsh Partridge whatever may be the natural flies on the water, although probably one would not be far wrong in calling it a nymph-suggesting pattern.

I have fished it only as a floater or semi-submerged, although friends tell me that it is quite as good when fished wet, and I imagine that, wet or dry, it would be as deadly in Scotland and Ireland as it has proved to be in other parts of Great Britain. It has the merit of attracting the larger trout, although why this should be so I do not pretend to know. The same claim has been made for other patterns and never once have I found that it could be substantiated, but in the light of experience, I believe it to be true of the Welsh Partridge.

Having thus commended the fly with a full realization of how easy it is to over-praise one's own inventions, I can only hope that other anglers who care to try it on river or lake will find it serves them as well as it serves me.

The dressing is:

Body: Claret seal's fur, ribbed with fine gold.
Hackle: Snipe rump feather (or from the back of a partridge), with a short stiff claret hackle behind.
Whisks: Two strands from a partridge's tail.
Hook: 14 to 12.

WHIRLING BLUE DUN

In *The Compleat Angler* this pattern is referred to as "The Little Dun, called the Whirling dun . . . one of the best flies we know", and ever since then angling authors have been writing about both the natural and artificial Whirling Blue Dun. Yet exactly what is the natural insect is still a mystery, for the old authorities name different flies, and the moderns, for the most part, are delightfully vague about the whole question. Those bold enough to mention a particular insect appear to do so with little confidence and less warranty. It was left to Major J. D. D. Evans, the Usk entomologist, to survey this intriguing problem in No. 93 of the *Salmon and Trout Magazine*. After sifting the matter very thoroughly, he came to two definite conclusions: firstly that there is no such fly as a natural whirling blue dun, and secondly that the artificial is a most killing pattern.

Few anglers will quarrel with his second conclusion and personally I accept his first with some reservations. In approaching a problem of this nature, one naturally turns first to those authorities whose entomological reputation stands highest and in this instance one naturally looks up Ronalds as being one of the soundest naturalists of the old order and because his valuable work is noteworthy for being very many years before its time in accuracy of observation and record. We find that he concludes his note about the W.B.D. in these words: "It has been supposed to be a second edition of the Yellow Dun of April. If compared with that, it will be found rather smaller and more ginger in colour."

That alone does not take us very far and many guesses have been made as to the identity of the fly which he describes as being smaller than the Yellow Dun. Now it so happens that the "models" from which Ronalds made the sketches for his book are (or were) housed in the Hope Department of the Oxford University Museum, a fact which must be known to few fishermen. A perusal of the collection has revealed the fact that Ronalds's Whirling Blue Dun was almost certainly what we now know as the autumn dun, or august dun as it is sometimes called.

Leonard West was another author whose careful observation is beyond dispute and on page 31 of his *Natural Trout Fly and Its Imitation*, we read that "Fig. 49 is the Whirling Blue Dun, which by the casual observer is sometimes mistaken for the March Brown on account of its size and dusky upright wings"—which is a pretty accurate description of the autumn dun.

The modern school are less inclined to commit themselves, although that good entomologist, Roger Woolley refers to the W.B.D. as being "a large autumn dun". It would appear to me, therefore, that the natural prototype of the pattern known as the Whirling Blue Dun may well be the autumn dun (*Ecdyurus longicauda*).

Yet there is no real proof of that and it is only speculation on my part, because it must still be admitted that there is no general agreement amongst writers as to which of the duns was, or is, meant by the term Whirling Blue. Several observers have noted the fact that in a certain light, all duns as they take to the air from the water occasionally look in flight as if they were spinning or whirling, and that being so, the name could have been applied to any dun.

But whether the autumn dun was the fly referred to by the old authorities as the W.B.D., or whether it has no prototype in nature, there can be no question that the artificial is a first-rate pattern. Actually there are several variations of the artificial fly such as those known as the Dark Whirling Blue Dun and the Light Whirling Blue Dun, but, as Major Evans has pointed out, they all have one common feature, for, as all the ancient and moderns agree, the pattern must always be dressed with a ginger hackle. There is no doubt in my mind that a hackle of this colour has some fascination for trout which will frequently take a pattern tied with one, irrespective of whatever natural fly may be on the water.

Halford's dressing for the W.B.D. is as good as any, although incidentally he was not one of those who hazarded a guess as to the insect it was intended to imitate. He did, however, make the following comment upon this pattern: "It is continually being reproduced as the 'Invincible' or 'Infallible' of some amateur or professional and is generally successful." And that remark is as true to-day as when he penned it just half a century ago.

His dressing is:

Wings: Medium starling.
Hackles: Two ginger cock hackles.
Body: Water-rat fur.
Whisk: Gallina dyed brown-red.
Hook: 16 to 14.

Another excellent tie is:

Wings: Starling, medium, light, or dark.
Hackle: Ginger cock's.
Body: Hare's fur spun on olive or yellow tying silk.
Tail: Three whisks ginger cock.
Hook: 14.

This is a very similar pattern to the Ginger March Brown and both are good autumn flies. Major Evans, in the article to which reference has already been made, expresses a view, which, I am sure, will be endorsed by most anglers of experience: "For myself, I like to dub its body with a spot of the fur from a young hedgepig's belly, whether it be mingled with squirrel, fox-cub, or what-not. Others may care for a quill or other body material. Some may differ as to the winging. But all this matters not one jot! We *must* have ginger and that is that."

WHISKERS
This fly is an ordinary Red Palmer but tied with long stiff hackles and is always fished as a floater. The invention of the late Harry Powell, the Usk professional fly-dresser, it is a favourite on the Usk and the Teme. A good general utility pattern, it kills best in June (on a size 12 hook) and during July, when a rather smaller pattern gives better results.

WHITCHURCH DUN. See LITTLE MARRYAT

WHITE MOTH

This is the fisherman's name for any light-coloured member of the Lepidoptera, of which there are numerous species. The artificial serves to suggest any of them and consequently it can be very useful. When a moth accidentally gets on to the water, its struggles to rise again create a disturbance which attracts any fish near it: and if it happens to be a large specimen, it forms a hefty mouthful which may cause a big trout to take it with a rush. The artificial is nearly always fished at dusk or after dark when the larger fish are on the move and I have known it account for some really fine specimens.

Whether on river or lake, and whether fished dry or semi-dry, the White Moth is entitled to be looked upon as one of the best patterns for use after dark, especially on warm sultry nights during August and September. The tie varies slightly but a usual one is as under:

Body: White wool, rather thick, ribbed with fine silver wire.
Hackle: White cock's, from shoulder to tail.
Wings: White owl, usually split for the floating pattern.
Hook: 10 to 14.

This is an effective pattern, although personally I consider that that other excellent fly, the Ermine Moth, is generally more deadly.

WICKHAM'S FANCY

A fancy fly which does not appear to approximate to any natural insect, but which, nevertheless, is a most useful pattern for general work especially in a small size for smutting fish. Used wet and dry, it is infinitely better fished as a floater.

A first-class trout fly, it is also effective for rainbows, dace, and chub, is by no means to be despised for grayling, and is a most killing pattern for sea-trout, particularly in low clear water. As a late evening fly on river or lake, it is a useful suggestion of a sedge.

The fly is generally understood to have been invented by Dr. T. C. Wickham and to have been first tied for him by Hammond of Winchester. It resembles the older Cockerton Fly of which Dr. Wickham wrote: "I used to fish with it when a boy at Sutton Scotney, five miles from Whitchurch on the Test, but I think that it had more hackle and less gold. But not being able to obtain a pattern of the Cockerton I went my own way, and the gold appeared to me to be essential as, according to Hammond, when held in a glass of water, it gave an olive tint. Whether this was true or not, the result was a killing fly. At one time I used it dressed with a pale olive hackle." The dressing of this popular pattern is:

Wings: Medium starling.
Hackles: Two ginger-red cock hackles at shoulder.
Ribbing Hackle: Ginger-red cock hackle.
Body: Flat gold, ribbed with fine gold wire.
Whisk: Gallina dyed brown-red.
Hook: 14 to 16.

Having given the credit of the invention to Dr. Wickham, it is only fair to add that as long ago as 1884 George Currell, of Winchester, claimed to have been the first professional to have tied the fly and stated that it was designed by Captain John Wickham, whose dressing was as that given above except that amber-coloured silk showed between the ribs of tinsel.

The Pink Wickham was evolved in 1885 by Francis Francis. It differs in no way from the original Wickham's Fancy, except that a landrail wing is used instead of starling. Still favoured for trout and grayling, many fly-fishers consider it a more killing fly than the older one. Possibly fish take it for a greenish-bodied sedge, and it is one of the most useful patterns for "tailers", providing, of course, that one can induce them to take notice.

My personal preference is for the hackled fly which I am convinced is a better killer. Although, except for the elimination of the wings, it is exactly the same as the standard pattern, it generally floats in a more natural manner and shy fish are less suspicious of it.

WILLIAMS'S FAVOURITE

This pattern was first tied by my father when fishing the Dysynni, at that time a good trout and sea-trout river, and was consistently used by him throughout the sixty years of his angling life. Undoubtedly he found it more successful than any other wet pattern and he must have taken thousands of trout and sea-trout on it, and not a few grayling.

Ignoring a natural family prejudice in its favour, I must confess that for most of my life this pattern has been my stand-by from May to September, fished wet or dry. I have given it a good trial in most parts of Great Britain, in France, Belgium, Germany, Austria, and Czechoslovakia, and in every country it has proved its worth.

As an all-round wet fly when a dark pattern is required, Williams's Favourite is first rate and is particularly useful as a lake pattern; in fact on some lochs it is now regarded as a standard fly. Personally because I so seldom fish with a wet fly, finding dry fly-fishing so much more pleasurable and interesting, I generally use this pattern as a floater and many times have taken fish all day long on it when far better-known dry flies have failed to produce a rise.

When trout are taking black gnats, there are few better patterns than this one tied on a very small hook, and fished dry, with or without the whisks removed.

Nevertheless, Williams's Favourite is a typical wet fly of the spider variety and without doubt it is one of the very best for use in muddy or peat-stained water, with the proviso, of course, that the stream is not so thick to warrant the name of "pea-soup", in which case it is next to impossible for fish to see a fly at all. But when heavy rain causes the river to rise and again when it is clearing after a spate, fish seem to see a black fly better than any other, and in these conditions the black and silver Williams's Favourite gives more chance of fish than any other wet pattern known to me.

The dressing is a simple one. A black hackle for the wings, a black silk body ribbed with silver, and two or three black whisks. Hook size 12 to 16, with 14 as the most generally useful. The dry pattern should be hackled with a stiff black cock's hackle.

A somewhat similar fly but dressed palmer fashion and fished in a large size, is popular at Blagdon. In appearance, Williams's Favourite is much like one of Charles Cotton's three-hundred-year-old Dove patterns for which he gave the following tie: "A black body of the whirle of an ostridg-feather, rib'd with silver twist, and the black hackle of a cock over all."

My father's fly has always been one of my own favourites for sea-trout and in this connection I received a letter some time ago from Mr. R. d'Oyly Hemmingway, the author of *Fly-Fishing for Trout*, in which he suggested a useful variation. He wrote: "I have often registered thanks to you for your praise of 'Williams's Favourite'. I find, however, that a few short red whisks on the longer black ones, sometimes make the fly more attractive to sea-trout."

WILLOW

One of Canon Eagle's favourite patterns, which he used to imitate the dark olive and iron blue duns. In his time, many good anglers looked upon it as a veritable sheet-anchor and it still bears a very high reputation amongst the few flyfishers who know the correct tie. Although a close relative of Colonel Rollo's Blue Dun Hackle, the Willow is always fished wet. It is well worth a trial for the Canon never used any pattern which did not bring him a lot of fish. The dressing is:

Body: Peacock quill, bound with finest silver wire.
Hackle: Grizzled blue dun cock, taken half-way down from the eye of the hook.
Hook: 10 to 12.

WILLOW FLY (*Leuctra geniculata*)

There are several flies rather similar in appearance, of which the best known representative of the smaller ones is the needle brown (*Nemoura inconspicua*) which is abroad in April. In autumn, the larger willow fly (*L. geniculata*) appears and is so like *N. inconspicua*, except in size, that anglers can treat them as one. The willow fly is widely distributed and is exceedingly abundant on many rivers, so that it is known to most anglers. In many parts of the country, it is known as the withy fly and in some districts in Devonshire it is called "Old Besom".

It is quite easy to recognize, its main features being an elongated brownish body with transparent brown wings, two antennae and no setae. About half an inch in length, or sometimes slightly over, the insect carries its four wings folded flat over its back in the characteristic manner of the perlidae, and although the general colouring of these is brown, they often take on a steely blue tint. The most accurate manner of identifying this insect, as Mr. Martin Mosely has pointed out, is to examine its antennae which carry strong hairs, arranged in groups, although a microscope will be required to reveal them. Neither *L. klapaleki* (which is usually found with it), nor, in fact, any other British species is thus adorned. During September *L. geniculata* is often blown on to lakes in considerable numbers.

In flight, the willow fly flutters in a clumsy manner and, for some reason or other, always looks considerably bigger than it actually is. Like some of its near relatives, it makes its presence known to fishermen by settling on their hands, necks, or clothing.

Anglers should get to know this fly because it is well liked by trout and grayling, although they pay far more attention to it in rough tumbling rivers than they do on the placid southern streams. Probably this is because other food is more abundant on the latter, for the natural fly is extremely plentiful on the Test and Itchen and fish have every opportunity of feeding on it if they feel so inclined. That is not to say that trout will entirely ignore the willow fly on the chalk streams, for, at times, they will take it freely, but that in the fast rocky rivers of the north and west, species of the perlidae family form a much more important part of the trout's diet.

The female fly deposits her eggs on the river by fluttering above it and dropping them from a height, of often several feet, on to the water where they soon sink to the bottom. As soon as the operation is completed, the insect falls exhausted on to the surface and it is whilst she is floating in this spent condition that fish get the best chance of securing her. It is because of this that spent artificial patterns are generally the most effective.

There are a good many well-known north-country wet patterns which serve to imitate this class of insect. They include the Brown Owl, Dark Spanish Needle, Light Needle, and the Winter Brown.

Of the several dry patterns, the Blue Upright is good, but the best of all, in my experience, is the Grey Duster. On some Herefordshire streams on which the willow fly is of importance in the early part of the season and again in September, the ordinary stock patterns are not always successful, although superficially they seem to be fair imitations of the natural insect. Canon Wilfred Knox tells me that the right answer would appear to be an Orange Tag. He ought to know, for he has killed hundreds of trout on this pattern, which is generally regarded as being more suitable for grayling.

For a spent fly, Mr. Skues has given particulars of a dressing which he used first on the Coquet as long ago as 1888, and which has served him well ever since. The tie is:

Tying silk: Orange.
Dubbing: Mole's fur.
Hackle: Rusty dun cock behind, between, and in front of the wings.
Wings: Hen blackbird. Four thin strips tied so as to lie flat to right and left of the hook shank, giving the effect of a spent fly.
Hook: 14.

As an alternative, the body may be represented with a brown quill from the shaft of the eyed feather of the peacock. On occasions, when there has been a hatch of the larger willow fly, Mr. Skues states that he has used slips of moorhen primary or secondary feathers from the wings, with marked success.

I would call the attention of amateur fly-dressers who are fond of experimenting, to a floating pattern evolved by Mr. T. J. Hanna, because his method of making the wing is very simple and highly effective. It can be used for copies of many insects but is especially suitable for those of the perlidae. The folded wings of stone flies, willow flies, yellow sallies and other perlidae are, of course, considerably narrower and in copying them, the feather used for the wings should naturally be cut to shape according to insect it is desired to imitate. Mr. Hanna's dressing for the willow fly is:

Body: Dark olive silk ribbed with brown silk.
Hackle: Honey dun cock, or yellowish badger over. The hackle is spread to each side of the body in the spent fashion.
Wing: Cut from speckled hen (bustard can be used), with the quill left on, the fibres being trimmed up each side, and the lower end of the wing slightly rounded. It is then tied on so as to lie flat over the body.
Hook: 12, long shank.

WITCH

This well-known grayling pattern, sometimes known as Rolt's Witch, was invented by H. A. Rolt, of Wimbledon, some fifty years ago. He made some wonderful bags with it on the Wylye and other streams, and its popularity grew unusually quickly. Writing of it in his book, *Grayling Fishing in South Country Streams*, Rolt said: "Although I am not a 'one-fly' man, and although I do not desire to blow unduly my own trumpet, I would rather pin my faith to an improved and glorified green insect I have discovered. It has been named the 'Witch', and with it I have killed more grayling than with any nondescript or natural I have tried, the red tag not excepted. Dressed on a No. 16 hook, it may be fished dry, especially when the grayling are midging. Being well hackled, it floats well with a little assistance from the brush of the paraffin bottle. As a wet fly, it cannot be too highly recommended. In rough, windy weather, trout will take it well, fished close to the bank and slightly worked."

That sums up the Witch very fairly, although to-day its reputation as a trout pattern is by no means great. As a grayling fly, wet or dry, it must be regarded as a standard pattern and for these fish there can be few better flies. The original dressing was:

Body: Bright green peacock herl from the sword feather, two or three strands twisted together and ribbed with flat gold.
Hackle: Light honey dun from shoulder to tail.
Tag: Red floss.
Hook: 14 to 17.

A white cock's hackle is preferred by some fishermen and red ibis is often used for the tag.

There are some other rather similar patterns such as the Silver Witch, the Gold Witch and the White Witch, but I do not think that generally speaking they are quite as good as Rolt's dressing. A possible exception is the Grayling Witch, invented, I believe, by Mr. Woolley. My opportunities for grayling fishing are infrequent, but on the few occasions I have tried this pattern, it has proved a much better killer than most. Woolley's tie for it is:

Body: Green peacock herl, ribbed with flat silver.
Hackle: Pale blue dun.
Tag: Red floss.
Hook: 17 to 14.

As a general rule dry grayling flies should be tied on small hooks, the largest hooks being more useful for wet fly for late autumn and winter fishing. In the winter grayling patterns are often leaded by wrapping the bodies with thin lead strip to make them sink, another idea invented by Rolt and since widely adopted.

WOODCOCK SERIES

The Woodcock flies, like the Teal, Mallard, and Grouse series, are standard wet patterns for trout, particularly for lake fishing, and all are good sea-trout flies.

The best known are the Woodcock and Green, Woodcock and Red, Woodcock and Hare's Ear (of which the dressings are given below), Woodcock and Orange, Woodcock and Yellow, and Woodcock and Black.

WOODCOCK AND GREEN
Tail: A few strands of golden pheasant tippet.
Body: Green wool or seal's fur, ribbed with silver wire.
Hackle: Ginger and red.
Wings: Inside of woodcock's wing feather.
Hooks: 8 to 14.

WOODCOCK AND RED
Tail: A few strands of golden pheasant tippet.
Body: Red seal's fur·ribbed with oval silver.
Hackle: Red.
Wings: Inside of a woodcock's wing feather.
Hook: 8 to 14.

WOODCOCK AND HARE'S EAR

Tail: Two fibres of brown mallard.
Tag: Flat gold tinsel.
Body: Dark hare's ear slightly tinged with dark olive-green wool and left rather long at shoulder for hackle.
Wings: Inside of woodcock's wing feather.
Hook: 8 to 14.

WOOD ANT. See ANTS

WORM FLY

A fly or lure of the tandem variety, mostly used well-sunk, on rivers and lakes after dark but sometimes deadly on still waters in rough weather. In these conditions, a really large fly—say on a No. 8 hook—may tempt the biggest trout.

It is a fly of which I know very little beyond that the usual pattern (which is subject to variation) has a peacock herl body with a red hackle, either at the head only or wound palmer-wise down the body. Normally the leading fly is tied on an eyed hook and is connected by a piece of stout gut to the second fly, which is dressed on a tapered shank hook.

The origin of the Worm Fly is attributed to William Black, the novelist, who is said to have invented it sometime prior to the year 1880.

WINTER BROWN

An old northern wet pattern designed to imitate the smaller perlidae —the needle flies and, possibly, the rather larger willow fly. A killing pattern for Yorkshire and Welsh rivers in the early spring. Pritt recommended its use on wild cold days in March and April.

Dressing (Pritt):

Wings: Hackled with a feather from the winside of a woodcock's wing.
Body: Orange silk, not too bright.
Head: Peacock herl.
Hook: 14 to 12.

Later in the year, when the needle flies are rather lighter in colour, the Little Winter Brown (or Light Woodcock) is said to be a more likely killer. The old Yorkshire dressing for this pattern is:

Wings: Hackled with a feather from the outside of a woodcock's wing.
Body: Orange silk, dubbed lightly with hare's ear.
Hook: 14.

WRENS

The Wren series of flies have long been looked upon as standard patterns in southern Ireland, although they are scarcely ever heard of on English waters. They are always fished wet.

The most popular patterns are the Green Wren, Black Wren, Gold Wren, Orange Wren, and Yellow Wren. All are sometimes described as Wren and Green, Wren and Black, etc. The only difference between the various flies lies in the colour of the body, so that the dressing of one of them only need be given. The Green Wren will serve for this purpose. It is tied as follows:

Body: Light green silk, sometimes ribbed very lightly with gold.
Hackle: Wren's tail.
Wing: Wren or woodcock.
Hook: 14.

Many anglers prefer starling for the wing. A tail is sometimes added and when this is done, it is usually made of rat's whiskers.

WRENTAIL *(Aphrophora alni)*

This is the fisherman's name for the froghopper or cuckoo-spit, a small mottled brown insect which is found, during summer, in the little frothy masses attached to grass and vegetation.

In the autumn, the insects emerge and sometimes large numbers fall or jump into the water, when trout will feed upon them with avidity. The name Wrentail seems to have originated with Ronalds. It has never occurred to me that a copy of this small insect is necessary but apparently some anglers think otherwise, since several dressings are available, although perhaps they are more used for grayling than trout. A common one is as under:

Body: Ginger-coloured seal's fur, ribbed with fine gold oval tinsel.
Hackle: The brown speckled feather from a wren's tail.
Hook: 16.

This is fished wet on hot days in September.

YELLOW MAY DUN *(Heptagenia sulphurea)*

Known in Ireland as the yellow hawk. The nymph, one of Pictet's "flat larvae", is rather like that of the march brown, but the insect is known to most anglers in the dun stage only.

Appearing sometime during May, it lasts for four or five weeks. The hatch is a daytime one and to the best of my knowledge, never an evening affair. Fishermen generally recognize this insect as being the

yellowish dun which is often on the water at the same time as the mayfly. Abundant on the Test and other chalk streams, I do not think it
appears in much strength elsewhere.

It is a largish dun with four wings and two setae and is of a bright
sulphur colour with metallic-looking eyes and opaque wings. Its
spinner has transparent wings with black neuration excepting towards
the roots, where the main nervures are sometimes tinged with greenish
or yellow amber. The spinner seems to be almost unknown to anglers
and had no popular name until Mr. Martin Mosely suggested that it
should share the name yellow upright with the imago of *Rhithrogena
semicolorata* to which it bears a very close likeness. In this instance there
may be some justification for this course which I have not fully
appreciated, and as a general rule I feel sure that the use of one name for
two different species (however alike they may be) is to be deprecated.
I must confess that my experience of the yellow dun is very slight and
I have never seen it in an autopsy. This is not very surprising, because,
to the best of my knowledge, trout seldom, if ever, pay the slightest
attention to it, and it is one of the very few species of the Ephemeridae
of which no fly-fisherman will require an artificial copy.

YELLOW PARTRIDGE. See PARTRIDGE AND YELLOW

YELLOW SALLY (*Chloroperla grammatica*)

Typical of the needle or willow flies, the yellow sally is known to
most fishermen, being easily recognized by its four pale yellow wings
and its yellow body. Measuring about three-quarters of an inch across
the wings, from tip to tip, with two setae and two antennae, it is a
very common insect on many rivers from June till August. In Yorkshire, Wales, and the Midlands, it is found in abundance and is common
on the Test.

The general opinion is that trout do not relish this insect, but I do
not think that is true of streams where there is a scarcity of other fly
life. On the Usk and Teify and many similar rivers a smaller relative,
known as *Isopteryx torrentium*, will often cause fish to rise freely. Incidentally the yellow sally is sometimes confused with the Little Yellow
May Dun (*Heptagenia sulphurea*) and it should therefore be remembered
that the yellow sally is a small member of the perlidae (stone-flies) with
long narrow wings which fold flat over its back, whilst the other is an
upright-winged dun.

Whether trout and grayling appreciate the natural insect is of no
great importance to fly-fishers because unfortunately neither of these

fish show much interest in the patterns expressly designed to imitate it. Yet, presumably because the yellow sally occurs in such large numbers, most fly-tiers have attempted copies and many dressings are available to choose from.

Pritt gives an old Yorkshire tie and adds that it does not kill well. The following modern dressing may prove more killing:

Tying silk: Primrose.
Body: Pale yellow wool, teased out before spinning it on to the silk.
Hackle: White cock dyed pale yellow.
Hook: 14.

Although I have yet to discover a satisfactory dressing, I tied a fly in Yorkshire some years ago which deceived a few fish. The dressing was:

Body: Pale yellow quill.
Hackle: Strands of very fine gut, dyed canary yellow, and mixed with three or four strands of the same material dyed scarlet. This hackle should slope well over the body.
Whisks: Three strands of fine yellow gut.
Hook: 14.

To-day, I should use nylon in preference to the silkworm gut.

Mr. C. J. Hughes has recently published another tie which would seem to be a good copy of the natural fly, although as yet I have not had an opportunity of testing it. His dressing is as under:

Body: Pale apple-green silk, ribbed with crimson silk.
Hackle: White bantam cock, first dyed yellow in a solution made by boiling the outside skin of an onion, and afterwards steeped in blue-black ink—a process which gives the required almost-transparent effect.
Hook: 15.

There is also a simple pattern with which my acquaintance is short, but which is much used, I am told, on the Usk and the Monnow, and probably on other rivers. My own experience of it is slight but sufficient to suggest to me that it may be a very happy suggestion of the natural insect. On the two occasions I have used it, the fish took to it very kindly and friends have told me that in June it can often be fished with striking success. The tie is:

Body: Light canary quill or wool.
Hackle: Two pale ginger cock's hackles.
Hook: 14

YELLOW UPRIGHT (*Rhithrogena semicolorata*)

Probably a great number of fishermen see this fly without recognizing it, for although rare on the chalk streams, it is common enough on many of our rivers and, indeed, throughout Europe. That so many anglers fail to identify it is due, I imagine, to two causes. Unless they look at it closely they may well be under the impression that it is a large early olive (which superficially it resembles) and also because they will reasonably expect it to be a yellow insect. But the yellow upright is certainly not yellow, the general colour effect being slaty-grey. It is a large dun with four wings and two setae, which occurs from late April until July, although I fancy that in most districts in England, it does not appear in any strength until the third week in May. Towards the end of that month, there are enormous hatches of it on many rivers such as the Welsh Dee and the Usk. The hatch starts as a rule in the late afternoon and continues right up to dark and is comparable to a typical b.-w.o. hatch. Often, also, there is a sparse but continuous hatch during daytime on shady brooks. As already indicated, the sub-imago bears some likeness to the large early olive but an examination, both in the case of the dun and spinner, will reveal the typical Rhithrogena "hall-mark", a dark triangular blotch on the middle of the femur, viz., on the top joint of the leg.

The imago is of less interest to fishermen because it is not much liked by trout but it is easier identified than the dun. The male spinners when dancing in the light of the setting sun often appear to be of a faint sulphury-yellow colour and it is on account of this and also because of their habit of ascending vertically in an upright position when in flight, that their popular name originated. The yellowish effect is probably caused by the bronze "stain" on the inner or basal portion of the wings, a feature which I believe is peculiar to this species. When once it has been observed, it will not easily be forgotten, but it is found on the imago only. The wings of the sub-imago are of an even pale slaty hue.

Since the yellow upright occurs in such huge quantities and trout take it freely, it is surprising that few imitations are available, but this is often the case with insects which are not indigenous to the chalk streams.

One of the most effective patterns is, without doubt, a Pheasant Tail, dressed with a dark rusty dun hackle of high quality. Major J. D. D. Evans, of Brecon, knows more about the yellow upright than most people and I am much indebted to him for letting me have particulars of a pattern which he states is the best known to him, and of which the dressing is as follows:

THE H.P.B. (or HEDGEPIG'S BELLY)

Whisks: Eight or ten fibres of pale golden-blue game from a spade feather.
Body: Belly fur from a half-grown hedgepig, blended with a little rusty-yellow seal's fur.
Rib: Finest gold thread.
Hackle: Best quality old English game honey dun—enough to ensure maximum buoyancy; anything else means failure.
Hook: 14.

In spite of the rather close resemblance of the yellow upright to the large early olive, patterns generally used to imitate the latter are seldom effective. The two ties given above are more likely to produce good results. In broken water, a suitable nymph pattern often proves excellent as a trout pay special attention to the insect just as it emerges from the nymphal shuck, some suggestion of it in the nymphal dun stage should be particularly useful. For this purpose, Mr. Eric Taverner has suggested the following:

Body: Light yellow-orange floss silk.
Hackle: Mottled brown partridge feather.
Hook: 14.

ZULU

It is with some diffidence I write of this fly for it is known to almost every fly-fisher as a good pattern, but I can never remember ever having had any success with it. Many friends have assured me that they find it a most effective trout fly for river and lake, for sea-trout, and for grayling; but although I have tried it dozens of times, I can't remember having taken a trout on it, although once it relented to the extent of catching a few chub and dace for me.

Purely a fancy pattern, always fished wet (except occasionally for grayling), the Zulu has long enjoyed a good reputation in many parts of the world, especially as a loch fly. Fished well sunk off the reeds fringing a lake, it is said to attract fish which will not be tempted by other patterns, whilst in the smaller sizes, it is effective for grayling.

Possibly I am rather prejudiced against this fly, for not so long ago, on the Usk, in clear low water, on a hot bright summer's day, I toiled hard and caught nothing, whereas my companion produced a creel full of trout, all of them of about a pound apiece; and every one of them was taken on a Zulu! In the conditions which prevailed, I could not (and still cannot) imagine any pattern which seemed less likely to attract trout.

The dressing is:

Tail: Short red wool.
Body: Black wool or seal's fur, ribbed with fine flat silver tinsel.
Hackle: Black cock's from tail to head.
Hook: 12 to 14.

The Blue Zulu is the same fly, but with a dyed blue hackle and, like the Zulu, is considered an effective loch pattern, especially in June or July.

For sea-trout I have found the following useful, when a dry fly is wanted. The dressing was sent to me by a friend some years ago, but I do not know who originated it.

Tag: Red ibis.
Body: Peacock herl, ribbed with silver twist.
Hackle: Himalayan pheasant.
Hook: 10 to 12.

PART III

A LIST OF MODERN
NATURAL AND ARTIFICIAL FLIES
By T. Donald Overfield

INTRODUCTION TO PART THREE
BY T. DONALD OVERFIELD

In 1932 A. and C. Black published A. Courtney Williams' classic volume *Trout Flies; A Discussion and a Dictionary*. The book was an immediate success, for here was the first attempt to write the individual histories of certain trout and sea-trout artificial patterns. The book is now a collectors' item, and rightly so.

The year 1949 saw the publication, again by A. and C. Black, of a much enlarged, and modified, edition now called *A Dictionary of Trout Flies and of Flies for Sea-Trout and Grayling*. The author had spent the years following the publication of his original volume in a tremendous amount of research, gathering together over 400 dressings, plus new colour plates. This book has remained the fly-dressers' bible and such was its quality that editions have appeared in 1950, 1961 and 1965, being reprinted in 1968.

During the early part of 1972 I was approached by A. and C. Black who suggested that I should undertake the up-dating of this classic book. The prospect elated me, though this feeling was rapidly tempered by the realization that here was a task of some magnitude, and one that must be approached with care. To attempt to don the mantle of Courtney Williams was no easy task and therefore at this point I will borrow a line from his original 1932 introduction.

"I trust that those who criticize this book will do so in the spirit of the true disciple of Izaak Walton; not searching out its errors for condemnation but rather seeking for that which they may fairly commend."

Some thought was given as to the form this new, revised, edition should take, and it was agreed that the material should form a separate chapter, while the artificials to be included should be, in the main, those that have been devised since Courtney Williams' first edition in 1949. The format of the material to follow that of the original publication.

Literally hundreds and hundreds of artificials have been devised in the intervening twenty-three years, since 1949, some to burst forth from nymph to dun and just as rapidly become spinners, having but one brief moment of glory in some angling paper before being washed downstream, never to be heard of again.

Others have stood the test of time, possibly within their own local area, where they have found their way into the fly-boxes of countless thoughtful fly-fishers, both in this country and abroad. The upsurge of still-water angling over the last few years has brought the fastest development in the design of new patterns. Man-made fibres, fluorescents and the increasing use of furs and hair have all played their part.

In selecting the new artificial patterns that appear in this book I have used a two-fold yard-stick. Firstly, patterns that have proved their worth both in this country and overseas. American, French and Scandinavian flies are included for they are equally successful on the waters of the British Isles, from the hill burns to the chalk-streams. Secondly, those patterns, some of them quite local creations, which never the less are effective trout takers and which I have tried on many rivers and streams.

Readers will note that I have not written in depth on the entomology of the naturals herein represented by the many artificials, other than to give the Latin nomenclature where applicable. To do so would have been to duplicate what has been well covered by Courtney Williams in part one of this volume.

To single out individual persons who have contributed in so many ways to the research of this chapter would present me with a most unenviable task, and the list of names would be almost as long as the list of flies, therefore just let me say to one and all, without your help and enthusiasm for the project it could not have been achieved.

My remaining hope is that I have done justice to all, not least the memory of that great angling historian who first wrote *Trout Flies; A Discussion and Dictionary*, and *A Dictionary of Trout-Flies and of Flies for Sea-Trout and Grayling* . . . A. Courtney Williams.

T. DONALD OVERFIELD

Solihull, Warwickshire, 1972

AIN SPIDER

The pattern of Dr. Yves Rameaux of France, based on a fly devised by Maurice Simonet, a well-known river keeper on the Ain in Franche-Comte. Rameaux is a fly-dresser, and angler, of note in his own country and his tying of the Ain Spider, a dry fly to represent the ecdyonurus forcipula, has been used by many fly-fishers.

The dressing is interesting in that it uses extremely long fibred hackles, these, coupled with the sharply downward pointing tails, makes for a very "high riding" fly. That well-known angler, the late Oliver Kite, spent many hours in the company of Dr. Rameaux on the Ain where the former's Imperial provided a tempting fly for the French trout.

Silk: Red.
Body: As tying silk.
Rib: Black silk.
Tails: Dark olive cock hackle fibres. Note that these are tied down so that they stand sharply downwards to the hook shank.
Hackle: Very long fibred steely ginger furnace.
Hook: 13 or 14.

Another of his patterns, tied in the same way, is the representation of the blue-winged olive.

Silk: Medium yellow or brown.
Body: As tying silk.
Tails: Blue dun cock hackle fibres.
Hackle: A very long fibred steely blue dun cock.
Hook: 15 or 16.

AMBER NYMPH

A pattern first devised in 1971 by Derek Bradbury, a most thoughtful fly-dresser. He readily admits that the term "nymph" is something of a misnomer, for the artificial is an imitation of the sedge larvae. Designed primarily for use at Grafham where it has taken many trout under the most difficult conditions.

Silk: Black.
Body: Rear two thirds, amber seal's fur ribbed with narrow orange lurex. Front third, dyed dark brown ostrich herl.
Back: Fibres from a dark brown speckled turkey tail feather. This is tied in from hook bend to eye, in the manner of a shrimp dressing.
Hackle: One turn only of brown partridge.
Swimming legs: Two fibres, one each side tied in at the head. From the centre tail feather of a golden pheasant. The fibres to be twice as long as the body, and pointing rearwards.
Hook: 10 D/E wide gape.

APRICOT SPINNER
   The late Oliver Kite's dressing of the cloëon dipterum spinner,
generally known as the Apricot Spinner due to its distinctive apricot-
coloured body. Though generally regarded as a still-water fly the pond
olive can be found on a number of our more sluggish-flowing streams
and rivers.

Silk: Golden olive.
Body: Swan primary herls dyed apricot colour, doubled and re-doubled at the
   thorax.
Tails: Pale yellow cock fibres.
Hackle: Pale honey-dun.
Hook: 14 U/E.

ASSASSINE
   This extremely effective dry fly was evolved in France during 1964,
since when it has achieved considerable success, not only in the hands of
its originator, Dr. J. P. Pequegnot, but when fished by countless others.
The dressing does not represent any particular insect, or group of
insects, and could rightly be called an abstract pattern. That it is most
effective there is little doubt. Pequegnot is a most experienced French
fly-fisher and fly-dresser, and his book *L'Art de la Peche a la Mouche
Seche* is a classic in his own country.

Body: Olive waxed nylon, or better still light yellow. One layer only.
Head hackle: Grey or brown well mottled partridge hackle. One or two turns
   only.
Body hackle: Smokey-grey cock. Not too dense. Shorter in the fibre than the
   partridge feather.
Hook: 12 to 15.

   Though not a particularly difficult pattern to dress it should be noted
that the head hackle is wound on first, the concave side of the feather
towards the eye so that when wound the fibres point forward. The
body hackle is then wound in, again with the concave side to the eye.
Several close turns are taken immediately behind the partridge hackle
in order to stiffen the forward curvature. The remainder is wound
palmer fashion to a point close to the bend. Note that the silk is tied off
at the tail, not at the head as in a normal dressing.

BARE HOOK NYMPH
   This must surely be the most austere dressing ever to achieve success.
Devised by the late Major Oliver Kite its value lies not so much in its
dressing, even if it could be so called, but rather in the method of presentation of the artficial and the manner in which it is fished, what Kite

cared to call the "induced take", manipulating the nymph in such a way as to impart a lifelike action.

Thorax: Built up turns of fine copper wire.
Hook: 14 or 16 D/E.

BEACON BEIGE

This pattern was originally known as the Beige. It is thought to be the invention of a member of the Wills family of Dulverton, who devised the fly when on leave from France in 1917. The fly was a great local success over the intervening years, and when that most expert professional fly-dresser Peter Deane commenced his business following the 1939–45 war, he was given the pattern by the late Frederick Tout, a well-known Dulverton tackle dealer.

Deane experimented with the fly on the Devonshire Culm and found that its taking ability was considerably improved by the use of a well-sprung Indian dark-red game hackle, long in the fibre.

Following the design change, and its appreciation by many anglers as a good representation of an olive, Deane renamed it the Beacon Beige; the Beacon being inserted because in the early days of his business at Hemcock his work-room window looked across the Culm Valley, which is dominated by Culmstock Beacon. I trust that the inclusion of this detail will prevent some angling historian, two-hundred years hence, searching for the reason why "Beacon" was attached to "Beige"!

Body: Well marked, stripped peacock eye quill.
Tails: Four strong fibres from a Plymouth Rock cock hackle.
Hackle: Plymouth Rock cock, with a dark-red Indian game cock wound through it.
The dressing to be kept quite light.

BELLE DE NUIT

A "fore-and-aft" style of dressing devised by Dr. J. P. Pequegnot of France. A dry fly that is suitable for poor light conditions in view of its white wing.

Body: Yellow nylon.
Tails: Dun cock fibres, tied with a positive downward slant over the hook bend.
Rear hackle: Dun cock tied at the rear extremity of the body.
Head hackle: Dun cock, wound hard up behind one turn of grey partridge feather.
Wings: Pure white cock hackle points.
Hook: 12 or 13.

BLAE AND BLACK

This version of the traditional fly, the Blae and Black, was devised by Thomas Clegg of West Calder, Scotland, who must stand extremely high on the list of thoughtful professional fly-tiers. No man had studied the effects of fluorescent materials to a greater degree than Clegg. The thought that has gone into his dressings can be gauged by the variations to be obtained from this basic Blae and Black dressing, and how very effective they are. By omitting the early season silver-wire rib for May and June, and replacing the black silk body with a well-marked peacock quill, a great many natural flies can be represented, ranging from the hawthorn fly to the black gnat and gravel-bed. When the black hackle is replaced by black ostrich herl and the artificial dressed upon the smallest hook then a first-class representation of the black smut is achieved.

By the addition of Fire-red gantron fibres as a tail you have a most effective sea-trout fly. Indeed, Clegg caught sixty-six sea-trout in thirty hours of daylight fishing on a fly so dressed.

A recent angling article stated that history will record Clegg's dressing of the Blae and Black as one of the most effective general-purpose river flies ever devised for the taking of trout. With that I agree.

Basic dressing:

Silk: Black Gossamer, well waxed.
Wings: Six lengths of Electron-white DRF floss, tied spent.
Body: Black Gossamer.
Rib: Five turns of silver wire.
Hackle: Small black cock, one turn behind the wings and two turns in front.
Hook: 18 to 12, singles and doubles.

BLACK GNAT

Tied by Commander C. F. Walker who acknowledges Dunne's first use of the green and red hackle fibres, however, this pattern differs from the Dunne dressing in both wound hackle and body materials.

Body: A fibre taken from the darkest part of a turkey tail feather, preferably one showing a bronze sheen effect.
Wings: Hackle fibres dyed bottle-green and wine-red in the proportion of twenty of the former to ten of the latter. These fibres being thoroughly mixed and tied in flat over the body. The fibre points being then clipped into a "V".
Hackle: Black cock.
Hook: 16 U/E.

BLACK MAGIC

Originally tied for fishing on the Wharfe in Yorkshire by Frederick E. Mold, author of *Presenting the Fly to the Trout*, this pattern is one that I would be loath to leave out of my fly-box. Like its originator, I have taken trout on this dressing on water ranging the length and breadth of the country and have found it to be effective at most times, fished up or down stream.

Silk: Black.
Body: The rear two-thirds of the body made from turns of tying silk. Forward of that point is a small hump of copper wire. Over this is wound two twisted strands of copper-coloured peacock herl, over-ribbed with the tying silk.
Hackle: A very small black hen hackle, two turns only.
Hook: 15 or 16 round bend. D/E.

BLOODY WILLIAMS OTHER MATE

Excellent sea-trout pattern by James Nice of Devon. He has taken grilse up to 6¼ lb. from the Axe on this fly and it has accounted for salmon also. The pattern is easy to dress and combines what are, to Nice's eye, the essential colours of a good sea-trout fly: red, black and silver.

Silk: Dark brown or black.
Body: Rear half black silk, front half black ostrich herl.
Rib: Fine oval silver.
Tail: Ibis or red dyed swan, goose or golden pheasant topping.
Hackle: Black henny cock.
Hook: Any size, but 10 most effective.

BLUE DUN

Thomas Clegg's excellent tying of the large spring olive, *Baetis rhodani*. This pattern shows the restrained use of fluorescent materials, at which Clegg is a master. I have had considerable success with this fly.

Silk: Primrose.
Body: Medium blue-grey squirrel, or similar dubbing.
Rib: Phosphor-yellow DRF floss, or a single fine DRF filament.
Hackle: One medium blue-grey and one medium olive, wound together.
Hook: 12 fine wire U/E.

BLUE-WINGED OLIVE (Collyer)

David Collyer's pattern of that most frustrating fly, *Ephemerella ignita*. This pattern has accounted for many trout from the Test and Itchen and would seem to be a first-class pattern.

Silk: Olive.
Wings: Dyed blue-dun cock hackle points, tied semi-spent.
Body: A strip of barred teal feather, wound over varnished hook shank.
Rib: A strand of dyed olive goose herl and a strand of cock pheasant centre tail feather fibre.
Tails: Three strands of barred teal feather.
Hackle: One olive cock and one Plymouth rock cock, wound together.
Hook: 12.

BLUE-WINGED OLIVE (Jacques)

This is a good representation of the male *Ephemerella ignita*. This method of constructing the body, by winding the PVC over the herl, tends to trap air pockets within the herl and aid flotation. Devised by the well-known angling entomologist, David Jacques.

Silk: Orange.
Wings: Two pairs from the wing of a coot. Rather fully dressed.
Body: Underlay of white ostrich herl dyed a dirty yellow. The best results being obtained by dyeing a greenish strand of herl. This body is over-wound by a thin strip of PVC dyed olive. This can be achieved by immersing in picric acid. The overall effect should be that of a ripening greengage.
Hackle: Light olive, with pronounced coloration of the stem.
Tails: Light olive hackle fibres.
Hook: 14 U/E.

BLUE-WINGED OLIVE (Law)

This particular wet-fly dressing of the b.-w.o. was brought to my notice by that well-known angler, Terry Thomas. Though not a pattern of his own devising, it was originally dressed by the late William Law, river keeper on the Usk at Buckland, it is one that Thomas has used with considerable success. I too have taken a fair number of trout on this pattern, especially from the rougher streams of the northern counties. Fished upstream when the b.-w.o. is hatching this simple fly is good medicine.

Body: Green wool.
Rib: Gold wire.
Hackle: Greenish-blue hen hackle.
Tails: Greenish-blue hen hackle fibres.

Thomas varies the dressing by using swans herl dyed emerald green.

BLUE-WINGED OLIVE (Nice)

Devised in 1947 by James Nice of Devon. It is of interest to quote from one of Nice's letters . . . "I have given the b.-w.o. some thought at one time and another and, in common with all fishermen, I have experienced the frustrations that the little beast can incur. I have studied the living insect for hours on end, and if it could blush it would have done so. The pattern is devised to give a general impression only, DFM being used for good colour, and it allows for the shading of the bodies. A simple pattern but effective, especially early mornings".

Body: Front half blue DFM. Whole body, including the front half, covered with lime DFM. This gives shading to the overall body.
Tails: Blue dun or olive cock fibres.
Hackle: Blue dun or olive cock.

BLUE-WINGED OLIVE (Walker)

Excellent representation of the male and female duns, *Ephemerella ignita*, originated by Commander C. F. Walker. These patterns were the result of much patient experimentation on the southern chalk-streams in order to arrive at flies that would be suitable for both day and evening fishing.

BLUE-WINGED OLIVE (MALE) (Daytime)
Body: Condor herl dyed bright orange.
Rib: Fine gold tinsel.
Wings: Medium coloured waterhen fibres.
Tails: Bright ginger cock fibres.
Hackle: Bright ginger cock, lightly dyed in orange dye.
Hook: 15 U/E.

BLUE-WINGED OLIVE (FEMALE) (Evening)
Body: Condor herl dyed bright olive.
Rib: Fine gold tinsel in close turns.
Wings: Medium coloured waterhen fibres.
Tails: Mallard scapular fibres.
Hackle: Bright olive cock.
Hook: 15 U/E.

BOWTIE BUZZER

This pattern, by Frank Sawyer, is a first-class representation of the hatching larvae of the buzzer, known so well to reservoir anglers. A refinement to this dressing is the incorporation of the white celia, noticeable in the natural, however, Sawyer does not tie it into the fly but attaches it to the cast point. This is done by passing the leader through the hook eye, making a slip-knot in the leader through which is passed a small portion of white nylon wool. The leader is then pulled tight up to the hook. It is important that the leader point is threaded through the down-eye of the hook from the *lower* side of the eye. This ensures that the artificial hangs almost vertically in the water, as does the natural. Also, slight retrieve action on the line can cause the artificial to spin round the leader in a most realistic manner. All in all a most worthwhile dressing.

Body: Underlay of fine gold-coloured copper wire, for weighting purposes, overwound by even turns of flat silver tinsel. Leave a length of wire hanging from the tail.
Rib: Four or five fibres from the cock pheasant tail feather, tied in at the bend and wound in conjunction with the hanging body wire to form the body covering. Leave space between the turns to show the silver under-body.
Tails: Ends of the pheasant tail fibres that form the ribbing.
Thorax: Pheasant tail herls, doubled and re-doubled.
Hook: 12 D/E.

BREATHERLIZER

Devised by Alec Iles for use at Chew Valley lakes as a representation of the stickleback. The artificial is generally fished near the surface at a fast rate.

Body: Flat silver tinsel.
Wings: Two hot-orange cock hackles, with two Green Highlander hackles on the outsides, dressed streamer fashion.
Tails: Soft black cock hackle fibres.
Eyes: Jungle-cock tied close to the head.
Hackle: Badger cock.
Head: Black varnish.
Hook: 6 to 8 D/E.

BROWN NYMPH

Devised by David Collyer of Redhill, Surrey, a well-known fly-dresser who has contributed much to the design of the modern fly and lure. This particular pattern is one of a trilogy; brown, grey and green nymphs that have proved to be quite successful on lakes and reservoirs.

Silk: Red Spinner.
Body: Cock pheasant centre tail fibres.
Rib: Oval gold tinsel.
Tails: End of body material tied in before the winding.
Thorax: Ostrich herl dyed chestnut, covered by waste ends of body material to form wing-cases.
Hook: 10 to 12 D/E.

BROWN SILVERHORN

Geoffrey Bucknall's version of *Athripsodes cinereus*, more usually found on lakes than the rivers of this country. Though trout do not feed avidly on the naturals they do, on occasion, take them and when they do this pattern is as good as any, and better than most.

Silk: Olive.
Body: Tying silk.
Rib: Fine gold wire.
Hackles: Dark natural red palmered down the body, also a throat hackle of the same colour.
Feelers: Two stripped grizzle cock hackle stalks, to show contrasting bands of colour, tied in before the wings. About twice as long as the hook shank, pointing forward in a "V".
Wings: Two slips of grouse tail, tied flat on top of the hook to extend just beyond the bend.
Hook: 12.

CADDIS CASE

An interesting dressing of the caddis, originated by Geoffrey Bucknall.

Body: Ostrich herl wound over a base of weighting fuse wire. Colour to taste; brown, black, olive etc.
Back: Raffine of same colour as body material. Varnished.
Hackle: Cock hackle, near to the body colour, wound in front of the body, then clipped short.
Hook: 10 or 12, long shank.

CADDIS LARVAE

Another pattern from the Derek Bradbury stable. A good tying of the caddis larvae, the pheasant herls and gold twist suggesting the case composed of stones and sand.

The artificial should be fished very slowly along the bed of the lake. In the first two months of the season, when trout may well be feeding on the natural larvae of the sedge fly and silverhorns, it can prove most effective.

Body: Several fibres from a centre tail feather of a golden pheasant. Just in front of the body dub a small portion of hare's ear fur.
Rib: Gold twist, size 15.
Legs: One turn of brown partridge hackle.
Head: Peacock herl.
Hook: 10 D/E long shank, or similar size keel-hook.

CLARET SHERRY SPINNER

The original pattern of this artificial was given to Peter Deane some years ago by a knowledgeable amateur who had spent some considerable time experimenting with various dressings of the sherry spinner. Deane's experiences has confirmed this fly to be an excellent pattern.

Body: Claret seal's fur, well shaped.
Tails: Three strong fibres from a Plymouth Rock or grizzle cock hackle.
Hackle: Three or four turns of Plymouth Rock.

CHOMPERS

Richard Walker, that well-known all-round angler, has been responsible for many good fly patterns, both for stream and reservoir fishing, and his series known as Chompers have considerable merit, in two directions. That they are attractive to the trout has been proved by countless still-water anglers, secondly, they are so simple in design that they can be tied by the newcomer to fly-dressing. One could call these "flies" impressionistic rather than representational and variations on the theme are unlimited.

The basic tie is to cover the hook shank with close turns of ostrich herl, over which a back of Raffine is laid.

Some of the variations are:

CORIXA
White ostrich herl body. Light brown or green back.

SEDGE PUPA
Ostrich herl body, dyed amber or green. Light brown back.

BEETLE
Black ostrich herl body. Black back. Alternatively peacock herl body, tied fat.

DRAGONFLY NYMPH
Green ostrich herl body, with a few strands of herl at the rear of the hook to suggest tails. Green raffine back covering only the front half of the body. Tied on small hooks this dressing can represent olive nymphs.

CAMASUNARY KILLER

This wet fly, popularised by Peter Deane the professional fly-tier, is one of the best sea-trout flies ever devised. It is thought that it was designed by Stephen Johnson of Jedburgh, whose family owns the famous Camasunary Fishery in the Isle of Skye, and who is the author of *Fishing From Afar*.

Deane originally received the dressing from one of his clients, Francis Williams of Melrose, Roxburghshire, in 1961 and from that day it has been one of Deane's most popular items. He recalls that it has taken two grilse and twenty-one sea-trout during one afternoon's fishing in Sutherland, and it has proved equally successful at Waterville, Co. Derry. It has also proved attractive to the salmon.

Tag: Royal blue wool.
Body: Two equal halves. Firstly royal blue wool followed by red DFM wool.
Rib: Oval silver tinsel, rather broad on the larger hook sizes.
Hackle: Black cock, long in the fibre, with plenty of turns on the larger hooks.

CRANE FLY

A good dressing of the Daddy-long-legs. Following on in the tradition of Hanna and West this variation was devised by Geoffrey Bucknall.

Body: Detached mayfly body of dun colour.
Legs: Six knotted strands of ginger horse hair, tied in front of the body, divided by figure-of-eight turns into three sets of three, sloping backwards.
Hackle: Two large brown cock hackles tied in close. The points tied down and divided on either side of the hook shank to simulate spent wings.
Hook: 12.

CREAM SPINNER

Devised by John Goddard, a first-class entomologist and fly-dresser, and author of *Trout-Fly Recognition and Trout Flies of Sill Water.* This dressing is a representation of the male spinner of the small spurwing, *Centroptilum luteolum,* the species being one of the few male spinners to be found upon the streams in any quantity.

It is also a useful artificial when other pale-coloured spinners, such as pale watery, large spurwings and pale evening spinners are about.

Silk: Cream.
Wings: Tips of two small pale-blue dun cock hackles, tied spent.
Body: Baby seal's fur, cream.
Rib: Fine gold wire.
Tails: Pale-blue cock hackle fibres.
Hackle: Cream cock, two turns only.
Hook: 15 U/E.

CREE SEDGE

A general sedge pattern, and a good floater, originated by Roy Masters. Though designed in the first instance as a lake fly I have found it a useful fly on the chalk-streams, particularly from mid to late season as darkness closes in.

Silk: White.
Body: A cree hackle, wound closely down the hook shank. The fibres are then cut down, preferably with curved scissors, to a slim cigar shape.
Wings: Natural red cock hackle fibres, tied in at the head to lie over the body. Ends trimmed off into a fan shape.
Hackle: Cree cock.
Hook: 13 U/E wide gape, or smaller.

DADDY-LONG-LEGS

Another pattern by Richard Walker, and one that is an excellent representation of the natural insect. When fishing this fly it is important that the legs trail backwards, and even more important that the fly is not pulled or dragged upon the water. It must remain completely immobile. It will be noted that the natural insect has only six legs. Walker ties in eight because some are apt to be broken off in the process of taking fish . . . and it is doubtful whether trout can count!

Body: Pale cinnamon turkey tail fibres.
Thorax: Body fibres wound double.
Wings: Two badger cock hackle points tied slanting back over the body, well divided.
Legs: Eight cock pheasant tail fibres, each knotted in two places, tied under the thorax and trailing backwards past the hook bend.
Hackle: Pale ginger grizzle.
Hook: 8 or 10 long shank.

DARK TUP

A somewhat similar pattern to the Half-stone, except that the hackles are of honey-dun and not blue-dun. Also the hackle is wound only in front of the thorax and does not cover it.

The Dark Tup has proved to be an excellent general-purpose fly and has done especially well on Blagdon and Chew, in the late evening, for its originator David Collyer.

Silk: Red spinner.
Body: Lemon floss silk.
Thorax: Mole's fur.
Tails: Honey-dun or very pale ginger cock hackle fibres.
Hackle: Honey-dun or very pale ginger.
Hook: 12 to 16. 12 being generally most effective.

DEVON DUMPLING

This good general pattern, largely unknown outside the west country, was devised in 1942 by James Nice of Sidmouth, Devon, one of the most original and deft fly-tiers in the British Isles.

Of the body variations Nice has a personal preference for DFM on water that is fining down. Over the last few years this fly has proved equally effective for lake fishing in the larger sizes. A good pattern to imitate a number of olives.

Silk: Yellow.
Body: Orange or lime DFM. Alternatively just tying silk.
Rib: Finest gold or silver wire.
Body hackle: Blue dun cock.
Head hackle: Blue dun cock.
Tails: Blue dun cock fibres.
Hook: River 14. Lake 12.

DAILY DUN

A useful fly when pale wateries are on the water. Originated by Eric Horsfall Turner and initially used on the Hampshire Test where it accounted for a number of good trout on its first outing. The following day Horsfall Turner was fishing with the late Oliver Kite near Netheravon, Wiltshire, and he found that the trout of that stream were just as interested in the fly. At the time the artificial had no name and Horsfall Turner, on Kite's insistance, gave it the name of Daily Dun. Why Daily Dun? Simply because the body material came from rabbits owned by a woman who at that time was the "daily" in the Horsfall Turner household! How many other flies down the ages have been so simply named, and have proved to be enigmas to future fly-dressing historians.

Silk: Light olive.
Wings: Bunch of mallard breast feather fibres tied with a positive forward slant.
Body: White angora rabbit fur, dyed light yellow.
Tails: Dark ginger cock hackle fibres.
Hackle: Dark ginger cock.
Hook: 18 D/E.

DARK SEDGE

A sedge pattern originated by Capt. Terry Thomas, a fly-fisher of some experience. His dressing differs from most in the use of deer hair for the wings, such material having an excellent floating capability.

Body: Black wool or chenille.
Wings: Black deer hair tied on flat. The thicker roots towards the bend of the hook and tied in such a fashion as to splay out the fibres. The ends are then cut off to the required length.
Body hackle: Black cock palmered down the body.
Head hackle: Black cock, wound over the wing roots.
Hook: 4 to 14.

DRY SEDGE

Richard Walker's well-known sedge dressing. Occasionally trout show a preference for a similar dressing but with a grass-green dyed swan's herl body,

Body: Bright ruddy pheasant tail fibres, or chestnut ostrich herl, clipped short, with a tiny tip at the rear of Arc-chrome DRF.
Wings: A bunch of barred or speckled cock hackle fibres, tied slanting backwards, then slipped square, level with the bend of the hook.
Hackle: Two barred natural red cock hackles, wound at the head over the wing roots.
Hook: 8 to 12.

DUCK AND COCK DUN

Another artificial created by the French angler and fly-dresser, Dr. Yves Rameaux. An interesting point about the construction of this fly is that the body is tied last, and the turns of silk are taken hard up against the rear portion of the back hackle, thereby forcing it upright.

Silk: Pale yellow.
Body: Yellow tying silk. Ribbing optional.
Tails: Blue dun cock hackle fibres.
Hackles: Two. A mallard rump feather wound in front of a stiff, short fibred, blue dun cock hackle.
Hook: 15 or 16 U/E.

ERIC'S BEETLE

A first-class general representation of the order Coleoptera. Originated by that doyen of fly-fishers, Eric Horsfall Turner, in 1940 for use on the Yorkshire Derwent. This fly was the subject of much careful experimentation evolving into its final, successful, form only after a number of years. Initially it was dressed with red wool, followed by other colours, but documented experiments proved that yellow wool was the most successful colour. To achieve the correct plump form is not easy, therefore it is proposed to quote at length from the dressing instructions laid down by the fly's originator.

"Wind the silk from the eye to about halfway down the shank. Wind back, with widely-spaced turns and trap in a small black hackle, then wind the silk back to a point level with the barb. Tie in at barb-level the yellow wool. Take the silk forward in close turns for approx. one-eighth of an inch. Give the wool two close turns behind the silk to act as a yellow butt, then wind the wool forward of the silk to within one-eighth of an inch of the eye, returning in close turns to the original position immediately in front of the silk. Tie in. Cut off surplus wool. Tie in two peacock herls, pale edge of the stems forward. Wind the peacock herl together, forward to the end of the wool, then back to the position of the tying silk. Tie in the herl and cut off the waste. Wind the silk over the peacock herl to the point where the hackle is tied in. Give the hackle feather two or three turns only and tie in. Complete tapered head with a whip finish."

The Beetle is fished up-stream with the leader greased to within three or four inches of the point, the fly drifting downstream, sinking the while. Casting under bankside bushes can bring good results.

Many flies have been called "deadly" but this one, in my opinion, deserves that title more than most. I am never without it.

Silk: Brown or black.
Body: Underlay of yellow wool, the wool to be left exposed at the tail for two turns. Overlaid with peacock herl.
Rib: Tying silk.
Hackle: Blackbird feather taken from the base of the wing.
Hook: 10 or 12 D/E.

FIRE FLY

Devised by Edward Arthur of Birmingham for use on the well-known Midland water, Shustoke Reservoir. This pattern has been very successful mid to late evening, during the rise, and has also accounted for many trout on other still-water fisheries. It is quite effective during the day when fished at the edge of a ripple.

Silk: Amber.
Body: Natural red cock hackle. Fibres cut down to approx. one sixteenth of an inch. Tied in by the tip at the bend of the hook and wound forward. Trim the fibres to a cigar shape.
Tails: Furnace cock hackle fibres.
Hackle: Furnace or C.Y.B. cock hackle.
Hook: 12 or 14 U/E.

FLUORESCENT ARTIFICIAL FLIES

Following the end of the 1939–45 war a material developed during that period, known as Daylight Fluorescent Material, became available to the fly-tier. It took the form of fibre floss and the original was marketed under the name of Gantron. The two main types sold in this country to-day are DRF (Depth Ray Fire) and Firebrand DFM (Daylight Fluorescent Material).

Many fly-dressers have experimented with one or other of these materials over the years, but few have studied the matter to the extent of Thomas Clegg of West Calder, Scotland. Clegg's contribution in this, and other matters appertaining to fly-dressing, has been considerable and all who wish to know more about the effects of fluorescents would do well to read his most erudite volume, *The Truth About Fluorescents*, published in 1968. In that book one will find many dressings, nymph, dun and spinner and wet flies, however, I will confine myself to the artificials that I have tied to Clegg's formula, and which have taken many trout from the rivers of this country.

PARTRIDGE AND ORANGE

A good variation on a traditional pattern and one that I have found most effective on the Wharfe.

Silk: Yellow.
Body: Orange DFM floss.
Rib: Brown Naples silk.
Hackle: Grey partridge.
Hook: 14 to 16 D/E.

DARK OLIVE

This dressing has provided me with some of my best days' fishing.

Silk: Olive.
Body: Dark olive wool, dubbed onto tying silk.
Rib: Electron-white DRF floss.
Tails: Dyed dark olive cock hackle fibres.
Hackle: Slate blue and dark brown-olive cock, wound together.
Hook: 14 U/E fine wire.

AMBER SPINNER

Though Clegg's dressing of this particular fly does not include tail fibres I have usually added them to my own particular tying, using light-ginger hackle fibres. I have found this tie to be effective when the b.-w.o. are about, but equally good as a general pattern.

Silk: White.
Body: Orange DFM floss.
Rib: Brown Naples silk.
Hackle: Two light-blue grey-dyed cock hackles.
Wings: Six lengths of grey DFM floss, equally divided.
Hook: 14 U/E fine wire.

DARK RED SEDGE

Silk: Primrose.
Body: Fire-orange DRF floss.
Rib: Fine gold wire.
Body hackle: Natural dark-red cock, palmered down the body.
Wings: Chestnut coloured mallard breast feather, rolled and tied in flat over the body.
Head hackle: Natural dark-red cock.
Hook: 12 D/E round bend.

FLYMPHS

The transitional stage in the life cycle of the natural fly, when the nymph struggles through the surface film and emerges onto the surface as a dun, is frequently a time when the trout feed with great voracity. It is not always easy to determine just what the trout are taking and many anglers cast various patterns of the dry fly to the rise forms with little success. When fish are feeding on hatching duns they are unlikely to be tempted by a floating pattern. And yet, despite this fact being common knowledge amongst thoughtful fly-fishers little research has been done into that stage of the natural's life cycle.

It has been left to an American, Vernon S. Hidy, to study that period in the fly's life and attempt to devise artificials to represent that transitional stage.

His dressings aim at creating an impression of the struggling insect breaking through the surface film; hackles somewhat larger than those found on the artificial traditional nymph, body and thorax of rough furs and wools, simulating life and vibrancy.

I have had success with Hidy's patterns, on streams ranging from Northumberland to Hampshire. Three "flymph" dressings are given, but in the tying due regard must be given to the overall impression of the natural at the critical moment of emergence.

Why "flymph"? Could a better name have been found for the stage between nymph and fly? I think not.

BLUE DUN

Silk: Primrose.
Body: Muskrat fur, blended with blue wool fibres.
Rib: Gold wire.
Tails: Light-blue dun cock hackle fibres.
Hackle: Medium blue dun cock, or starling feather from marginal coverts.
Hook: 13 to 15 U/E.

BROWN HACKLE

Silk: Brown.
Body: Brown mohair blended with hare's poll fur.
Rib: Narrow gold tinsel.
Hackle: Brown badger hen, or gold furnace.
Hook: 12 to 16 wide gape.

LIGHT CAHILL

Silk: Primrose or white.
Body: Hare's cheek and creamy fox fur spun onto silk.
Rib: None.
Tails: Ginger cock hackle fibres.
Hackle: Ginger cock.
Hook: 12 to 16.

FOOTBALLER SERIES

The original pattern was the result of careful observation by Geoffrey Bucknall, and it has rapidly found favour with many still-water anglers in its original, and varied, forms.

The Footballer represents the pupal stage of the buzzer family. The dressing came about after Bucknall examined the stomach contents of countless trout and viewed blown-up photographs of the pupa. The original dressing given here accounted for four Blagdon trout on its first outing, all over the 3 lb. mark.

It will be noticed that the dressing is not strictly representational in that the filaments are absent. This deliberate omission is due to Bucknall's belief that nothing must prevent a swift entry through the water surface when the fly is cast to a cruising fish. On calm evenings the water can be "sticky" and any filament, represented by a hackle, is likely to prevent the required penetration.

Since the original Footballer there have been many colour variations; white, black, red, olive, brown, green, orange, claret etc., the colour being obtained by using the appropriate tying silk. Fluorescents have also been used.

All the patterns can be tied as floaters by the addition of a pair of glassy-white hackle point wings, tied to slope backwards. Also the tying in of a badger cock hackle. Bucknall maintains that the black centre of the badger hackle gives a fore-shortening effect, as if the pattern were closer to the water surface, as is the natural image of the chironomid. The larval form is dressed as follows:

Body: Clear horsehair, or nylon, over red silk.
Tail: Strands of red goose cossette. Lengths to be same as hook shank.
Head: Two turns of fluorescent scarlet chenille.
Hook: 10 or 12.

FRESHWATER SHRIMP

This dressing, devised by Eric Horsfall Turner a number of years ago for use on the Derwent in the North Riding of Yorkshire, has proved to be one of the most successful, when fished correctly.

It should be fished downstream, allowed to sink and then, holding the line steady, let the play of the water slowly bring the artificial to the surface. The fly is most effective under given conditions; when there are no sign of surface rises, and in cold conditions and clouded water. Horsfall Turner has experimented with the addition of a gold rib but has found this to make very little difference to the taking ability of this artificial.

A recent modification has been to substitute a sliver of toe-nail paring for the back fibres. This makes for a most durable fly. The artificial is then known as the Toe-nail Shrimp.

Body: Underlay of fine (0·014 in.) fuse wire, wound over with pale brown wool. A hump-backed effect should be aimed for.

Hackle: Red cock, palmered evenly over the body.

Back: Golden pheasant tippet fibres, tied in at the bend. The hackle fibres being cut down on top of the body, and the top being treated with Durofix or some similar adhesive. The G.P. tippet fibres are then pulled over the top of the body and tied down at the head.

Hook: 11 D/E.

G. AND H. SEDGE

The joint development of Clifford Henry and John Goddard in an endeavour to obtain a more natural silhouette than is possible with the standard dressings. It is an excellent floater and a most killing pattern. While this artificial is tied to represent the *glyphnotaelius pellucidus* it is also a good general pattern for any of the lighter sedges.

Silk: Green.

Body: Deer hair, spun onto the hook in the manner of the Muddler Minnow. After the spinning of the hair the fibres are trimmed to the shape and silhouette of the wings of the natural sedge.

Under body: Dark-green seals fur, dubbed onto the silk and tied in at the bend of the hook. After the shaping of the deer hair fibres the strip of seal's fur is stretched the length of the underbody and tied in at the eye.

Hackle: Two rusty-dun cock's tied in together at the eye. Both being wound just a short distance down the body. The top of the hackles then being cut down to the approximate shape of the head of the natural. The stripped butts of the two hackles may be left intact to form the antennae of the sedge.

Hook: 8 or 10 long shank.

GRAYLING FIDDLER

Devised by Eric Horsfall Turner in 1967 and first used on Oxfold's Beck, a tributary of the Costa chalk-stream in Yorkshire. A good fly when the grayling are "nipping".

Silk: Brown.

Body: Tying silk wound down to a position just forward of the barb, then carried forward for three turns. These turns to constitute the rear of the body. Remainder of teased red wool, or DRF floss, spun onto the tying silk.

Hackle: Very small grizzle cock.

Hook: 18 D/E.

GREEN APHIS

This ingenious pattern, imitating two or three flies together, was devised by Derek Bradbury following a day's fishing at Tittesworth reservoir in June 1970. During a flat calm the water was covered by the minute natural insects, these being taken by the trout with considerable relish. A size 16 spent winged spinner with a pale green body was the nearest artificial Bradbury had and, despite cutting the wings down to a more realistic size, it was still too large to tempt more than the odd fish. He observed that there were so many greenfly on the water that many had drifted together to form small solid areas, some as large as a 2p. coin. It occurred to Bradbury that two or three flies could be tied on one hook, tandem fashion, thereby simulating this grouping.

Fished as a dry fly this pattern has proved effective on both rivers and lakes during falls of aphis. The wings can be so arranged as to project at different angles from each side of the hook to present a more random silhouette.

Silk: Olive.
Body: Signal-green DRF floss.
Wings: White DRF floss, two strands per wing. Two or three pairs tied spent down the hook shank.
Hackles: One for each set of wings. Tiny light olive cock hackles. All fibres being removed from the underside of the hook.
Hook: 14 or 16, preferably the latter.

GREY MIDGE PUPA

Another of Collyer's simple, but effective, dressings. Especially suitable on calm warm days on the reservoirs. The leader should be greased to within half an inch of the fly and an extremely slow retrieve used.

Silk: Black.
Body: Well-marked stripped peacock herl.
Thorax: Dubbed mole's fur.
Hook: 14 to 18.

GREY NYMPH

Possibly the more famous of the trilogy of nymphs devised by David Collyer. It was with this particular pattern that Norman Fance took the largest rainbow trout caught on fly in the United Kingdom, the fish going to 9¾ lb.

Silk: Black.
Body: Natural heron herl from the primary feather.
Tails: Ends of body material tied in to form short tails prior to the winding of the body.
Rib: Oval silver tinsel.
Thorax: Natural ostrich herl, grey with white tips to the flue, covered by the waste ends of the body material to form the wing cases.
Hook: 10.

GREEN NYMPH

Third in the trilogy of David Collyer's general nymphal representations.

Silk: Olive.
Body: Goose or heron herl dyed olive.
Tails: Ends of the body material tied in to form short tails prior to the winding of the body.
Rib: Oval gold tinsel.
Thorax: Olive-dyed ostrich herl, covered by the waste ends of the body material to form the wing cases.
Hook: 10.

GREY WULFF

A most successful American pattern devised by the well known U.S. angler, Lee Wulff. Its popularity over here as a mayfly dressing is due in no small measure to Peter Deane of Eastbourne, Sussex. The story of its introduction onto the chalk-streams of this country is worth recounting and I can do no better than repeat the gist of recent correspondence with Peter Deane. He says. . . . "In a remote way I can claim a little responsibility for the popularity of this version of Lee Wulff's wonderful fly. In the 1950's a client of mine, the late Lord Brand, was fishing the Houghton Club water with Lewis Douglas, then American Ambassador over here, as his guest. We rather pride ourselves on our artificial mayflies but on this occasion the Club trout would not look at them, so in sheer desperation Lewis Douglas tried a Grey Wulff and gave one to his host, and both found trout accepted them like a baby takes milk. That evening Lord Brand sent me the pattern Lewis Douglas had given him and I examined it with great care, noting particularly the forward hair wing was not divided but stuck out in front like a single bar. I tried some the following day and sent them off to Stockbridge, where the original success was repeated, and since that time the Grey Wulff as a mayfly tied in this fashion has proved one of our most successful mayfly artificials, and dressed on small hooks an equally effective small 'floater'.

The reason for its success I have no doubt is that trout accept the single forward wing as a stage in the hatching nymph when the wings have come out of the thorax but are still stuck together, the circulation not having properly gone through the wing veins themselves. Be that as it may, we never split the wings of a Grey Wulff, big or small, unless requested to do so, and 99 per cent of our flies of this pattern are dressed in this manner. It has proved an outstanding success in any size in this country and throughout Europe on rivers, streams, lochs and lakes. It is also first class as a dapping fly or floater for salmon and sea-trout."

GREY WULFF MAYFLY

Whisks: Natural bucktail fibres.
Body: Grey squirrel fur.
Hackles: One dark red cock and two blue dun cock, well mixed.
Wing: Single forward wing of small brown barred squirrel tail fur.

SMALL GREY WULFF

Whisks: Small brown barred squirrel tail fibres, short.
Body: Grey squirrel fur.
Hackle: Medium blue dun cock.
Wing: Small brown barred squirrel tail.
Size: 11 to 16.

HACKLEPOINT COACHMAN

One of the favourite patterns of David Collyer. If in any doubt as to which fly to use this is the one he chooses. It is especially effective in the evening when small flies of the sedge variety are hatching. Like the famous W. J. Lunn of river Test fame, Collyer has a distinct preference for hacklepoint wings.

Silk: Red spinner.
Wings: White cock hackle points, tied semi-spent.
Body: Bronze or green peacock herl wound over wet varnish for durability.
Hackle: Ginger or red cock.
Hook: 10 to 14.

HARLOT

Another of Collyer's patterns, dressed in the traditional style with married wing fibres. A good reservoir and lake fly, fished on a floating line and drawn across the bows of surface feeding fish. More effective in the evening than during the day.

Silk: Black.
Tail: A few strands of blue gallena.
Butt: Peacock herl.
Body: In three parts: black, scarlet, black in floss silk.
Hackle: Fibres of blue gallena, tied "beard" fashion.
Wings: Married strands of scarlet, black and scarlet dyed goose fibre.
Hook: 6 to 12.

HATCHING MAYFLY NYMPH (Rivaz)

A pattern devised by that thoughtful fly dresser G. F. G. Rivaz of Hungerford. The artificial owes its origin to the well known American pattern, the Grey Wulff, however, its final form bears little resemblance to Lee Wulff's creation. It is an excellent floater.

The hook size should be in accordance with the size of the natural mayfly, though if the same dressing is tied onto a number 14 hook the resultant pattern is most effective in late Spring as representative of the larger olive duns at the point of emergence.

Body: Pheasant tail fibres, wound forward to a point approx. one-eighth of an inch behind the eye.
Tails: Pheasant tail fibres. Use the tips of the body fibres, prior to winding the body.
Wings: Deer hair fibres. Tied in front of the body with a pronounced forward slant.
Hackle: Blue dun cock. Tied in behind the wings and extending halfway down the body.

HATCHING MAYFLY (Goddard)

A pattern tied by John Goddard to represent the adult mayfly emerging from its nymphal case in the surface film. It should be fished with the tail section submerged.

Silk: Yellow.
Wings: "V" shaped hackle fibre wings from a large pale-blue dun cock hackle.
Body: Rear half of body of pheasant tail fibres. Forward half cream seal's fur.
Rib: Gold wire, or narrow gold lurex.
Hackle: Small furnace cock tied thickly.
Hook: 8 fine wire long shank.

HATCHING MIDGE PUPA

Another of John Goddard's patterns dressed to represent the pupa (buzzer) and particularly effective during calm conditions on the reservoir. The colour and size of the artificial should be dictated by the colour and size of the pupa hatching at the time.

The red pattern tied to represent the orange-silver midge pupa should be ribbed with wide silver Lurex, leaving only a narrow band of red showing between each turn of lurex. Goddard also, on occasion, ties in a hot-orange pad on top of the thorax to represent the distinctly orange wing cases of this particular natural. For tag and head filaments strands of white glass-fibre cloth can be used, or Firebrand fluorescent wool. The method of fishing this artificial is important. A floating line is used with a lightly greased leader. A large floating sedge type pattern is tied on the point, with two or three pupae tied directly onto the leader at twelve inch intervals, the nearest should be at least three feet from the sedge. This method has proved most effective during calm spells when a widespread rise to the pupae takes place; a time when trout can be most difficult.

An effective method of fishing these artificials when the trout are not feeding on the surface is to use a weighted nymph on the point and one or two pupae as droppers. Use the sink-and-draw retrieve with a floating or "sink-tip" line in water of medium depth, but retrieve as slowly as possible.

Silk: As body colour.
Underbody: Black, brown, red or green marabou silk, or Firebrand fluorescent wool.
Rib: Silver lurex.
Overbody: Strip of opaque PVC overall.
Tag: White hen hackle fibres, projecting approx. one-eighth of an inch from end of body, tied in well round the hook bend.
Thorax: Green peacock, buff condor or turkey tail fibres.
Head filaments: A bunch of white hen hackle fibres tied through the thorax but facing upwards and forwards over the eye of the hook.
Hook: 10 to 14 straight eye, round bend.

HATCHING OLIVE NYMPH

This pattern, by John Goddard, is a first class dressing of the nymph at the moment of emergence from nymph to dun. It should always be fished in the surface film, and it is therefore fished as a dry fly.

Silk: Brown.
Underbody: Olive green condor herl, three fibres, leaving short tips projecting to form the tails.
Rib: Silver lurex.
Overbody: A strip of olive-dyed PVC.
Thorax: Three brown turkey tail fibres. Later in the season peacock herl is used to give a darker silhouette.
Wing cases: Three dark pheasant tail fibres, doubled and re-doubled.
Hackle: Two turns of pale honey dun, tied in front of the thorax.
Hook: 13 to 16 D/E.

HAWTHORN FLY (JACOBSEN)

A good pattern devised by Preben Torp Jacobsen, a veterinary surgeon from Norager in Denmark. Jacobsen is a most observant amateur entomologist and a thoughtful and inventive fly dresser. His book *Torflue Fiskeri*, published in 1965, has become a standard work on fly fishing and fly dressing in his own country, and 1973 will see the publication of his work on nymphs. For many years he has carried out practical experiments into the breeding of birds for the production of top quality dry fly hackles.

Silk: Brown.
Body: Three strands of black condor herl twisted round the tying silk.
Hackle: Two black cock hackles.
Legs: Two black condor herl tips.
Hook: 12.

HAWTHORN FLY (KITE)

Another of the late Major Oliver Kite's patterns, this one to represent the species *bibio marci*. Some still water anglers claim to have had good sport with this fly during the short period when the natural is about. I have had more success when fishing it as a sedge in the late evening.

Silk: Black.
Body: Strands of green peacock herl, dressed plump.
Rib: Fine gold wire.
Body hackle: Black cock dressed palmer fashion.
Head hackle: Black cock.
Hook: 13 U/E.

HEATHER MOTH

A salmon and sea-trout pattern popularised by Peter Deane. The dressing was given to him in the 1950's by the Hon. Edward Davies, who swore by its appeal to sea-trout and salmon. His enthusiasm was not misplaced for it has proved to be a most excellent fly. In 1971 the Hon. Edward Davies took thirteen salmon in one morning with this pattern on the river Polly, trying out other flies that the fish would not look at. Tied in smaller sizes it is a good pattern for reservoir and lake trout.

Tag: Fine silver oval.
Body: Grey squirrel fur, well picked out.
Rib: Flat silver tinsel, and wire.
Hackle: From the start of the tag a Plymouth Rock cock hackle palmered up the body. In the bigger sizes, especially for salmon, two or three extra turns can be added at the head.

Sometimes a golden pheasant crest feather is added as a tail, but that is optional.

HERON AND YELLOW

This general pattern, originated by Arthur Dew of Solihull, Warwickshire in 1967, has proved to be a good dry fly for reservoir angling. It was originally tied for use at Shustoke but has been equally successful on other still water fisheries such as Chew Valley, Draycote, Clywedog and Clatsworthy. Cast into the path of a cruising trout, or left to dance upon a good ripple, it appears to be equally effective.

In one respect the fly bears some resemblance to Lunn's Winged Caperer, the use of a body bearing a central ring of swans herl dyed yellow, however, the Heron & Yellow has no other similarity and can, I think, be justly claimed as an original pattern.

Silk: Brown.
Body: Natural heron herl in two equal parts, divided by a narrow ring of dyed yellow swan's herl.
Hackle: Top quality coch-y-bondhu cock. Preferably two hackles for maximum flotation.
Hook: 12 or 14 D/E wide gape. On very choppy water a size 10 can be used to advantage.

HØSTRUP

A pattern originated by one of Denmark's leading amateur fly dressers, Johannes Laursen of Faarbaek, near Karup. Laursen has been responsible for a number of excellent patterns, all wet flies, usually fished across and down they are equally effective for sea-trout and brown trout. His patterns have taken many fish in British waters.

Body: Dark brown floss.
Rib: Oval silver.
Wings: Two tips of medium red brown leghorn bantamcock spade hackles, laid back over the body.
Hackle: Medium red cock hackle, fully wound over the wing roots.
Hook: 4 to 6 for sea-trout. 8 to 10 for brown trout.

IMPERIAL

This fly was invented by the late Major Oliver Kite as a representation of the *baetis rhodani* dun. The date of origin was 1962 since when it has gained a considerable, and well deserved, reputation. The Imperial can also be used to good effect as a general pattern. In the latter period of his life Kite, who died in 1968, used this fly almost to the exclusion of any other pattern when fishing the dry fly.

Just before he died he gave me some Imperials tied with light ginger hackles, commenting that they seemed just as effective as the more rare honey-dun hackle. I have dressed them with twin hackles; one of a short fibred slaty-dun wound through a longer fibred light ginger hackle. This gives a fair imitation of the honey-dun.

The true original pattern however is as follows:

Silk: Purple.
Body: Four undyed heron primary herls, doubled and re-doubled to form the thorax.
Rib: Fine gold wire.
Tails: Greyish-brown hackle fibres in Spring. Honey dun later in the season.
Hackle: Honey dun cock.
Hook: 14 U/E early Spring. 15 or 16 U/E from mid May.

IRON BLUE

Over the years artificials representing the iron-blue, *baetis pumilus* and *baetis niger*, have been devised in countless numbers. Few natural flies have so many different imitative counterparts, from the sparsely dressed Dark Watchet of Yorkshire to the double split-winged floater of the early nineteen hundreds.

Of the more recent dry fly dressings, with a special place on the chalkstreams, that of Commander C. F. Walker must rank high.

Body: Dark-grey condor herl.
Rib: None, so as to preserve the dark effect.
Wings: Darkest Waterhen.
Tail: Dark-grey cock hackle fibres.
Hackle: Dark-blue dun cock.
Hook: 16 U/E.

IRON-BLUE HATCHING DUN

The name of W. H. Laurie is respected wherever the talk turns to fly fishing and the dressing of the artificial. A man of considerable experience and the author of many books on both subjects, he has given thought to the evolvement of patterns to represent the stage between nymph and dun. That period in the life cycle of the natural insect when trout feed with gusto, frequently ignoring the dun that has successfully emerged.

This pattern of the iron-blue, *baetis pumilus/niger*, has been used with excellent results.

Silk: Claret.
Body: Mole or water rat's furs.
Thorax: Blue rat's fur dyed a purplish shade.
Tails: Three fibres of soft white or cream hen hackle.
Wing hackle: Medium slate-blue cock. After winding cut away the lower fibres.
Leg hackle: Dark-blue cock. After winding cut away the upper fibres.
Hook: 16.

Only sufficient leg hackle is applied to float the fly with the wings and thorax above the surface film. Silicone floatant should be applied to the thorax and legs only.

JOHN STOREY

This particular fly, of north-country origin, is most certainly not a new dressing, however, its usefulness is well known on the rivers and chalk-streams of Yorkshire and a recent interest has been shown by many south-country fly fishers.

Its origins were somewhat obscure but recently I have been able to authenticate the original dresser. It was John Storey (1834-1914), river keeper to the Ryedale Anglers at Helmsley, North Yorkshire. His pattern was dressed with the wing slanting over the body in wet-fly fashion. The present, and better known, style of winging was devised by Arthur Storey, grandson of the old gentleman, in 1935. The true present day dressing is as follows:

Hook: No. 14 down-eye.
Silk: Black.
Whisks: None.
Body: Copper coloured peacock herl.
Wing: Small whole breast feather of the mallard, from an adult bird, tied in with a distinct forward slant, bunched, not split.
Hackle: Rhode Island Red dark red cock.

It is of passing interest that the Storey family have served as river keepers to the Ryedale Anglers Club for one hundred and fifteen years.

JONAS

Invented by the Danish fly dresser, Johannes Laursen of Faarbaek, this pattern can be used for sea-trout and brown trout. It is also a good fly for still water rainbows when dressed on a size 10 or 12 hook.

Body: Cock pheasant tail fibres.
Rib: White floss silk.
Wings: Two badger spade hackle tips, tied sloping back over the body.
Hackle: Grizzle cock, fully wound over the wing roots.
Hook: 4 to 6 for sea-trout; 8 to 10 for brown trout.

KENNY'S KILLER

A good pattern by Kenneth Burns of Gordonbush, Brora. Initially designed as a sea-trout fly for the waters of Sutherland but has since proved its worth as a good all round fly.

Body: Flat silver tinsel.
Rib: Oval silver.
Tails: Golden pheasant tippet.
Hackle: Cock hackle dyed yellow. Tied "beard" fashion.
Wings: A sparse bunch of black squirrel tail hair, or hairs from the tail of a black retriever.
Hook: 8 to 12 D/E.

KILLER BUG

This fly, so simple to dress but most effective in action, was originally designed by that most experienced flyfisher, Frank Sawyer, for the taking of grayling in the upper reaches of the Wiltshire Avon. The pattern has since that time proved capable of taking river, reservoir and lake trout, also salmon. Sawyer is most emphatic that no other wool has the required attractiveness, when wet, for use on the fly body as Chadwick 477.

Body: A double underlay of fuse wire. Following the final layer the wire must end up at the bend of the hook. A triple layer of Chadwick wool No. 477 is then wound over the wire underlay, the final layer to end at the bend where it is secured with the hanging length of wire.
Hook: 9 to 12 for lake flies; 7 to 4 for salmon.

KNOTTED MIDGE (*or* MATING BLACK GNAT)

Patterns of the mating gnats have been with us for many years, though in the main those artificials do not take into account that the male differs in colouration to the female.

This dressing by G. F. G. Rivaz does allow for this variation and it has proved a good fly for trout and grayling.

Body: Black silk.
Rib: Very fine silver wire.
Tails: Three long cree hackle fibres. These should be cocked up at almost 90 degrees to the hook shank.
Front hackle: Short fibred badger cock.
Rear hackle: Red cock, wound at rear of body near the bend of the hook.
Hook: 16 U/E long shank.

KROGSGAARD SERIES

The following patterns, though devised during the twenties, I consider to be worthy of inclusion in this book. They represent the most well known flies originated for Danish waters and yet can be used with great success in this and other countries.

They are the result of the combined observations of a dentist, Olav Krogsgaard, and a school-master J. Kr. Findal. Together they collected examples of the natural flies found on their Danish rivers and arranged them in nine groupings, each group consisting of insects that bore certain similarities to each other in regard to size and colour. From each of these nine groups they chose one fly as being representative of that particular group. These naturals were preserved in fluid and shipped over to Hardy Bros., of Alnwick, Northumberland where they were translated into fur and feather.

They were never named, being given only the numbers 1 to 9. For many years Hardy's were the only firm to tie these patterns and the flies were consistently successful in both wet and dry styles.

All the flies are dressed in a similar fashion. The wings, rather full, are tied in sloping well back over the body, strangely this applied to the dry fly as well as the wet. The only difference being the head hackle, cock for the dry flies and hen for the wet. A sedge-like appearance should be aimed for.

Hook sizes can vary; 10 to 12 for trout and grayling, 4 to 8 for sea-trout.

Number One

Body: Olive floss.
Wings: Two strips of white and two strips of brown hen wing fibre. The brown to the outside.
Hackle: Red.

Number Two

Body: Brown floss.
Rib: Oval gold.
Wings: Two strips of cinnamon turkey or hen wing fibre, and two strips of goose or white duck fibre. The cinnamon on the outside.
Hackle: Ginger.

Number Three

Body: Chocolate-coloured floss.
Wings: Two strips of brown and two strips of white hen fibre. The brown to the outside.
Hackle: Dark red.
Antennae: Two strands of brown mallard fibre.

Number Four
Body: Woodcock quill.
Wings: Waterhen or jackdaw feather.
Hackle: Black.
Antennae: Two strands of black horsehair.

Number Five
Body: Black quill.
Wings: Two honey hackle tips.
Hackle: Furnace.

Number Six
Body: Mixture of olive and brown seal's fur with a slight tinge of white. More brown than olive.
Wings: Four cream hackle points, tied flat on dry fly and upright on the wet fly.
Hackle: Two- black and red.

Number Seven
Body: Hard quill dyed fawn.
Rib: Chocolate-coloured floss.
Wings: Four blue dun cock hackle points, tied on flat on the dry fly and upright on the wet fly.
Hackle: Ginger.
Antennae: Two strands of brown horsehair.

Number Eight
Body: Originally dark-brown raffia. Brown floss now used.
Wings: Grey turkey dyed mauve.
Hackle: Light red.
Antennae: Two strands of brown horsehair.

Number Nine
Body: Yellow and brown floss, alternate bands, four of each.
Wings: Light-grey turkey fibres.
Hackle: Ginger.

LARGE DARK OLIVE

Another original pattern by P. T. Jacobsen. Although his flies were originally tied for fishing the streams and rivers of his own country, the Simested, the Binderup and the Guden, they have proved just as well suited on the waters of the British Isles. Many thoughtful anglers are now tying their flies to his laid down patterns and this dressing of the *baetis rhodani* is one of the best.

Silk: Amber.
Body: Two natural blue heron herls and two heron herls dyed olive. All four
  twisted together around the tying silk prior to winding down the hook shank.
Rib: Fine silver wire.
Tails: Ginger cock hackle fibres.
Hackle: Three. A medium size pale olive and a small ginger cock, wound
  together. A large dark rusty dun wound at the head.
Hook: 13.

LARGE PALE WATERY HATCHING DUN

W. H. Lawrie's "emergent" pattern representing the transitional
stage between nymph and dun.

Only sufficient leg hackle is applied to float the fly with the wings
and thorax above the surface film. Silicone floatant should be applied
to the thorax and legs only.

Silk: Primrose.
Body: Blue cat fur.
Rib: Fine gold wire.
Thorax: Primrose floss silk, or wool.
Tails: Three fibres from a ginger hen hackle.
Wing hackle: Pale smoke-grey cock. After winding cut away the lower fibres.
Leg hackle: Medium ginger cock. After winding cut away the upper fibres.
Hook: 14 or 15.

LARGE RED SEDGE

This pattern was designed by G. F. G. Rivaz of Hungerford after
much experimentation. It is recommended for fishing dry in the shel-
tered bays of the great chalk-stream lakes of Western Ireland, the time
to fish this fly being in the later part of a summer evening. A slow,
steady, draw across the surface to simulate the insect struggling towards
the land will often attract the feeding trout.

Body: Pheasant tail fibres.
Rib: Fine gold wire.
Body hackle: Furnace cock, palmered down the body.
Wings: Speckled turkey wing quill feather fibres. Generous in size and extend-
  ing half an inch beyond the bend.
Head hackle: Red cock, eight to ten turns.

LAST HOPE

Originally devised by John Goddard to represent the pale watery
dun, *baetis bioculatus,* however, in practise the artificial has proved
most effective to simulate the adult caenis, or any other small, light, fly.

The artificial should always be tied on very small hooks and it is essential to use a very small sharp hackle, extremely short in the fibre. Such hackles are very hard to find and therefore a clipped hackle may be used.

For the body the ideal is two or three herls in a dark grey stone colour, or alternatively light buff, preferably from the breast feather of a Norwegian goose. Condor herl may be used as an alternative. The lighter buff bodies are used early in the season while the darker ones are used from mid June onwards.

Silk: Pale yellow.
Body: Goose primary or condor herl, buff colour.
Tails: Honey dun cock hackle fibres, at least six in number.
Hackle: Cream or honey cock hackle. Very short in the fibre.
Hook: 17 or 18 U/E fine wire.

LECKFORD PROFESSOR

A good dry fly by Ernest Mott, for many years Head Keeper on the Leckford water of the River Test. Will frequently bring results when the trout are being very choosy. It is someti. ..es known by the unfortunate name of Cow's Arse!!

Note that the hackle is tied in at the bend of the hook, not at the eye.

Body: Dark hare's ear fur.
Rib: Fine flat gold tinsel.
Hackles: Two. A bright-red cock and a white cock.

LIGHT OLLIE

A good floater created some years ago by Jacobsen but un-named until after the death of Oliver Kite in 1968. The originator then decided to name the fly after his good friend and angling colleague.

A variation to this dressing is made by substituting a dark honey-dun hackle for the head hackle and a dark blue dun for the body hackle. It is then known as the Dark Ollie.

Silk: Primrose.
Body: Four heron herls dyed primrose in picric acid, then twisted around the tying silk before winding the body.
Rib: Fine silver wire.
Tails: Buff Orpington cock fibres.
Body hackle: Natural blue dun cock, henny in texture, palmered down body.
Head hackle: Light honey dun cock.
Hook: 15 U/E.

LIGHT SEDGE

A sedge pattern devised by Terry Thomas. I have found this to be a good dressing.

Body: Light cock pheasant tail fibres, wound on as thickly as possible.
Wings: Brown deer hair tied on to slope backwards over the body. The hair is tied in by the tips with the thicker roots over the bend. Cut ends to shape.
Body hackle: Ginger cock palmered down the body.
Head hackle: Ginger cock, wound over wing roots.
Hook: 4 to 14.

LITTLE CLARET SPINNER

This is one fly that I would be loath to leave out of my fly-box. Though the dressing has its origins in Denmark, being designed by one of the old school of fly-tiers in that country, Johs Vangsgaard of Odense, I have taken trout from all kinds of waters, the length of the country, and have found it to be especially useful in the late evening.

Silk: Claret.
Wings: Two dark rusty dun cock hackle points, tied half spent.
Body: One strand of condor herl dyed brownish-red.
Rib: Gold wire.
Tails: Dun cock hackle fibres.
Hackle: Two. One brown-olive and one light-greenish-olive cock hackle, wound together.
Hook: 15 U/E.

LONGHORNS

These dressings, by Richard Walker, imitate various *trichoptera* coming up to hatch. All the four body colour combinations have their uses, dependent on the species of sedge pupa the trout may be feeding on at the time.

Body: Rear two-thirds ostrich herl dyed pale blue-green or amber. Front one-third sepia or chestnut dyed ostrich herl. Tie the body fat.
Rib: Gold thread over rear two-thirds of the body.
Hackle: Brown partridge.
Horns: Two pheasant tail fibres tied in at the same attitude and position as the wing of a conventional wet fly, but extending to twice the length of the hook.
Hook: 8, 10 or 12 U/E.

MAJA

A well-known Danish brown trout and sea-trout wet fly, originated by Johannes Laursen, his flies being held in very high regard by Scandinavian fly-fishers.

Body: Bronze peacock herl.
Rib: Narrow embossed gold tinsel.
Wings: Two jungle-cock neck feathers, tied back over the body.
Hackle: Brown Leghorn medium red bantam cock hackle, wound over the
. wing roots.
Hook: 4 to 6 for sea-trout; 8 to 10 for brown trout.

MARCH BROWN HATCHING DUN

Another transitional stage pattern by W. H. Lawrie, this time of
Rhithrogena haarupi. Only sufficient leg hackle is applied to float the
fly with the wings and thorax above the surface film. Silicone floatant
should be applied to the thorax and legs only.

Silk: Yellow or orange.
Body: Medium hare's ear fur.
Rib: Fine gold wire.
Thorax: Dark bronze-red hair from a red setter, or for variety, seal's fur dyed
to a sepia colour.
Tails: Three short cock pheasant tail fibres.
Wing hackle: Dark partridge feather. After winding cut away the lower fibres.
Leg hackle: Dark-red cock. After winding cut away the upper fibres.
Hook: 12 to 14.

MATUKA'S

The Matuka style of dressing is generally associated with the southern
hemisphere, yet flies dressed in this distinctive style have proved their
worth over recent years when used on the reservoirs of this country.

The name "Matuka" originally referred to the bird from which the
feather was obtained, however, the term now covers a range of patterns, the similarity between them resting on the manner of winging
the artificial. As an example I shall describe the dressing of the Ace of
Spades, a pattern devised by David Collyer and one that has proved
consistently successful on the many still-water fisheries of this country.

Silk: Black.
Body: Black chenille.
Rib: Oval silver tinsel.
Hackle: Guinea fowl fibres, tied "beard" fashion.
Wings: Two dyed black hackles, back to back, with bronze mallard over all.
Hook: 6 to 10 long shank.

Having wound the silk down the hook shank to the bend tie in the
oval silver tinsel and the black chenille. Take the silk back to the head.
Wind the body material, in close even turns, up the hook shank.
Secure and cut off the waste end. Tie in the throat hackle fibres. Take
the two black hackles, ideally they should be almost twice the length of

the hook shank, and strip off the fibres from one side of each hackle, approximating to the length of the hook shank. Placing the hackles over the top of the hook shank, the stripped fibre sides being directly on top of the body material and the side with the intact hackle fibres pointing upwards. The unstripped portions of the hackle, where intact on both sides of the stem, should be beyond the bend of the hook forming the tail. Now tie the hackle stalks to the head. Ensuring that the hackles are even and upright on the body, wind the ribbing tinsel down the hackle stalk and over the body in even turns, trapping down the hackle stalk. Tie in the tinsel at the head, remove the waste and whip-finish the head.

Another pattern devised by Collyer is the Red and Grey:

Silk: Black.
Body: Silver-grey chenille.
Rib: Oval silver tinsel.
Hackle: Scarlet hackle fibre.
Wings: Hen pheasant body feathers.
Hook: 6 to 10.

Matuka's so dressed overcome the problem of using long-hackled lures where the trailing feathers, tied in only at the head, have the annoying habit of twisting under the hook when casting.

MAYFLY

This floating mayfly pattern was originated by Derek Bradbury in 1968, for use on a twenty-acre lake in Cheshire which produces what is possibly the best mayfly hatch in the whole country. The duns hatch for several weeks and odd stragglers have been seen as late as mid October.

That this is a good pattern I can confirm, for artificials tied to Bradbury's dressing have taken trout from two rivers that I fish, where we are still fortunate to have a few natural mayflies.

Silk: Olive.
Body: Seal's fur dubbing mixture. 60 per cent yellow, 39 per cent light olive, 1 per cent hot-orange.
Rib: Oval gold tinsel, size 15.
Wings: Tied forward, two bunches of hair from a small brown squirrel tail, this having a light, dark, light coloration. Wings divided by figure-of-eight turns of silk.
Tails: Three or four fibres from a cock pheasant tail, approximately the same length as the body.
Hackle: Two. Yellow-olive cock, two turns behind the wings, remainder in front.
Hook: 10 U/E Partridge wide gape.

A nymphal pattern has also been designed. The tying of this follows standard nymph-tying techniques with one exception. To achieve the colour variations between dorsum and venter on the body Bradbury uses the tail fibres in the following manner.

Having tied in the tail and the ribbing tinsel he then lifts up out of the way the forward-facing waste tail fibres, completes the winding of the dubbed body, then lowers the waste ends onto the top of the body. Ensuring that they are correctly aligned he then traps them down with the turns of ribbing tinsel. A simple, but effective, method of imitating the distinctive colouring between the top and bottom of the naturals body. This method can also be applied to the dun pattern.

Silk: Olive.
Body: Yellow-olive seal's fur.
Rib: Oval gold tinsel, size 15.
Thorax: Yellow-olive seal's fur, thickly dubbed onto the silk.
Tails: Cock pheasant centre tail fibres.
Wing cases: Thick bunch of cock pheasant centre tail feather fibres.
Hackle: One turn of brown partridge.
Hook: 10 D/E long shank.

MAYFLY HATCHING NYMPH
This dressing was devised by Commander C. F. Walker. The hackles are tied in such a way as to suggest the first stages of the wings emerging from the case.

Body: Medium-brown hare's ear fur.
Thorax: Darkish hare's ear fur.
Rib: Fine gold twist, wound only over the body, not the thorax.
Tails: Short tips of three strands from cock pheasant tail feather.
Hackle: Greyish-brown speckled feather from the breast of a partridge, dyed light olive, followed by the same sort of feather, undyed.
Hook: 11 U/E long shank.

MEDIUM OLIVE DUN
Commander C. F. Walker's representation of *baetis vernus*, or *tenax*. It is interesting to note that despite the inclusion of one strand of greyish-olive herl in the body make-up the general effect is certainly not one of a pronounced olive hue. This is deliberate, for Walker considers that the natural does not possess the olive colour generally

attributed to the natural. An excellent pattern that has had much success.

Body: One strand of pale brownish condor herl and one strand of greyish olive herl.
Rib: Fine gold tinsel.
Wings: Brownish-grey waterhen breast feather fibres, bleached in peroxide.
Tails: Pale grey cock hackle fibres.
Hackle: Pale olive cock.

MINNOW STREAMER

Devised by one of this country's formost exponents of streamer and bucktail styles of dressing, Taffy Price. This pattern, in general with many fish representing flies should be retrieved with a slow action, interspersed with occasional pauses and sudden darts. In fact, the natural movements of a small minnow. In Price's words "it should not be fished as a jet-propelled aquatic rocket".

Price's many patterns, and details as to his method of tying and fishing, can be found in his book *Lures* (A. & C. Black).

Body: White floss silk, wound so as to achieve a minnow-like shape.
Rib: Silver lurex.
Tail: Blue dun cock hackle fibres.
Wing: Two cock hackles, dark olive in colour, tied streamer fashion. On either side are mounted strips of black and white barred teal feather.
Hackle: Scarlet cock hackle fibres, tied beard fashion for male minnow. Blue dun for female fish.
Cheek: Very short jungle-cock.
Head: Olive green, white underneath.
Hook: 8 D/E long shank.

MISTIGRI

Another famous French pattern, devised by J. P. Pequegnot of Besoncon during the 1965 season. It came about after Pequegnot examined the stomach content of several trout taken in April from the Doubs near Goumois and found they had been feeding almost exclusively on *nemouridae*, the smaller types of stone-fly. Such insects being plentiful on the Jura streams during early April.

Pequegnot realized that to date no classical French or English pattern really gave a true representation of these smallish black insects with their elongated silhouette and so he came up with the following pattern, now renowned throughout France.

Silk: Black.
Body: Black peacock herl.
Wings: Bunches of hackle fibres from a black cock, mixed with a few fibres from a partridge feather.
Hackle: One or two turns of black cock.
Hook: 14 to 16.

The important step in dressing this artificial is the build up of the wing fibres that are tied in to form a thick cone around the hook shank with the fibres spreading out at an angle of 20 to 25 degrees, only the hook point emerging.

To achieve this three or four bunches of hackle fibres are successively distributed rotationally around the shank, all being tied in at the head. The head hackle is then wound over the wing roots. In the absence of good quality black hackles then slate-grey, such as those obtained from the Gaulois blue cock may be used.

The Mistigri can be tied more simply by omitting the partridge fibres, and substituting a body of black tying silk for the peacock herl. This applies especially to the smaller hooks.

This artificial can suggest with equal effectiveness the small brown stoneflies, *Nemoura cinerea*, *N. avicularis* and *N. picteti*, also the needle-fly, *Leuctra fiesca* and *L. hippopus*. It may also imitate the smaller dark species of sedge flies, while tied upon the very small hooks it does good service when diptera are about.

MISTY BLUE DUN

A most effective tying of the medium olive, found in some quantity on the rivers and streams of this country, and in particular on the chalk-streams. This dressing was evolved by Tony Waites, head river keeper for the Driffield Angling Club that fishes many miles of that superb chalk-stream, the Driffield Beck. It has been my good fortune to fish this water and the associated streams and feeders and I have found the Misty Blue Dun a most excellent fly.

Silk: Yellow.
Body: Yellow tying silk.
Rib: One strand of natural heron herl, closely wound but allowing the yellow to show through.
Tails: Three long fibres from a light blue dun cock hackle.
Hackle: Two. A light brown and a light blue dun cock, wound together.

MUDDLER MINNOW

A most effective representation of the native cockatush minnow of the American Nipigon waters, the local name of the minnow being "muddler". Don Gapen of Anoka, Minnesota was the originator and the fly reached this country around 1967 when it was an immediate success, particularly with the still-water anglers. The fly has accounted for many large fish in its original, and varied, forms.

Body: Flat gold tinsel.
Tail: Section of turkey wing quill, slightly larger than the gape of the hook.
Wings: A moderately thick bunch of grey squirrel hair, on each side being a section of mottled oak turkey wing feather tied on to almost the same length as the squirrel hair and pointing upwards at an angle of 30 degrees.
Shoulders: Natural deer hair spun onto the hook shank in front of the wings, clipped to shape. The method of spinning deer hair is fully described in the Veniard series of books on fly-tying.
Hook: 1 to 12 long shank.

NEVAMIS MAYFLY

Originated by John Goddard as a river pattern, it has proved a good fly on some of the large Irish loughs.

Silk: Yellow.
Wings: "V"-shaped hackle fibres, using the large pale blue dun cock.
Body: Cream seal's fur wound thickly.
Rib: Oval gold tinsel.
Tails: Three long cock pheasant centre tail fibres.
Body hackle: Large honey cock tied palmer style from tail to shoulder, then clipped to a quarter of an inch of shank at the shoulder, sloping to one-eighth of an inch at tail.
Head hackle: Small, half-inch fibres, furnace cock.
Hook: 8 U/E long shank fine wire.

NICE'S FAVOURITE

First tied in 1967 by James Nice, this lake and reservoir fly has been consistently successful. Dressed with a stiff cock hackle it has also taken lake trout when fished along the margins.

Silk: Brown or claret.
Wings: Speckled game hen. Dark.
Body: Peacock herl dyed magenta.
Rib: Scarlet DFM, four to six turns wound close together at the rear to form a tag.
Hackle: Black hen, or henny cock.
Hook: 10 or 12 D/E.

NO-HACKLE FLIES

These patterns are the result of much patient research by two Americans, Carl Richards and Douglas Swisher. Both men being skilled entomologists and fly-dressers of considerable experience.

Briefly, they hold the theory that the traditional hackle, particularly on smaller hooks, masks the important part of the artificial that triggers the reaction of the trout . . . the body and the wings. Having accepted that premise they then evolved a series of patterns, duns and spinners, from which the hackle is deleted.

One problem that faced them was that they had to devise a method of maintaining stability on the water surface. A winged hackleless fly generally lands on its side when cast. They overcame this problem by the wide angle spreading of the tail fibres. To achieve this they tied in at the bend of the hook a small wad of fur, divorced from the body material. The tail fibres were then carefully tied in on either side of the hook shank, the small wad forcing the fibres apart into a wide angle.

The body material was, in the early stages of development, mainly composed of dubbed fur. Swisher and Richards found that such bodies, dressed on fine wire hooks and well treated with floatant, did not require the aid of a hackle.

Recent further development has led them to use polypropylene fibres in place of fur. This material having a specific gravity of 0·94 and therefore possessing good floating qualities.

I have tried out a number of the dun and spinner dressings and they do take fish. It is early days yet to form concrete opinions but the no-hackle fly is one aspect of the craft that is worth investigating.

The following dressings are only some of the many patterns devised by Swisher and Richards. A comprehensive list, and a full record of their researches, can be found in their book *Selective Trout*, published in 1971 by Crown Publishers Inc. of New York.

B.-W.O. Dun (Family *baetidae*)
Body: Medium olive, or medium olive and medium brown rabbit fur, mixed.
Wings: A bunch of light or medium grey hen hackle fibres.
Tails: Light grey cock hackle fibres, widely spread.
Hook: 14 to 24 U/E.

B.-W.O. Spinner
Body: Medium or dark brown rabbits fur.
Wings: Light grey hen hackle tips, cut to shape and tied spent.
Tails: Light grey cock hackle fibres, widely spread.
Hook: 14 to 24.

Dun Quill Gordon (*Epeorus pleuralis*)
Body: Pale yellow and dark brown rabbit's fur, well mixed.
Wings: Dark grey duck quill feather fibre.
Tails: Ginger cock fibres, widely spread.
Hook: 12 to 14 U/E.

QUILL GORDON SPINNER

Body: Pale yellow and dark brown rabbit's fur, well mixed.
Wings: Light blue hen hackle tips, cut to shape and tied spent.
Tails: Dark brown hen hackle fibres, widely spaced.
Hook: 12 to 14.

BLACK QUILL DUN (*Leptophlebia cupida*)

Body: Brown rabbit's fur.
Wings: A bunch of dark elk hair.
Tails: Dark bronze blue dun cock fibres, widely spread.
Hook: 12 to 14.

BLACK QUILL SPINNER

Body: Dark reddish brown seal's fur, or buffalo fur.
Wings: Bronze blue dun hen hackle tips, cut to shape and tied spent.
Tails: Dark bronze blue dun cock fibres, widely spread.
Hook: 12 to 14.

PALE MORNING DUN (*Ephemerella lacustris*)

Body: Pale yellow and olive rabbit's fur, well mixed.
Wings: Light grey duck shoulder, or light grey hen hackle tips, cut to shape and tied spent.
Tails: Light olive hackle fibres, widely spread.
Hook: 16 to 18 U/E.

PALE MORNING SPINNER

Body: Light green and light tan rabbit's fur, well mixed.
Wings: Light grey hen hackle tips, tied spent.
Tails: Light olive hackle fibres, widely spread.

OLIVE AND GOLD

A fly dressed in the old traditional style by David Collyer. It proved most attractive to the trout of Weirwood reservoir in Sussex during the 1970 season and could well be worth a try on the northern lochs.

Silk: Olive.
Tails: Golden pheasant crest.
Body: Gold tinsel or lurex.
Hackle: Ginger cock.
Wings: Married strands of olive dyed goose with a strip of gold dyed goose fibre in the centre. Six separate strands in all.
Hook: 6 to 12.

OLIVE HATCHING DUN

A good general pattern by W. H. Lawrie, covering a range of olives at the point in their life cycle when struggling to change from nymph to dun through the surface film.

Silk: Primrose.
Body: Soft blue cat's fur dyed greenish-olive in picric acid.
Rib: Fine gold wire.
Thorax: Hare's ear fur mixed with primrose worsted.
Tails: Three short fibres from a dingy olive-brown hen hackle.
Wing hackle: Medium blue cock. After winding cut away the lower fibres.
Leg hackle: Dark centred cock with olive tips. After winding cut away the upper fibres.
Hook: 14 or 15.

Only sufficient leg hackle is applied to float the fly with the wings and thorax above the surface film. Silicone floatant should be applied to the thorax and legs only.

OLIVE NYMPH

A nymphal pattern devised by P. T. Jacobsen to cover various olives. Used to good effect by the writer on many waters.

Silk: Primrose.
Tails: Plain blue guinea fowl neck feather dyed olive.
Body: Mole's fur dyed olive in picric acid.
Rib: Signal-green DRF filament.
Thorax: Dark-red cow's hair.

ORANGE SEDGE

A dry sedge pattern originated by Christopher Pudley of Tunbridge Wells, designed for use at Weirwood reservoir. It has taken many good trout and, as recorded in Veniard's book *Reservoir and Lake Flies*, it rose and caught four trout in succession on its very first outing.

Body: Hare's ear dubbing.
Rib: Flat gold lurex.
Wing: Partridge wing feather fibre, rolled and tied flat along the body.
Hackle: Cock hackle dyed hot-orange, tied in front of the wing.
Hook: 12 to 14 U/E.

OTTER RUBY

A representation of the iron-blue, by James Nice, that was first used in 1957. The choice of condor herl in place of the more usual mole's fur was an attempt to avoid a material with a tendency to water-logging.

Silk: Brown or claret.
Body: Condor herl dyed magenta.
Rib: Gold wire, optional.
Tails: Iron blue or brownish-black cock fibres.
Hackle: Iron blue or brownish-black cock.
Hook: 14 to 18 U/E.

PHANTOM LARVAE

David Collyer was requested by Alex Behrendt of the famous Two Lakes fishery to design a pattern to imitate the almost transparent natural. This artificial was the result of his experiments.

Silk: Olive, well waxed, use only as a ribbing.
Body: Overlay of stretched polythene, approx. one-sixteenth of an inch wide.
Hackle: Badger cock, or hen.
Hook: 14 long shank. Silvered. It is important that a silvered hook be used for the colour is the body base.

PALE EVENING DUN

A good representation of the natural, *procloeon pseudorufulum*, first tied in 1959 by the late Oliver Kite. Also a useful pattern for a number of light-coloured naturals.

Silk: White.
Body: Grey goose primary herl, doubled and re-doubled at the thorax.
Tails: Cream cock hackle fibres.
Hackle: Cream cock.
Hook: 15 U/E.

PALE WATERY DUN

The interest in the use of various furs for the winging of flies has grown apace over the last few years and this particular artificial is a good example. Devised by Thomas Clegg of West Calder, Scotland, the author of *Hair and Fur in Fly Dressing*, this pattern is one that has taken a good number of trout for me when the natural, *Baetis bioculatus*, has been about.

Body: Opossum fur.
Rib: Primrose silk.
Wings: Marmot or cream tips of Japanese fox fur.
Hackle: Two blue dun cock hackles, wound behind and in front of the wings.
Hook: 16 U/E.

Another good pattern of the pale watery is that devised by Commander C. F. Walker.

Body: Pale watery-olive condor herl.
Rib: Fine gold tinsel.
Wings: Palest waterhen.
Tails: Pale grey cock hackle fibres, with honey tips.
Hackle: Pale honey cock.

PALE WATERY HATCHING DUN

Another artificial in the emergent series by W. H. Lawrie.

Silk: Primrose.
Body: Pale blue cat's fur, spun very thinly onto the silk.
Rib: Fine gold wire.
Thorax: Blue cat's fur mixed with primrose worsted.
Tails: Three short fibres from a blue hen hackle.
Wing hackle: Pale blue cock. After winding cut away the lower fibres.
Leg hackle: Grey cock, or henny cock. After winding cut away the upper fibres.
Hook: 16.

Only sufficient leg hackle is applied to float the fly with the wings and thorax above the surface film. Silicone floatant should be applied to the thorax and legs only.

PALE WATERY/OLIVE

A good lightish pattern general-purpose fly, originated by Preben Torp Jacobsen. The fly is equally at home on the streams of this country as those of its native land, Denmark.

Silk: Primrose.
Body: Two strands of natural blue-grey heron herl, twisted around the tying silk. Three or four turns of silk left exposed at the rear of the body.
Rib: Signal-green DRF filament.
Tails: Fibres from a Buff Orpington cock hackle.
Hackle: Dun cock wound in front of a Buff Orpington hackle.
Hook: 15 U/E.

PALE SEDGE

One of the most effective sedge patterns of recent years. Evolved by David Jacques, this artificial has been consistently successful.

Body: Cinnamon turkey tail fibres.
Rib: Gold twist.
Wing: Natural hen pheasant wing fibres, bunched and rolled, tied down flat over the body.
Body hackle: Ginger cock, palmered down the body.
Head hackle: Ginger cock.
Hook: 14 U/E during the day; 11 D/E late evening.

PANAMA

A great dry fly from France. Its originator is unknown, however, the first time the dressing was committed to print was in *A La Mouche* by Tony Burnand and Charles Ritz. It also bears some resemblance to that other good French fly, the Irresistible, created by M. Cuvelier.

The pattern does not purport to represent any particular insect, though it is a fact that it is effective when the mayfly or the sedge are on the water. Dr. Pequegnot is of the opinion that it is one of the very few artificials that will tempt the trout of the Loue when the great stone-flies make their appearance.

Silk: Black.
Tag: Four or five turns of black silk.
Body: Natural raffia.
Tails: Golden pheasant tippets.
Wings: Two grizzle cock hackle points, tied spent. Two dark red cock hackle points tied over the grizzle points, but clearly separated from them.
Body hackle: Small fibre light-red or ginger cock hackle, wound palmer fashion.
Head hackle: Light red or ginger cock. In front, near the eye, a few turns of grey partridge hackle.
Hook: 10 to 14.

That first-class French angler Andre Ragot devised a "female" of this general pattern, as a joke of course. This pattern differs from the original in that the wings are of furnace hackle, the black silk tag is replaced by one of peacock herl and the grey partridge is replaced by a very dark partridge hackle.

Knowledgeable French anglers have had many a quiet chuckle when they have overheard other fly-fishers discussing the relative merits of the two sexes!!

PALMER NYMPH
Nymph's, palmer hackled, are not new. Skues was of the opinion that a nymph so tied could give the impression of the buzz effect, i.e. movement, to the artificial representing the activity of the gill plates and legs.

This particular dressing was devised by Conrad Voss Bark and features prominently in his book *Fly-Fishing for Lake Trout*, published in 1972. The artificial has proved most successful when fished in the correct manner, that is slowly. It can be fished either sub-surface or deep, but with an occasional "induced take" action imparted to it by a fast movement lasting for a very short period.

Under body: Lead or copper wire to form a pronounced thorax shape.
Body: A mixture of yellow and green seal's fur, darkening towards the thorax.
Rib: Fine gold or silver wire.
Body hackle: Short fibred cock, one red and one golden-olive, wound round the body to the tail where they are secured by the ribbing, which is wound back to the head.
Head hackle: Reddish-coloured cock.
Tails: Golden pheasant topping, or tippet, short.
Hook: 12, but for deeper fishing up to size 8.

PINK PERIL

A most gaudy fly that may convince anglers that trout are colour blind! However, the pattern, by A. B. Bourne, has accounted for hundreds of fish, both brown and sea-trout.

As stated in John Veniard's book *A Further Guide to Fly-Dressing*, Mr. Bourne says "It is essential that the fly be tied with a fat, succulent body." Well worth a try, if only out of curiosity as to the fishes reaction.

Body: A fat cork body covered with pink DFM floss.
Tails: Ibis, or substitute.
Hackle: Light red game cock.
Hook: 14 fine wire, long shank.

POND OLIVE SPINNER

The *Cloeon dipterum* is often referred to as the Apricot Spinner due to its very distinctive colouring. It is one spinner that does call for a specific artificial. This pattern, by John Goddard, should be fished in, not on, the surface film.

Silk: Orange.
Wings: Pale blue hackle tips, tied spent.
Body: Apricot coloured condor herl, covered with pale olive PVC.
Tails: Pale badger cock hackle fibres.
Hackle: Fibres from a dark honey cock hackle, tied in under each wing in place of the traditional wound hackle.
Hook: 12 or 14 U/E.

POLYSTICKLE

Possibly the best-known reservoir fly devised since the war. The idea of Richard Walker to simulate a small fish. There must be few still-water anglers who do not carry at least one pattern of the Polystickle within their fly-boxes. The pattern given here is, as a rule, most effective, however, various colour schemes can be tried.

Body: Well-spaced turns of black tying silk over the silver hook shank, with a few turns of red silk, or wool, about a quarter of an inch back from the eye. Over this is wound clear polythene strip, about 0·003 in. to 0·005 in. thick, to form a fish-shaped body.
Back and tail: A strip of brown Raffine tied in with black silk at the front and rear of the body, then clipped at the rear to form a fan-shaped tail. The Raffine must be damped and stretched when tying in.
Hackle: A bunch of hot-orange hackle fibres, tied "beard" fashion.
Head: Made up of black silk, large and bold, then well varnished.
Hook: 6 or 8 long shank, silvered finish.

For muddy water conditions the Raffine back and tail can be hot-orange. At dusk a Polystickle having two or three layers of polythene strip wound over a fat white fluorescent wool body is often effective, with orange hackle and brown back.

For very deep water in daylight, or at any depth after dark, the Glowstickle may prove deadly for brown trout. It is tied like a Poly-stickle but with luminous plastic strip instead of polythene. When used after dark is requires re-activating every five minutes or so with the aid of an electric torch.

A variation on this pattern has a large stiff white cock hackle wound at each end of the body, and the Raffine back and tail is omitted. This dressing can be cast out and allowed to lie on the bottom, stationary, or moved in very small twitches.

PVC NYMPH

Another of John Goddard's patterns. The use of PVC, tied over the herl, gives the body a most translucent appearance, closely simulating the natural nymph.

This pattern represents a number of different olive nymphs.

Silk: Yellow.
Body: The shank of the hook is covered with fine copper wire. Start at the eye and work along, building up a thorax just behind the eye by winding more thickly at that point. Continue on to the bend of the hook and use the wire to tie in the body materials. Then cut the wire.

Body materials are three golden-olive condor herls and a thin strip of clear PVC. The points of the herls should protrude one-eighth of an inch at the rear to form the tails. These herls are then wound up to the eye. Tie in with the yellow silk, then take the silk in wide turns to a point just behind the thorax. Wind the PVC over the body, terminating at the rear of the thorax. Tie in and cut off waste.

Take the silk back to the eye and tie in three blackish pheasant tail fibres; these are then doubled and re-doubled over the top of the thorax to form the wing cases.

To imitate the translucent effect of some nymphs, sparsely wind silver tinsel over the body herl, but under the PVC.

Hook: 12 to 16.

REED SMUT

A good general dressing by Preben Torb Jacobsen. Worth a try on most waters when the naturals are in evidence.

Silk: Black.
Body: Black condor herl.
Hackle: Black cock tied parachute fashion, in the centre of the body.
Hook: 16 to 18.

RED SPINNER

An excellent dry fly that has taken many trout, particularly from the Otter and the Axe, for which it was designed by James Nice.

Silk: Pale brown or red.
Body: Scarlet DFM.
Rib: Brown silk.
Tails: Blue dun or ginger cock hackle fibres.
Hackle: Two. Red and blue dun cock. The former to be wound through the latter.
Hook: 14 to 18 U/E.

RED SQUIRREL NYMPH

Another American pattern, devised by one of the foremost fly-dressers in that country, David Whitlock. This nymphal pattern, though originally designed for the White Water river, has proved equally effective in this country, particularly in sizes smaller than 12. It is worth noting that the fur is from the body, not the tail, which is usually the case in fly-dressing. Whitlock is on record as saying that if he were to be restricted to one nymph pattern then this would be his choice.

Silk: Black.
Body: Underlay of fine lead wire, followed by a mixture of the fur from the underside of the red fox squirrel and the bleached under-fur from a beaver; 75/25 mixture.
Thorax: Back fur from the red fox squirrel.
Rib: Fine oval gold.
Wing case: Dark brown speckled turkey quill fibre.
Tails: Red fox squirrel back fur.
Hook: 6 to 16 D/E.

RED QUILL

An American pattern originated by that famous angler and fly-tier, Art Flick, author of the classic *A Streamside Guide.*

Though this artificial bears the name of an old English pattern, it is in fact, a representation of an American east coast natural fly, the *Ephemerella subvaria.* Despite this natural having no British counterpart I have found Flick's Red Quill to be a good general pattern when any darkish fly is on the water.

Body: Quill of a large Rhode Island Red cock hackle, stripped of all fibres. After winding in lacquer the body.
Wings: Bunch of fibres from the flank feather of a mandarin or wood duck drake.
Tails: Dun spade hackle fibres.
Hackle: Natural blue dun cock.
Hook: 12 to 16.

ROACH FLY OPTIC

Devised by Geoffrey Bucknall. The eyes that form the optic component of this fly can be either silver or gold, and can be obtained from the small ornamental chains sold by haberdashers, or more recently, from fly-dressing material stockists.

By altering the basic coloration of the artificial, patterns can be devised to represent the fry of the perch, minnow, stickleback, gudgeon etc.

Body: Open turns of red lurex covered with a strip of clear polythene, built up to the natural shape of the roach fry.

Back and tail: Dark-green nylon raffia. The back being varnished.

Hackles: Dyed red cock fibres, tied "beard" fashion.

Eyes: A pair of beads tied in by the figure-of-eight method, under the shank of the hook at the head of the fly.

Head: Polyurethene varnish or Venglaze.

Hook: 4, 6 or 8. Gold-finished Aberdeen.

RØJBAEK

Another famous Danish wet-fly pattern for brown and sea-trout, devised by Johannes Laursen.

Body: Dark brown floss.

Rib: Claret floss.

Wings: The tips of two Brown Leghorn medium red spade hackles, tied back over the body.

Hackle: Brown Leghorn medium red bantam cock.

Hook: 4 to 6 for sea-trout; 8 to 10 for brown trout.

RUSTY BLUE

This general pattern was devised by James Nice of Sidmouth. The fly has its origins on the River Otter and is described as a "damp air" fly. As such it requires to be well hackled, and would seem to be most effective in the early morning or late evening.

There is a wet-fly version of the Rusty Blue, the main change being the substitution of a single dark rusty hackle, edged in white, and dyed in blue dun dye. The hook size can also vary between 10 and 16. If tied on hooks larger than 14 then the body ribbing is changed for oval gold. The sizes preferred by Nice, when fishing wet, are 10 or 12, and the fly to be fished as the bob on a two-fly leader.

Body: Hare's ear fur mixed with a small amount of orange and red DFM wool. The wool to be cut into very short lengths.

Rib: Fine gold.

Tails: Medium blue dun cock fibres.

Hackle: One medium blue dun cock and one dark red cock, wound together.

Hook: 14 to 16 U/E.

SEDGE PUPA

A most killing pattern from July onwards, devised by John Goddard. It is intended to represent the pupae of various sedge-flies, as they ascend to the surface. It should be fished rather slowly in medium to shallow water. The artificials are dressed in several colours to represent the most common natural shades. This is basically a still-water, not river, pattern.

Silk: Brown.
Body: Cream, dark brown, orange or olive-green seal's fur. The latter two colours may be covered lightly with fluorescent floss of the same colour, all ribbed with narrow silver lurex.
Thorax: Dark brown condor or turkey herl.
Wing cases: Pale brown condor herl. Four strands are brought over the top of the thorax and tied in at the eye, then doubled and re-doubled to form the wing pads.
Hackle: Honey or rusty hen hackle, tied sparsely. One and a half to two turns only.
Hook: 10 or 12 long shank, wide gape.

SEPIA DUN

Major Oliver Kite's representation of the *Leptophlebia marginata*. It is true to say that this pattern is generally of more use to the still-water angler than the stream fisher. Hatches of the natural are not large, but being one of the first flies to appear on the lakes it has a special appeal to the angler.

Silk: Dark brown.
Body: Dark heron herls, doubled and re-doubled at the thorax.
Rib: Fine gold wire.
Tails: Dark brown or black cock fibres.
Hackle: Black cock tinged with a brownish shade.
Hook: 14 U/E.

SHERRY SPINNER (Featherstonhaugh)

A good pattern of the *Ephemerella ignita* originated by H. A. D. Featherstonhaugh.

Silk: Orange.
Body: Claret fur dubbed very lightly onto the silk so that a translucent effect is obtained.
Tails: Cream badger cock, with black tips.
Hackle: Badger cock with a lightly-marked centre. Two turns maximum.
Hook: 14 to 16 U/E.

SHERRY SPINNER (Nice)

A most effective pattern that works well on all streams. Tied by
J. Nice.

Silk: Pale brown or orange.
Body: Front half scarlet DFM. Whole body then covered with orange DFM,
   giving a darker shade to the thorax.
Tails: Light red or ginger hackle fibres.
Hackle: Blue dun and red cock. On smaller hooks, blue dun only.
Hook: 14 to 18 U/E.

SHRIMPER

John Goddard's version of the shrimp of still-water. It should be
fished on a floating, or sink-tip, line in the shallow margins near to
weed. It should be retrieved slowly, along the bottom, with frequent
pauses.

Silk: Orange.
Underbody: Copper wire wound from eye to bend, thickening in the centre
   to form the typical hump-back shape of the natural.
Overbody: Tie in a strip of natural PVC, about one-eighth of an inch at the
   bend. The PVC should be wider in the middle of the strip. This is followed
   by a honey-coloured hackle and olive marabou silk. Wind the latter to the
   eye, followed by the hackle, palmer fashion. Stretch the PVC over the top
   of the body and tie in. Trim excess hackle along the body side.
Hook: 10 to 14 D/E Limerick.

SINFOIL'S FRY

This fry representation, devised by Kenneth Sinfoil, head water
bailiff at Weirwood Reservoir, has proved to be consistently successful
when trout are feeding in the margins on the fry of fish.

The dressing is quite simple, though one or two points are worth the
mention.

The flat silver tinsel underbody is wound from the head, two-thirds
down the shank, and then returned to the head. The overlayer of
polythene is wound backwards and forwards over the length of the
hook shank, building up the while into the typical shape of a small fish.
The collar of scarlet floss silk is wound immediately behind the head
position, approx. $\frac{1}{8}$ in. wide. The brown mallard fibres do not of course
represent a "wing", they simply provide the illusion of movement.
The head should be built up quite large and painted eyes can be added
if desired.

Silk: Black.
Underbody: Flat silver tinsel, wound two-thirds down hook shank.
Overbody: Heavy polythene strip, approx. one-tenth of an inch wide.
Collar: Scarlet floss silk.
Back: Fibres of brown mallard feather.
Head: Large build up of tying silk.
Hook: To suit.

SILVERHORN

Though there would seem to be some divergence of opinion as to the value of a representation of the natural species covered by the name "silverhorn" this particular dressing, by James Ham of Birmingham, has proved successful at Shustoke reservoir when that natural is about. The artificial should be cast among the rising fish, then twitched for a few inches over the surface, the action being repeated every few seconds.

Body: Dubbed fur from the body of a light brown, almost blonde, labrador dog. A similar material as used in the well-known fly, the Dogsbody.
Rib: Fine gold wire.
Hackle: Grizzle cock.
Hook: 12 to 14 U/E.

SMALL HATCHING MIDGE

J. Goddard's pattern of the midge transposing from the pupal stage. At certain times during the summer, on most still-waters, occurs quite large hatches of some of the smaller midges, usually brown, red or green in colour. When these small pupae are hatching the trout often become preoccupied with the species and are very difficult to catch. With this pattern Goddard has achieved a measure of success. It must be fished only partly submerged in the surface film. When trout are feeding on the emerging midges Goddard considers that the rise-form is unmistakable, for the trout usually rise repeatedly upwind in a ripple, or in a circular pattern during a flat calm, barely breaking surface with their neb as they sip down the midge.

This pattern should be fished with little or no movement, on the point, or on the point and top dropper, using a light rod and line and casting directly into the path of a rising fish.

Silk: Brown.
Body: Two turns of silver lurex round the bend of the hook, followed by the main body material of dark-red, green or brown condor herl.
Rib: Narrow silver lurex.
Thorax: Buff condor herl.
Hackle: Small honey rusty dun cock, tied in immediately behind the eye.
Hook: 14 to 16 D/E.

SNAIL

A pattern devised by Clifford Henry for use when the trout of still-waters feed avidly upon the snail during their periodic migration to the surface.

Silk: Black.

Underbody: A pear-shaped section of cork, with a flat top, is fashioned. This is split halfway through, placed onto the hook shank with the flat end facing the eye, and bind tightly in position with the tying silk.

Overbody: Stripped peacock quill, other than the last two or three turns next to the flat end against the eye; this is covered with bronze peacock herl.

Hook: 10 to 14 D/E wide gape.

SPENT MAYFLY

Yet another good pattern devised by Richard Walker. Useful for the fly-fisher who is still fortunate enough to fish a water that can boast a mayfly hatch. The fly should be fished within the surface film. When viewed in the hand the fly may look rather garish, however, when viewed from the trouts' point of view, the underneath, the resemblance to the natural spent female spinner is remarkable.

Silk: Dark brown.

Body: Three or four strands of white swan's herl.

Rib: Dark-brown silk, or horsehair, wound on the opposite spiral to the body material. Two bands, made up of four or five turns near the rear of the body, followed by open spirals up to the wing roots.

Tails: Four or five pheasant tail fibres, dyed sepia.

Wings: Two light Sussex hen hackles, tied flat with figure-of-eight fixing. These hackles should have pronounced black centres, such that when cut down to size the centres have a diamond shape.

Hackle: Natural dark-red cock, not too long in the fibres, or too dense.

Hook: 10 long shank.

STANDARD SEDGE

A good general sedge pattern, originated by Terry Thomas. This fly, along with his Dark Sedge and Light Sedge artificials, covers all the naturals one is likely to meet with.

Body: Dark cock pheasant tail fibres, wound very thickly.

Wings: Grey deer hair, tied in by the tips, flat along the body. Well splayed out.

Body hackle: Ginger cock, wound palmer fashion.

Head hackle: Ginger cock.

Hook: 4 to 14.

SWEENY TODD

A well known and much used still-water pattern, jointly devised by Peter Thomas and Richard Walker.

Body: Black floss. A few turns of neon-magenta wool behind the wing root.
Rib: Silver thread.
Wings: Black squirrel hair.
Hackle: Crimson cock hackle fibres, tied "beard" fashion.
Hook: 6 to 14, and two-hook tandem, two and a half inches long.

TEAL-WINGED BUTCHER

David Collyer's adaptation of the old established lake and sea-trout pattern. He has found this variant especially useful under hot, difficult, conditions.

Silk: Black.
Tail: Ibis sub.
Body: Silver tinsel or lurex.
Wings: Barred teal.
Hackle: Black hen hackle fibres, tied "beard" fashion.
Hook: 10 to 14.

TERRY'S TERROR

This dry-fly pattern was devised by two angling compatriots, the late Ernest Lock, well known Andover fly-tier, and Dr. Cecil Terry of Bath. It represents all the stages of the olives from hatching nymph to dun and spinner. Dressed small it is accepted as an iron-blue and on bigger hooks makes a first-class sedge pattern. For many south country chalk-stream anglers it is a sheet-anchor.

Peter Deane, a most knowledgeable fly-dresser, is of the opinion that this artificial is the best all-round dry-fly pattern for any river or stream.

Tag: Equal parts of orange and yellow goat's hair, cut short and flared.
Body: Peacock herl, one strand only.
Rib: Flat copper tinsel.
Hackle: Fox-red cock. The bottom half of the hackle may be trimmed but this
   is a matter of personal taste.
Hook: 10 to 16.

Though rarely dressed as a wet fly it has on occasion proved its worth. Tied on a small Limerick double, and fished by Cdr. Ralph Martin, it took the following trout in one morning's fishing: 1½ lb., 9½ lb., 6½ lb. and 7½ lb.

TORP'S REED SMUT NYMPH

Jacobsen's original pattern of the simulium nymph. When dressing this pattern he pre-treats the cow's hair with silicone floatant in the belief that this substance traps air within the body, lending the artificial an attractive sparkle under water.

Silk: Brown.
Body: Blood-red cow's hair, over an underlayer of fine copper wire. At either extreme end of the body a whipping of fine silver wire, four or five turns, close together.
Hook: 16.

VICTORY

Devised by Dr. Yves Rameaux of France, where it has achieved considerable success on that superb water, the Andelle in Normandy. Rameaux has found it particularly effective on slow-flowing, smooth-surfaced waters where duns frequently stay, slightly in the surface film, for quite some time.

Body: Greenish-yellow silk.
Rib: Brown silk. Optional.
Tails: Blue dun cock hackle fibres.
Hackle: Pale blue dun cock. After tying in, the fibres are divided by figure-of-eight turns to form a semi-spent wing style.
Hook: 15 or 16 D/E.

WHISKY FLY

This pattern, the brainchild of Albert Whillock of Hayes, Middlesex, has gained considerable popularity following reports of its trout-taking capabilities during the 1970 season. Whillock recommends that it be fished a few inches under the surface and retrieved at a moderate speed. The fly has accounted for many limit catches on various waters and feats such as Whillock's own in taking six rainbows, up to 2½ lb. in less than half an hour, at Grafham, has given this pattern an almost mystical quality to some still-water anglers.

Silk: Hot orange.
Body: Gold or silver lurex.
Rib: Red silk.
Tag: Red silk.
Hackle: Hot orange dyed cock hackle fibres.
Wings: Four cock hackles, dyed hot orange.
Cheeks: Jungle cock. Optional.
Head: Red varnish.
Hook: 8 long shank.

The fly has been tied with the tag omitted and a tail of red hackle fibres included. It also performs creditably on most hook sizes.

WOLDSMAN

 My own pattern of the *Ephemerella ignita* dun, devised some five years ago for use on the Wolds chalk-streams in the Driffield area of East Yorkshire. Time has shown that it is also a most useful general pattern and I can fish it with confidence on any water.

Silk: Pale yellow.
Body: Three strands of condor herl, one natural buff, one dyed light olive and one dyed dark claret, wound side by side.
Wings: Bunch of summer-duck feather fibres, tied upright and not split.
Tails: Summer-duck fibres, well splayed out.
Hackle: Golden-olive cock, maximum number of turns.
Hook: 14 to 18 U/E. Fine wire.

PART IV

APPENDICES

APPENDIX I

HOOKS AND HOOK SIZES
BY JOHN VENIARD

I have many requests for information on hooks—the best to use for different types of fishing. Salmon flies do not present much difficulty as far as hooks are concerned, as the range is very limited these days, but trout flies can be tied on a wide variety of irons.

The kind of fish to be caught, where it lives, and the type of fly to be used, must, of course, determine the type of hook to use. A heavy hook in clear, placid water is as much out of place as a fine wire hook would be in heavy water where large fish can be expected. Furthermore, different kinds of hooks must be used for different flies, streamer patterns, nymphs, etc., as no hook is appropriate for all fly-fishing conditions.

The range of all types of hooks is much smaller than before the war, when it was possible to get a greater variety. If anyone worked out a new design which the manufacturers thought practical, they were often prepared to manufacture and market it. Such is not the case these days, as present-day costs of retooling, etc., make the introduction of a new pattern a costly business, and not a practical proposition unless a very big quantity is made. However, the range of types available for fly tying is still quite extensive, and one soon decides on preferred patterns for one's types of fishing. Fig. 1 illustrates the descriptive points of modern usage, and in this case it is a forged upturned-eye pattern.

Salmon flies can be divided up into four main groups: those using standard hooks which have a Dublin or Limerick Bend; summer or low-water hooks which are of lighter wire and longer in the shank for the same gape; dry-fly hooks which are of very light wire and which can also be used for low-water flies, and trebles for use with the now very popular tube flies. The standard and low-water hooks are also used as doubles.

The "shape" is the index to the hook pattern and I have illustrated one or two of the most popular of these. Incidentally, the "shape" is quite often referred to as the "bend". "Bend" really refers to any lateral

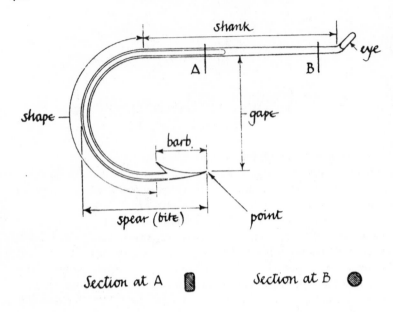

Section at A ▮   Section at B ⬤

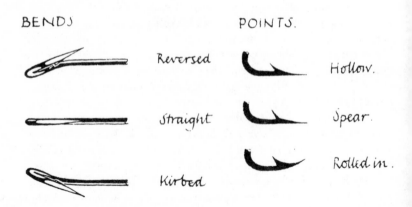

BENDS

Reversed

Straight

Kirbed

POINTS.

Hollow.

Spear.

Rolled in.

SHAPES   EYES.

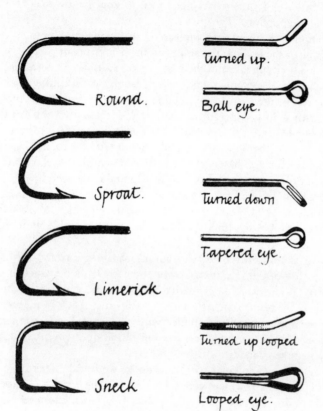

Round.

Turned up.

Ball eye.

Sprout.

Turned down

Tapered eye.

Limerick

Turned up looped

Sneck

Looped eye.

WIRE SECTIONS

Forged.   Regular.   Oval.

offset to the point and barb, i.e. when the point is offset to the right it is called a "reverse bend" and when it is offset to the left it is called a "kirbed bend". Another misnomer is that of "snecked bend" instead of "kirbed", although it has been used so much now that it is an accepted description. The purpose of these bends is to direct the penetration of the point at an angle to the shank, which helps to prevent the release of the hook as the point and the shank are not parallel.

For dry-fly fishing, one of the best patterns to use is one with a sproat shape and turned-up eye, a slight reverse bend, and, of course, made of light wire. An alternative, and second in popularity, is the same type of hook with a turned-down eye, although I think that much of its popularity is due to the fact that it is considered easier by some tyers to dress a fly on a downturned eye hook. Hooks with the round shape are also popular for dry flies in its smaller sizes, but as the wire increases in weight in the larger sizes they are also admirable for wet flies.

A good hook for all-round types of wet flies is the Limerick pattern, which is usually of quite stout wire. Another type of hook, which is self-descriptive, is the long-shanked. They are obtainable with either up- or down-eyes.

I am grateful to Mr. S. A. Shrimpton, managing director of Messrs. Allcock & Co. Ltd., for the following notes on hook nomenclature.

"BEND". This is definitely a trade term for the shape of the hook, such as kirby bend, Limerick-bend, round bend, sneck bend, etc. To shape the hook, barbed and pointed wires were pulled round on a hand "peg-bend"; later the bend was fixed in a hand-operated machine, and the wire pulled round to shape.

As regards the different parts of a hook, we usually describe as the "depth" that part which you call "spear". The machine point (as distinct from the old hand-filed point) is generally termed "spear point" so that there could be no confusion.

Gape/Length Combinations for a Typical Hook.
(№ 8)

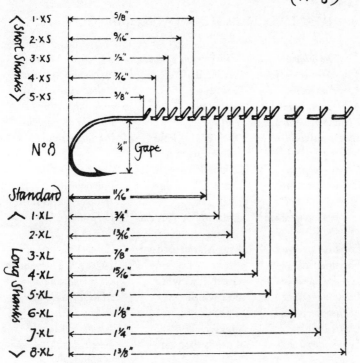

⟨ 1·XS
⟨Short Shanks⟩ 2·XS
3·XS
4·XS
⟩ 5·XS

5/8"
9/16"
½"
7/16"
3/8"

Nº 8   ¼" Gape

Standard   11/16"
⟨ 1·XL   ¾"
2·XL   13/16"
Long Shanks 3·XL   7/8"
4·XL   15/16"
5·XL   1"
6·XL   1⅛"
7·XL   1¼"
⟨ 8·XL   1⅜"

NOTE. Measurements do not include the hook eye.

Further variation (not shown) include differences
in the gauge of wire, to suit hook purposes,
ie., for dry, wet & salmon flies.

APPENDIX II

RE-CLASSIFICATION OF NOMENCLATURE

Old Name	Fisherman's Name	New Name
Anisomera burmeisteri	Gravel Bed	*Hexatoma fuscipennis*
Aphodius foetens	Cowdung	*Aphodius aestivalis*
Aphrophora alni	Wrentail	*Aphrophora spumaria*
Chlotoperla grammatica	Yellow Sally	*Isoperla grammatica*
Cloëon rufulum	Sail Wing, Pale Evening dun	*Procloëon rufulum*
Corixa geoffroyi	Water Boatman	*Corixa punctata*
Ecdyurus insignis	Large Green dun	*Ecdyonurus insignis*
Ecdyurus lateralis	Dark Dun	*Heptagenia lateralis*
Ecdyurus longicauda	Autumn or August Dun	*Ecdyonurus dispar*
Ecdyurus venosus	Late March Brown	*Ecdyonurus venosus*
Ecdyurus volitans	Brown May Dun	*Heptagenia fuscogrisea*
Hemerobius alba	Green Lacewing	*Chrysopa ciliata*
Lasiocampa rubi	Fox Moth	*Macrothylacia rubi*
Leptis scolopacea	Oakfly	*Rhagio scolopacea*
Leptis lineola	Oakfly	*Rhagio lineola*
Leptophlebia sub-marginata	Turkey Brown	*Paraleptophlebia sub-marginata*
Leuctra klapaleki	Willow Fly	*Leuctra fusca*
Nemoura geniculata	Willow Fly	*Leuctra geniculata*
Nemoura inconspicua	Needle Brown	*Nemurella picteti*
Nemoura meyeri	Early Brown	*Protonemura meyeri*
Otiorrhyncus picipes	Beetle	*Otiorrhyncus singularis*
Pachyprotasis rapae	Saw Fly	*Macrophya rapae*
Perla cephalotes	Stone Fly	*Dinocras cephalotes*
Perla maxima	Stone Fly	*Perla bipunctata*
Phyllobius alneti	Beetle	*Phyllobius pomaceus*
Pterostichus madidus	Rain Beetle	*Feronia madida*
Scatophaga stercoraria	Cowdung	*Scopeuma stercorarium*

PLATE 1

WINGED DRY FLIES
(1⅓ of actual size)

1	Alder Fly	9	Lunn's Particular
2	Iron Blue	10	No-Hackle Fly
3	Hawthorne Fly	11	Red Ant
4	Cinnamon Sedge	12	Blue-Winged Olive
5	Little Brown Sedge	13	Grey Wulff
6	Orange Quill	14	Little Black Gnat
7	Crane Fly	15	Light Cahill
8	G & H Sedge		

PLATE 2

Invicta

Greenwell's Glory

Mallard & Claret

Peter Ross

Alexandra

Butcher

Polystickle

Matuka

Muddler Minnow

Sweeny Todd

Missionary Fly

Whisky Fly

Woodcock & Green

March Brown

Connemara Black

WINGED WET FLIES
(actual size)

PLATE 3

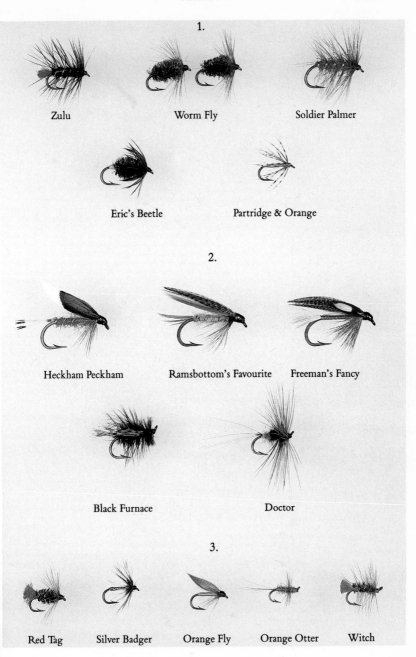

1.

Zulu   Worm Fly   Soldier Palmer

Eric's Beetle   Partridge & Orange

2.

Heckham Peckham   Ramsbottom's Favourite   Freeman's Fancy

Black Furnace   Doctor

3.

Red Tag   Silver Badger   Orange Fly   Orange Otter   Witch

1. HACKLED WET FLIES
2. SEA TROUT FLIES
3. GRAYLING FLIES
    (all shown actual size)

PLATE 4

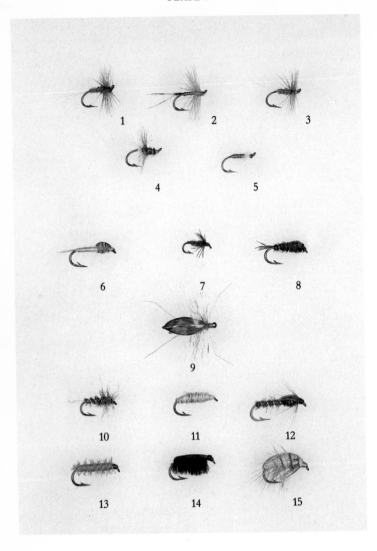

HACKLED DRY FLIES
(1½ of actual size)

1 Kite's Imperial
2 Ginger Quill
3 Orange Spinner
4 Leckford Professor
5 Blagdon Midge

NYMPHS, ETC.
(1½ of actual size)

6 PVC Nymph

7 Iron Blue
8 Bowtie Buzzer
9 Water Boatman
10 Gold-Ribbed Hare's Ear
11 Killer Bug
12 Sedge Pupa
13 Green Caterpillar
14 Chomper
15 Freshwater Shrimp

APPENDIX III

CLASSIFICATION OF NATURAL INSECTS

Order	Principal Representatives
Coleoptera (*Coleos*, sheath; *pteron*, wing)	Beetles
Diptera (*Dis*, two; *pteron*, wing)	Mosquitoes, Midges, Crane Flies, Gnats, Smuts, Blowflies, etc.
Ephemeroptera (*Ephemeros*, lasting for a day; *pteron*, wing)	Mayfly, Blue-winged Olive, Olive Dun, Pale Watery, Iron Blue, March Brown, Turkey Brown
Hemiptera (*Hemi*, half; *pteron*, wing)	Water Crickets, Water Boatmen, etc.
Hymenoptera (*Hymen*, membrane; *pteron*, wing)	Wasps, Ants, Bees, Ichneumon Flies
Lepidoptera (*Lepis*, scale; *pteron*, wing)	Moths and Butterflies
Megaloptera (*Megas*, large; *pteron*, wing)	Alder
Neuroptera (*Neuron*, nerve; *pteron*, wing)	Lacewings
Plecoptera (*Plecos*, plaited; *pteron*, wing)	Stonefly, Willow Fly, Yellow Sally, Needle Fly
Trichoptera (*Trix*, hair; *pteron*, wing)	Sedges, Grannom, Silverhorns

APPENDIX IV

GLOSSARY OF TERMS

Abdomen: The main hinder part of an insect's body which contains the most important organs of the body.

Advanced Wings: Very similar to split-wings, but tied forward in advance of the eye of the hook. Originally this method of winging was applied only to the Mole Fly, but in recent years its use has been extended to some other patterns.

Antennae: The sensory organs or feelers found in pairs on the heads of insects.

Anterior Wings: The fore-wings of an insect.

Barbless Hook: A hook without a barb is sometimes used to permit of the return of under-sized fish without injuring them.

Bob Fly: The top fly on a cast when two or more are used. Its function is to "bob" or skate on or along the surface. Also called the top dropper.

Bulging: A type of underwater rise causing a bulge on the surface made by the sudden turn and consequent swirl when fish are chasing sub-surface insects, usually over or near weed-beds. Hence "bulgers".

Buzz: A hackled fly is sometimes described as being tied "buzz".

Dapping: A method of angling in which the fly is not cast but is lifted and lowered on to the surface of the water. Normally a natural insect is used (less often an artificial one) with a short line so that only the fly touches the water. Favourite natural flies for dapping are the mayfly, blue-bottle, daddy-long-legs, and grasshopper (Ireland). Hence the verb to dap. Also know as dibbing and shade-fishing.

Detached Body: A term applied to a semi-detached body of an artificial fly. The body curves up and away from the hook instead of being wound round the whole length of the hook up to the bend as is usual. Sometimes used for flies imitating the Ephemeridae (and more especially mayflies) which, when at rest, carry their bodies in this position.

Drag: An unnatural movement of the artificial fly on the water, due to some part of the cast travelling at a different pace than the fly. Usually caused by a faster current between fisher and fly.

Divided Wings: A type of wing sometimes used for wet flies. A slip of feathered fibre is taken from the right wing of a bird and a slip from the corresponding feather on the left wing, the two slips then being placed back to back. The final appearance is of two separate wings.

Dropper: One of the artificial flies above the tail fly when two or more flies are used on a cast as is customary in wet fly-fishing. There can thus be a "first dropper", "second dropper", etc. The same term is also used for the piece of short gut fixed to the cast to which a dropper (fly) is attached.

Dry Fly: An artificial fly which is fished floating on the surface usually aided with a little paraffin or some proprietary substance.

Dry Fly-Fishing. When using a dry fly, it is customary to fish with a pattern which imitates or suggests a natural insect on the water. In normal practice, one fly only is used on the cast and on the chalk streams is cast to rising fish only. Hence the phrase "fishing the rise".

Dubbing: Various materials, generally fur or wool, teased out and wound round the hook to form the body of an artificial fly. It is usually spun on waxed thread.

Dun: The first winged state of a fly belonging to the Ephemeridae.

Elytera: Outer hard wing-cases of beetles.

Entry: An artificial fly (wet) which swims naturally without skirting or offering undue resistance to the water, is said to have a "good entry".

Fan Wing: A type of wing for dry flies, of little importance to British anglers, but popular in parts of U.S.A. The illustration on Plate II shows its general appearance.

Fancy Fly: An artificial fly which is not designed to represent any particular insect, or class of insect.

Flotant. A liquid or solid substance applied to artificial flies to assist them to float.

Gallina: Guinea-fowl.

General Fly: An artificial fly which roughly suggests not one but many natural insects.

Hackle(d) Fly: An artificial fly in which hackles are used to represent wings.

Hackle-point Wings: Two bright stiff fibres from a cock's hackle used to suggest wings. A method advocated by Mr. Roger Woolley and particularly effective for spent patterns.

Hackles: The tapered feathers from the neck, upper back and shoulders of fowls used in fly-dressing.

Herl or Harl: A strip of plumed fibre usually taken from the peacock, ostrich, or pheasant.

Imago. The final and perfect state of an insect after all metamorphoses.

Iron: Old name for a fish-hook.

Larva: Insect from time of leaving egg to transformation into a pupa.

Leader: Term used in U.S.A. for gut cast.

List: The centre of a feather, such as a poultry hackle.

Naiad: Nymph, more especially of a dragon-fly.

Nymph: Larva of the Neuroptera order of insects of which the Ephemeridae family are of chief interest to anglers. (2) An artificial fly dressed to suggest a natural nymph.

Nymphing: Fish feeding on nymphs are said to be "nymphing".

Palmer-wise: An artificial fly tied as a Palmer, viz., hackled along the length of its body instead of at shoulder only.

Point: The end of a cast nearest the hook, hence a fly fished "on the point". (2) The business end of a fish-hook.

Primaries. The main long feathers growing on the first joint of a bird's wing.

Pupa: Form taken by an insect in the torpid stage of passive development between larva and imago. A chrysalis.

Purist: Usually applied to an angler who fishes exclusively with a dry fly which is intended to be a definite copy of the natural fly on the water and who fishes the rise only.

Quill: Herl from which the down has been scraped off.

Raffia: Fibre from the leaves of a kind of palm.

Reversed Wings: Same as advanced wings (q.v.); inclined over the head of an artificial fly instead of towards tail or upright.

Rolled Wings: A type of wing made with one feather only (instead of normal two) which is folded in the shape of a V. The final appearance is like a single split wing.

Ribbing Hackle: A ribbing down the body of an artificial fly which consists of an ordinary unstripped and unclipped hackle feather instead of silk, wire, etc. In a wet fly, it vibrates in the current and so gives "life" to the fly, whilst it assists a dry pattern to float.

Secondaries. The feathers growing on the second joint of a bird's wing.

Setae: The tails of an insect.

Shade Fishing: See Dapping.

Shuck: The nymphal case or husk discarded by the sub-imago in its metamorphosis from nymph to dun.

Smutting: Fish feeding on or very close to the surface on smuts, midges, the so-called curses, or other very small insects, are said to be smutting.

Spent Wings: A type of winging for artificial flies in which the wings lie flat on each side of the body and extend outwards horizontally in imitation of a spent and drowning spinner with wings out-stretched.

Spider: A hackled wet fly tied with a short stiff hackle, sparsely wound to cover completely that part of the hook which corresponds to the thorax of the natural insect. Probably suggests a nymph.

Spinner: The imago or perfect state of a fly belonging to the Ephem-eroptera.

Sub-imago: The penultimate or dun stage of a fly belonging to the Ephemeroptera.

Split Wings: A usual form of winging dry flies. The wings are divided to form a V and in an erect position are used to imitate the natural upwinged duns. They may also be set on at other angles, viz.

(a) tied low over the back in "penthouse" style, to imitate the wings of the alder, sedges, and other roof-winged flies; (b) tied flat on the back in imitation of the wings of the willow fly, needle flies, and other perlidae; (c) tied erect and well forward as in the case of the Mole Fly and similar patterns. In this position they are known also as "advanced" wings.

Strike: The act of tightening on a fish which has just taken the fly in order to drive home the hook.

Tag: A short tail in trout and grayling (not salmon) flies, usually of wool, red ibis, etc., which takes the place of whisks.

Tail Fly: The artificial fly at the extremity of a cast when two or more flies are used at the same time.

Tailer: A fish rooting amongst weeds with nose on the bottom or when feeding in an almost vertical position so that its tail, or part of its tail, protrudes above the surface of the water, is said to be "tailing" Fish thus engaged are known as "tailers".

Taper: A tapered line or cast is one in which the material gradually decreases in thickness towards the fly end, the object being to have sufficient weight to ensure easy casting, but at the same time to allow the fly to fall lightly on reaching the water. A line of which the heaviest part is in the middle and which decreases in size towards each end, is known as a "double tapered" line. When one end shows signs of wear, the line can be reversed on the reel, thus providing two lines in one length. A taper which is sharp and not gradual is called a "steep" taper.

Thorax: The part of an insect's body between neck and abdomen which carries the legs and wings.

Tippet: Barred black and orange feather from the golden pheasant.

Topping: The long golden crest feather from a golden pheasant. Used for some sea-trout and salmon flies.

Upwinged Dun: A contraction of "upright-winged dun", called by old writers, "cock-winged", and used for the duns and spinners of the Ephemeridae, all of which, when at rest, carry their wings folded and erect in butterfly fashion.

Waters: In Scotland, the term indicates small streams and tributaries as opposed to big rivers. In some districts, it is used for lakes and is then possibly a contraction of "still-waters". Often, however, it is employed loosely as a generic term for rivers and lakes.

Wet Fly: An artificial fly used below the surface of the water to imitate or suggest larvae, shrimps, etc., moving in the water, or a winged insect when hatching, waterlogged, or drowned. In Scotland and the northern counties, a distinction used to be drawn between wet fly and sunk fly. The former was used for an artificial fished just under the surface, whilst the term sunk fly was reserved for one fished several inches (or more) below the surface.

Wet Fly-Fishing: When fishing a wet fly, the angler casts where he expects fish to lie, irrespective of whether he sees a rise or not. For this reason, it is sometimes termed "fishing the water". Three or more flies are commonly mounted on the same cast.

Whip: To whip an artificial fly is to bind it with silk, etc.

Whisks: Strands of feather or hair used on artificial flies to represent the setae of the natural insect.

Winch: Old term for a reel, seldom used to-day.

GLOSSARY OF TERMS RELATING TO HACKLES

Badger: Black or dark in the centre, with white or cream points.

Blue Dun: Blue-grey or smoky-grey.

Brassy Dun: As blue dun but with a tinge of gold or brass in it when held against a dark background.

Coch-y-bondhu: A black list with reddish-brown points tipped with black.

Dun: A dingy brown or mouse-colour.

Furnace: Black list and reddish-brown points. Very similar to a coch-y-bondhu.

Ginger: A pale or yellowish-red.

Grizzly: A grizzly or grizzled hackle is grey with alternate bars of black and white. Also known as "cuckoo". Comes from the Plymouth Rock.

Honey Dun: Golden ginger points and a centre which varies from grey and light blue to pale brown.

Red: Means fox-red. The darkest shade is generally termed "dark red game".

Rusty Dun: Same as blue dun but with a tinge of rusty brown in it.

INDEX

This index is in four consecutive parts, in this order: Artificial Flies, Natural Flies, *Personae,* and Rivers.

The names of artificial flies, and the popular names of natural flies, are included in the index only when they are to be found elsewhere than in the main headings of the alphabetical list on pages 75 to 346, and 351 to 407.

NATURAL FLIES, ETC.

PERSONAE

Rivaz, G. F. G., 373, 379, 382
Rogan, Michael, 169
Rollo, Lt.-Col. Keith, 93, 106, 336
Rolt, H. A., 211, 338, 339
Ronalds, Alfred, 54, 90, 136, 138, 140, 146, 152, 169, 189, 194, 210, 211, 214, 224, 271, 279, 283, 303, 308, 314, 325, 330, 331, 341
Rountree, G. H., 30
Routledge, R., 286
Rudge, M., 160, 161

Sanctuary, Dr. T., 303
Sanders, W., 304
Sawyer, Frank, 130, 262, 263, 264, 357, 379
Senior, W., 134
Sheringham, H. T., 114, 135, 136, 193
Shrimpton, S. A., 149
Simonet, Maurice, 351
Sinfoil, Kenneth, 402
Skues, G. E. M., passim
Smith, T., 211
Stewart, W. C., 102, 165, 297
Stoddart, T. T., 23, 182, 290
Storey, Arthur, 378
Sutton, J., 314
Swarbrick, J., 289
Swayne, G. C., 112
Swisher, Douglas, 390

Taverner, E., 54, 58, 105, 128, 132, 146, 203, 279, 297, 329, 345
Taylor, Major-General Sir John, 57, 73
Terry, Dr. Cecil, 405
Theakston, M. 213

Thomas, Peter, 405
Thomas, Terry, 356, 363, 384, 404
Tod, E. M., 99, 198, 284, 317, 326
Tout, Frederick, 353
Turing, H. D., 10, 276
Turle, Major W. G., 81

'Val Conson', 222
Vansgaard, Johs, 384
Vavon, Lt.-Col. A., 11
Veitch, J., 194
Voss Bark, Conrad, 396

Wadham, P., 196
Waites, Tony, 389
Walbran, F. M., 90, 107, 274, 298, 304, 326
Walker, Cmdr. C. F., 354, 357, 377, 387, 394
Walker, Richard, 360, 361, 363, 384, 397, 404, 405
Walton, Izaak, 206, 296
Wauton, C. A. N., 58
Wells, H. P., 282
West, Leonard, 95, 96, 98, 146, 150, 155, 324, 331
Whillock, Albert, 406
Whitlock, David, 399
Wickham, Capt. J., 334
Wickham, Dr. T. C., 333
Williams, Francis, 360
Wills family, 353
Wilson, James, 291
Wilson, John, 290
Woolley, Roger, 54, 58, 140, 186, 207, 269, 331, 339
Wright, James, 56, 197
Wulff, Lee, 371
Wyers Frères, Messrs., 321

RIVERS

Ain, 351
Aire, 116
Alwen, 199
Andelle, 406
Anton, 9, 44
Arrow, 80
Avon, 276
Avon (Wiltshire), 379
Axe, 399

Bean, 253
Binderup, 381
Blythe, 303
Border rivers, 119, 193, 232, 300

Clun, 10, 80, 125
Clyde, 105, 194, 195
Colne, 9, 222
Coquet, 337